LIFE

OF

HENRY ALFORD, D.D.

Henry Alford

(ANNO 1867.)

Engraved by J. H. Baker.

LIFE

JOURNALS AND LETTERS

OF

HENRY ALFORD, D.D.

LATE DEAN OF CANTERBURY

EDITED BY HIS WIDOW

Philadelphia
J. B. LIPPINCOTT & CO.
1873

CONTENTS.

CHAPTER I.

1810—1828.

CHAPTER II.

1828—1832.

CHAPTER III.

1832—1840.

CHAPTER IV.

1840—1847.

CHAPTER V.

1847—1851.

CHAPTER VI.

1851—1853.

CHAPTER VII.

1853—1857.

CHAPTER VIII.

1857—1860.

CHAPTER IX.

1861—1862.

CHAPTER X.

1863—1867.

CHAPTER XI.

1867—1870.

CHAPTER XII.

1870—1871.

APPENDIX.

ILLUSTRATIONS.

CHAPTER I.

1810–1828.

PARENTAGE—BIRTH—CHILDHOOD—AT SCHOOL AND WITH A PRIVATE TUTOR.

HENRY ALFORD came of a Somersetshire family. His great-great-grandfather, the Rev. Thomas Alford, who died in 1708, was vicar of Curry Rivell, near Taunton. His wife was Frances Powell, sister of Mr. Powell, of Heale House, in the parish of Curry Rivell, and aunt of Mary Powell, heiress of the Heale Estate. His son the Rev. Thomas Alford, was vicar of Ashill near Ilminster, and died in 1777, leaving two sons in holy orders, of whom one Thomas, succeeded his father as vicar of Ashill, and the other, Samuel, became vicar of Curry Rivell. The latter appears to have had a larger share than his brother of worldly prosperity. The parish of Curry Rivell included in its boundaries Burton Pynsent, one of the seats of the Chatham family, and he became Dean of St. Burian's, Cornwall, on the nomination of Lord Eliot, of St. Germans, who was related by marriage to the first Lord Chatham. He also inherited considerable property, including Heale House, from his cousin Mary Powell. The patronage of the Chatham family appears to have been extended to his son and namesake, the Rev. Samuel Alford (my father), who was chaplain to Lady Chatham from 1801 to 1803, when she died. I have heard him say that Lady Hester Stanhope, who resided with her grandmother at Burton Pynsent, was on terms of great intimacy with the family at Heale House, and Mr. Pitt became well-known to them in his frequent visits to his mother at Burton[1]. A memorial of that distinguished family remained with us long after those days. A table on whose plaster surface were etched some incidents from Ovid's Metamorphoses, which once stood in the apartment of Mr. Pitt at Burton, was transferred on my husband's death in 1871 from the Deanery at Canterbury to the Library adjoining the Cathedral.

My father, the Rev. Samuel Alford, was perpetual curate of Muchelney, a small parish about three miles distant from Heale House where he resided. There he brought up a family of thirteen children, and died in 1853.

His brother, the Rev. Henry Alford, the father of the subject of this memoir, was born in the Vicarage of Curry Rivell in 1772, and entered Wadham College, Oxford, 1800. He had obtained some success as a special pleader, when, in 1809, he married Sarah Eliza Paget, a sister of a College friend, whose father was a banker at Tamworth. This lady, to whom he had long been deeply attached, is described as "a very pleasing, amiable, and interesting person," intellectual, and a good musician. On October 7, 1810, their only child, HENRY ALFORD, was born at 25, Alfred Place, Bedford Row, London, and in the following February the young mother died.

Her son writing in 1854, thus refers to these two events:—"The meditations and prayers contained in my mother's journals for some months previous to this event (the birth) are very touching, and such as prove her mind to have been beyond doubt under the workings of God's Holy Spirit. He indeed was already preparing the way for the completion of her course here below; and it is by His providence that there has been left to us such precious signs that this was so. Almost from the time of my birth her health seemed to decline. For this various causes were assigned; but in looking back over the bereavements of the past, it is well to dwell on one cause only and that the first. On

---

[1] See Lord Stanhope's "Life of Pitt," for an account of the time spent by Pitt at Burton Pynsent during his father's life, and of his visits there to his mother after his father's death in 1778 at Haynes.

the 13th December my father wrote cheerfully about her, as having nearly regained her usual strength. But on January 29th she had become much worse, and there was every reason to fear a vessel had been ruptured in the head. The worst fears were realized on Sunday evening, February 4th, but not before she had been mercifully favoured with an interval of sensibility, in which she recognized all around her. She was buried at Tamworth, her native place."

Under this deep sorrow the whole course of the widower's life was changed. Though he was afterwards called to the Bar, he never resumed special pleading. He left his infant son at Tamworth, and after once going the Western Circuit, he changed his plan of life and returned to Oxford to attend divinity lectures, and was ordained Deacon on Trinity Sunday, 1813, at a place with which his son was afterwards associated, Quebec Chapel, London. His character is thus described by a legal friend who knew him intimately[2]:—"I should say that he had a cheerful and even temper, an affectionate disposition and delicate feelings, combined with great courage, which prevented him from assenting to or acquiescing in any thing he disapproved of, and yet screened him from ever giving offence. He was very sensible and straightforward; he had not, I think, any decided taste for general literature, at least his study appeared confined to one science, and there he was indefatigable. He had a clear, discriminating, and, I think, sagacious mind."

The circumstances connected with his own birth, and his earliest recollections, are thus recorded by Henry Alford in a memorandum written in 1830 when he was at College:—

"I was born 7th October, 1810, at No. 25, Alfred Place, Bedford Row, London. My father then was a special pleader, and making rapid progress in legal eminence. About four months after my birth, my mother died, and this severe stroke my father has never recovered. I knew very little of her, as he seldom or never mentioned her to me, unwilling,

---

[2] The late W. H. Tinney, Esq., Q.C., Master in Chancery, who died at the advanced age of eighty-eight, in November, 1871.

doubtless, to tear open afresh a wound which time may have begun to heal. They say I am very like her. She was buried at Tamworth, and there I was christened. My father, after her death, determined on going into the Church. I was sent to Tamworth, to my grandfather and grandmother and aunts there; when I was about two years and a half old we went into Somersetshire, and arrived at Heale on the night when my cousin Mary was born; that I distinctly remember. I have a distinct idea of my cousin Fanny, a baby. I recollect when I was three years old at Heale, Bel, who was my nurse, set me on a chair, and told me I must behave like a man, for I was three years old. My father and I went to Tamworth. I remember my grandfather Paget showing me what poppies were, and I remember riding before him on his horse to Tamworth. I remember singing to the piano at prayers, and being asked one morning to choose a hymn. I remember having to drink healths all round one day after dinner, when there was a party. After this (1813) we went to Steeple Ashton; I remember the very severe winter of 1813-14, and I had desperate chilblains, I remember I used to be left at home with 'old Sarah' when my father went to church, and I used to read the 'Pilgrim's Progress' to 'old Sarah.' I pondered one day a long time, thinking why the word 'four' should signify the number more than any other word. I remember a snow man that winter being made at a house near us on the green. I remember going with my father to some valley, and up to a gate which led out on Salisbury Plain, and my father killed a snake. One day I remember looking out of the back window and seeing my grandfather's carriage coming. I then went, I think, back to Tamworth, and stayed some time under the care of my aunts. We then went to Wraxall."

Here the autobiography ends abruptly.

Wraxall in Somersetshire was his father's second curacy, on which he entered in the midsummer of 1815. In 1814 an aunt describes young Henry "as a tender, delicate plant; his extreme sensibility makes him often ill." It was about this time, whilst he was staying with his grandfather, Mr. Paget, at Comberford Hall, near Tamworth, that he had a very narrow escape, to which he often referred in after-life. As he was standing on the lawn, the scythe of the gardener actually cut through his little shoe, without touching foot or sock. This shoe was carefully preserved by his aunt, Miss Harriet Paget (afterwards Mrs. Freeman), residing near Tamworth. She was peculiarly attached to him, and through her care many memorials of his early life were preserved. Already he appeared a very precocious child, wonderfully ready in acquiring knowledge, and in reproducing what he acquired. One of his amusements was to make little books, in which, between the years 1815—1819, he wrote histories, or copied texts of Scripture. One of these books, which is preserved, is remarkable as an early indication of his employment in mature years. It was written apparently before he was six years old; it consists of fourteen pages (five only being filled), each about three inches by two. It is called "The Travels of St. Paul, from his Conversion to his Death, with a book of Plates," containing three drawings of St. Paul, the Stoning of Stephen, and the Conversion. In the text these plates are referred to by an asterisk; there is also a reference at the word Damascus to "Wells' Geography, p. 299."

Another little book, written when he was between eight and nine years of age, shows that his father had made some progress thus early in teaching him Latin. It contains some brief Latin sentences (apparently his own composition) which he entitles odes. Another book, dated 1819, contains some fables evidently his own composition. There are also a prayer against evil thoughts, and a very short sermon entitled, "Be not conformed to this world."

At eight years old he wrote (probably under his father's guidance) a chronological scheme of the Old Testament, called "History of the Jews," beginning from the Creation and going down to B.C. 456. This is written in a larger-sized book and extends over fifty pages. Another specimen, dated 1820, of the early bent of his mind may be placed on record exactly as it is written.

"Looking unto Jesus, or the believer's support under trials and afflictions.

"By Henry Alford, Jun. 1st edition.

"Contents. Chap. 1. What looking unto Jesus means.
Chap. 2. When we ought to look to Jesus.
Chap. 3. Looking unto Jesus is the believer's comfort.
Chap. 4. Texts of Scripture which order looking to Jesus.

"Chap. 1. Looking unto Jesus is not, as some would suppose, looking to him with our bodily eyes, for we cannot see Jesus as the Apostles did, and other holy men; but it is here taken in a spiritual sense, and means first, a looking unto him by faith, second, praying to him."

The other chapters are written only in pencil, and consequently are scarcely legible.

Before any of these little books were written, his father was ordained, and went with his son to reside at Steeple Ashton, as curate to old Mr. Samuel Hey.

Here was his home for two years, and a recollection of his intercourse at this time with his father is recorded in the Second Lesson of the "School of the Heart."

"Evening and Morning—those two ancient names
So link'd with childish wonder, when with arm
Fast wound about the neck of one beloved,
Oft questioning, we heard Creation's tale,
Evening and Morning brought to me strange joy."

His father was his teacher and companion, and so great was his anxiety for his son, even at that tender age, that he kept a daily account of his conduct.

The parochial work of Steeple Ashton was too hard for his father's delicate health, and he left in the summer of 1815, and undertook the curacy of Wraxall, near Bristol, from whence he took his son on occasional visits both to his mother's relations in Staffordshire, and to his father's relations in Somersetshire.

In July, 1815, he and his father were staying for a time at

Torquay, where they saw the "Bellerophon" in which Napoleon was waiting to be sent to St. Helena[3]. To this visit the following passage from the Second Lesson of the "School of the Heart" refers.

> " I ever loved the ocean, as 't had been
> My childhood's playfellow: in sooth it was;
> For I had built me forts upon the sand,
> And launch'd my little navies in the creeks,
> Careless of certain loss; so it would play,
> Even as it listed with them, I were pleased.
> I loved to follow with the backward tide
> Over rough rocks and quaintly delving pools,
> Till that the land-cliffs lessen'd, and I trod
> With cautious steps on slippery crags and moist,
> With sea-weed clothed like green hair of nymphs,
> The Nereids' votive hair, that on the rocks
> They hang, when storms are past, to the kind power
> That saved their sparry grottoes."

A change was now coming on the child's hitherto peaceful hours with his kind and patient father, who, compelled by infirm health, gave up his curacy at Wraxall, and accepted an offer to accompany as chaplain the late Lord Calthorpe in a tour on the Continent. Accordingly in April, 1817, the travellers left England, and the little Henry was sent to a small school kept by Mr. Mercy at Charmouth, in Dorsetshire, from whence he went to spend his holidays partly with his uncle (the Rev. Samuel Alford) at Heale House; and partly with his paternal grandmother, Mrs. Alford, at Ilminster.

In the "School of the Heart" he refers to Charmouth as "that steep built village, on the southern shore," and speaking of it at this time, he says,—

> " Then with strange joy
> Forgetting all, I gazed upon that sea,
> Till I could see the white waves leaping up,
> And all my heart leapt with them :—so I past
> Southward, and near'd that wilderness of waves."

During his father's absence abroad, which lasted till August, 1818, many letters were written by him which show

---

[3] He set sail from England July 24, reached St. Helena August 8, died March, 1821; disinterred and taken to the Invalides, Paris, 1840, by Louis Philippe.

his constant carefulness for his child. Some of them were printed in the "Memorial of the late Rev. Henry Alford," page 53.

A fever which broke out in Charmouth in 1818 led to the withdrawal of Henry from this school; and on going to Ilminster he had a severe attack of whooping-cough. Another ailment, ophthalmia, caught from an old soldier who taught him to ride, fell on him in the following year.

In 1819, his father undertook the curacy of Drayton, in Somersetshire, and bought a house in the neighbouring village of Curry Rivell, within a mile of Heale House, where the Rev. Samuel Alford lived with his numerous children, who were as brothers and sisters to Henry; and here his father carried on for about a year the education of Henry and some of his cousins. Once more his father's useful life was interrupted by a failure of health and strength; and Henry was again sent from home for education to Charmouth, this time to a school kept by a Congregationalist minister, the Rev. B. Jeanes[4]. From this time he seems to have written constantly to his father and to his cousins at Heale, and to his aunt in Staffordshire.

The following letter is written to his aunt whilst he was still in his home at Curry; and here, it may be noted, we

---

[4] In an article in the "Contemporary Review," September, 1866, p. 57, the Dean of Canterbury has described this teacher of his boyhood, referring to Mr. Lyon, the Congregationalist Minister in George Eliot's novel, Felix Holt. The Dean writes:—"It was not our fortune to be much in company with Independents at the precise date given in this story, but we can speak from experience of a pedagogue of that denomination in 1820-21, and certainly talk from him like that which is attributed to old Mr. Lyon would have astonished his scholars not a little. The characteristics of our old friend, and of the brethren who came to officiate for him, were rather an avoidance than an inculcation of any thing like high doctrine. There was an abundant flow of florid rhetoric, garnished with frequent quotations from Dryden and Goldsmith; not a word of conversion, nor an approach to the normal state of religious thought, which George Eliot seems to imagine natural among Independents. One saying of his may be worth recalling:—'You may see,' said he, speaking one day of his status as Dissenter, 'that I am a conscientious Nonconformist, because I regularly and cheerfully pay my church-rates.' It was in the midst of the unhappy strife which divided the land into King's-men and Queen's-men (the trial of Queen Caroline). Our good old friend was a staunch upholder of the injured Princess, and employed all hands in the school in decorating for the illumination on her acquittal. Peace to his memory, and to the memory of the days before theological rancour had set in between Churchman and Dissenter."

have the first indication from himself of his love of flowers, which afterwards developed into that taste for gardening which was shown at Wymeswold and at Canterbury:—

To Miss H. Paget.

"*Feb.* 4, 1820.

"My dear Aunt,—As Mr. Bird is going to Lichfield on Saturday, I will now take the liberty of writing a few lines to you. I have sent you some flower-seeds, which I hope you will accept, as they are the first-fruits of my garden. I have got coming up three hyacinths, four crocuses, four snowdrops, two tulips, and some more crocuses in a pot. Over the seed that is called convolvulus major you must place a long stick, and the plant will adhere to it and crawl up it. The convolvulus minor will grow to a bush of itself. All the lupins had better be tied up to a stick. Yesterday I planted peas, and to-day beans. I have got a green-and-blue tulip in my garden. I have sent you a plan of my father's house and garden. I sleep in a room by myself, and have done for half a year nearly, and have got a drawer for my playthings, a drawer for my clothes, a washing-stand, a large bed, a chest of drawers, a little red box to keep seeds in with two bottoms, half a dozen pill-boxes, a large box to keep my books in, and pens and slate, some silk-worms' eggs, an Ovid's Epistles of Heroes in Latin, which I am learning, Cornelius Nepos, Clarke, and a large Bible which my father gave me. Please to give my love to my uncle, and tell him I am going to send him a line. Believe me, my dear aunt,

"Your affectionate and dutiful nephew."

About a year after this, he writes thus to his father from Mr. Jeanes' school:—

"*Charmouth, March* 10, 1821.

"My dear Father,—As Mrs. Shute[5] is going to Heale, I will now take the opportunity of writing to you. I com-

---

[5] My maternal grandmother, who lived at Charmouth, and was very kind to the motherless boy. She died in 1824.

menced Horace last week, and to-day I have begun the 7th Ode, 1st Book, 'Laudabunt alii,' &c. We missed the 5th and 6th Odes. I was so pleased with your seal of Diogenes, and desire you to send me Regulus, and also a stick of sealing-wax. I have sent you one of the Sphinx, with ΑΙΓΥΠΤΟΣ on it, which I believe means Ægyptian. Do not break the seal. I have several bread seals, which is now the fashion in our school.

"We must all die: it is no good to resist death. 'Pallida mors æquo pulsat pede pauperum tabernas Regumque turres.'—*Hor.* I received your letter yesterday. My knee, which was injured by the bowl, is now very well. I should be very glad if by Mrs. Shute you would send me some paper, pencils, string, a letter, and 1*s.* 6*d.* There came a man the other day with three very curious cards, containing an alphabet of capitals in such a small compass that I could hardly read it; the second card, a perpetual calendar; and the third, tables, weights, and measures, elegantly coloured; all three for a shilling, a set of which I bought. I have sent a marble with my name marked in it for Fanny, a curious card of my own marking to Shute, and another to Polly, and another to Octavia. Please put 3*s.* 6*d.* of my money in the Missionary-box towards that Society. I was very much pleased with the seal of Brutus which you sent me. I was sorry to hear of the illness of poor James House: I hope he will not die. And how is old Betty Low? I continue to take in the 'Cottage Magazine.' Please to give my love to all, and accept the same kindly yourself. I shall write a short note to Fanny. I remain

"Your affectionate son."

The coast between Charmouth and Lyme Regis is well known to students of geology (see Dr. Buckland's "Bridgewater Treatise," vol. i. pp. 377, 437), and Henry Alford's recollections of his school-boy days there are recorded in an article in "Dearden's Miscellany," 1839, p. 310.

"We remember in our boyish days how we loved the sea; how we were at school in a seaside village, a pleasant, warm nook on the southern coast; how we used to get up soon after the sun on the bright, warm summer mornings, and rush down on the firm sands to bathe; how we used to bask and sport in the clear, green sparkling water, and run leaping and plunging into the spray, and get knocked down by the waves; and then the breakfasts of hot rolls and prawns, and the appetite for them! And there was a river, a small, irregular, alder-fringed, playful river, full of strange fish, such as inland streams yield not—dabs and flounders, and the like—and after spring-tides or storms this river used to have its course over the beach changed, never twice alike. Sometimes we used to go down, and find it flowing in one full, unhindered stream into the sea, and were fain to strip and ford it to pursue our path; sometimes it was split into two or three respectable streams, and then it was who could leap them, and many a ducking used there to be; then, again, it would trickle down in hundreds of little rillets not shoe-deep, making the pebbles bright and clear, like pearls and cornelians and onyxes; and sometimes it was not traceable at all, but found its way into a bank of pebbles which the waves had cast up, and there sunk away. On half-holidays it used to be put to the vote—the fields or the sea? and our rambles were directed accordingly. And what a beach it was! Fossils of all descriptions strewed lavishly about; bright bronzed ammonites, or cornus, as we called them; other sparkling nondescripts, known as mushrooms and buttons; and many a stone, which we polished with sand and water. And what a delight it was to ramble away at low tide over the queer fields of green sea-weed, studded with gleaming pools of salt water! and to see the awkward crabs sideling away from us, and the purple and crimson and white polypi, with their long fringes floating in the hollows! And how grand and glorious were the storms, when we used to sit all in a heap on our dormitory window-seat, looking breathlessly over the meadows into the sea, which flashed, and foamed, and roared in the moonlight! And what fun was the havock the next morning!—the village bridge broken down, the coaches all in a body the other side of the stream, now itself raging like a sea; the passengers crossing in boats; and then the odd things washed ashore—star-fish and jelly-fish, and shells of all shapes."

About the year 1821, he made a set of Hymns, and called them "A Collection of Hymns for Sundry Occasions." One specimen we will give:—

> "Life is a journey, heaven is our home,
> While round this wicked world we sinners roam.
> What joy will fill the true believer's heart
> When earth he leaves, from earth for heaven to part.
>
> "Here trouble and anxiety distress;
> There lasting joy and Jesus' presence bless:
> Here never-failing sin and death remain;
> There, free from trouble, we with God shall reign.
>
> "There we no more shall darkly Him perceive,
> Whom to have hurt on earth our hearts will grieve,
> But face to face we shall behold Him there,
> Exempt from fear, anxiety, and care.
>
> "Just as a school-boy longing for his home,
> Leaps forth for gladness when the hour is come;
> So true believers, eager for the skies,
> Released by death, on wings of triumph rise."

The longing expressed in the beginning of the last verse, may have been felt with peculiar strength, from his experience in the new school to which he was removed in the autumn of 1821. It was kept by Mr. Elwell at Hammersmith, and his reminiscences of his time spent there were not the happiest of his school life.

In the winter of 1821, he accompanied his father on a visit to Lord Calthorpe, at Ampton Hall. Whilst on this visit he wrote the following letter to his aunt:—

TO MISS H. PAGET.

"*Ampton Hall, Dec.* 30, 1822.

"MY DEAR AUNT,—You received, I hope, my letter from London. I came here on Tuesday week in the Bury coach and arrived about six in the evening. The house is in the form of an E, with a modern front on the back of the E. It stands in a large park which is well wooded with cedar and firs, and such like trees. In it there is a large lake (about three times as big as the pond at Lichfield) which is now quite frozen over, so that we have famous skating and sliding on it. There is a great deal of game about here, such as partridges, pheasants, hares, and rabbits, and, consequently, there are a great many poachers about here, most of the people in Bury Gaol are poachers. The other day there was a hare frozen into the ice, which was about four inches thick. I went to work with hatchets and pickaxes, knives, &c., and got it out; but, alas! the ice magnified it, for never did I see such a skinny, poor lean thing, in all my life. It was not worth carrying home, so I left it down at the lake. There are no deer in this park, but in a gentleman's park that is only separated from this by some rails there are a great many.

"I will tell you in what manner we spend the day. At eight o'clock the bell rings to get up, but we generally get up before to skate and slide, &c. At nine the bell rings for prayers, when we all assemble in the hall, and Lord Calthorpe expounds a chapter and prays, which generally takes up till ten, when we go to breakfast; after breakfast we separate, and go out or do what we like till two, when the bell rings for luncheon, which takes up but very little time. After luncheon we separate as before till five o'clock, when the first bell rings to dress for dinner; at half-past five the bell rings again to go into the dining-room for dinner, which takes us up altogether till half-past seven, when we retire into the drawing-room, where tea and coffee are immediately brought in; we remain there till the bell rings for prayers, which are the same as in the morning, only no expounding; after prayers we some of us go to bed, others stay longer.

"Your most affectionate nephew.

"P.S.—Lord Calthorpe is such a nice man, his crest is two men with clubs, standing on each side of a boar's head. I cannot send a seal, as my father is going to enclose this in his letter; however I can send you the seal of my affection for you, which will never be erased from my mind."

Some pieces in verse and prose are preserved which seem to have been written by him in his holidays about this time. They relate to subjects which occupied his mind in later years; one is entitled, "The Believer's Home," one is on "The Improvement of Time."

There is also a "Litany," an address on the "Bible Society," and an essay on "The All-sufficiency of God," and a little book entitled, "Christianity Extended."

In the Christmas of 1823 he left Hammersmith, and was sent in the beginning of the year 1824 to Ilminster Grammar School, almost within sight of his father's house at Curry. This change was most agreeable to his own wishes. Mr. Allen, the head master, was one who could discover and appreciate the peculiarities of his pupil's character, and give that kind of training which was best calculated to develope his abilities. The time which he spent at this school, three years and a half, was full of happiness, and marked by an uninterrupted progress. In after-life he often spoke most gratefully and affectionately of Mr. Allen and his wife, who showed a careful interest in her husband's pupils. She still survives (1871) her husband: and the following lines, extracted from a letter recently written by her, contain her recollections of Henry Alford as a schoolboy. She recalls the image of "the delicate, gentle boy, whose wondrous powers of memory were shown at a standing-up" (a Winchester exercise), able, when put on at the will of the examiner, to repeat an immense number of lines in Greek, Latin, and English. She remembers among his peculiar amusements a practice of cutting out shades to represent the head of the Blessed Saviour, and other objects; his arrangement of fragments of glass to imitate peals of bells, and his habit of writing verses. In connexion with this, she remembers as the cause of the only habitual complaint against him his inclination, which many impositions failed to correct, to write in forbidden hours of and to the members of his home circle. She remembers only one evil tendency which seemed to be sufficiently marked to rouse his teacher's apprehension, and that was selfishness, which," she says, "as being so entirely one, I only mention, to show my desire to tell you all I can, and to be impartial."

The feelings which impelled him to keep up so frequent a correspondence with his cousins are expressed in one of the letters of this period. He says, "It has pleased God that I should be blessed with neither brothers nor sisters: this is a misfortune at which I have often grieved, and (I blush to own it) have sometimes even repined. Since this, therefore, is the case, I must write to my cousins, and I must have some one to whom I may write fully and freely; therefore don't deny me this pleasure."

Times and seasons much affected him at that age. On the approach of his fourteenth birthday, October 6, 1824, he says to his Cousin Fanny (afterwards his wife), "What a different sensation the mention of the 7th of October produces in me now from what it did formerly. I think now upon the troubles and temptations which I must necessarily be exposed to, and tremble at the prospect of them. I think on the many snares which necessarily await me in the gaieties and frivolous pleasures of youth, and fear I shall never be able to withstand them. I look on the vices and failures I think I have discovered in myself, and which others have mentioned to me in my character, and think that the nearer approach of manhood can but confirm these in me and stifle what little seeds of virtue it has pleased God to implant in me. My two greatest failings among, as you know, many thousand others are idleness and inconstancy; when I undertake a thing I set about it eagerly, and I have no doubt if I continued it all the way through should not make a bad job of it (as we say in this country), but my ardour is like a storm, it soon abates, and leaves behind it a sort of lethargy."

To the same cousin he writes:—

To Miss Fanny Alford.

"*August* 8, 1825.

"You have been confirmed; an event no less important as it regards your advancing years, than as it respects your serious views and eternal welfare. I hope you have thought more seriously of religion since you have been confirmed; in my letters I have often mentioned these things to you, and more and oftener perhaps than you have liked. But I am afraid that my conduct has not been on a level with the standard which I have prescribed in my letters: indeed the negligence and pride of my youth, the thoughtlessness to which I am so prone, and the weight of sin so pressing upon me, often, much too often, lead me into follies and excesses, which in my more sober and thoughtful hours I bewail and repent of. Example is a great thing to those who pretend to give advice to others. I need not explain to you (as I, of course, think you know it already) the serious nature of the engagement you have entered into. You will not be offended if I insert a few short maxims for behaviour which I once laid down for myself, but, alas! I have but badly observed:—

"1. When about to do any thing, first consider whether it pleases God, then if others would like it, and lastly whether myself.

"2. When inclined to passion or anger, to stop and consider God sees me.

"3. Never dispute any trifling thing with any one, even though I should be in the right.

"4. Whenever any one calls me names or otherwise reproaches me, to return it by saying, perhaps I may be what you say; or, perhaps I may have done it.

"5. To weigh a question before I trouble others by asking it, whether or not it is of any consequence, if not, to drop it.

"6. Never to be ashamed of any thing which is right by God's law.

"7. Never to affect any thing, but follow nature.

"8. In company to consider myself absent.

"9. In study to consider all others absent.

"10. To try persuasion as far as possible in every thing before I enter upon force.

"11. Strictly to adhere to truth in every thing in relations, that is, narratives of any thing I have undergone or seen, rather to speak within the mark than otherwise; and if there be any thing which I exaggerate, to let it be my own vices and failures.

"12. To pray incessantly to God that He would send me grace to perform these resolutions, through Jesus Christ our Lord."

On his fifteenth birthday he sends an address in poetry to his father, who replied in a letter which has been published in "Memorial of the Rev. H. Alford," page 82.

The following extracts from it will show with what judicious and tender sympathy the father soothed his son's ardent temperament without discouraging the natural exercise of his promising talents:—

"Beware, my dear boy, how you indulge in poets' dreams, which are proverbially unreal. Bring your mind to view things through a more sober medium, and lower your expectations of happiness from earthly objects. Thus you will experience fewer disappointments, and have a more real enjoyment of the comforts which this chequered life affords. On the other hand, do not give way to a gloomy and melancholy state of mind. Refuse not to gather the flowers, though they be but daisies and buttercups, with which it pleases God sometimes to strew the path of life; but remember that perennial and thornless flowers bloom only in the Paradise above."

His tendency to judge himself with severity, and his desire to exercise a religious influence on his associates, are shown in a letter to his cousin and schoolfellow, Walter Alford, a youth only three years older than himself.

The letter is dated from Winkfield, a village near Bradford in Wiltshire, where his father resided as curate between the summer of 1825 and October, 1826, when he removed to Ampton, Suffolk, the rectory of which was presented to him by Lord Calthorpe.

To Walter Alford.

"*Dec.* 31, 1825.

"Poor old 1825 is now stretched on his dying bed, with all his friends around him, and ready to breathe his last. People seem very glad to get rid of the old fellow, for they salute him off with bells and rejoicing. He has been the death of many, and will be the doom in judgment to many more; to-morrow will be 1826.

"I well remember when I might have said, to-morrow will be 1814. Twelve years have gone since that, and what use have I made of them? Why, as good as none. I have been trifling away what has been more important, if possible, than life itself, and shall still continue to do so, till I not only know but feel the precious worth of time. God grant that I soon may; I have now no time to lose, but am continually doing so for want of firmness of character and steady application. I have a study here, and all my books about me, and a nice fire, but the misfortune of it is, that I am so confoundedly lazy and idle. There is a great difference, though you may not think it, in these two words. Laziness is that kind of stupid mood when one stretches oneself, and yawns, and wishes it were the next meal. Idleness, on the contrary, is the sitting with one's books before one, and scribbling poetry, or reading names in the dictionary, or talking with your neighbour. We might encourage one another in good practices; we should have no very inconsiderable influence on those about us; let us discontinue all improper and irreligious conversation, let it be with whom it will, at school and at home, as far as our influence extends to discountenance such talk in others: will not you join with me in a practice which may be beneficial both to ourselves and others? I am persuaded you will, and not only so, but will set me an example of following this precept."

In another letter to Walter, dated July 25, 1826, after describing an excursion with his father up the Wye, he thus adverts to his confirmation. "I am, you know, about to be confirmed, about to enter on a solemn covenant with God, to renounce the pomps and vanities of this wicked world, and all the sinful lusts of the flesh; about to profess a public belief of all the articles of the Christian faith, and to endeavour, by God's help, to keep His holy will and commandmandments, and to walk in the same all the days of my life: what a solemn covenant is this! If we regard covenants made with our fellow-creatures as sacred, and not to be broken through, what should we think of a covenant made with the Father of spirits? I am afraid that indeed I often shall break through it. I hope God will grant me seriousness on that occasion."

It was at this time that Henry Alford appears to have begun the practice of keeping a daily record of his pursuits and feelings. His journals, extending over forty-four years, still remain. A few years before his death, he came across these earlier volumes, that had long been laid by and forgotten, and he was on the point of destroying them when his intention accidentally became known to his wife, and in deference to her entreaty he spared them, and gave them to her custody. It is obvious that they were written for his own eye alone; but some portions of them may, without impropriety, be used to serve the purpose of this book, which is to delineate his character, and record the principal incidents of his life. The entries of the first week will be extracted almost verbatim, as a specimen of the whole. In these memoranda it will be instructive and pleasing to trace the early germs of most of those varied gifts which distinguished him in later years. Not only the ardour with which he applied himself to the study of classics, and mathematics and general literature; to music, and drawing, and mechanical contrivances, and his strong love for poetry, and precocious facility for composition; but also the constant communion of his soul with God, his unselfish desire to live for the service and pleasure of those who were nearest to him; his industry and activity, amounting almost to restlessness, may be traced in the following record of a week.

"*Winkfield, Friday Night, July* 28, 1826.

"Received my 'Burton Pynsent' from Messrs. Baldwin and Cradock [see page 23], with a kind note; rose at seven, made a sundial, learnt some tunes, among which the bass of the Evening Hymn.

"*Sunday, July* 30.—Mr. Longmire performed the morning service, text, Rev. xii. 10, sermon half an hour long. My father's afternoon's text, Acts viii. 17, half an hour long;

read the lessons for him; evening lecture on Confirmation read Deut. viii. to xi. at night.

"*July* 31.—Added a month's index to my sun-dial, wrote out two tunes for the singers, read a bit of Foster's essays on the term 'Romantic;' (remember, the clock is ten minutes slower than the sun) intensely hot, thunder, rain, and lightning, bed at eleven. τῷ θεῷ δόξα, ὅς ἐμαυτὸν ἀπὸ τῶν τῆς ἡμέρας κινδύνων ἔσωσε.

"*Aug.* 1.—Rose at six, arranged octaves of musical glasses, no use, could not make them answer. Read part of the life of Rev. D. Brown by Mr. Simeon; after dinner walked a little with my father; he remarked that there are moments when, if we could look no farther than this world, we should be truly the most miserable of men, and that ever since my dear mother's death he had no one to whom he could open his mind; why may not I become such? cannot I try to accommodate my habits to his, my notions to his, and to soothe and allay his sorrows; (five o'clock) came into my room and prayed for grace to do so, may God grant this prayer. I am constantly making resolutions, and as constantly breaking through them, O may they not rise up in judgment against me in the last day; where, O Lord, can I then fly? whither can I take refuge? my head knowledge says to Christ, my heart gives me no answer. It is the contrary in spiritual from what it is in worldly matters; there if the arrow reach the heart, immediate death ensues; till God's arrow reach it there can be no life; draw Thy bow, O Lord, make ready Thy shaft; send it, O Lord, deep into this wall of stone; Thou before whom the mountains melt, canst Thou not melt this rock of my heart? Prayer is irksome to begin, how sweet when begun. Evening, read Romans xiii. and xiv. in Greek, had a conversation with my father on these subjects; even in writing a journal Satan sometimes says 'well done,' and so elates the heart. N.B.—Avoid argument. Went to Trowbridge and bought 'Hervey's Meditations' for Fanny, and 'Falconer's Shipwreck' for myself.

"*Aug.* 3.—Read some of Mr. Brown's life: may I be enabled to imitate him in his zeal for God and in his private practical pi[illegible]: must learn Hebrew. My father gave me Wolfe's Rema[illegible] He talked of the stings of conscience after the death o[illegible] friend.

"*Aug.* 4.—Read, [illegible]r rather devoured Falconer's 'Shipwreck,' certainly not inferior, but much otherwise to any thing Walter Scott ever produced. A thunderstorm coming on. 'Tu me, Deus, per noctem e periculis eripe, Sancto tuo Spiritu illumina ut ab impuris omnibus et levibus cogitationibus abstineam et in te mediter. Amen.'

"*Aug.* 5.—Rose at half-past six, read twenty-four Propositions of Euclid; after breakfast read 'Bridge's Algebra' to adfected Quadratic Equations, tried Hebrew, and wrote out an alphabet; no Grammar, only a Dictionary; must apply at Christmas. After dinner translated the Latin notes in 'Hervey's Meditations' for Fanny, the verse into verse, the prose into prose, and marked some passages in Hervey, 'Among the Tombs,' and 'On a Flower Garden.' Evening, played the flute, practised my tunes, and now another week is ended. Do Thou, O God, forgive me all the sins I have committed therein, and keep me, during the following and every week, from adding to the number of my transgressions. May the knowledge which I may acquire not puff me up, but rather humble me, as always finding out more which I ought to learn.

"*Aug.* 7.—Rose at six, read Euclid, cut fragments from newspapers, drew a likeness of myself. Evening, thought on confirmation; may I truly be able to take upon myself these promises and vows, and perform them to the utmost of my power; Lord, give me grace to do so.

"*Aug.* 8.—Rose at half-past five, read Algebra and Greek Testament, made a secret drawer in my writing-desk. My father showed me a memorandum of my mother's. When I consider my ingratitude to him and God, for the many favours received by me, I am ready to sink as it were into nothing with shame and abhorrence with myself. Copied out Lonsdale's L. M. tune. Talked with my father of my poem of the Crusades. Entered too much into argument; I must keep in my feelings. I sometimes feel carried away with that romantic spirit, that I want, oh I want to write; I want to produce something famous; but my mind is so full of things that I don't know what to say, just so now.

"Pie Jesu Domine,
Dona mihi requiem. Amen.
O! ab hœdis me sequestra
Statuens in parte dextrâ.

"O for a spark of living fire
That blazed in Wolfe's poetic lyre!
O for a brand from out the flame
That burns in Byron's endless fame!

"Or rather for a sacred breath
From old Isaiah's fragrant wreath;
To sing in bright, in rapturous lays
My glorious Maker's worthy praise.

"*Aug.* 9.—Read Euclid. Took a drawing of the parsonage from the wood, in a blank page of 'Hervey's Meditations' for Fanny. The church I have begun there too.

"My father read some of Mr. Marsh's letters to him in 1808-11. The confirmation as it approaches nearer and nearer, in reality seems to recede further and further from my heart. O Lord, do thou fix firmly on it the vows I am about to confirm in my own name, and assist me in the right performance of them.

"Lord, I my vows to Thee renew;
Scatter my sins as morning dew;
Guard my first spring of thought and will,
And with Thyself my spirit fill.

"*Aug.* 10.—Read Euclid. Completed my sketch of Winkfield Church. Set to music one verse of Wolfe's 'Not a drum was heard.' Finished my Ode on F.'s birthday."

In addition to the journal from which the foregoing extracts are taken, another memorial is preserved of the thoughts and feelings which were stirring in him during his pupilage at Ilminster. His "Commonplace Books" of this date contain about 150 pieces of poetry, original and translated, in English and Latin, interspersed with drawings and musical airs. The longest poems are in blank verse. One entitled "Burton Pynsent," in 705 lines, with a Preface and Notes, which, as the journal has already recorded, he offered to a London publisher.

Another an unfinished drama, entitled "The Persecution under Diocletian." Some of the smaller poems on subjects of passing interest were published in the country papers. A few specimens of this collection of poems may be interesting to the reader.

TRANSLATION (ANTIGONE, 775) SOPHOCLES.

" O Love, that in the dimpled cheek
Of virgin youth dost dwell,
Nought can thy powerful influence break,
Nor e'en all conquering riches can avail:
Thou rid'st triumphant on the waves,
And mak'st the abject wind thy slaves;
All feel alike thy thrilling power,
Both gods above and men below."

ODE TO MUSIC.

IRREGULAR.

" I had the note! ah! was not that a part?
These should be they! ah! treacherous heart!
'Tis gone! The melody evades my art!
Hush, let fav'ring silence reign!
There! I touch'd the string again!
These are the notes—once more with pleasure
My ear recalls the favourite measure!
Move with gentle cadence on,
All ye harsher sounds be gone," &c. &c.
Sept. 1825.

This Ode goes on in this wild strain for about fifty more lines.

MY MOTHER'S GRAVE, TAMWORTH.

" My mother, if thy spirit blest,
Enthroned in bliss on high,
Can from its place of endless rest,
'Midst joys that never die,
One placid look of pity cast
Upon life's troubled scene,
Behold thy son."
1825.

MORNING PRAYER.

" Through the night Thy love hath spared me;
Lord, accept my morning praise:
O be with me, keep and guard me
This and all my future days.

"When assaulted by temptation,
O permit me not to fall;
May Thy love and consolation
Bless my meat, my drink, my all."

EVENING PRAYER.

"Guard me, O Thou gracious Saviour,
Through the perils of this night:
Let Thy presence and Thy favour
Turn my darkness into light.

"Whether waking, Lord, or sleeping,
May my thoughts be still on Thee;
Take me to Thy care and keeping,
Watch, preserve, and comfort me."

In an article in Dearden's "Miscellany," 1840, vol. iii., he thus speaks of his poetical taste at this time, and his schoolboy days at Ilminster.

"It was in the month of May, 1826, that we first became acquainted with the poems of Byron. It was such a May as glows over all nature while we are now writing. Balmy and voiceful and flowerful; a season which always affects the mind (for what reasons we inquire not now) with an undefined, faint melancholy languor, which, however, ranges side by side with the purest and deepest joy arising from the loveliness of all around; is not this a mode for reading Byron? Those who know the town of Ilminster, in Somersetshire, know also a quaint and mossy hill rising to the south-west of the town, and retaining from its ancient tenants the name of Heron Hill. Far across the timbered vales and green hill-tops may be seen its clump of dark firs; and wide and glorious is the prospect which he may see stretched beneath him, who walks therein, or lies, as we lay in our schoolboy days, half covered with scented woodbine and bright blue periwinkle, looking through the old trunks of those same windy giants. Here in those golden days of schoolboys, yclept half-holidays, did we repair, and amidst the speaking beauties of nature, did we read and read again, even till they became part of our minds, the 'thoughts that breathe and words that burn' of Byron. The underlying town, with its rosy belt of blossoming orchards, and venerable fretted tower, the misty woods stretched away into faint distance, the uplands and bright green flats, and the far off blue of the everlasting hills, are bound up in our recollection with many a passage in 'Childe Harold,' and the repetition of the well-known lines, brings about us the air of spring, the scent of hawthorn and woodbine, and the hum and song of the happy legions of air. What wonder then if we became idolizers of Byron? What wonder if even now, when we can read him 'with calmer pulse and judgment more attent,' our hearts still dwell fondly round those old poetic haunts, and receive pleasure from those same strains!"

A few more extracts from his journal may be introduced by the following letter to his cousin, Mary Alford, afterwards Mrs. Trenchard.

"*Oct.* 3, 1826.—I am now pretty well got into my school business again; 'tis plod, plod, plod, step by step, dull work, but I have to console myself, while labouring up the hill, on the fine prospect and fresh breezes I shall enjoy on the top, should I ever arrive there. Diligence, my dear Mary, is the only way of becoming famous or acquitting yourself honourably in any station of life; it is what you owe to yourself and to Him who gave you your talents. . . . . When we are a little put out of our way, then it is those Christian graces, humility, resignation, and meekness, have an opportunity of shining forth to the glory of God in Christ. It is not going over a smooth and even road which tries the springs of a carriage; but when the road is rough and the ruts deep, and the stones high, then it is that we fear the springs, and that their goodness or badness appears.

"You seem to like that which really constitutes a letter, viz. mutual advice and comfort."

Extracts from his journal:—

"*Ilminster, Oct.* 4.—Rose at six, learnt Wolsey's lamentation on his greatness. Began copying the anthem. Verses, subject, 'The restoration of the Fine Arts by the French after the Revolution.' Went to the playground and made up the quarrel between Jay and Day. Thucydides and mathematics.

"*Oct.* 11.—Learnt the story of Lavinia in Thomson. Missed dinner by staying in the church to hear the new organist play. Practised the flute.

"*Oct.* 13.—Rose at six. Livy; Greek epigram, subject, 'non prodest quod non lædere possit idem;' helping about a play; heard Thring his 'gatherings' for to-morrow; began a play, and wrote the scene and plot.

"*Oct.* 19.—Rose at six, continued verses. Thucydides, Homer, mathematics.

"*Oct.* 20.—Mr. Whitfield gave me a drawing lesson. Latin verses, subject, ἀμουσία; wrote to my father, asking him to let me learn music[6]. Eve, Thucydides.

"*Oct.* 23.—Theme, 'Why does Genius flourish most in free states?' Construed all the time from five to six, and from seven to eight, did 200 lines of Juvenal, five chapters of Thucydides, and ninety lines of Homer.

"*Nov.* 1.—Seven weeks to the holidays. Mr. Cope came and agreed to give me three music lessons a week; learnt a piece of Wharton's Pleasures of Melancholy, began trigonometry, drank tea at my grandmother's, let off fireworks.

"*Heale House, Dec.* 28.—Went to Muchelney and took two sketches of the church; was never so cold in my life.

"*Dec.* 30.—With Tom to Owlstreet, repeating and practising Brutus and Cassius. Evening, acted Alfred four times with my cousins. I took three different characters. Tom and I did Brutus and Cassius.

"*New Year's Day*, 1827.—My uncle at Heale had all his family assembled (thirteen of them), and gave them each a New Year's gift, and me also. I must take care what I write to Fanny at school, as her letters are looked at. Took

6 "Would you have any objection for the ensuing quarter to my learning the piano? I can easily manage so as for it not to interfere with my other studies by having my lessons in play time; and if you should think the money not sufficiently well applied, I will willingly, with your consent, apply some of that money which lies in your hands of my own to paying for it. My only reason for wishing to learn is for my own private amusement. I do not aspire above mediocrity. I think eight weeks will be quite sufficient practice for every purpose that I shall want."

leave of all my cousins and went by the North Devon coach to town, and stopped at night at Salisbury[7] to have tea.

"*Ampton, Jan.* 5.—Came here, ground covered with snow. At 9 p.m. the Duke of York died.

"*Jan.* 7.—My father read in at Ampton, and performed three full services; thank God for having given him strength to do so.

"*Jan.* 13.—Went to the other side of the lake and cut reeds for arrows, dined at Lord Calthorpe's five times in eight days; company, Lord Calthorpe, Mr. and Lady Charlotte Calthorpe, R. Benyon de Beauvoir, Esq., Lord and Lady Barnard, Mr. Barnard, an Etonian, and Mr. Gough. They are going to present a petition about the game laws next session."

After his return to school, his journal tells us that in March he lost his grandmother, Mrs. Alford of Ilminster, whose house was to him a sort of home whilst he was at school in that town. His journal records that he had attained the privilege, customarily accorded to the head boy in the school, of "full liberty" to go in and out as he pleased. He says at this time he was reading "May you like it" and did like it, and describes himself as one

> "That's eaten up with care for circle, line, and square;
> That's worn away with classics, rubbed out with mathematics."

Shortly after he heard from his father that it was fixed that he should go as a private pupil to the Rev. John Bickersteth, of Acton, in Suffolk, to be prepared for college: and on June 20th he left Ilminster school[8], and spent a week with his cousins at Heale, to which place he then bade adieu for three years.

---

[7] This view of Salisbury first suggested to him those lines in his poem, "A Doubt," first published in 1835:—

> "I know not how the right might be;
> But I have shed strange tears to see,
> Passing an unknown town at night,
> In some warm chamber full of light,
> A mother, and two children fair,
> Kneeling with lifted hands at prayer."

[8] A few weeks before his death, in a sermon preached at Canterbury Cathedral, first Sunday in Advent, 1870, he refers to the end of these schoolboy days, "Truth and Trust," p. 23.

In a letter to his cousin, Walter Alford, written July 11, Ampton, after his return home from school, he expresses a strong feeling of regret at parting with some of his companions, particularly one Walker Thring, younger than himself:—

"I dare say you think me a most unaccountable sort of creature, to take such curious likings to two or three different persons, and so sudden in their beginnings and indescribable in their causes. It was very hard parting with Thring: we attempted three times to part,—

'τρὶς ὀρέξαι ἰὼν τόδε τέτρατον'

but could not reconcile our minds to it. You know how to pity me, but I may venture to say you can never feel the like. I will send you some pretty lines from Heber on Farewell.

'When eyes are beaming, &c.'

"There is something that has bound me almost irresistibly to that boy, he is so affectionate, and so almost instinctively averse to all improprieties of word or thought. Forgive me for running on thus. You are well aware that mine is a mind of warm emotions, and most easily worked upon, and too much elated and depressed by trifles. You will rather wonder, with all the bad things that I often say of myself, that I would not change my disposition for any other in the world. I have thoughts peculiar to myself, and parting from these would be like separation from old friends.

"Never mind answering my Latin letter; I would sooner have an English one."

The reference in the last sentence is to a long Latin letter which he wrote to his cousin from school a few weeks previously. This letter is preserved.

With the schoolfellow whom he regarded with so much affection he kept up a correspondence for some time; but as they did not often meet, even the correspondence died out. There was an accidental renewal of acquaintance in 1860; and when Henry Alford died, his widow received (in

February, 1871) a kindly letter, in which this early friend thus refers to their schoolboy days:—

"I have never forgotten our old and unusually warm friendship at Ilminster, and how kind, good, and patient Henry Alford was to me in those days; and probably, how much I am indebted to his guidance and teaching, that I have since then been preserved from harm, in a course through a life of many changes and much early trouble."

Some letters have been preserved which he wrote to his cousin, Walter Alford, during his stay with Mr. Bickersteth at Acton; that is, from August 6, 1827, to October 6, 1828. He describes his life there as very happy. He visited the poor and taught in the Sunday-school, helped to play the organ at church, and in various ways seemed to be preparing himself for the occupation of a clergyman.

One of his letters contains the following expression of his opinion concerning Lord Byron:—

"How do you like Lord Byron? What a genius for noble themes! If, instead of prostituting his muse to the service of licentiousness and infamous blasphemy, he had employed her in the praise of his God, of what service might he have been to the cause of religion!"

A hymn written at this time shows how much attention he gave to the Sunday-school:—

WHAT CAN YOU DO FOR CHRIST?

A QUESTION ADDRESSED TO ACTON SUNDAY-SCHOOL.

"What, children, can you nothing do
For Him who did so much for you?
He left His throne above the sky
For you to suffer and to die.

"In your imperfect nature born,
He bore reproach, contempt, and scorn:
For you He left—amazing love!—
His kingdom and His power above.

"And can you, children, nothing do
For Him who did so much for you?
Oh, you can love Him, you can try
With His commandments to comply.

"You can beseech Him to impart
A humble, new, and contrite heart;
And He will never send away
The children who sincerely pray.

"Oh, you can read His holy word
To those who ne'er its truths have heard;
So children, you will something do
For Him who did so much for you."

Sept. 1827.

His journals supply evidence of the healthy development of his religious character in the year which he spent as a pupil in the family of Mr. Bickersteth.

A few fragmentary extracts may be inserted:—

"*Aug.* 8.—Mr. Canning died ten minutes to 4 a.m.

"*Aug.* 26.—First took the Sacrament.

"*Sept.* 3.—Saved Robert's[9] life in the Stour.

"*Sept.* 13.—Swam with my clothes on.

"*Sept.* 24.—Made an Æolian harp. Drew Acton Church.

[Written in a Bible.] "*Sunday, Nov.* 18, *Acton.*—I do this day, as in the presence of God and my own soul, renew my covenant with God, and solemnly determine henceforth to become His, and do His work as far as in me lies.

"So one more Sabbath is gone to his rest,
And our Sabbaths below are imperfectly given:
They are broken and chill'd and imperfect at best,
But types of the Sabbath in heaven."

"*Dec.* 30.—Played the organ first time in Ampton Church.

"*Dec.* 31.—Bought Milton's works. At night examined the past year, and prayed for grace for the next.

"So ends 1827, spent not as it should have been, valued not as it ought to have been, improved not as it might have been. Lord, give me grace not only to feel really thankful for mercies past, but learn from past sins and past deliverances to be more circumspect in time to come! Help me solemnly to ask myself the question, 'Where art thou?' and my conscience to faithfully answer it!

---

9 One of his fellow pupils.

"The clock strikes twelve: 1827 is ended. 'What is your life?'

"*Jan.* 19.—Learning Horace's Odes, I. II., and finished Aristophanes. Heard I was entered at Trinity College, Cambridge."

The following lines, which were written in his Bible, contain a reference to Henry Kirke White, whose poems and biography made a deep impression on him about this time:—

"*Acton, Feb.* 20, *half-past* 12 *a.m.*—

"'Tis midnight, palely burns my waning lamp,
And gladly I turn from worldly cares to thee,
Blest Messenger of Heaven—and scan thy page
With high and fervid joy—and written there
Is all my lot—past, present, and to come,
And disappointment, and unhail'd success,
Sickness and death—now here the prospect ends.
Wide-stretch'd beyond the grave are realms of joy
And crowns of astral brilliance—heaps of gold,
The meed of faith—and be those treasures mine.
Now to my couch—a few hours' brief repose,
Then back to busy life, but why complain?
Am I as he who sung his mournful strain,
Both time and place alike o'er health destroy'd,
And chilling penury, and sharp ambition
Goading behind, while veiling all before?
Ah, no! but far from me be aught but love,
And strict regard unto the memory
Of him I sing of—pardon, gentle night,
This dull intrusion on thy wonted bounds,
And take my service—world of sin, farewell!"

"*May* 14.—News came of the Catholic question having passed through the first reading in the House of Commons; did Hesiod, wrote notes from Porson, began translating third chapter of Habakkuk into Greek verse. Frewen Turner gave me a cast of a head for phrenology."

From Ampton, where he spent his summer holidays with some of his cousins, he writes:—

"*June* 30.—Copied music, and played the tunes on the organ to my cousins, rowed them round the lake in Lord Calthorpe's grounds; fine sunset. Sketched the Wadgate cottages, sung 'From all that dwell below the skies,' to the Old Hundredth tune (sung bass for the first time); most cosy with all. My father gave me a Shakspeare."

"*July* 11.—Read six hours; getting very fond of algebra; did questions on proportion and Eumenides; made part of a tune for 'When the threatening tempest scowls!'"

This was his last quarter with a private tutor. His journals tell us he was "getting up the Georgics, reading trigonometry, and reading, writing notes, and drawing plans of the Theatre of the Greeks."

For some days this month his journal was written in Latin.

"*Sept.* 30.—Did verses nearly all the morning, read Adams after dinner. Discovered Capella by altitude. Astronomized till past twelve; very beautiful night; wrote down the names and situations of several primary and secondary stars, *α* Lyræ, &c., and watched for Procyon in Canis Minor; he rose at half-past twelve."

The two following letters were written at this time:—

TO WALTER ALFORD.

"*Acton, Sept.*

"I am going to Cambridge in October, so that I must fag. I hope to go up with the first six books of Euclid, plane and spherical trigonometry, and algebra, at my fingers' ends; and in classics I hope to have mastered the Iliad (which I have never read), Sophocles; the four Porsonic plays of Euripides, two or three of Aristophanes, Thucydides, Herodotus, and Xenophon's Cyropædia and Anabasis, Virgil, Livy, Tacitus, Cicero's Orations, Horace, Sallust, and if I can, Pindar. I think that if I can really cram these, as we Cantabs call it, by October, it will be a very respectable set out in classics. In mathematics, as I have often told you, I shall attempt little or nothing, a Senior Optime is at present the ἀκμή of my wishes, though I own the word Wrangler sounds very pretty, but is more like a distant star in the horizon, which work as far as I will I can never reach, than any thing attainable by me."

As the time approached nearer he again wrote to the same cousin.

"You cannot think how I dread Cambridge; I quite

shrink from the thoughts of going there, and fear I shall fall. I have no stamina as yet of religious principle, at least so I fear, and all as yet is talk and pride. People want me to get into the first class at Trinity. I hope I shall be enabled to do my best as in the sight of God, and not to regard the praise or dispraise of men, and then if I fail of my object of attainment of earthly honours, I can be calm and contented under the will of my Heavenly Father, who I can be assured would not have frustrated my expectations, unless it were good for me that it should be so. I have been advised by those who wish for my good to fight shy of new acquaintances, and rather be sought than to seek associates. In such doubtful circumstances, on what can I rely, but on the kind guidance and Fatherly care of Him, who has promised to be a guide to them that love Him?

"I am very busy, and can hardly find time even for letter-writing, of which you know I am so fond. Mathematics I fear comes off but poorly; never fear of my being Senior Wrangler, or a Wrangler at all, or even a Senior Optime, or, I am afraid, even a Junior Optime; however, I hope this stupid head of mine, will get a little more sense knocked into it at Cambridge, or I don't know what I shall do. I am very much afraid of going there, chiefly because I fear I shall disgrace my profession, and dishonour my Saviour; don't forget me about that trying time, during the end of October and the beginning of November, for I expect that during that time my character will be formed in the University."

Before going up to Cambridge, he spent a few pleasant days at Ampton, which are recorded in his journal:—

"*Oct.* 9.—Pleasant day altogether; read to my father an article in the 'Quarterly' on astronomy, and looked at Adams on Astronomy, got the carpenter to make me a quadrant; went to Lord Calthorpe's to dinner, met Mr. Wilberforce [1],

[1] It must have been now, or at an earlier period that Lord Calthorpe, to prevent the consequences of Mr. Wilberforce's earnestness in conversation, which constantly impelled him to advance nearer and nearer to the edge of

and was much pleased with him; Mr. and Lady Harriet Gurney, and Mr. Spencer were there, and Mrs. and Miss Wilberforce.

"*Oct.* 10.—Fixed the globe, put a stay on the quadrant, read Adams' Planets, very interesting indeed; in the evening went to the Hall again, and had a very pleasant time. Lord Arthur Hervey there, Mr. Wilberforce very agreeable, we looked for the comet, looked at plates with Miss Wilberforce.

"*Oct.* 11.—Pleasant day, particularly with dear Mr. Wilberforce. He and Miss Calthorpe called on us, and we walked with them down to the gamekeeper's; pleasant walk and delightful conversation; found a curious fungus in the evening; wrote out about the light on Sept. 29, for Mr. Wilberforce.

"*Oct.* 15.—Wrote an account of the Aurora Borealis; went to the Hall, dear Mr. Wilberforce went, and Mrs. and Miss; played on the organ with Mr. Bickersteth. So ends my career of boyhood; from this time I hope a new era in my life. Lord, support me in it for Christ's sake.

"*Oct.* 16.—Set out for Cambridge with my father. Dined at Professor Farish's, very pleasant. We went to Trinity Church, Mr. Simeon preached there from 'My soul is like a weaned child,' a very delightful sermon, calculated to do much good."

---

the chair on which he was seated, employed young Henry Alford to watch and take suitable opportunities of pushing the chair forward by degrees so that it might keep pace with the advance of the speaker's person.

CHAPTER II.

1828—1832.

LIFE AT CAMBRIDGE AS AN UNDERGRADUATE—GOES TO READ AT PORTSMOUTH—MEETING WITH W. WORDSWORTH—BELL'S SCHOLAR.

THE following extracts from his journal at this time will show the industry, the severity towards himself, and the religious earnestness with which he entered on his college course. The early hours (averaging six) at which he rose, his regular attendance at morning and evening chapel, and the three chapters and a Psalm which constitute his daily portion of the Bible, are set down; and, besides this, under every day a description of the weather, which could scarcely have been more minute and careful if he had been specially studying meteorology.

"*Oct.* 23.—Breakfasted in a great hurry, went to Evans' lecture, very good, a preliminary one on criticism; went to mathematical lecture, Coddington's.

"*Oct.* 24.—Called on Peacock; he recommended me Hodson as a tutor. He set me to do the third part of algebra, some Latin verses, and gave me an order for the library.

"*Nov.* 10.—Lectures, read mathematics, called on Professor Farish, learnt four Odes of Horace.

"*Nov.* 11.—Lectures, read hard till two, then rowed down the river, returned to Hall, worked hard and finished the New Testament. Always estimate men in proportion as they estimate this Book.

"A man may be deep read in the Scriptures, and full of commentaries and criticisms, and yet not be a lover of them;

as a man may be intimately versed in the character of another, and yet not be his friend.

"This Book hath that advantage above the Old Testament which the second temple had over the first, and for the same reason: but in this respect they differ; the glory of that temple is past, and the building destroyed, whereas this book hath its glory to come; for an hour is at hand when all nations shall come hither to see what God hath done, is doing, and will do for their souls.

"*Nov.* 13.—Matriculation, wrote music, went to Senate House, got matriculated, went to Smyth's lectures, very good, and very full, hired a piano, worked at Iambics. Rather idle day, and dilatory.

"*Sunday, Nov.* 30.—Read Bible, went to Scholefield's to the communion, very delightful indeed, beautiful sermon; St. Mary's afterwards, tremendous long sermon, one hour twenty minutes, men scraped with their feet, chapel, good anthems.

"*Dec.* 2.—Very cold, lighted my fire and read till chapel, at the lecture Evans gave a quantity of cram about the choruses in the Eumenides, read till two, walked to Granchester.

"Bleak blows the wind along the moor,
And whistles at the cottage door,
While the poor houseless wanders on
Unpitied, friendless, and alone.
How thankful then ought I to be
For all Thy favours, Lord, to me.

"*Sunday, Dec.* 7.—Simeon, a very good sermon, a divinity sermon; then St. Mary's, a most magnificent sermon from Melvill, made an extract in my common-place book.

"Deeply, Lord, upon my heart
This important truth engrave;
'Tis Thy mercies that impart
All we are, and all we have.
Heavenly Father, what are we,
Left alone, and reft of Thee,
Left without a prop to stand,
Left to sin's overwhelming hand?

"*Dec.* 12.—Continued verses, Evans' lecture all cram about Thucydides. He wished us a pleasant vacation.

"Prayed in Latin, any thing to keep up the attention.

"Full many a beam of mercy shines
  Upon our pilgrimage below,
And oft along the thorny way
  The beacon lamps of mercy glow;
Well if they wean from vanity
And draw our wishes, Lord, to Thee."

In addition to the facts recorded in his journal, his thoughts and feelings at this time will be shown by the following extracts from his letters.

To Miss R. S. Alford (afterwards Mrs. Morgan).

"I am now entered on my life of temptation and have begun to think and act for myself, and have brought upon my own shoulders that weight of cares, in a measure at least, which till now others have taken from me; do, dear Shute, write soon, and give me spiritual comfort, and let me know that I have friends somewhere. It is now above all other times, that I feel the want of such friends as the members of a large family have in their brothers and sisters: do write me soon a long and hearty letter."

To his cousin Walter, then at Oxford, a month later he writes:—

"I am reading for the University Scholarship with a private tutor. I read eight hours a day, have few friends, and attend Simeon's preaching and evening parties."

The following letter refers to his work at college, a visit from his father, and his future prospects.

To Walter Alford.

"I am afraid I am expressing myself very intricately and indistinctly, for I am so muddled between Thucydides and Æschylus, and Virgil and Euclid, and the Binomial Theorem, &c., that I write a letter as if I was doing a problem, all in confusion. I was so pleased to see my father here, and to lionize him. These are blessings which call for thanks and praise in many points of view, and in one, not the least, that I have been most graciously upheld by the power and grace of my Heavenly Father while I have been here hitherto. For how could I meet my father with a smiling welcome or a light heart, had I been giving way to temptation, and falling into open sin? is not this a mercy?

I often look forward with very mingled feelings to the time when, by the good pleasure of our God, I shall be a labourer in His vineyard; how awful, yet how delightful a thing the cure, as it is emphatically called, of souls! how overwhelming a responsibility, yet how pleasing an office. I have very much to say to you on various subjects, and on none more than on religion. I do indeed feel cold and dead, and I am afraid my coldness arises from pride and self-conceit: I wish I could think, I mean act, as if I thought myself all vile and unworthy of pardon. But here is the misfortune, that then the world thrusts in its opaque shadow between me and the Sun of Righteousness, or my Saviour seems to hide His face under clouds of doubt and fear. I have, I trust, now and then bright gleams vouchsafed, and sometimes I can bask myself in His sunshine, and delight myself in Him. I did so remarkably yesterday morning. It was a beautiful warm day, and almost cloudless, and I took a solitary walk in the grounds at Queens' before Simeon's service, and certainly did enjoy meditation very much; but delightful as these seasons are, they are times of peculiar temptation; for as Newton says, 'A robber will not attack a man on his way to the bank, but when he is returning loaded with money.''

He writes about the same time:—

TO MISS R. S. ALFORD.

"Excuse the liberty I have taken in sending you these few lines. I used to write nonsense in this way once, on things which I have since bitterly repented of. You may get an appropriate text for the heading of them from Num. vi. 24—26, or Psalm xx.

"Gracious Saviour, here behold us
Kneeling at Thy mercies' throne;
In Thy arms of love enfold us,
Claim and take us for Thine own.

"Though in distant regions sever'd,
Still unite us, Lord, to Thee;
Dead to earth from sin deliver'd,
Pilgrims of eternity.

"In the moments of temptation
Hold us by Thine arm of power;
Arm our hearts for peril's station,
Shield our heads in danger's hour.

"When we pass the last dark river,
Bear us o'er the swelling tide;
Hear and answer and deliver,
Land us safe on Canaan's side,

"There in measure never ceasing
Sweeter songs we hope to raise;
Thee our God for ever blessing,
Wrapt in love, and lost in praise.

"As often as you have time, I shall be most happy to hear from you, and I shall want something like the advice and open-hearted freedom of a friend, to relieve my solitary hours at Cambridge. It makes a great difference to me to be placed in a state of solitary independence.

In December from Ampton, where he spent his Christmas vacation, he thus writes:—

To Walter Alford.

"Now my first term is passed, I can look back with cool reflection on my manner of life and pursuits at college, and the more I look at the time spent there, the more I like the method of life. I know two or three good men. How very refreshing is Christian communion of this sort! After the dry pages of mathematics, and though not quite so uninteresting, yet quite as unsatisfying, of a classical author, I find nothing but the Bible satisfy me. I read Æschylus and Homer, and then turn to Isaiah and Joel; and the heathen poetry, sublime as it is in itself, is mere prose in comparison. I read algebra and Euclid, and then turn to the Epistle to the Romans, and all the reasoning of ancients and moderns appears weak and inconclusive, every store of spiritual and intellectual knowledge is hid in that divine book. We heard this morning of my Aunt Cordelia's death; her gain, though our loss. Whilst she was here she had a presentiment of it in her mind.

"There is a soft and friendly voice
Which calls the saints away,
And bids them look to brighter joys,
When life and health decay.

"There is a sweet unearthly smile,
A calm and heavenly breath,
While earth's frail body wastes the while
Beneath the tomb of death.

"Excuse this, as you know it is an old fault of mine."

It was about this time that he wrote a hymn, published long afterwards in the "Year of Praise," No. 181, "Forth to the land of promise bound."

The following extracts from his journal will show how he was employed at home:—

"*Ampton, Jan.* 1, 1829.—Read till breakfast 'Oratio contra Leptinem,' read some of the first book of Cicero's 'Offices' whilst walking; dined at Lord Calthorpe's, rather interesting conversation about statuary and painting.

"I humbly thank Thee, O Lord, for thus preserving me to see the beginning of another year. May it be spent in Thy service.

"Heard from Fanny.

"*Jan.* 2.—Wrote letters and diary. After breakfast condensed 'Oratio ad Leptinem,' made Latin epigram on 'splendide mendax,' read some Juvenal. In the evening at the Hall again, very pleasant. How can I be grateful enough, not only for being permitted to live and enjoy health, but also all the advantages which the best society affords?

"*Sunday, Jan.* 11.—Read Doddridge's Paraphrase on 1 Tim. i., and also read Bishop Hall and made notes on it.

"So sabbath after sabbath flies,
And each is noted down above;
And tears are wept by angels' eyes,
O'er grace refused and slighted love.
Lord, may my every sabbath be
A stage upon my road to Thee.

"Wrote in my original album some remarks on Instruction of Children[1].

---

[1] The beginning and ending of these remarks were as follows:—"Excess of feeling is rather a failing of mine; when I hear it urged against a man who intends well, that he is too apt to let his feelings overbalance his judgment, I always hope well of that man. Perhaps this may be from the general willingness to think well of one's own weak points which so much prevails; but, I think, if we were to lay fact against fact and reason against reason, we should generally find that the most useful among men have been men of warm hearts and feeling minds; men who could not only say they sympathized in the distresses of others, but really were themselves afflicted with their afflictions; who not only affirmed that to see others happy gave them pleasure, but actually themselves rejoiced in their joy: [and ending with] I have been induced to write the above few remarks from a persuasion that much more than is usually thought depends on the manner of ministers towards their flock, and especially the younger part of them. If these

"*Jan.* 12.—Not quite well. Rose at eight, having woefully overslept myself, prayers almost immediately, talked much to my father, thought much of death. I am disposed to fear it, but it should have no horrors for me. I do not fear it, but I fear my separation from many worldly objects, which should be to me but as loss for Christ. Oh! the being with Him.

"*Jan.* 14.—Bad cough, read two books of Euclid and some Agamemnon. My father read to me in the evening.

"Lord, teach me conformity to Thy will, humble my proud heart, subdue my high spirit, if Thou have work for me to do, O keep me here, I beseech Thee; if not, take me to Thyself.

"*Jan.* 15.—Wrote to Fanny. It is very pleasant for me to write to her once again after so long a silence. This has been a trying week to me, as, not having been well, I have not been able to do my accustomed work."

Just after his return to Cambridge he wrote to his cousin, Miss R. S. Alford, on Jan. 26, with reference to a correspondence which had been temporarily interrupted. "Forgive me for a freshman not managing his time well enough to have time for every thing. I heard from Fanny and Mary on New Year's-day, and I assure you it was no unacceptable New Year's present to me especially, the beginning of the year with so pleasing and long-wished a change, and that we are once more on the footing of Christian friends and relations. And not only should I rejoice, but show it in thankfulness to God for His mercy, to whom I have so often prayed that it might be so. What a delightful feeling it is when some unexpected mercy reaches us, and we are too full to speak our gratitude to God; but a sort of unutterable burst of thankfulness escapes like that of David, 'What shall I render to God for all His benefits?' I remember a very pleasing verse from the new version of the Psalms, I think,—

[remarks] be any part of that right path which I am to pursue, when I shall become one of Christ's ministers (if it please God to spare me), do Thou, O Lord, fix them in my mind deeply and firmly; if any of them be incorrect or detrimental, may I remember and act on the rest while I forget and reject those."

> 'The Lord is good! fresh acts of grace
> His bounty still supplies,
> His anger moves with slowest space,
> His willing mercy flies.' "

His next term at Cambridge was marked by a visit from his father, and by his passing through three examinations, two of which, for the Craven and for the Bell Scholarships, he undertook voluntarily in addition to his college examination. From January 26—31, he went to the schools for the Craven Scholarship examination, which he describes as "very tough—Scholefield, Haviland, Tatham, and Turton examiners." On February 23 he records, "Craven decided in favour of Wordsworth" [afterwards Bishop of Lincoln]. His journal next refers to the examination for the Bell scholarship.

"*March* 5.—Went to the schools, Tatham examiner; Greek poetry, did pretty well; out at half-past two. Walked with Oliver and Dalton on the Trumpington Road; returned to Hall. Went to Simeon's, good sermon about Catholic question (night of the Catholic debate); returned and read till twelve. O Lord, I commit the ensuing contest to Thee; Thou knowest, and Thou only knowest, what will be best for me, and I trust in perfect confidence in Thee that Thou wilt settle it as it may be best for my spiritual welfare.

"*March* 6.—Schools at nine. Goldcut examined. Out at half-past two. Did pretty well. Had Persius set. Fifth Satire, which I had read last night. Hall afterwards. Got paper. Went to Simeon's rooms. Returned to tea at eight. Read mathematics very fiercely, being afraid of the paper to-morrow. Read till four o'clock, and then went to bed.

"*March* 7.—Intended to be up for Chapel, but too late. Read mathematics till ten, and then went to the schools. Did better than I expected; fifteen out of thirty questions. Out at two. Went to boat race. Returned to Hall, chapel, and tea. How can I enough thank Thee, O gracious God, for having brought me through this long and fatiguing examination; and if it please Thee, may I be able to assist my dear father."

The following extract is taken from a letter from his father during an examination:—

"*Feb.* 28.—My expectations are not sanguine, and should you prove unsuccessful my disappointment will be very little. I mention this to ease your mind on my account. Do your best, and I shall be quite satisfied with the result, though it may be against you. The issue of the contest rests with your heavenly Father, who knows what is best for you far better than I do."

And after the close of the examination his father says:—

"*March* 13.—Your mind I hope as well as your body is released from the burden which it imposed upon it, and that you can now breathe freely again. You have done, my dear boy, your part, and whatever may be the result of the election, I shall be satisfied. The progress you have made in preparing for the examination, the habits acquired by it, the temptations prevented by it, the experience which it has given you, are all advantages of more value than the 40*l.* a year, of which the determination of the electors cannot deprive you, and you have moreover the consciousness of having done your duty."

The visit of his father to Cambridge occurred shortly after the examination, and is thus noticed in his journal:—

"*May* 8.—Rose at half-past five, read till chapel, to chapel and returned to breakfast, and then my father came and left just after, went to Peacock's lecture, read till two to Hodson, read steadily all the evening. O Lord, I thank Thee for this short relief from the severity of study in the company of my dearest father[2]. May I be thankful, my wish is now accomplished. I am to go to read mathematics with Mason at Portsmouth this summer, when the long vacation begins."

A letter which he wrote from Portsmouth, 16th June, will show how much self-control he exercised in applying himself to mathematics. He calls the letter a strictly scholastic and mathematical communication:—

---

[2] The habit of reviewing each period of study with prayer became so much a part of his nature, that he was known on one occasion, as he closed his books after a hard day's reading, to stand up as at the end of a meal and thank God for what he had received.

TO WALTER ALFORD.

"Having a good deal of MSS. mathematics to send you, I have taken a sheet of Cambridge mathematical paper, that I might be the better able to get it all in, and now to proceed to business. [Then follow three well-filled pages of mathematical figures.]

"I have arranged the MSS. in order, and you must read them, please, according to the figures prefixed to them, as the proofs of some depend on others already proved. We read Boucharlat at Cambridge, and indeed I am now just in the middle of the Differential Calculus, but I am sure I should never have mastered it without a tutor, it is of so much importance to get a right idea of it at first. We read Whewell. I have now finished my first year at Cambridge and entered on quite a new course of reading. The second year's subjects are much more difficult; they are the second part of Wood's Algebra, conic sections, mechanics, eleventh book of Euclid, the Differential and Integral Calculus, and three sections of Newton. You will say we have enough of it, and so say I, especially as I intend to make classics my principal study, as I cannot get on in mathematics, having very little liking for them. Our college examination was a very tough and fatiguing one, being for five days, eight hours a day. I did not feel in the least anxious, for I knew I had done all I could, and I was only anxious to know what that all was. I have been this morning over the *Victory,* the ship in which Nelson fell, of 120 guns. It is a very fine sight to see a large man-of-war in perfect order. We saw the place where Nelson fell on the quarter-deck, they have put a small plate of copper, with 'England expects every man to do his duty' engraved on it. We saw also the cabin where he died. What emotions are excited on visiting sights like these. I am writing to Fanny and Mary, giving them an account of the Dockyard. I am going to Tamworth in July, and from thence to Ampton, where my father intends remaining all the vacation."

The following is the letter which he mentions :—

To Fanny Alford.

"*June* 16.

"As you know how fond I am of scribbling by long experience in former days, you can make allowances for my intrusion on you, especially as I am here all alone, and writing answers now and then the purposes of society and conversation. The rain has at length come, how many a scheme is frustrated by a summer's day's rain, and how very applicable to all things is that adage, 'Make hay while the sun shines.' I need not mention one particular application which your own mind will doubtless suggest, how often do we put off that all important business from one fine day to another, from the spring of childhood to the summer of youth and mature age, till at last the cold and rainy season of old age comes on us unawares, and the blasts of death begin to howl about our frail tenement, and the recollection of squandered talents, unimproved opportunities, and misspent years of advantages, adds its bitter pang to the sad repentance which a life spent without God gives cause for. But you will say, this is your old strain, moralizing again, as formerly; to this I must answer, I am very sorry for it, but I cannot help it. It seems natural to my mind to think on things which are going on around me, as if they carried an instruction with them, and were meant in some measure to bear a secondary meaning, and teach a lesson of spirituality and heavenly-mindedness. Simplicity and openness of character is the characteristic of a servant of Christ. O may I be led farther and farther in the way that leads to this enviable attainment, and may I become more humble and single-minded.

"I am now lodging in a place which is as it were the rendezvous of British naval preparation and strength. The country about Portsmouth is not pretty, there are no cliffs on the seashore, but the beach goes up quite in a flat; the three towns, Portsmouth, Portsea, and Southsea, are all situated on the island of Portsea, the water at high tide surrounds them all. Portsmouth and Portsea are strongly fortified with very broad turf walls, on which sentinels are always stationed. It seems very odd to be shut round with walls and gates, and makes me fancy myself in some old Grecian town. There is a large garrison of soldiers always kept up here, and they frequently exercise them on the common, which is a very fine sight. There are some very good military bands here, and they play on the fortifications every night at nine o'clock, till nearly ten. The music is very fine: you can imagine me highly delighted with it. Every morning at daybreak they fire a gun from the walls, which is answered by the ships in the harbour. In the evening at sunset they fire another, and another at nine o'clock, then the various bands strike up, and play on different parts of the walls till nearly ten, when they play 'God save the King' and stop. After that they won't allow any one to go on the walls. I shall reserve a description of the Dockyard for Mary, and tell her the naval, as I have you the military lions of the place. I am busy at present reading mathematics, and am determined if I can to make myself like them. I am almost afraid to send this, lest it should cross one from you on the way; if so I hope they will have the good manners to wish one another a pleasant journey."

On 15th of July, he left Portsmouth and spent some days in London, for we have this entry in his journal:—"19, *Sunday, half-past six*:—Went to hear Irving in Regent Square; liked him very much. Sermon two hours long, on 'Give diligence to make your calling and election sure.'" Then he spent a week or two with some friends whose late breakfasts, and want of any fixed employment much tried him, being so contrary to his own habits of early rising and regular occupation—of this visit his journal notes.

"*July* 30.—This has been I think the dullest day I ever spent in my life, no mind, no body in exercise, but a sheer determination and regular system here, to do nothing and let others do nothing. O how thankful should I be that I am not always cast into such a place, and with those whom, although I love them sincerely, I must say I blame for their waste of that precious time which was given for better purposes."

On his return to Cambridge he writes:—

TO WALTER ALFORD.

"*October.*

"Feeling myself indisposed for work, and especially mathematics, I cannot do better than answer your last kind epistle (I use this word to avoid a rhyme). You may imagine I easily fall in with my college habits again, and return with increased relish to that Academical life, of which I am by this time become very fond. 'College certainly has charms,' says Kirke White, and he was a Johnian; *à fortiori*, then, must Trinity have charms, and I can testify that it has a comfortable set of rooms[3] though with sixty stone steps to get up to them. A blazing fire and a door which, secures my independence from without, are comforts not to be despised, nay, on the contrary, I cannot help feeling how graciously I am dealt with every time I look around me, both with respect to outward, and also intellectual and spiritual advantages. My comforts this year have much increased, and with them also my temptations, and I feel more than ever the need of watchfulness. It is not so much the gross outward temptations of this or any other place that I have to fear; my inmost feelings recoil, and turn with disgust from the brutality and sensuality of many men whom I see around; but it is the insidious undermining, if I may say so, which study and literary habits, carry on against the work of God in the soul, it is the springing up of those seeds of pride which an enemy hath sown in my heart, and which are working slowly, but I fear surely, towards maturity, the pride of intellectual, philosophical, or classical acquirements, it is these I have to dread; O the chilling influence of literary pursuits and literary society. My father was here last week. I always enjoy myself when

---

[3] Attic rooms, Letter B, New Court, left-hand side of the staircase, entered by a door on the left side of an archway leading to the back of the college. These rooms, although they would not seem desirable to many undergraduates, were so satisfactory to him that he never changed them. The window of his sitting-room looked out on the avenue, and its sills were always decked with flowers. The sixty steps, which had a tendency to repel loungers, increased the value to a student. After he had left college, when he next visited this room, he was sorry to find a fresh paper had obliterated a cathedral he had drawn on the wall.

he is here, it is such a pleasure to show people things when they are determined to be pleased, besides there is not a little pleasure in turning host, and entertaining him as my guest, and thus inverting the order of things."

After a single life of twenty years, his father contemplated a second marriage. The remarks in the following letter refer to this:—

TO HIS FATHER.

"*Trinity College, Oct.* 24.

"All the plants came safely, and are now thriving in my window, but these severe frosts will try them. On the subject we talked of on Monday, I can speak more freely on paper than *vivâ voce*, and will make this an opportunity of saying something about it; and first, believe me, dearest father, when I say that for many years it has been my wish and continual earnest prayer that it might take place, both on your account and my own, both for our spiritual and temporal good. I could never for a moment allow the consideration of self-interest to enter into the question; because, in the first place, I consider it my privilege to be able, and my duty to endeavour, to work my own way, and at least to spare you all I can of expense and labour; and secondly, because even if I were entirely dependent on what should come from you, I should reject with indignation the bare idea of my being an obstacle in the way of what is so decidedly for the good of both of us. Do then, I pray you, rather consider me as a furtherance than a hindrance to such a step, rather as an additional cause that you should, than as a reason why you should not take so desirable a step."

On the subject of working his own way, an extract from a former letter must be quoted.

"You have, my dear father, given me an education for which I can never be sufficiently thankful, and have promoted the cultivation of a mind in itself indolent and lethargic. I often reflect with pain on the privations I know you submitted to on my account, and am not a little angry with myself for not having ever done any thing to mitigate your expenses, or at all in the way of providing for myself. However soon an opportunity may offer; and I am satisfied, in reliance on God's blessing, that if I am not successful it shall not be for want of exertion on my part. I look upon these few years through which I am now passing as peculiarly dedicated to the cultivation and improvement of my mind; and as in some measure differing from any other time, either that I have passed or shall pass. Hitherto, or at least in former years, I have been getting the ὕλη, or matter for work together; now comes the time for working on that matter, and making my work the employment of the mind instead of the mere mechanical drudgery which it once necessarily was. Hereafter, if spared, I shall have occasion to call into practice the knowledge now acquired; and the more diligent I am in the acquiring it now, the more valuable store I shall have hereafter."

To Fanny Alford.

"*November.*

"I am now once again settled in at Cambridge, amid all the advantages and all the temptations with which this place abounds; advantages for having every opportunity for enlarging my understanding and informing my mind, and, what is more, of hearing the truth as it is in Jesus continually; and temptations in being constantly brought into contact with men who live without God in the world, and in the chilling effects of study on the religious affections and communion with God in prayer, and in being surrounded with professors of religion, who are, many of them neither moral nor religious. I hear you are reading Wilberforce's 'Practical View;' don't you like it very much? I know of no book which opens so much the present state of society, and the godlessness which now is so prevalent. I think a few things are a little overstated. Oh, if you knew the man himself you would read that book with double interest.

"I envy your domestic fireside and family party, and often look forward with pleasure to joining myself to it for a few days. It is now going on for three years since I was at

Heale. We may come next summer. My father talks of it. I remember you and myself six years old. Some difference between six and eighteen."

His journal at Cambridge continues :—

"*Nov.* 9.—Met in Allen's rooms, and debated on whether Luxury is necessarily an attendant on Civilization.

"*Nov.* 13.—Met in Burrowes' rooms; debated on Painting and Sculpture.

"*Nov.* 20.—Made useless calculation about the vibration of musical sounds. At Christie's rooms debated about the Diffusion of Knowledge; read at night till two.

"*Nov.* 23.—Wasted most of the morning in doctoring a clock; made it strike the half-hours; bed at half-past one.

"*Dec.* 11.—Last meeting of the Debating Society. Subject, Duelling."

That Christmas was spent partly with his cousin, T. Paget, at Ampton; but, as he was working hard, he soon returned to Cambridge.

In the following term he became a candidate for a scholarship at Trinity College, and soon after the following letter was written we heard that he was successful.

TO FANNY ALFORD.

"I am going on much as usual, only reading rather hard just now, as the examination for the Trinity scholarships comes on in a few weeks. I am afraid I shall not get one; I wish, however, to do my best, and leave the issue in the hands of Him who will ordain all as it should be. Remember me on the Friday and Saturday after Easter, for those two days are our scholarship examination."

His journal at college continues :—

"1830. *May* 16.—Breakfasted with Sedgwick: very pleasant. Sedgwick a wonderful man indeed. I am going out, after some Greek Testament, to adore the God of Nature in His works, and to be filled with beauty and grandeur. Read St. Matthew. I think our Saviour's prophecies on the destruction of Jerusalem, and its mystical connexion with the final judgment, the most sublime thing I ever read.

"*May* 18.—I shall not easily forget this night, when I have been writing out cram till I cannot actually write legibly, and am brimfull of the examination. I must work very hard, or I shan't do. 'Tis only for my dear father and Fanny that I am thus working. I don't care a fig for the first class.

"*June* 12.—Winkfield since I wrote last. The whole of the Trinity examination has passed, and I have got in the first class and fourth.

"Well, now I am on the confines of my own beloved country, and I am now looking forward to seeing them all. I don't know how it is, but I certainly am not in the vein just now. I have been working my brains for the last five minutes, but not a subject or a line will come.

"*June* 15.—Went to Heale after an absence of three years.

"*June* 27.—Delightful walk to Burton with my cousins. Went to the top of Burton Pynsent[4] last night. A most beautiful sunset.

"The King George IV. died at 3 a.m. that day. Some proposed to sing 'God save the King!' I said, perhaps his sun is set by this time. It was, and this morning we heard of it. May God be gracious to our country!

"*June* 30.—Went to Ilminster, and dined with my former master, Mr. Allen. Bought an album for Fanny and Mary. Walked back to Heale in an hour and three quarters. Beautiful night.

"*July* 2.—Wet all day. Cleaned, new-leathered, and

---

[4] Since the house at Burton Pynsent became a ruin, that name has been transferred to the handsome column of white Portland stone, 140 feet high, which was erected by the Earl of Chatham to commemorate the former owner of the estate. The inscription on the pedestal is:—

SACRED TO THE MEMORY OF SIR WILLIAM PYNSENT, BART.
HOC SALTEM FUNGAR INANI MUNERE.

This monument is frequently mentioned in the letters and journals in this volume, and it is referred to in a sonnet written about this time. (Poems, page 162, Sonnet xv.) In Lord Stanhope's History of England, vol. v., pp. 61, 62, there is a full account of the noble bequest of this estate in 1765 to the Earl of Chatham by Sir William Pynsent, the last baronet of an old Somersetshire family.

tuned the dining-room piano. Played 'Graces' in the nursery, and afterwards 'Birds and Beasts' and 'Blind Man's Buff.' It put me in mind of five years ago. Fanny and Mary have asked me to write the first things in their albums. Now, of all things, I hate writing an introductory piece the worst. I have made several ineffectual attempts.

"*July* 3.—Walked with Fanny and Mary to Wick Hill, and picked flowers for them. One place particularly beautiful, where all kinds of grasses were luxuriating in the fertility of the soil. After went, *per se,* to call on my father's old servant, W. W.; had a long conversation with him, and read to him the 71st Psalm. Then walked home with my cousins by Westfield. At night drew a cathedral for Octavia.

"*July* 6.—Went, a large party, to see the tesselated pavement near Pitney. Well worth seeing. We drew a plan of it. I drew some, Fanny some, and Walter some. One room is in the shape of an octagon. We saw also a Roman bath near. Delightful view of Huish Tower as we were returning.

FOR FANNY'S ALBUM.

" From flower to flower the singing bee
Hath bounded on exultingly,
And stow'd upon her honied thigh
The sweets that in the blossoms lie :
And when the daylight beam hath fled,
Her journey she hath homeward sped
Back to the hive where all things sweet,
All essences and fragrance meet.

" From flower to flower of melody,
Ye writers in these pages fly,
And cull the beauteous and the sweet,
Upon the album's leaves to meet;
And as the bee hath never flown
But where the sun's bright beams hath shone,
Let every strain you cull be bright
With beams of grace and heavenly light."

"*July* 7.—Nice talk with my cousins by moonlight. After drinking tea at Wiltown, we talked on creation in connexion with geology, on the exquisite beauty of nature at that still and solemn hour. The full moon was clear and bright in the south-east, and Jupiter beamed not far from her; and such clouds, such shadows! Oh, the rarefied atmosphere of my soul! ideas sported or entertained! the atmospheric influence of people on each other's minds!

"*July* 8.—Stood with Fanny and Mary at the school-room window, looking at the most unclouded and beautiful moon[5] that summer evening ever beheld."

To a college friend, Mr. John [now Archdeacon] Allen, he writes from Heale House, July 6:—

"I have been here for three weeks; and enjoying myself in the midst of an affectionate, unreserved Christian family, my spirits are apt to run riot. All that I wish is, that it may be the riot of the blushing and fragrant hedge-rose, not that of the rampant and intruding briar. I have all kinds of things to say to you, but can't write them now, for I have to draw a plan of a tesselated pavement near here for the girls. It is now half-past eleven, and I want to be up at six. I have just parted with my old (and yet young) master, your namesake. He is one of a thousand: a rare fellow, a genius, a perfect, accomplished gentleman, and the interest and life of every company in which he is found."

About the middle of July he went to Portsmouth, to read with a mathematical tutor, visiting his friend W. Thring by the way, as his journal shows.

"Warminster, St. Swithin's; rained all day. Went with Mrs. Thring and the boys to Longleat: very pretty place. The King was buried to-day.

"*July* 16.—Left Warminster, and went by Heytesbury, then through a pretty valley, and by bleak downs on the left of Salisbury—most magnificent spire—and on to Southampton and Portsmouth."

To Fanny Alford.

"*July* 19.

"With respect to the subject which furnished us matter for two or three conversations—the probability of meeting and recognizing friends in heaven—I thought a good deal, and searched Scripture yesterday. The passage, 1 Thess. iv. 13—18, appears to me almost decisive. Do read it over again. . . .

---

[5] See Poems, "A Night Scene." July, 1830, page 209.

"Tennyson says—

> 'To search the secret is beyond our lore,
> And man must rest till God doth furnish more.'

Certainly if there has been one hope which has borne the hearts of Christians up more than another in trials and separations, it is this. It has in all ages been one of the loveliest in the chequered prospect of the future, nor has it been confined to Christians; I mean the idea. You will excuse me; nay, you will thank me, I know, for transcribing an exquisite passage from Cicero's treatise on Old Age. It is as follows: 'O glorious day, when I shall go to that divine assembly and company of spirits, and when I shall depart out of this bustle, this sink of corruption; for I shall go not only to those great men of whom I have before spoken, but also to my dear Cato (his son), than whom there never was a better man, or one more excellent in filial affection, whose funeral rites were performed by me, when the contrary was natural, viz. that mine should be performed by him. His soul not desiring me, but looking back on me, has departed into those regions where he saw that I myself must come; and I seem to bear firmly my affliction (viz. the loss of him), not because I did not grieve for it, but I comforted myself, thinking that the separation and parting between us would not be for long duration.' I am at present reading Plato's book on the Immortality of the Soul, and may have a quotation to give you out of that before I have finished this letter. The passage from Cicero which I have copied is considered one of the finest, if not the finest passage, in all the heathen authors. It certainly is very fine; but now, when you have admired it enough, turn to 2 Tim. iv. 6—8, and compare the two. Blessed be He indeed who has given us such a certainty of hope! Let us adore His grace in Christ which could put such strains of triumph into the mouth of the aged and persecuted apostle. Pardon my digression a little. You cannot think how beautiful it is to select and admire the sublimest and finest parts of the classical philosophers and poets, and then to find parallel passages in Scripture, as may almost always be done, and compare, not to destroy the faculty of the first, but to exalt and bring into light the divine sublimity of the latter. I have been reading Plato to-day, and have met with a passage singular enough, as it expressed a doubt on the subject. The whole of Plato's book on the Immortality of the Soul is related as a dialogue between Socrates and his friends the evening of his death. You remember Socrates was put to death by the Athenians for asserting the unity of the Supreme Being in opposition to the many deities of Paganism; and he was executed, according to the Athenians' custom, by drinking hemlock juice. This was always done after sunset, as the Athenians accounted it unlawful to put any one to death during the day. On the afternoon then before his death he conversed with his friends on the immortality of the soul, which conversation Plato has recorded. The passage to which I allude is as follows:—'If, my friends, I did not expect to go to a wise and good God, and to men who have died and are better than those whom I leave here, I should do wrong in not grieving at the prospect of death. But now be assured that I hope to go to good men, but this I am not entirely certain of; but that I shall go to God, a Master wholly good, be assured, if I am certain on any such subject, I am on this.'"

His journal at Portsmouth continues.

"*July* 27.—Calmest sea I ever beheld, not a ripple on the water, moon very beautiful: read Aristotle and Phædo. Drew Portsmouth, also drew from memory the view of Ilminster from the new road. Strongly put in mind of those 'noctes cœnæque Deum.' I must collect things from Wordsworth to write to Fanny. Childhood, it strikes me, would be a good subject.

"*July* 29.—Spent an idle and hot day; read Southey's Life of Nelson. I repeat what I have so often said, no one is fit for any thing great, unless he have enthusiasm on some one subject. Glorious example in Nelson! I feel I am to do something some day, in what way He only knows who has the ordering of my life. My mind at present is of such a dissipated and indolent cast, that I cannot imagine it raising itself to any thing great. Yet that it can, I cannot help feeling; this body—ah! there is the clog—if I am not to accomplish a career of greatness, I am at least to begin one. Oh! the misery of being a promise and nothing else; but hush, God's will be done; let me then collect my scattered energies, and endeavour to rise superior to the body and its feelings and weaknesses, and may my God assist me therein. One wish, one prayer I have; that in all I may hereafter acquire, in the way of honour or fame, though I desire neither, I would rather be unappreciated in mine own age, or appreciated only by a few that she may have an equal share, and more than half, if it be at my disposal, shall be hers. I have to serve my country as well as Nelson; our course will be different, their end the same. He on the ocean of danger, in the action and hour of peril; I by labour of mind, and doing by writing and thinking my best in my way. O Lord, grant me decision and true steadiness to pursue this course for Thy honour and for the good of my country, undeviatingly, for Christ's sake. Amen.

"*July* 30.—Sad news of an approaching revolution in France. Paris in an uproar, the royal standard pulled down and burnt. The Chamber of Deputies refuses to obey edicts, and declares itself the true representative of the French people, and declares its sittings permanent. All the papers except those on the Ministerial side are stopped.

"Lord, heavily Thy scourge hangs o'er that land,
For they have felt the terrors of Thy hand.
The die is thrown for liberty or life,
And happy they alone whose hearts are fix'd on Thee.

"*Aug.* 8.—Glorious walk to Fort Cumberland over the sands, saw some names written on the sands.

"So on the shifting sands of life
Our feeble joys we trace;
So soon the refluent waves of time
The fleeting lines efface.

"Learnt Montgomery's lines on prayer 'per se;' had beaming and burning thoughts, a thousand phosphoric sparks of poetry leaping about in my mind, but no settled or fixable beam: was intensely happy. The sea was calm, the evening lovely, and Hesper was mildly looking down on the face of the waters. I, in anticipation of the future, the prospective and anxious view of many a bud of hope expanding into a blossom of joy, and the certainty of the care and love of an all good and all gracious God, who will order all things as shall be best for me; grounds indeed of happiness, why am I not always happy?

"*Aug.* 17.—Had a glorious pull in the evening with Blakesley[6], and Spedding and his brother, round the French King's vessel, which is at Spithead.

"*Aug.* 19.—Finished the third book of Herodotus. I hope this day will be to me the beginning of regular and steady reading. When I think of the things I have to urge me forward, I am ashamed of myself for my want of energy, and my listlessness of mind in not grappling with subjects which I might overcome without very great difficulty. I may repent when I come to take my degree every hour I waste now.

"*Aug.* 22.—Let me record a few of the workings of my mind, and the effects which those workings have produced upon the body.

" O, when shall this frail tenement of clay
Be emptied by Death's peremptory call,
And its celestial guest be fetch'd away
From mortal tenure and corporeal thrall:
A beam to mingle with the flood of day,
A part to join unto the glorious All?
When shall the kingly Intellect have fled
From this his dull material servitude,
And Thought exalt her long-abased head,
With pomp of heavenly majesty endued?
And when shall the affection, here below
Broken by parting in its stream of light,
Dash off the earthly vestiture of woe,
And shine with everlasting radiance bright?"

SONNET XXVIII. *Poems,* p. 169.

" Who would have thought that I should have committed a sonnet on life, death, and immortality, in a five minutes' diary on a Sunday evening?

---

[6] Now Dean of Lincoln.

"*Aug.* 29.—Ryde. A glorious walk to-day and intercourse with the universe and Him who made it. Passed through Brading, on the Down, magnificent divine view; had Wordsworth with me: repeated the Platonic Ode, and thought on it; reflected on faith in old age. Plato's Elysium as applied to it, fear in small dangers, courage in great ones, self-sacrifice and many multifold subjects naturally occurring to an active and restless mind, naturally flowing from a full and grateful heart. Felt much of the beauty of love in the universe, the resignation which nature shows in autumn, in fact of every thing which earth, and sea, and air had to suggest of inward worship in that awful and infinite temple. Thought of an old age of conjugal love. . . .

"*Sept.* 7.—After finishing Herodotus, lib. iii., and reading Spherical Trigonometry to-day, I rowed with the other men to Ryde. It was rather rough, but the waves carried our little gig over their backs in fine style, and we arrived there safely and triumphantly; we settled that it would be advisable to row along shore to Netherstone and proceeded to embark, the other men got in, and I had to get in last. I aimed directly at the middle of the boat, but some how or other, either by the boat's moving before I was well in her, or by a wave carrying her on one side, I stepped far from the middle and over she went, I found myself with the sound of mighty waters in my ears, and in an instant after had hold of the keel of our boat which was now *ἄνω κάτω*, the other men were some swimming, and some clinging to the boat. Blakesley and I got into a wherry which was near, Spedding swam to the pier with the greatest composure, and came in like a first-rate under sail, Allen was clinging to the boat, and at last got into the wherry, so we were all safe. Spedding and I bought grotesque dry things. Blakesley, very gaily equipped, found us out, and brought us to a most hospitable lady's house, a Mrs. Good, who gave us all that was required from her husband's wardrobe, and was exceedingly kind and gave us some tea. Home by steamer. *Τῷ Θεῷ δόξα.*

"*Sept.* 13.—Very delightful walk to-day, cliffs, grand coast, sea-views, and dark and luxuriant timber, all my favourites. Oh the delights of nature as connected with reflection and anticipation, and the worship of the human mind, and our great and bountiful Creator! I think that the scraps which I have written in this book, with a few more would make a book, but then I like them so well in their rough state, and it would be such a silly, unprofitable book, that I shall not take the trouble. The truth is I must furnish my mind with more materials before I think of it. I know little of history, less of philosophy, least of all of criticism. Just let me call over the muster-roll of my mind.

"*Sept.* 22.—Walter here to see the place, took him a walk round the walls, went to Dusautoy's church, considerable disturbance caused by a mad man coming in and crying 'fire.'

"*Sept.* 30.—Reading hydrostatics, and like them very much. One month more of dreams, instead of as much of life. O when shall we wake to reality, when shall we be borne into eternity? This progression of time is a veil cast over the truth, we are formed for other objects than change and passage can afford us. The world is a channel into which God lets a partial and elapsing stream of the great deep of eternity; all seems flowing onward here because we can see no farther, but existence is not a lapse, being cannot be a progression.

"We see things fleeting round us," &c.[7]

From Ampton, where he spent a short time before returning to Cambridge, he writes in his journal:—

"*Oct.* 9.—Took out the tune 'Bedford' from the organ in the church, and set it fresh with longer intervals. Reading Butler's 'Analogy.'

"*Oct.* 10, *Sunday.*—Read and extracted some of Chalmers' sermon on 'The unvarying course of Nature and the expulsive power of a new affection,' very good and fine; read

---

7 Sonnet xxix., altered thus:—"All things are dying round us." It was during this summer that five of his lyrical pieces were written. "Poems," pp. 209—214.

at night Leighton's sermon on 'What is that to thee? follow thou Me.' O for the zeal and unction of some of those elder divines, especially of Leighton, when I have to declare the truths of the Gospel to men; I long for the time, I know not how it will be with me. I lie in the hand of God, let Him do what seemeth good unto me.

"*Oct.* 12.—Looked over both the Tennysons' poems at night: exquisite fellows. I know no two books of poetry which have given me so much pure pleasure as their works."

It was at this time that he wrote the lines entitled "Midnight Thoughts," Poems, page 127. On his return to Cambridge he continued his journal:—

"Found a letter from my uncle asking me to become godfather to his last child. So opens my career of responsibility, where to end He only knows in whose hands are all our matters and prospects. Reading Gray's 'Letters,' finished Irving's 'Life of Columbus,' a most interesting and useful book, with some eccentricities of style and diction, but much true talent, much of the penetration of genius. What an example of human and civilized depravity is the ruin and desolation of those lovely spots by the Spaniards! truly such things tempt one to wish for 'a lodge in some vast wilderness, some boundless continuity of shade,' but then the delights and sympathies of social and domestic intercourse, and the holy communion of heavenward pilgrims, and the joyous participation of hope, and the lightening division of sorrow, and the kindle of imparted smiles, the glisten of sympathizing tears spread light and loveliness over the haunts of men, and the soul loathes as ungenial the distant and solitary waste.

* * * * *

After dinner Vaughan called; chapel. Blakesley came to tea and asked me to become an Apostle, Heath came too. Walked with him in the cloisters and talked of Coleridge and Shelley, &c.

* * * * *

Met Tennant, Hallam, Merivale, and the three Tennysons at

Alfred Tennyson's rooms, the latter read some very exquisite poetry of his 'Anacaona,' and 'The Hesperides,' Tennant read a very beautiful sonnet to a little child. Found at my rooms a notice for an English declamation, wasted almost all the morning in looking for subjects. A man named Bland chose the character of Edward I. as a subject, and I to defend him. After went to the first meeting of the 'Fifty,' a society for true practice in speaking culled from the Union; a very pleasing meeting; they elected Blakesley president and myself secretary, and Cameron, Hallam, and Spedding committee-men.

"*Oct.* 30.—Just elected an Apostle[8]. Blakesley proposed me.

"*Oct.* 31.—Went to a poetical society at Tennant's, read them my two sonnets—

'I love thee, Poetry,'

and

'We see things fleeting round us.'

Hallam read some beautiful things, Kinglake a pretty little piece.

"*Nov.* 7.—I have opened a debate in the Union about Wordsworth, and have been elected their treasurer. I must work hard next week for many reasons.

"*Dec.* 3.—Dreadful state of the country. Fearful fire at Coton last night, went there and worked engines. Peacock assembled the men in the cloisters and organized us in bodies of ten or eleven, in case of an attack on Cambridge which is meditated.

"*Dec.* 19.—Though it is now two o'clock, and I am bedward disposed, I must stop to relate a most glorious evening spent in the company of and in conversation with Wordsworth It was at Spedding's rooms, present—Wordsworth, Spedding, Blakesley, Thompson, Tennant, Brookfield, and myself. If I remember rightly the first thing we spoke of

---

[8] A very small society of reading and thinking men, meeting weekly at each other's rooms, for the discussion of literary, historical, political, and philosophical questions, and living at other times in habits of close intimacy.

was the great work of Coleridge. Wordsworth said his MSS. were in such a state of forwardness, that should he die, they would be intelligible to the public. Thence to the 'Christabel' the transition was easy. Wordsworth does not believe the story to have an end and had rather have it without the second part; inasmuch as the second part creates an expectation, and he thinks the daylight—at least so abrupt and so short a notice of them in that state—divests the persons of much of their charm; thus if Milton had only just brought Satan out of Hell to this earth and there left him, he had much better have kept him in Hell, where he showed to so much more advantage. It takes some time to give the characters a charm in their new situation, and to make us acquainted with them. Milton pursues it through several books and thus we become familiar with it. He next spoke of the 'Aids to Reflection,' which Wordsworth considers rather to have been a collection of marginal notes which Coleridge made in the books from which the aphorisms are taken, than any settled writing on the subjects, and to have been published by the request of friends. Coleridge has not laboured many of his published poems, many of the others he has overmuch. Wordsworth considers the conclusion to a part of the 'Christabel' too minute and laboured. Then we spoke of the 'Kubla Khan,' as to whether it was actually composed in a dream, certainly Coleridge believes so. Wordsworth thinks it might very possibly have been composed between sleeping and waking, or, as he expressed it, in a morning sleep; he said some of his own best thoughts had come to him in that way. Then to Walter Scott's 'Demonology' and spectral appearances. He said he was inclined to detract much from the invention of the romances of the middle ages, from the multitude of natural appearances which might be taken for supernatural; mentioned amongst others a remarkable appearance of an island, which he had once seen on Grasmere lake, produced by a reflection from the rocks and woods on the sides on a sheet of ice on the lake, which made it appear, as if an island of about four or five acres stood out from the lake, covered with wood and variegated with rocks, &c. He was with his sister at the time, and came upon it suddenly. The first idea which struck him was (although he was well aware that such an event could not take place without much noise), that part of the mountain had slidden down into the lake; but this only crossed his mind and was not there the hundredth part of a second; and afterwards by comparing and examining the image, they found it an exact reflection of a part of the sides of the lake. He went in to call Mrs. Wordsworth, but before she came it had subsided into an inverted reflection, not so bright as some he had seen on the lakes. Reflections are unusually bright there, so that often you cannot tell where the land terminates and the reflection begins; the reflection is the brighter of the two, owing to the smooth polish of the lake, in the same way as a picture which is varnished is brighter than one which is not. He likewise spoke of the reflection of a star on a lake which was contracted and obscured by invisible bays. Spedding asked him whether he had actually seen the phenomenon which he describes in 'The Excursion' from the mountain. He said he had, but not all at the same time, but had filled it up with others seen at different times and something of his own imagination.

"Described having seen a castle (in company with Coleridge) at the bottom of a lake, where the building itself was hid in mist, and the rays from it had found a passage under the water. Spoke of thunderbolts, &c., and said that fables and superstitions might have been built upon all these appearances in the middle ages. Spoke of thunder, and thunder-storms. He gave a grand description of a thunderstorm in Savoy (I think) where there was a very extensive prospect, and the lightning seemed to come in floods, and bathed the whole country in a sulphurous kind of light. He then inquired about the state of religion in the University, had been trying to use his influence and should do so, to get men better prepared at the public schools before sent up to the University, and course of reading enlarged. Talked much of Eton, and famous men there produced; he considered it odd that Eton had produced so few famous literary men, naming Harris; he had not much respect for Harris, thinks his 'Hermes' a very shallow book; thinks Coleridge speaks highly of him from having had his thoughts called out by him, and having been put into a good humour by writing marginal notes about him, and then fancying his own thoughts were in Harris: thinks much of this is in Coleridge's way. Spoke of his darkening things by illustration, or at least dazzling our sight which is much the same. He said Southey had compared it the other day to hunting with a piece of bacon to confound the scent. Proceeded to talk of the effect upon the public mind—of what effect should be produced; of De Quincey; the article on Kant in 'Blackwood;' does not think he would abuse Berkeley; of passive obedience—thinks things would be much better if men would observe its doctrines more than they do; thence we came to the state of the country, the general effects of revolution—the general unfitness of nations to receive them—ought to be prepared by knowledge; is apprehensive of an increasing desire of reform in this country, and a reign of terror, got exceedingly eloquent on this subject; said he should talk till nine to-morrow, if he did not go; however, we kept him longer on the same subject; he showed the exceeding importance of the middle or resisting classes, as he called them, who will not bestir themselves till occasion really requires, but then he hopes will effectually resist the rabble; thinks ministers will disagree and Lord Grey secede, and that the more reform is granted, the more the people will want. He said any discerning man might have seen that when the bone of contention given by the Catholic Bill was removed, something else would engage parties. Spoke of the press inciting the people, and the shameful temporizing and fear of the magistrates. He said also he had frequently had dreams of gliding about in the air without wings, and that this was always connected with a sense of being admired and with self-conceit, and he had sometimes thought that the line in Milton,

'High conceits engender pride,'

had reference to some such dreamy appearances; and much

more, which I shall no doubt remember bit by bit hereafter, for this is a night I shall never forget. I count it one of the proud passages of my life, to have met and conversed with Wordsworth. Bed at three.

"*Dec.* 22.—A Bell's Scholarship has fallen vacant; I must read hard, especially mathematics, and try for it. I have been very happy and very busy throughout this term; laden with work and with mercies, I have been happy in the accession of several very valuable acquaintances in the 'Apostles,' who have done my mind much good, and contributed I hope, to make me less desultory and ill-arranged than before. I have become intimate and internal with two men whom I shall ever love and respect, Hallam and Tennant. Certainly, I have done more to improve myself this term than during any one that preceded it. I have been able to unbosom myself more to Hallam and Tennant than to any men I have known here; full of blessings, full of happiness, drawing active enjoyment from every thing, wondering, loving, and being loved. Thus another term has passed in full, and almost unclouded sunshine of mind and spirit. Oh, may the fountain of this my light be no mock sun of this earth's impure atmosphere, which a cloud has made, and which, at the return of the blue sky, will vanish away, but the Sun of Righteousness itself!

"At night Hallam came full of love and happiness, sat up with him till four a.m.; promised to write to him."

From Ampton, where the Christmas was spent with his father, his journal says:—

"*Dec.* 24—Just come here. I have this year got a scholarship; in April became an Apostle; treasurer to the Union in November; secretary to the Fitzwilliam; member of the English Club; obtained many valuable acquaintances and opinions; or rather had those now to whom I could without restraint confess my old ones. My new acquaintances have been Hallam, Tennant, and Alfred Tennyson. Read principally classics, and met Wordsworth.

"*Dec.* 27.—Finished Wordsworth's 'Platonic Ode,' which I have copied out for Fanny, and wrote a long and philosophical letter to her. I said much in this letter I should like to keep, but it is safe in her hands."

The following extracts are taken from the letter thus referred to:—

TO FANNY ALFORD.

"*Ampton, Dec.* 27.

"I mean to write a long and philosophical letter. Under this frank, I have sent you a very exquisite ode of Wordsworth's, commonly called his 'Platonic Ode; or, Evidence of Immortality from Recollections of Childhood.' I will first give you an analysis of the ode. . . .

"This ode was written at that time of life the feelings of which you and I cannot yet fully enter into—the decline and autumn of man's days, when the green leaf grows sere, and the temples are sprinkled with grey. It consists of a recalling and contemplating the feelings of early childhood, and deducing from them evidences, or rather intimations of immortality. Permit me again to say, that this ode requires study and thought; it is not a sort of thing which you can read over, and say, 'it is pretty,' but it contains high and secret sentiments, and deep philosophy, which deserve a considerable share of thought and meditation." [Then come two closely written pages of criticism.]

"I should much like to send you frequently pieces of poetry and prose which are favourites of my own, with my remarks, such as they are, upon them. My view would be, to let you into the pleasure which I have myself felt from this kind of contemplation, aud to form your mind and improve my own.

"It appears to me, Socrates was the one of all others most enlightened among the heathen, and to whom God appears to have vouchsafed some dim and indistinct glimmerings of the truth. His knowledge, so far as it was good, must have proceeded from that one overruling principle whom we acknowledge, and for the belief of which he died; so far we are certain, all beyond is not for us, but for God. Some day or other, even when we arrive at the heavenly Jerusalem, we shall know, even as we are known, and be permitted to look into the deep things of God. To that blessed time let us all look; for it let us pray that an abundant entrance may be ministered unto us unto the Kingdom of God our Saviour." [Then a quotation from Seneca on the reason why good men suffer affliction.]

Journal continued:—

"1831. *Jan.* 1.—Dined at Lord Calthorpe's. Pleasant evening. Heard account of evidence before the House of Commons on the Scotch Poor Laws by Dr. Chalmers.

"*Jan.* 3.—Finished 'The Revolt of Islam,' and wrote a sonnet thereon. Dined at the Hall again. Met ——— there; she played 'The Heavens are telling.' I do not like encumbering and beclouding thus fine airs with such a multitude of variations; she has good execution.

"*Jan.* 5.—Wrote to Hallam to-day; the letter had an atrociously long sentence in it. Dined again at Lord Calthorpe's. Read Malden's 'History of Rome' yesterday, and to-day a delightful book written in a most enchanting legendary style. Give us the legends as they are, and let us exercise our own judgment upon them, instead of giving us truisms and stripping off the glorious mist which enwraps ancient and heroic times; that historian insults the common sense of his readers who does not leave them to pursue narratives of facts for themselves. Composed part of a poem on the Polar regions. Dined at Lord Calthorpe's. Fancy me mistaken for an unmusical and unpoetical person.

"*Jan.* 7.—Cold and frosty. In the evening saw a magnificent Aurora Borealis; certainly the finest I ever saw. It began by a bright light, like that produced by a fire, in the north, and extended in the form of an arch to the west, where it was of a bright rose colour; then there came a bright arch of white flame all across the sky, like that I saw at Acton (October, 1828). Afterwards twenty or thirty pillars of white fire stood up in the north, and coruscations took place in all quarters; the bright arch faded, and another began to be formed, but did not unite. The pillars increased in size and number, and were bent in all directions, seeming as if blown aside by wind and waving about; in some parts they were of a pure white, in others flame-coloured, and in others again deep crimson. Then the sky appeared smeared or dented with all these tints in confusion; and lastly turned into a pure calm brightness in the north, which now continues (eleven o'clock), and makes it as light as on a moonlight night, although there is no moon. A truly glorious and magnificent sight, one I have long wished to see, and now at last have seen. I saw no quick waverings about of bands of light such as take place in the Polar Auroras, and which are compared by Scoresby to the waving of ribbon held in the hand. I should think this must be one of the finest ever seen in this country; at least if the descriptions I have read be correct."

The following lines, which were not retained in the last edition of his poems, were written on this day:—

WRITTEN DURING AN AURORA BOREALIS, JANUARY 7, 1831.

"Lo, where they play, the fiery squadrons bright,
Along the spangled azure of the night;
Waving aloft their ensigns, where the while
Wheels to the spherèd music many a file
Of heavenly soldiery, and pour'd on high
Far o'er the orient and the southern sky,
Fair stations of still fire their watches keep,
O'er half the world entranced in slumber deep.
Or, issuing into brightness, dome and hall,
And palace front distinct with columns tall,
In mystic maze of varied light are driven
Along the pictured conclave of the Heaven:
And ever and anon upon the North
Vistas of rosy flame are opening forth,
And centres of intense and throbbing light
Pour eddying brilliance o'er the arch of night.
So, in the primal infancy of man,
Ere yet the desolating curse began,
Hues of celestial sheen were wont to rise
Far o'er the blos'my groves of paradise;
While the blest pair stood wondering to behold
Shiftings of myriad gleams from wings of gold,
And in a deeper glory faint descried,
Mid blazonry of banners floating wide,
Some seraph Hierarch, on his airy way,
'Companied earthward by that high array."

The following letter was written on January 19 to Mrs. R. Gibson, a cousin, then recently married:—

"I despair of equalling the pleasure which your letter gave me. I rejoice that it has pleased our Heavenly Father to give you so fair an heritage, as I know from your letter you have. Might we not all find our heritages fair, if the will to do so were present with us? I am sure ever since I saw you I may say always I have been happy; I have nothing to complain of, rather every thing to give thanks for. I dare say you know what I mean, and at such times the thought is delightful. What shall I render for all His benefits? Poor, poor indeed, are my returns. As good old delightful Bishop Beveridge says, 'My very repentance wants repenting of, and my holiest acts want purifying afresh in the blood of Christ.' What a delightful thing it is, after all the doubts and controversies of science and philosophy, to turn to the pure simple truths of Scripture, 'We have all sinned. Jesus died for sinners. Believe, and thou shalt be saved.' It is like turning from the flickering and dancing of a meteor to the pure fixed stars that beam for ever, and are of a brightness that fails not. You spoke of my future prospects. I always feel that they are in the best hands. Next to Him who will do all things well for me, I have unlimited confidence in my dearest father; I believe he would do nothing which did not, in his ideas, most conduce to my real benefit and substantial good; I believe (and not without reason and evidence) that he would surrender his own particular wishes and designs for me."

One of his lyrical pieces, "Refresh me with the light blue violet," Poems, p. 215, appears to have been written early in this year.

His journal proceeds as follows:—

"*March* 21.—Well, the Bell is out, and I have got it. So far, so good. I must now read mathematics rather fiercely.

"*March* 25.—Left Cambridge for a few days' holiday in the West. Tennant[9] joined me at Reading. We went to Clifton by Barley Wood (Mrs. H. More's former abode), and walked

---

[9] Afterwards British Chaplain at Florence, where he died.

from Cross to Cheddar, and up the cliffs, very magnificent, rising immediately above the road on each side, some of them between three and four hundred feet high, and covered with clustering ivy and yew. Went to the top, and had a view all over Sedgmoor, Glastonbury, and Bridgwater, the Quantock Hills as far as Minehead. Sketched an old cross, then set off for Wooky-hole. It is at first narrow and winding, with a considerable descent by natural steps; then an ascent, which leads to a magnificent opening of immense height and breadth, where the rushing of the water is heard underneath, and sounds particularly awful: here dwells in her tall cathedral cavern, surrounded by all her fixed implements of stone, the Witch of Wooky, a tall figure of rock with an awful spirit-like aspect. Then we went on to Wells.

"*March* 30.—Reached Heale with Tennant.

"*April* 4.—Walter returned from his ordination at Wells. 'The Rev.' How curious it looks. We have been playfellows, and schoolfellows, and every thing together, except at college. Well, my time next. May God grant I may be as well prepared and fitted for the ministry as this dear friend and cousin is. Tennant is reading some of Tennyson's poems to them here.

"*April* 5.—Left Heale with Tennant for Nether Stowey, came to Taunton in my uncle's carriage, and walked from thence to the Bladown Hills by Enmore Castle, a very large princely-looking house which I sketched.

"*April* 6.—Porlock at one. Started off, and inquired for Coleridge's cottage and sketched it, and talked with a very old man who remembered the rescue of some labourers who were pressed in the American war.

"Another day we walked to Culbone, and I sketched; and to the Valley of Rocks, the oddest heap and jumble of great and little rocks of all shapes, and in all forms of combination whatever."

From Linton, he wrote as follows to his friend Mr. J. Allen:—

"Behold Tennant and myself in Devonshire, among hills sky high, and crags and roaring streams and the sea, and inland the wildest country ever devised or trampled over; hills piled on hills, covered with heath and fern; no houses or trees, except here and there a luxuriant valley (or 'combe,' in Devonshire and Somersetshire language), with its *ain* stream bubbling and leaping down its rocky channel, and canopied with budding branches of elm and oak, and bordered with myriads of primroses and wood anemones. We passed yesterday the highest hill in the West of England, —I forgot I was speaking to a Welshman; however, even you must acknowledge it is respectable,—called Dunkery Beacon.

"We have been at Heale (my uncle's) for nearly a week. We go back there on Wednesday, and I shall start from thence on Friday night, and get to Cambridge on Saturday night. I shall be anxious to know who are scholars next week. It sounds so odd to talk of Cambridge matters. I had almost forgotten there was such a place, till (an actual fact) a woman, an old gossip of mine near Heale, congratulated me on having extinguished myself lately, only think! The houses about here are full of rats, and the hills rabbits: that puts me in mind I saw Burrows in town.

"*March* 12.—Heale; came here from Ilminster this morning; rose at half-past five, and walked here: of course they were all surprised to see us.

"At twelve we walked to the hollow tree; in the evening all walked to Burton, and ascended Burton Pynsent. I took back the keys to the old house, and saw some of the old pictures; one of Sir W. Pynsent, and one of Charles the Second, I should think by Vandyke, a particularly fine one. Walked in front of the house at Heale; a most lovely moonlight evening. 'New moon with the old moon in her arms,' and various signs of bad weather. This evening sketched the old house at Burton; at night in my old room at the top of the house[1]."

---

[1] "Looking from a chamber casement high
Over paternal groves, beneath the moon
Listlessly pondering, hear the village clock
Strike in the noiseless night."
"School of the Heart," Lesson iv.

After his return to Cambridge, his journal states:—

"*June* 15.—Got the second essay prize; Thompson the first.

"*July* 9.—Recited my essay, and got fifteen guineas, and immediately paid my bills and bought books."

In the following month, August, his father married Miss Susan Barber, a daughter of John Barber, Esq., a lady whose amiable qualities had already secured the affection of her stepson; he spent his long vacation at Cambridge, and from thence paid more than one visit to his father at Ampton. The following letter was written about this time to Lady Millicent Barber, the sister-in-law of Mrs. Alford:—

"I have been spending a month full of happiness at Ampton, and happiness which went to my heart. I dare say you can feel what I mean. There are many joys and sorrows which skim lightly over, and leave no mark, but some that leave their footprints as they go. I have never known domestic comfort or enjoyment in the bosom of a family; and though my life has been an unbroken series of mercies, and I have every body to thank for every thing; yet I have always felt in this one respect lonely and disheartened. I had never known the care and love of a mother. You may therefore conceive the change to me, I cannot describe it; and certainly the thanks which I owe for it are beyond all measure. It has been in my case a very special answer to prayer; and God has done it all so gently and tenderly for me, like a kind friend, who, in preparing for you, has anticipated a thousand little wishes which you would have thought of after your arrival. If you have at any time a few minutes to spare—the conclusion I leave to you. I long to know of the welfare of your harp. If any thing happens to it, 'The harp that once through Tara's halls' will not have been sung in vain; especially in these degenerate days. If you read the song, or recollect it, you will see my allusion."

The following extracts are taken from his journal, beginning with his twenty-first birthday, October 7, 1831:—

"I have this day completed the twenty-first year of my age. Gently, indeed, and with a kind hand has the Author of my life led me up to manhood, moving every danger from my way most carefully, and preserving me safely through those to which He saw it good that I should be exposed. O Lord! make me thankful. I have never been thankful to Thee as I ought. As a child I was wilful and stubborn and undutiful; as a youth, petulant, ungodly in heart, and hasty. And now what shall I say but this: 'Hold Thou up my goings in Thy path, that my footsteps slip not.' O Lord, hear me; and if I forget, do not Thou. Check my wanderings with a look of love divine; in the snares and allurements of the world; in the evils of ungodly society; in the perils of close mental application, good Lord, deliver me. In my approaching hour of trial, in all my studies, in all my thoughts and words, good Lord, deliver me. From all bad tempers and risings of pride, good Lord, deliver me. In that matter wherein I am now especially solicitous, good Lord, direct me. O Thou holy and most adorable Redeemer, who didst die for me, and didst rise again for my justification, hear and answer; and may not these, the great ends of Thy mighty love be frustrated in Thy servant. Amen.

"*Nov.* 4.—Heard of the riots at Bristol, and that a third part of Queen's Square and the Mansion House, &c., are burnt. Heard too of the cholera being at Sunderland; but I am not alarmed. We are in safe keeping; and I hope the little words, 'Thy will be done!' will fence me against a thousand fears. What must not those suffer who are at sea upon the wide ocean of uncertainty, without a star to guide them?

"*Dec.* 13.—Heard they have established a family newspaper at Heale, called 'The Family Mirror,' and Tom is the editor. October term seems fated to be a cause of my neglecting my little books. Confound these conic sections! I cannot write letters, the world goes hard with me. Oh these body-destroying, mind-destroying mathematics! Next Saturday three weeks, D.V., and it will be all over.

"1832. *Jan.* 1.—A new year, a new pen, but no new thoughts; the old ones will do very well again, even these. May all I love be preserved through this year, even as through last. God has been gracious to us, and will be gracious again.

"Next Friday week the degrees begin. I shall do about as well as I expect, not better I think; for I cannot get through my subjects, I think, as —— complains, so fast as they get through me; however I shall be most happy when it is over. It's all these plaguy mathematics. I find a sort of spell on me that won't let me read or any thing else; however, I can't complain, for I am not anxious, or perplexed, or melancholy. . . . Health to the poets, fine fellows: I haven't seen much of them lately. My 'Divine Poem' gets on badly.

"*Jan.* 19.—(The evening before the Brackets.) I feel very nervous, more so than I ever remember to have felt before. I have very great cause to be thankful for having been so well preserved through this examination."

The next extract from his journal records the most important events in the career of an undergraduate:—

"*Jan.* 21, half-past three a.m.—Thirty-fourth Wrangler. Heath, Thompson, Allen, all glorious; nothing could be possibly better. Hurrah!"

The mathematical examiners were Dr. Hymers, of St. John's College, Dr. Philpott (afterwards Bishop of Worcester), of St. Catherine's Hall. In the interval between the above entry and the next he paid three visits to his father at Ampton, each including a Sunday.

On 25th of February, he writes, "To-morrow the classical tripos comes out. To-day I have spoken to Bridge about my volume of poems. He estimates the expense at 12*l.*"

His place was eighth in the first class of the classical tripos; the examiners were Dr. Kennedy (afterwards Head Master of Shrewsbury, and Regius Professor of Greek), Dr. Thirlwall (afterwards Bishop of St. David's), and R. W. Evans (afterwards Archdeacon of Westmoreland).

On March 16, he writes in his journal:—"Medals this

week; hard work. Must begin now reading right away for next October twelvemonth, when I hope to make a push. I will now mark out roughly, a course of reading, which I hope to pursue."

His journal about this time tells nothing of his daily acts. He records his feelings and expectations with reference to a visit to Heale, which he intended to pay in June. Pages are filled, partly with rough drafts of some of his own poems, and partly with extracts from Drayton, Browne, Drummond, Daniel, Crashaw, and Donne, &c.

He writes:—

"*May* 6.—I have now four pupils, and I am attending Airy's Lectures, at least I shall begin to-morrow; so I shall have pretty full employment this term, till Friday three weeks, when the Trinity examination begins."

On June 1 he went in company with his friend Mr. Charles Merivale to Town, and on June 4 he went from thence to Heale.

CHAPTER III.

1832—1840.

First publishes Poems—Pupils—Curacy at Ampton—Fellow of Trinity—Marriage—Becomes Vicar of Wymeswold—Tour to Belgium, Switzerland, and North Italy—Edits Dearden's Miscellany.

THE severe toil of the last months of his undergraduate career was followed by one of the most joyous periods of his life.

The object of his visit to Heale was to make a proposal of marriage to his cousin, Fanny Alford. Three weeks before his arrival he considerately wrote a letter to prepare her for this step. How he himself regarded it is shown by two extracts from his journal. He thus looks forward to it on the eve of his leaving Cambridge:—

"Let me look at the step which I have taken. The choice is for life. Can I live with none else to depend on, none else to trust in, none else to love? I think, with God's grace, that I can. Sixteen years of attachment have done surely their part to rivet my heart stronger upon hers; and though I know my faults of temper and of want of forbearance, and also hers in some points, yet I hope to be able, if to any one to her at least, to be loving and kind always and by all means."

His reflections on the day of the engagement, dated June 5, 11 p.m., end with this prayer:—

"O Lord God, who art the God of love, and the guide of all Thy servants, look upon us two, who, in reliance upon Thy promise and Thine answer graciously vouchsafed to our prayers, have this day pledged ourselves to each other. May the step which we have taken be in accordance with Thy most holy will, that so we may be united in Thy fear and love unfeigned here below, and may be partakers of the marriage supper of the Lamb in heaven, through Jesus Christ our Lord! Amen."

He remained at Heale from June 5 to July 17. The details of every day in this season of pure and unalloyed enjoyment are recorded, with constant thanksgiving and prayer to the Giver of all good. It had been the study of the parents at Heale to bring up the family with a living faith in God, and in the habit of acknowledging Him in act and word. The earnest ministrations of the Rev. Henry Roberts in the parish church at Curry Rivell were such as harmonized with the religious teaching of their home, and helped to form their characters. Hence, while they were encouraged to follow their common occupations with ardour and cheerfulness, the stamp of religion was set upon their acknowledged motives and ordinary conversation.

In their summer walks amid the woods and terraces of Burton, and the heights above Sedgmoor, the betrothed cousins framed for their future life no more ambitious scheme than the care of some country parish. Together they learned to open their hearts unreservedly of and to one another; they read, learned, and reasoned on Scripture together, and prayed together; they formed, and very nearly accomplished, in those six weeks, the design of reading together the first volume of Dobson's edition of Hooker's works, his first five books of "Ecclesiastical Polity," and his sermon on "The Certainty and Perpetuity of Faith in the Elect." Archdeacon Evans' charming book, "The Rectory of Valehead," was twice read through, first by Henry alone, then by him to his future wife and her sisters. The good archdeacon had been his tutor at Cambridge, and exercised great influence on his mind at this time[1]. His volume of sermons on "The Church of God" was also read through, and one ("On the State of a Member of the Church of God") struck Henry as

[1] See Sonnet ix., dated 27th May, 1832, in "Poems," page 159.

"indisputably the finest sermon he had ever read," and he wrote out a copy of it for his future wife. He determined to enable her to read the New Testament in Greek, and for this purpose began a Greek Grammar, in the form of a series of letters to her, which grew to the extent of sixty folio pages. For the amusement of his cousins generally, he wrote some small pieces entitled "Guesses at Truth," &c., and gave them as his contribution to the "Family Mirror," a periodical which never attained the dignity of appearing in print, but was circulated in manuscript (see page 73) among various young members of the Alford family.

A design, of which in the enthusiasm of those days he was the originator, was contemplated for forming among themselves a society for the regulation of social intercourse: among its objects were to get rid of all frivolous conversation, and to give mutual aid in detecting and correcting faults. At intervals during this time he was reading the life of William III. in Tyndal's "History," and his attention was not entirely distracted from such passing events of modern history as those to which he refers in his journal on June 8:—

"Heard of the breaking out of new scenes of carnage and massacre in unhappy Paris. What will become of that thankless people? God seems to have given them up."

Some lines on "The Sign of the Cross in Baptism" (suggested by Hooker's "E. P.," v. 65) were written at this time ("Poems," p. 310). They were sung four years afterwards in Wymeswold Church as a hymn when his first child was christened, and since their publication they have come to be used not unfrequently on the occasion of a baptism.

Before the six weeks were ended the betrothed pair made an arrangement for a periodical interchange of letters—a matter of consideration in those days of costly postage; and on this subject his journal contains the following prayer:—

"O Lord, we beseech Thee to grant that whatever correspondence Thou mayest permit us to have with each other may tend to mutual edification and comfort. May we stimulate each other in the things belonging to our everasting peace; may our letters be means, under Thee, of acquainting us more and more with each other and with Thee, and fit us for living together here on earth, and hereafter in glory, for Jesus Christ's sake."

When these bright days came to a close on July 17, he looks back on them with the following reflections:—

"Oh, how many and how great have been the mercies of God to me during this my visit at Heale! First and foremost, that ever-memorable evening, June 5, and then all our sweet walks and talks since, many of them very profitable, and lasting monuments of His mercy, and all the admonitions on tender points. Oh, may all these not be without their due effect of drawing me nearer to Him! Oh, Lord, may it be so for Jesus Christ's sake! Amen."

The remainder of this Long Vacation (which lasted till Oct. 15) was spent by Henry Alford chiefly near Porlock, on the north coast of Somersetshire, whither he went accompanied by a cousin, Mr. T. Paget, of about his own age, and there pursued his reading with a view to a fellowship. They left Heale together on July 17; slept at Dunster; the next morning walked to Porlock, and hired lodgings for a guinea a week at Worthy Farm, just below Lord King's house, near Culbone. At this place he read Plato's 'Republic,' the 'Agricola' of Tacitus, Niebuhr, vol. i., various articles in the 'Philological Museum,' some of Peacock's 'Algebra,' Whewell's first three sections of Newton, Young's 'Differential Calculus,' some of Woodhouse's 'Astronomy,' besides three volumes of Gibbon, and some miscellaneous reading. The following extracts are taken from his journal:—

"*Aug.* 1.—Merivale is with us; walked with him to a great mountain east of Porlock Bay. Very grand rocks, and a cavern leading to the Minehead side; much grander than Black-gang Chine; no comparison. Ascended the mountain. Grand view over the Vale of Porlock and Dunkery Beacon.

"*Aug.* 4.—Now I do resolve, once for all, to get up when I am called every morning, for I have got lazy lately; God will give me strength to do it, for it is not a trifle."

"*Sunday, Aug.* 5.—Rose at six, conformably to the above resolution; thanks be to God for enabling me to keep it. Had some very sweet moments of prayer this morning. Learnt John xvii. Went to Selworthy Church; very beautiful among the mountains; fine church, but such a sermon! Sir T. Acland there. They rung him in and rung him out.

"*Aug.* 6.—Walked with Paget to the top of Dunkery Beacon; saw a most magnificent view, the finest I ever saw. I have drawn a panorama of it, so need not describe it; saw about thirty miles all round, forty or fifty in some directions.

"*Aug.* 14.—Finished my map of Italy. Read Niebuhr. Really he is one of the greatest men that have been in this ignorant and obstinate world. Finished the fourth book of the 'Republic.'

"Sketched this house (i. e. Worthy Farm). Walked with Paget to Culbone, along by the sea, and all manner of perilous places, to Glenthorn. Sent Fanny some things for the 'Family Mirror,' and three more sheets of Greek Grammar.

"*Sept.* 4.—With Walter (who is here for a day or two) and Paget to Linton, by Culbone-wood, and down to the beach at Glenthorn; had to walk through no small quantity of the Atlantic on account of the tide. Went to the Valley of Rocks, and after dinner up to Lyn Cleave to Waters' Meet. I don't know that I ever saw any thing so beautiful and grand. Returned by moonlight.

"*Sept.* 10.—Went with Paget to Worthy Dell. The stream, owing to the storm, very full and sonorous; grown into no end of a cascade. Reading lots of Plato in the evening. Sir T. Acland called, and asked us to dine there. Very pleasant evening. Met his eldest son, who is an Oxford Apostle, and a very nice religious person. He knew well many of my friends, and we had many common topics both literary and religious."

Many of his Sonnets, e. g. xviii.—xxi., "Poems," p. 164, several Lyrical Pieces, pp. 216—229, and various passages in the "School of the Heart," were written at this time.

The following letter was written from Worthy Farm :—

TO FANNY ALFORD.

"*September.*

"Cut this as a book before you read it, and tell me if they charge double[2].

"I pray God He will make us means of much usefulness to each other, and that we may make the interval which shall elapse before our union a time of preparation, solemn and earnest preparation for the duties of it, and every other situation to which it shall please Him to call us.

"I will not look higher than a curacy in the country. I have no idea of being ambitious, but perhaps this feeling is wrong, and I ought to accommodate myself to that sphere, whatever it may be, to which God has seen right to call me.

"You ask me how I get on with the poor at Culbone. A man and his wife and three children live in a little hole not above twelve feet square, but they are nice sober people, and I lend them books. An old woman here keeps a school and has a wonderful knowledge of Scripture. I am writing her out, in imitation of printing (for she cannot read writing), some hymns and prayers for her little school. The clergyman, poor man, is dying of consumption. He gives Bibles and Prayer Books to the people, and is thankful for any attention to them. I have sent you more sheets of the Greek Grammar, containing the formation and declension of the tenses, also three articles for the 'Family Mirror' at Heale.

"How can we be thankful enough! in that blessed state where we shall rest ever in His bosom, with all our hope turned into joy, all our jewels brightly polished, we shall have nobler and better engines of praise than we have here; our minds will then see into the depths of all His gracious dealings; our eyes will be dazzled with no false light, dimmed with no tears, and our tongues will be set free, to sound for ever and ever pure genuine praise, unmixed with display, excitement or enthusiasm, our feelings and motives all justly balanced, all rightly in subjection, a lasting quiet

[2] A sheet of any size might be used in those days of heavy postage, provided it was entire.

joy; for nothing can be lasting that is not quiet. The branch of improvement in which you most need cultivation is that, which by leading us to compare our opinions and information with those of others, enlarges our minds, and makes us take a more comprehensive view of subjects. Don't misunderstand me. What affection has dictated, affection will interpret aright.

"I am reading Gibbon's History of the 'Decline and Fall of the Roman Empire,' not from choice, for he is a very anti-Christian writer, and besides a very affected and disgusting one; but because it is a book that every one has read, and the portion of history of which it treats, always has been in my mind a perfect blank.

"In a few days I shall be twenty-two. I wish it were twenty-three, for I do so want to begin my ministerial course."

Soon after the above letter was written, his sojourn at Porlock was abruptly ended. On Sept. 11, he received a letter from Cambridge, which led him to resolve to become a candidate for the fourth classical mastership of Christ's Hospital. He immediately visited Heale, Cambridge, and Ampton, met with encouragement from his friends and family to proceed, and procured testimonials; but soon after arriving in London he found that the circumstance of his not having been educated at Christ's Hospital would effectually prevent his being elected; and thereupon, he withdrew his name from the list of candidates, and returned to his father's house at Ampton.

Here a letter reached him from his friend Mr. Tennant, concerning a recent election of four Fellows of Trinity; "which," he says, "fixes all my hopes more than ever on this time two years, for which I must work."

On his return to Cambridge in October, he occupied himself chiefly in the care of seven pupils, among whom was his friend E. Bickersteth, and also in reading metaphysics, divinity, and Hebrew. He "had some thoughts" (which were soon afterwards realized) of making a poem of the Muchelney Abbey Legend, and the first germ of the "School of the Heart" appears in the following entry in his journal:—"I have been thinking of my poem lately, and a plan is, I think, now gradually rising up in my mind. The progress and life of a soul to be the subject-matter. The title I cannot fix on, but there is time yet. Endeavour to get it in a train of publication by Midsummer, 1834, D.V."

Some of his poems were placed about this time in the hands of Messrs. Deighton, of Cambridge, and were published in the following February with the title of *Poems and Poetical Fragments*, but without his name. The volume contained only ninety-seven pages; and it included six poems which he did not print in later editions.

His work at this time was too severe for his health, as appears from the following letter:—

To Mr. J. Allen.

"*Trinity College, Nov.* 28.

"I had begun a letter to you as soon as I knew your direction, but other letters and seven pupils have caused it to be unfinished till now. I am not very well, having a cough, and rather an unpleasant fulness in my head; however, there is not much of this term left, and I must be wiser next term. Have you seen Hallam's pamphlet about the 'Spirito Antipapale' of Rosetti? If not, see it *quam primum*. Also if you have any means of seeing the 'Foreign Quarterly,' read an article on the 'German Origin of the Latin language,' by Kemble (who is here), and one on an Italian translation of Milton, by Hallam."

About the end of this term he wrote:—

To Fanny Alford.

"*Trinity College, Dec.* 21.

"I do not pretend to deny that my seven pupils are too much for me, i.e. considering how much I ought to be reading on my own account, but as to writing less frequently to you, I cannot think of it; for it is no hindrance to me, but rather a furtherance. We two have much to rejoice over at the end of this year. O may it all be blessed to our eternal good, may the union between us this year begun, be ripened into a deep, holy, and everlasting one, independent of sorrow and death.

"You say even now nature has some beauties to admire. Indeed she has, there is to me something very fine in the look of the rows of bare trees, tossed about by the winds, and the rooks sailing about and cawing wildly, and also in the deep green moss that grows now on the banks, and the full swelling rivers. One thing strikes me particularly in winter, every thing seems dead and stagnant, but all this time the earth is being prepared by rains and frost and snow to do its work in the spring; the buds are being filled with the young plants, the wool is thickening on the sheep, the birth of the young lambs is coming on and in a thousand other ways progress is taking place; is it not very often so in the spiritual nature, does not God often work in the souls both of others and ourselves, and we know it not?

"*Entre nous*, I am fully and over employed seven hours a day, entirely occupied by pupils besides reading for my fellowship. I generally get up between half-past five and six, and light my fire and read till eight. In the evening I read principally Hebrew or divinity; I am reading Hebrew with a view to understand thoroughly and critically and dogmatically the Epistle to the Hebrews, by Evans's advice."

The following reflections on the close of the year were written at Ampton in his journal.

"*Dec.* 31.—Thus ends another year, and by far the most eventful one of my life: full it has been both of events and interests, but of neither fuller than of mercies; it began with my degree, which so far surpassed my wishes in every respect. . . .

"These dying moments of the old year bring me into a strange mood, something which I cannot express. If I live another year, I shall most likely have entered on the work of my life, even the service of Christ. Oh, what pure and holy pleasure I anticipate in that work: may I have spirit to resolve, and strength to perform. . . . The old year is just dying, there is a strange feel in the air, the snow is lying scattered thinly here and there, and the swept gravel walks look brown like long worms. There is but one cloud in the sky, the shroud of the old year."

In the short vacation which was spent at Ampton, he chides himself for reading little or no Hebrew, but writing letters, poetry, &c., all the week. His "Hymn to the Sun" was finished January 5. He returned to Cambridge in January 25, and records that he then learnt to skate. He now became an author. A copy of his "Poems and Poetical Fragments" was sent to his tutor, the author of "The Rectory of Valehead," to whom a sonnet ["Poems," p. 159] is inscribed. Mr. Evans' letter of acknowledgment, which is subjoined, gave peculiar pleasure to his pupil.

"I return you many thanks for the present of your volume, a considerable portion of which I have gone through already with much pleasure, and profit too, I hope. Among the sterling qualities it possesses that of great purity of taste, no common thing in these days. With regard to the feelings in it, which may make it in a manner belong to me of right, I assure you that I consider the property of great value, and am not a little proud of such a claim. I trust that your work is the first-fruits of an abundant harvest."

JOURNAL. "*Trinity College.*

"1833. *Feb.* 2.—My book is out: may God bless it to my good, and that of others: had a delightful note from Evans about it, speaking of it far better than it deserves.

"I am sending an article[3] on 'Music' to Thirlwall, [Bishop of St. David's] for the 'Philological.' He talked about it most quaintly.

"To the health of my intellectual and spiritual faculties, that of my body is very necessary, and though it has pleased God to bless me with unbroken health all through my life hitherto, yet there is a certain buoyancy of spirit and absolute command of the mind's faculties, which is best preserved by early rising, strong and regular exercise, moderation and regularity in diet, and hardihood of habit respecting clothing, &c. I thank God sometimes that He has made me of a

3 Published in the "Philological Museum," vol. ii.

quick and lively temperament, because I think I have more tangible occasion for self-government, but still there is nothing I practise so little. I have bought Digby's 'Mores Catholici,' which is very delightful: also Thomas à Kempis. The service of Christ is sweet; the only calm, the only blessedness is in holiness; what do we not owe for the inestimable gift of the religion of the heart?

"Vigilandum est et orandum, ne tempus otiose transeat. [Thomas à Kempis, I. ch. 10.]

"O may I more and more feel that indolence is poison both to my intellectual and spiritual nature. Another poison is pride and self-adulation.

"I have been of late and particularly this morning, sketching in my mind the plan of a long poem which may be a bye-work of some years of labour or rest, bustle or seclusion, and as some have set apart a work for their old age, so do I this for my youth, thinking it one of the ways in which God has qualified me to instruct and benefit (if it may be) my generation. As far as my choice has yet proceeded, I mean the tendency of it to be, to recall those feelings of yielded obedience and ready faith which it seems to me our age hath too much cast behind it. And to this intent has my 'Marian[4]' already published been written, but not directly. As to the vehicle in which it shall enter the minds of men, I have rather of late inclined to allegory; not that of more modern times, but a mode of that of our sweet Spenser, and the great and holy Dante. Something approaching to the history of a blessed soul, including the various stages of its progress, and its nourishment and refreshment by the way. And as for the manner of it, whether it shall be a self-related history, or a dream or vision, &c., I have not determined, but I at present prefer the former. And may He who is the fountain of all intellectual knowledge and all perfect beauty, even the Redeemer of the mind and soul of man, direct and assist me; and may the work begun under His blessing, be

---

[4] This was published in the first edition of his Poems as a separate poem, but subsequently it appeared as the First Lesson in the "School of the Heart."

finished by His assistance and be of service to the end intended.

"Truly no time is to be lost. I do so wish I could habitually make a conscience of redeeming every moment. One of the great delinquencies of men here is waste of time."

In March, his uncle and aunt from Heale, and his cousins Fanny and Mary, came to Ampton. He spent his Easter vacation there. Sonnets x. and xi., "Poems," p. 160, were written now, also the piece in blank verse, entitled "Ampton, 1833," "Poems," p. 130, and four lyrical pieces, "Amor Mundanus," and "Cœlestis," "The Little Mourner," and "Ampton," pp. 229—236.

His future vocation was not absent from his thoughts. He records:—

"Reading aloud during our walks Isaac Walton's 'Life of Herbert.' I am determined by God's grace to be a follower of him, as he was of Christ." And in the same week, "I have been reading a review of the life of Felix Neff: many points to be imitated in it, particularly his entire devotedness to his work. O Lord, grant me the like."

After Easter he returns to Cambridge on April 19, and during a long walk after chapel "heard the first nightingale of the season sing most lustily in the brake in the Coton-road Lane." He records as books to be perused Bingham's "Origines Ecclesiasticæ," and Burnet "On the Articles." He proposes to read for the Divinity Scholarship in the long vacation Mosheim and Jennings; and in term time, between five and seven every morning, the historical parts of the Old Testament in Hebrew with "Critici Sacri;" also for the Fellowship, Plato's "Philebus" and Locke in term time, and Brown and Reid and mathematical subjects in the long vacation; and he looks forward to reading afterwards, with a view to his ordination, Grotius, Sumner's "Evidences," Burnet "On the Articles," and the "Pastoral Care."

In May 10 he writes to his cousin Fanny:—

"I am in high order this beautiful weather, enjoying it as much as mortal can enjoy any thing of its kind. Till two I am closeted, if you can call it closeted (sitting at a window which opens thus [then a sketch], with clematis and geraniums and your periwinkles outside), with pupils.

"I am so glad you are coming here with my father and Mary to see me. Who would have dreamt of seeing you at Cambridge? You will be pleased; you must not, however, expect too much, though I don't think you can well be disappointed. This place is looking so very beautiful, our trees are such noble fellows here, and our meadows so rich and luxuriant."

[Here follows a narrative of a meeting with an enthusiastic kinsman who had recently joined the followers of Edward Irving, and who earnestly endeavoured to induce him to quit the Church and follow the guidance of the "unknown tongues."]

"Let our motto be, 'Walk humbly with thy God.' It seems to me that five minutes of real thankfulness for the love of our dear Saviour is worth a year of hard reasoning on the hidden parts of our redemption. We have not fallen upon days of meekness: these are times of spiritual and carnal pride. Let us ever remember that while we give only our private hours to God, and banish Him from our social ones, we cannot expect that our social intercourse will be blessed by Him, or our social wants fulfilled. I know you will agree with me in praying for the joyful consummation anticipated in the last six lines in page 81 of my little book[5]:—

"We must pray for one another; then we shall be able to advise one another. Let the love of Christ hallow every word we speak to each other, whether of common talk, of affectionate advice, or of spiritual intercourse. Remember the world is near, and heaven is far off. But I am advising myself more than you; at least, I ought to be; but we should exhort and edify one another thus, for God does many things by weak vessels."

---

[5] "O glorious time! then may we wake at length,
After life's tempest, under a clear sky,
And count our band, and find with keenest joy
None wanting;—love preserved in all its strength;
And, with fresh beauty, hand in hand arise,
A link in the bright chain of ransom'd families."
"Poems," page 171, Sonnet xxxi.

His father and two cousins, on May 22, came to see him at Cambridge, and returned on the following day. Some lines in the "School of the Heart," Lesson iii., describe his solitary walk back over Newmarket Heath to Cambridge, after accompanying them out to Kentford.

"As one in Summer-tide pacing a weary road."

He left Cambridge for the long vacation on May 28, spent a few days at Ampton with his father, mother, and two cousins, and on June 3 the whole party set off for Heale, spending a night in London by the way. From Heale he went, on July 4, with his friend, and now pupil, E. Bickersteth (as he had done the previous long vacation with his cousin, T. Paget), to read at the north coast of Somersetshire.

A letter written in 1871 to myself by his companion at Porlock (afterwards Archdeacon Bickersteth, of Buckinghamshire) refers chiefly to this vacation, and may be most fitly inserted here:—

"I have been looking, I am sorry to say, in vain for such notes and reminiscences as you have asked of the time when I was in daily intercourse with the departed one. Changes of residence and lapse of time have obliterated these tangible memorials, though the heart's remembrance of those early days is still as fresh and as present as ever. My most familiar intercourse with the Dean was some forty years ago, at the time when he was preparing for Cambridge, as a pupil with my father at Acton. Our companionship then was of the most intimate kind, and we were as much together as it was possible for two persons to be. It was impossible not to be drawn very closely to one with so much thought and feeling and intellect, and I remember that it was a great sorrow to me when he left for Cambridge. When I followed him to Cambridge four years afterwards, he became my private tutor, and our personal intercourse was then renewed. In the long vacation of 1833 I read with him in Somersetshire, and I well recollect the interest of the occasional visits to Heale House. We took lodgings first at a house called Worthy Farm, close to the seaside and near Porlock, and afterwards we moved to Over Stowey. From these places we used to make frequent rambles over some of the most picturesque parts of Somersetshire; while Over Stowey, with its associations with Coleridge and Southey, was very congenial with the tastes of Henry Alford. It was about this time that he wrote some of those beautiful little sonnets and minor pieces in the 'School of the Heart.' I have often been with him, when in a fit of abstraction he was composing some of these verses, which will always remain for the delight and instruction of multitudes."

Worthy Farm, near Porlock, his lodging in the previous year, afforded him accommodation for the first three weeks of this vacation; he afterwards removed to a cottage belonging to Mr. Anstice, of Bridgewater. He formed strong resolutions for self-discipline:—

"I find I have several things to guard against, among which are,—sharpness of word or look upon slight occasions, and exaggeration of all kinds. May God give me grace to do so! I purpose giving my time before breakfast to theology, the fore part of the morning to mathematics, the latter to metaphysics, and what classics I do read in the evening. I have of late been given to be in bed much later in the morning than my philosophy or conscience can approve. I hereby make and record a solemn resolution (which may God give me grace to keep!) to rise, if I wake, never later than six."

An unforeseen occurrence at this time hastened the fulfilment of his intention to enter into holy orders. His father was pressed by the Rev. Thomas Spencer, rector and patron of Winkfield, to accept that rectory. Mr. Alford accepted it; but, feeling convinced that he should not long continue to keep it[6], determined not to resign Ampton, and therefore proposed to his son to take the curacy of Ampton as his title for orders, and to reside there. Henry's comment on this in his journal, July 18, is—

---

[6] The circumstances are stated in the "Memorial of the Rev. H. Alford," page 116.

"Δόξα τῷ Θεῷ. How graciously has every thing been managed, that we should settle once more in our dear old nest!"

During the months of August and September his journal records various walking excursions to Bridgewater, Bristol, the Mendip country, and Bath, in company partly with E. Bickersteth, partly with C. Merivale.

On October 2 he went to Norwich to be examined as a candidate for the order of deacon. He records that Mr. Drake, the chaplain, whose examination he passed, was very civil to him. But it happened inconveniently for him that the ordination was fixed for October 5, when his twenty-third birthday being October 7, he wanted two days of the requisite age. He, therefore, returned on October 4 to Ampton, and then received letters dimissory from the Bishop of Norwich to the Bishop of Exeter.

His journal states on Saturday, October 26: "At 10 a.m. I went to the Cathedral (Exeter); a very fine interior and venerable exterior, with those two grand old towers, which I shall never (for many reasons now) forget. Very beautiful chant in the morning at twelve. Went to the Bishop's palace and heard his Charge. Altogether it was the most solemn thing I ever heard. He talked to us most seriously for nearly two hours on the inward call, the ministerial duties, &c. Oh! may I never forget it, and may this be to me a lesson, among many others I have had of late, not to judge of men harshly, or before the time, as I certainly had of the Bishop of Exeter.

"Next day to the Cathedral at ten, and I was ordained. What a service it is! and the Bishop's manner was most solemn, and altogether all was most suitable and proper. I am very thankful to God for having brought me to such a place and such a man."

On his way back to Ampton he spent one evening at Heale in the society of very old and dear friends, and read to them the Ordination Service.

On his return to Ampton, not being quite well, a feeling of depression came over him as he approached a home from which his father had now removed, and where he was 200 miles away from his nearest earthly friends.

He makes the following entry in his journal:—

"First let me begin with an acknowledgment to the Author of all my mercies, and my Divine Saviour who has now vouchsafed to call me to His work, and given me a place in His vineyard. Never did I feel myself so wholly unworthy or incompetent as now that I have entered on the duties of the ministry; but His strength is perfected in my weakness."

To his friend, C. Merivale, he writes of his Ordination and his home life alone:—

"I had a most pleasant time of it at Exeter, was delighted with the Bishop in every way; dined with him on the Saturday, and sat near him, so had much talk on many subjects, among others the Anthology and you. His Charge was wonderfully solemn and to the point. Altogether he is a man whom I have put among my persons not to be despised. The luxury of being quite alone is something more than I can describe. It does one so much good to find out one's real place in the universe of things, and I seem to be growing almost perceptibly (like a plant under a glass) in things in which I before felt myself very deficient. Whether I shall ever 'unveil the blooming fruit of solitary hours,' as Evans has it, I know not.

"You say nothing more about Hallam[7], poor fellow. I do not remember any thing for many years which has distressed me so much as his death; I sometimes sit and think of it till I feel quite unhappy. It seems, indeed, a loud and terrible stroke from the reality of things upon the fairy building of our youth."

He gives this account of the first Sunday (November 3) after his ordination:—

"Performed my first service and preached my first sermon (I am happy to say without nervousness or inconvenience) from Matt. xxviii. end. Full congregations. Was not at all

---

7 The death of Arthur Henry Hallam, as is well known, is the subject of Tennyson's great poem, "In Memoriam." There is a humbler tribute to his memory in the "School of the Heart," Lesson v., "Poems," p. 63.

tired. Praise be to God who so graciously through this trying day has brought me.

"I see the absolute necessity of regularly undertaking the study of divinity; I think my best plan will be to study the Scriptures. At present going on with the Epistles in the early part of the morning, next Hebrew, and after that Ecclesiastical History. Mosheim for the present. My sermons in the morning; and what time I can spare from that for classics and metaphysics, in which department Butler must be the first book."

Soon after he had begun his work as a clergyman, he writes to his cousin Fanny:—

"I have now begun God's work in the strictest sense. I am now in an office to which I had often looked forward, and too often with a sort of indefinite pleasure, without laying before me the duties and requirements of it, and I must say I feel, what till now I never felt half so deeply or vividly, that I am most unequal to them[8].

"My inexperience may be in a few years remedied, but I feel as if I had no ground to go upon. My fancied fitness for the ministry, and my cherished schemes of usefulness, have all slipped away, and I am left a mere boy in understanding. My texts for next week are:—Thursday evening, Rev. xiv. 12, 13, an introductory sermon to the lectures on the history of the Church; Sunday morning, Matt. v. 3, a text which I feel will do me especial good at this time to think upon; on Sunday evening Phil. iii. 21, a glorious subject, and one which I think may be made useful by being put in the light of a strong contrast between our vile body and His glorious body, and showing by what power this change will take place. I mean to have the children to sing on Thursdays and Fridays; and on Sundays, boys ten and half-past three, girls half-past ten and half-past two.

"I have lately lost a very dear and intimate college friend, Hallam, who died suddenly at Vienna. He was a man of a

---

8 The poem entitled "The Ancient Man" refers to his experience at Ampton. "Poems," p. 225.

wonderful mind and knowledge on all subjects, hardly credible at his age—younger than myself. He was well acquainted with our own, French, German, Italian, and Spanish literature, besides being a good classical scholar, and of the most tender affectionate disposition; and there was something admirably simple and earnest in all he said or did. I long ago set him down for the most wonderful person altogether I ever knew."

From his ordination till Christmas he was working his parish and reading for his fellowship. His friend E. T. Vaughan (afterwards Vicar of St. Martin's, Leicester) thus describes him now:—

"Twice during the autumn of 1833, and the following winter, I stayed with him in the parsonage [Ampton] at the edge of Lord Calthorpe's beautiful place. I have the most delightful remembrance of rambles with him by the lake, and through the woods vocal, in the depths of a mild winter, with innumerable rooks. He was throwing all his heart and mind into his new ministerial duties, his sermons, and his pastoral intercourse with the simple villagers, in which already he seemed to find a happiness more congenial to his true taste than the restless intellectual activity of the circle in which he had lived at Cambridge; but he was as diligent in study as ever. He was thinking and feeling much on the *religious questions of the day*. He was taking pupils too, young men preparing for college; a work which occupied a large share of his time from henceforth to the summer of 1849, when he gave it up finally."

The following letter was written to his betrothed cousin, in answer to some remarks on the peculiarities of his character:—

"Never be afraid Fanny to tell me what you have. If for no other reason than that you do so I ought to consider you my best earthly friend. Now never spare to do so; whenever you see this in me, do tell me; not perhaps at the time, but the first opportunity afterwards. You are too much disposed to make allowances for me. I am afraid in very many instances it is much more than my manner, that I feel a sort of contempt for the opinions of others which leads me to show this manner towards them. Much of this is owing to the pride of my natural heart, which struggles in me, and sometimes gets the upper hand in a manner which makes me ashamed and grieved when I come to reflect upon it. But there are also minor causes, and one of these is, that my society at Cambridge has long consisted of a very exclusive set of men, of certainly very superior minds, who form a sort of aristocracy in the University, and I think their opinion of, and behaviour towards men who have not had the same advantages has been too haughty and self-important. Another reason is, I have got among them, and from them, much truly valuable mental instruction and discipline, and one consequence of it is, I never like or can bear to take any thing upon trust (always excepting the great mysteries of our faith, which rest on a different footing altogether), unless I can see my way very clearly to it. I cannot take up any opinion, however common it may be. But then the mischief of it is, I do not make allowances for those who have not had the advantages, whether real or fancied, which I have had; and if I find any persons holding opinions which I cannot subscribe to, or have satisfied myself of the error of, I set upon them without mercy or allowance, as if they were some terrible moral delinquents, or had done me some great personal injury. These explanations I give not in any way to justify myself, but to lay open to you the reasons, in many cases, of that otherwise unaccountable manner. But after all, whatever minor causes may have conduced to increase it, my natural pride and self-importance are the true and great causes of it—feelings very opposite to that true Christian humility which should be eminent especially in a minister of Christ.

"I entreat and conjure you by every thing you value, if you have any regard for my temporal and spiritual welfare, to do your utmost to cure me of that sharpness and spirit of opposition which so often shows itself in me. I am conscious very frequently of saying things from the mere desire of opposition.

"I was so pleased with your account of Tintern Abbey:

don't count those days wasted. You don't know what an effect such sights as these have upon the mind—an effect not observed, and working silently, but not the less sure for that, and one which is felt in after-life often in the most solemn and important things. We are too apt to think that we get nothing except by actual exercise of our mental powers; whereas very much of the growth of our minds, and more especially of our power of appreciation of truth and fitness in things, arises from little things which we take no note of, and which occur when we fancy ourselves unemployed, and are not on the look-out for any such teaching.

An extract from his journal will take us to the end of this year.

"*Dec.* 19.—Ampton. I have been here now seven weeks, not living in such active study and conscientious attention to duty as becomes me. O how the profession of God's ministry and the light of His countenance bring to notice all my many shortcomings, and set before me my secret sins. Sloth—sloth is my crying and most usual evil; many hours do I waste which hereafter will be more precious than diamonds, and I know not how to combat it, for at times I seem to have lost all my energy, and with it both the wish and the power to regain it. God grant that it may not be the beginning of a chilly and inactive manhood. Striving against it now is the only means to prevent it, and by His grace strive with it I will.

"*Dec.* 31.—It has pleased my Heavenly Father to bring me safe to the end of another year, a very eventful one to me, for what I anticipated has taken place. I have been admitted into the ministry, and there has opened before me a glorious work; the work indeed of a life. May I increase in the knowledge of Christ.

"I am now going on with my poems for a second volume, which I heartily hope may be blessed to bringing to a better mind many who are worth reclaiming from the nonsense now abroad, and bad taste becoming so common."

Two pupils, Dunbar Heath and Lawrence, came to him at this time, and in the spring of 1834 his first sermon was published; it was entitled, "An Address to the Inhabitants of Bury St. Edmund's on the Lord's Day[9]."

TO FANNY ALFORD.

"*March* 25.

"Every hour of every day is filled up; but I am quite happy in being employed in the service of Christ and being permitted to lay aside all points of contention and argument and doubt, and enforce the plain saving truths of the Gospel. Should God unite us together, I have often determined in looking forward to the time, that we would endeavour strenuously to avoid the indolence and inertness of mind which seem often to creep over people when they settle in life."

His journal notes:—

"*April* 4.—My third pupil Reynolds is come; I am afraid I have not been enough in the parish of late, I must therefore begin to be more so, not that I think it needful or desirable to keep up the system of espionage, which already is too much carried on here, but because the people have been accustomed to more attention, and so look for it. My poem and the fellowship go on but poorly, I seem to be consumed with things to do, and yet cannot find any solid fruit for all my work; my reading is a mere farce with, on an average, six hours per day employed in pupils and sermon work; by getting up at six o'clock I have managed to finish Butler's 'Analogy,' but I must read it again.

"*April* 22.—I have heard from my father in answer to my question about the fellowship; he wishes that I should exert myself as much as possible to get one; this then I must set about, though with my present occupation, reading is very uphill work, especially that of mathematics. I have been reading Berkeley, and Reid *versus* Berkeley, and I can't tell what to think of either of them, for my mind seems wholly incapacitated for thinking on any subject. I never was so stupid and worth nothing intellectually, and now I am to begin and accomplish the work of arranging

[9] During his stay at Ampton he printed another sermon entitled, "Faith Explained and Enforced:" preached in Ampton Church, and printed for the use of the parishioners.

all I ever knew, and bring it to bear upon one point. All I can say is, if they elect me fellow, they must be grievously in want of fellows."

He was now settled with his pupils at Ampton, and for some months his journal records chiefly the names of occasional visitors, and the sights and sounds which met him in the neighbouring woods; e. g. "April 18. First heard the nightingale; 19, saw swallows; 20, heard the cuckoo; 30, hawthorn in bloom; May 1, lilac in bloom; 2, swifts appear; 5, laburnum in bloom." Throughout his life he never failed to notice such occurrences with a fresh interest every year. In June and July he visited London, Somersetshire, and Cambridge.

The following letter, dated August, was written to Mr. J. Allen on his marriage:—

"I write immediately on hearing your direction, to congratulate you on the event which, in common with all our Cambridge coterie, I have been delighted to hear.

"And so you are married, and doesn't the world seem to have an end, and the ancient sayings of prophets to be accomplished; we bachelors go about in a constant state of seeking and imperfection; our talk is of fellowships and pupils and such like buffetings in the voyage of life; and you happy fellows have made your port, and are safe in the haven where you would be, with your white sails in the sunshine. We are cheated out of our better feelings by the importunate calls of worldly studies. You seem to have all the poetry of your life let loose upon you, and to have discovered an inexhaustible treasure of joy, quiet and *unintermeddled-with.* I used to think I knew you; but you are grown double, and I only know half of you. Mysteries, these deep things of life.

"May you, dear fellow, never have a moment's cause to repent your being in them. As to my own love affair, it begins to dawn to a close, I hope; provided I can obtain a settled residence, I believe Easter is to be the time; nineteen years' courtship, and three of engagement is, I should think, as long a time of pleasurable suspense as most people ever look back upon. With every wish and prayer for your future happiness."

He went on reading for his fellowship, of which he says, "I think I have about as much chance as I have of being Emperor of China." But he was agreeably disappointed. After the examination, he writes to his father:—

"*Oct.* 1. The fellowships have just announced themselves; the list is as follows:—

1. Lushington.	4. Hamilton.
2. Alford.	5. Dobson.
3. Thompson.	6. Birks.

I know you will rejoice with me at this unexpected result. I think you will both hope and pray with me that this increase of influence may be for my real good and that of others with whom I shall be concerned."

To his cousin Fanny he writes:—

"I have some good news for you, I am a fellow of Trinity; having got my fellowship, I shall now proceed to devise methods to rid myself of it as soon as possible."

The next month he was ordained priest; to his father he writes in November,—"I go to town on Friday to be ordained priest at St. Margaret's, Westminster, i. e. if it be not burnt; it is close to Westminster Abbey and the burning Houses of Parliament. May God's blessing rest on me in that solemn and responsible office. My tutor Peacock says, rather than I should marry without a living, he would give up a small one in Leicestershire which he holds with his fellowship, and which he has been thinking of doing for some time."

His journal says:—

"*Nov.* 6.—Went up to town and received the Holy Orders of a Priest; may I be a temple of chastity and holiness fit and clean to receive so great a guest; and on so great a commission as I have now received, O my beloved Redeemer, my dear Brother and Master, hear my prayer."

Eventually he was presented to Wymeswold, but it was not till March 4, 1835.

A week or two after this, having paid a visit to the place which was to be his home for eighteen years, he thus describes it to his father:—"Wymeswold is five miles east of Loughborough, twelve from Nottingham, fourteen from Leicester, and eight from Melton Mowbray; population 1200, value 110*l.*; fine church; but now comes the drawback, and a considerable one it is, the house is a very bad one; so bad (I have seen it) that I could not show a pupil into it as a bachelor, much less a wife. Give me your practical judgment on it, there seems to me to be much to be said on both sides. I hardly know which way my own inclination turns. I saw the place on Monday, my general impression was favourable. Country fine, having Charnwood Forest hills within a drive or ride. The parish is full of charities, and I am told a judicious application of the new poor laws would in a few years abolish poor-rates altogether."

After it was apparently settled he writes again:—

TO HIS FATHER.

"Now consider me as vicar of Wymeswold. I do indeed join with your kind wishes for my usefulness there in subservience to the will of my Heavenly Father, the fulfilment of which is with us as it was with Christ, the end of our being born into the world. It will, I expect, be a post of much increasing labour. The population is large, and the nature of it seems to require particular attention. The dissenters there will afford ample scope for the exercise of Christian charity and also of temperate zeal. The temporal concerns of the parish will also demand much attention; from all accounts the charities have been abused, the poor neglected or injudiciously treated for some years; some conflicts and difficulties must be expected in all these points, some striving to convince the short-sighted and ignorant, and to convict the interested, and stir up the indolent. It is a place where there will be much to do and bear with, full of good institutions, but apparently not efficient for want of proper management, or active superintendence of some leading person. This I look forward to with much distrust of myself, though, I hope, without shrinking from it; indeed I feel glad that God has thought it fit to appoint me to a place of duty, to put an office into my hands, and entrust me with such a charge. Pray for me, my dear father, that I may not fall into a state of indolence and indecision, which I feel strongly to be my temptation, being a reaction after some years spent in constant labour and frequent excitement."

It was in the interval between his ordination and his marriage that he met with an accident, the effect of which was visible as long as he lived. In November he had a fall from a tree of twenty-four feet in height, and was mercifully preserved with no further injury than dislocating his right elbow.

On December 29th, after having sent to press a new volume of poems, he left Ampton, to visit his father at Winkfield, and to make at Heale the final arrangements for his marriage. On his return to Ampton he writes to his cousin Fanny just before his marriage:—

"I was presented to Wymeswold on Monday, and am now, therefore, vicar of that place. God grant it may be for our good. Soon our joys will be doubled and our sorrows halved by mutual participation. I wish I could read you Jeremy Taylor's sermon on the Marriage-ring; however, I will, please God, ere long.

"I suppose you are infinitely busy, so am I, for what with writing letters, attending to my pupils and my volume of Poems, and finishing a new barrel to the organ[1] for the church here, which I don't like to leave unfinished, and the parish, I hardly know which way to turn myself.

"Time hath leaden wings.
"The days, though full of work, lag slowly on;
O for some wise receipt to make them fly
As fast as fly my wishes. The glad words
Should then have been pronounced which make us one:
And we (till God shall send and fetch us home),
Together bound for better or for worse."

The marriage took place at Curry-Rivell church, on March 10, 1835. We left Heale for Cheltenham and Malvern (see Sonnet xlii., "Poems," p. 177). Our road lay through Worcester and Birmingham to Tamworth, where a visit was paid to his mother's grave; and from thence, passing through

[1] With his own hand he set several tunes on the organ in Ampton Church, which he found simply a common barrel-organ.

Ashby and Loughborough, we arrived at Wymeswold, his new incumbency, where he officiated in the church, March 15; and afterwards made the necessary arrangements for coming to live there. We returned by Cambridge to his curacy at Ampton, where he officiated in church on Sunday, the 22nd. At Ampton we spent the first four months of our married life.

To his friend, C. Merivale, he says:—

"I wish you could come and see us, going hand in hand, and every day making me, and I may safely say both of us, more and more thankful to God for His mercy in bringing us together."

To his sister-in-law, Mary:—

"You cannot think how pleasant a thing it is to have known each other from childhood; it gives so much of common interest and retrospects for both to speak of and feed affection upon. You should see her bustling about in the house, or coming down to me with her bundle of books to be tutorized, with health and happiness on her rosy cheeks."

His entries in his diary are not now so regular (for a time). On May 1 he writes:—"How very much has happened since I wrote here; various employments and other reasons have caused it. I am now enjoying, as a quiet and usual thing, the daily company of that dear person who has been through my young life the chief object of my love here on earth. God has now filled up the measure of His mercies to me, while that of my gratitude is yet empty."

In July we went from Ampton to Cambridge to be present at the installation of the Marquis Camden. Our occupation of the rectory of Ampton now came to an end: his father resumed his residence there, and we removed to Wymeswold, where a house was hired sufficient to accommodate the pupils and ourselves. Whilst it was being furnished we took, as he says in his journal—

"*Aug.* 4.—An excursion into Derbyshire, to the Peak District and Dovedale. We walked the last day fifteen miles, and went in old style with knapsack. Delighted with Castleton and the Peak.

"*Aug.* 11.—Much is to be done as usual; or, rather more than usual. Hebrew must not be neglected, nor German; both, however, bye-works compared with the great end of my ministerial duties, and the scarcely less important object of my dear Fanny's improvement, which I have so much at heart. My pupils are now come back."

Soon after this time many circumstances combined to produce a depression of spirits. In addition to his ministerial duties in a large parish, and the trouble of becoming acquainted with the details of its "localities and politics," he had the care of four pupils. He was full of desire to advance in knowledge, and to "do some good among men;" and he could not fail to miss the refreshment and pleasure of frequent intercourse with men of intellect and cultivation, from whom he was now in a great measure secluded. These clouds, however, gradually vanished.

About this time the second edition of his Poems was published at Cambridge. It is in two volumes: the first [169 pages] containing "Sonnets and Minor Poems;" the second [129 pages] "The School of the Heart." With reference to this he wrote to the Rev. C. Merivale:—

"Do you see me outside Deighton's catalogue in the corner? 'The Passion of St. Agnes' is a sort of anomalous thing, taken in part from one of the *περὶ στεφάνων* poems of Prudentius, which are very beautiful. My long poem makes its bow, rejoicing in the name of 'School of the Heart,' an old title, I believe, to a sort of religious picture-book of Quarles [though I can find no mention of it in his life], and now adopted in lieu of a better, after a long search for one. I think it does very well to combine all the very miscellaneous matter which that poem doth, or will contain. The several parts are called Lessons i., ii., &c., embellished with appropriate mottoes."

The following letter to another friend also relates to this publication:—

". . . Whilst I am on this subject, my new poems, my wish has been to undertake a work for God and to promote His glory. I am determined by His grace to use any power

I may have to promote His cause, and for this reason I have undertaken to describe in a sort of conversational narrative what I conceive to be the food, natural and physical, of a renewed soul on its way to God; thus showing how all earthly beauty, natural and moral, has its right place and its purest enjoyment in a soul so ordered, and how revealed and spiritual truth and beauty bear on it."

The following letter from William Wordsworth, doubtless, belongs to this time, though no year is given:—

"*Lowthe Castle, Sept.* 26.

"MY DEAR SIR,—A few days before I left home I had the honour of receiving your two volumes, 'The School of the Heart,' and some time before, a letter from you, for both which marks of your esteem I beg to return you my sincere thanks. Being at present in a house where franks abound, and not purposing to return home immediately, I avail myself of this opportunity to say, that I was so much pleased with the 'Lessons' which I read that I have no doubt that the whole of the book will delight me when I shall be able to peruse it at leisure. The strains of sentiment are such as I have been in the habit of cultivating for my own great benefit (as I have lately had much cause to feel under severe domestic affliction), and also with no little service, as you encourage me to believe, to others. My right arm is suffering under a severe sprain, which must be my excuse for not writing at greater length, and so illegibly. Believe me to be, my dear sir,

"Very sincerely yours,

"WM. WORDSWORTH."

His Poems were criticized in the "Edinburgh Review," No. 126. He thus refers in his common-place book to the article:—

"The principal faults objected to me are carelessness in language and inconsistency of opinion, to both of which I frankly confess, having, in the first place, a strange aversion to correction of any kind; and again, being on many matters in such a state of progress and unsettledness, and having been still more so than I am—to wit, especially during the time while those poems were being written. The whole article is more one of praise than blame, but there is much of both. I certainly must endeavour to systematize more than I have done. Subjects for poetry must be chosen, and the 'patient labour of manly years' be at last undertaken. A subject for a long poem, some time thought of, doth not yet appear. Sonnets must be cultivated, and, for the sake of avoiding scandal, regularity of structure observed."

It may be mentioned here, that amongst other readers of the new edition of his poems was the Rev. John Moultrie, rector of Rugby. Though not personally acquainted with the writer, Mr. Moultrie felt so much delight with the book, that he addressed a poem of considerable length to Henry Alford.

The autumn of 1835 and the following winter were spent in the quiet discharge of ordinary duties at Wymeswold. We received visits from many members of our family. No letters have been preserved that were written at this time.

The strong feeling with which he dwelt upon the intellectual society at Cambridge, and its happy "days of youthful confidence and sacred joy," is shown in the "Lines written in a Gift Book" ("Poems," p. 131). The book, given to his wife, March 10, 1836 (the first anniversary of the wedding-day), had belonged to Arthur Hallam, and the lines in their degree are not less full of his memory than is the great poem of Tennyson.

It must have been in the spring of this year that his father, having occasion to call in a medical man at Havre, was treated with unusual kindness, because he was the father of Henry Alford, whose poems the doctor had lately read. This incident formed the subject of the following sonnet, which is only to be found in a small edition[2] of his poems, called "The Abbot of Muchelnaye, Sonnets, &c."

---

[2] Published in 1841, and dedicated to the Rev. J. Moultrie.

ON AN INCIDENT WHICH HAPPENED AT HAVRE,

APRIL, 1836.

"Since my first essay to the world went forth,
Twice spoke the critic from his seat severe
Words not unpleasing to my youthful ear;
Nor in my walk of life hath there been dearth
Of praising tongues, in earnest and in mirth:
Self-chiding it hath ask'd, and wholesome fear
Firmly against the Syren's voice to steer,
And measure praises by their sterling worth.
But when I learn that in a stranger land
My wandering fame hath in the hour of pain
Bespoke the soothing voice and ministering hand
For thee, my father—to resist were vain.
Nearer to tears my thankful heart it stirr'd
Than each approving page or praising word."

On May 28 he writes at Wymeswold:—

"I have passed in full employment two months with five pupils and my parish, and in great and increasing happiness. My poetical career seems for the present suspended—not, I would hope, for good, though in less hopeful moments I am led to suspect so. The 'Edinburgh' and 'Blackwood,' the latter especially, have noticed my book favourably, and I have had many encouragements; but this spring has not called out my poetic propensities in the same manner that former ones have done.

"My excess of employment generates a correspondent indolence at leisure times, which prevents me from applying to composition as I could wish. My subjects of thought are few in comparison with what they used to be; my mind is not so active, and yet my opinions are not one whit more decided on any point. The slow, unobserved course of experience seems to be my teacher, unfolding, as years go on, the nature of things as far as I need know.

"We promise ourselves four weeks this vacation of enjoyment in Derbyshire. I then propose writing something for publication, but feel no drawing as yet towards any particular subject; in fact, it would be exceedingly hard to say what is the bent of my mind at this time; it seems, intellectually speaking, to be acted on, on all sides, and therefore at rest."

Sonnets xxxv. and xlv. ("Poems," pp. 173, 178) were written at this time; and, taken together, they seem to represent the same balanced state of mind, the former showing a yearning after action; the latter, a mistrust of self-guiding freedom.

But he did not suffer his feelings and his literary plans to divert his attention from his parish. It was his habit at this time to preach unwritten sermons, morning, afternoon, and evening, every Sunday. They were, however, very far from being unpremeditated. A manuscript book is preserved which contains his notes for his parochial sermons throughout the last five months of 1836. The numerous divisions and subdivisions show how carefully the matter of each sermon was considered. Generally the texts are taken from a Lesson of the day or other appropriate Scripture, and the notes for a single sermon sometimes are so copious as to fill six pages. The notes, I believe, were carefully read before going to church, but nothing except the Bible was taken up into the pulpit.

At this date he published a letter on "Infant Baptism," addressed to one of his parishioners, a Baptist, and the father of one of his Sunday-school girls. The case of that family was a common one at that time in Wymeswold. Many children were unbaptized, some of whom, as they grew up, attended the Church Sunday-school, and actually offered themselves for confirmation! and the Sunday-school, which was partly held in the church, was then the only school belonging to the Church in the parish.

He formed the design of building two schoolrooms, one for a national school (for which he proposed to give up the old vicarage-house and garden), the other, for an infant school. He induced some of his parishioners to take an interest in the welfare of others and to act as district visitors. He compiled a small hymn book for the use of his congregation, and attempted to put in order the choir of the church, which he found in a neglected state.

Although he addressed himself with ardour to the task of organizing a large agricultural and manufacturing parish, it was not easy work to a poor man, and it was not the most congenial work to one of his disposition, endowed with a refined, intellectual, and sensitive temperament, and with a peculiarly generous, open nature. He was here brought into intercourse constantly with some who did not understand him, and into collision occasionally with some who could not sympathize with him. With all his energy and desire for progress, he was not a man of business in the ordinary acceptation of the term, and whatever skill and tact he possessed in the administration of a parish, and the regulation of its machinery, were gradually acquired in the course of his experience at Wymeswold.

His five pupils returned to their homes at Midsummer, and we went to spend our first and well-earned vacation near the wild scenery of the Peak in Derbyshire. Our head-quarters were at Ashford. The principal record of this time is a set of five Sonnets (xlix.—liii. "Poems," pp. 181, 182).

We returned to Wymeswold early in August, and in the following October our eldest child was born. The Poem entitled "Lines written October 23, 1836" ("Poems," p. 133), was composed a few hours after her birth. The Sonnets xlvi.—xlviii. (p. 179), and the Poem entitled, "Christmas Eve, 1836" (p. 135), and a Spring Scene (p. 140), followed in due course. Very early in her life the child was taken on a visit to her friends at Heale, which is thus recorded:—

"At Christmas, we went during a very deep snow to London, where we spent a week at the Bedford Hotel, Southampton Row. Thence, after an attack of influenza, with which nearly every one in town was laid up, went, taking our little Alice, to Betchworth in Surrey, Mr. Goulburn's [3]; and after spending a few pleasant days there, posted on through Winchester and Salisbury to Heale. Nearly all there were ill of influenza, and altogether it was a dreary time. We came home by way of Cheltenham, and went to Stratford-on-Avon, to visit Shakspeare's tomb, and see the room where he was born."

---

[3] The Right Hon. Henry Goulburn was at this time Secretary of State for the Home Department. His son Frederick was a pupil at Wymeswold.

The impression made on his mind by this memorable spot is recorded in a Sonnet (liv., "Poems," p. 18), and in the following portion of an article in "Dearden's Miscellany" (vol. ii. p. 452, 1839).

"To us there is hardly a dearer spot in fair England than that chancel in Stratford-upon-Avon church. The churchyard slopes to the Avon. Peacefully and tenderly does that famous stream glide by the solemn place. The scenery around is quiet but beautiful. Gentle swells and falls, and willow-peopled meadows, are the objects on which the eye rests, looking countryward; and townward, many a substantial dwelling, coëval with the glories of the place. Between these two prospects the spire rises, crowning a rich and massy pile of church architecture. You approach it by an ancient wall of limes, clipped and curiously interwoven overhead. Inside you pass through oak-carving, and by stately tombs. You enter the chancel, lofty and light, with full-embellished windows and fair proportions. On your left, somewhat more than half way, is a stone half-length in an arched niche. You know the figure: who does not? Beneath your feet is a slab, and a small plate let into it. Under you rests one who has formed more of your mind than you wot of—the parent of many a thought which you call your own. The lofty benevolence of Prospero, the pure gentleness of Miranda; Juliet and her Romeo—the dreaming moodiness of Hamlet—the lovely lady married to the Moor—the aged exile-king—with all their companions, joyous or sad. It may be, you think not of them, you feel them not; but the power of them is upon you. Truly if there be a place where memory strikes one dumb, the present is overborne by the past, the material by the spiritual—it is that chancel and that tomb."

Sonnets lx. and lxi. ("Poems," p. 186), written this spring of 1837, show how fully he appreciated such rural beauties as Wymeswold affords.

In the spring he had a severe attack of quinsy, and was otherwise incapacitated for officiating in church, where there were three full services every Sunday. A curate (Mr. Robinson) was temporarily engaged.

In June we went abroad for ten weeks, leaving our little girl to be taken care of at Heale. It was the first time that either of us saw the Continent. We went through Belgium, Ostend, Antwerp, Brussels, Waterloo, Namur, Liége, Cologne, up the Rhine, through Basle, Soleure, Berne, Geneva, over the Simplon to Lago Maggiore, visited Turin to get our passports viséed for Austria, through Milan, Como, Lugano, back to Geneva, and thence through Paris and Boulogne home. A poetical record of the tour is contained in nine sonnets, lxii.—lxx. ("Poems," p. 187) with a lyrical poem, "On a Cyclamen," p. 265.

An entry in a common-place book shows that he was inspired by the country now visited, with the first idea of a poem, which he did not complete till thirty-two years afterwards, when he published "The Children of the Lord's Prayer." He now writes:—"An idea has struck me, which it may be as well to record, if only to be relinquished again. It is to write a poem, to be called Visions [or records] of Time, connected perhaps with another to be called Visions of Eternity:—

"*Scene.*—The summit of Mont Blanc. Time, before sunset. The Hierarch of Europe. The inferior angels bending, as in prayer.

"*Chorus*—O Thou Eternal One!
Around whose central throne
This universe is poised in balance high.

"*Hierarch*—Our Father who hast made the night and day,
Thyself transcending all that Thou hast made,
By Thy high pleasure this our state we keep,
To watch and bless Thy earth," &c.

This same strain goes on for more than 100 lines, reproduced in 1869 in the illustrated book mentioned above.

We give a few extracts from his letters at this period. The first before starting, June 3:—

TO HIS FATHER.

"I look forward with much interest to witnessing the Romish religion; its acting and flourishing system in Belgium; its subsistence under toleration in Prussia; its very opposite extreme of anti-decoration and will-worship in Switzerland, and its results in the spread of spiritual indifference in France.

"*Namur, June* 16.—We came here in perfect safety by Brussels, where we had a most splendid dinner at two francs each. Waterloo we saw, and were pestered to buy relics. At Bruges the buildings in decaying grandeur looked like some old palaces. The cathedral at Antwerp is very fine.

"*July* 27.—Our excursion to the Oberland of Berne has given us exceeding pleasure. At Thun we went across the lake to see Unterlaken, then in a carriage to Grindelwald, where we saw the magnificent glacier, and slept with the Wetterhorn just over our bedroom window. At six a.m. one morning, we mounted our horses and went over the Wengern Alp to Lauterbrunnen. This was most beautiful; the ground as we ascended was covered with Alpine flowers. At Lauterbrunnen we saw the Staubbach, and next morning went up the Lake of Brienz to see the Giessbach. We have been to Chamounix, and by the Tête Noire to Martigny, thence through the Valais, by Sion and Brigue, over the Simplon to Baveno, where we slept. Our first evening in Italy was most delightful; the sky and the moon, and the quiet, clear smoothness of Lago Maggiore were to me like some strange place one dreams of rather than reality. Next day we saw the Borromean Isles, and crossed to Luvino, intending to go to Milan, but our passport had not been properly viséed, so we were obliged to go with it to Turin, for this purpose we recrossed the Lake to Arona. Saw the statue of St. Carlo Borromeo, and all night to Turin; a fine place.

"This unfrequented journey showed us the utmost of Italian dirt and discomfort; but we saw two most glorious views of the whole range of the Alps at sunrise. We were beyond measure delighted with the cathedral of Milan; from thence we came by Como, Menagio, Porlezza, and on to Luvino and Baveno, and over the Simplon by Sion, Vevay (saw the Castle of Chillon), and by steamer to Geneva. To-morrow we are off for Paris, three days there, and then, please God, Boulogne and London. We have both enjoyed ourselves much and walked a great deal."

We returned to England much delighted with our first experience of foreign lands. After a short visit to Heale, we settled again at Wymeswold.

During our absence from England, his father's household at Ampton was gladdened by the birth of a son, Bradley Hurt Alford. A change took place in our own household by the departure of four of his pupils for Cambridge, Messrs. Spring Rice, Courtney, Goulburn, and Rose, and the arrival of Messrs. Heathcoat, Dickinson, Bastard, and Sitwell. Mr. Law had left, and for a short time Mr. Peyton was his pupil. He now began to prepare a new edition of the works of Dr. Donne, which he had undertaken at the request of Mr. Parker, of Cambridge, the publisher. It was published in 1838, in six volumes, the first of which contained a short biographical preface.

In January, 1838, he visited his father at Ampton; and his Sonnet lix. ("Poems," p. 185,) gives a pleasing representation of the feelings which the sight of the place renewed in him. A record of this journey is contained in his journal.

Just after his return from Ampton he was surprised by receiving a letter from the Bishop of Lincoln, Dr. Kaye, whose diocese then included Wymeswold. The Bishop wrote to tell him that it was in contemplation to colonize and civilize New Zealand, and that a part of the plan was the selection of a Bishop, and asked to be informed, whether in the event of the appointment being offered, he would be disposed to accept it. A letter which he wrote to his father on the subject, shows what was his answer to the Bishop.

"Of course, as will have already occurred to you, my age[4] not being sufficient for the office, has enabled me to return a decisive answer as far as that is concerned, and has spared me a long and painful inquiry.

[4] The canonical age for a bishop is "full thirty years," and Henry Alford had not at this time completed his twenty-eighth year.

"But still as it might possibly occur, that the service of the future bishop might not be required for two or three years, the subject may be opened again. I can only lay it before Him who furthers His ends by His own means. How surprised I am at this mark of notice and confidence from one on whom I have no claim for any such, and with whom I never held any but official communication."

This proposal, however, was not again renewed. Bishop Selwyn, as is well known, became the first Bishop of New Zealand in the year 1841. A similar overture was made to him seven years afterwards when the Diocese of Fredericton was about to be created.

In the spring of 1838, the birth of a second daughter brought an additional happiness to the home at Wymeswold. Writing in June to her godfather, the Rev. E. T. Vaughan, (now Vicar of Harpenden, Herts,) he refers to a want which he often felt. "You must take an early opportunity to come over and see your little godchild, and us also; for I assure you we are so wearied by the utter dearth of congenial society in this place, that the sight of a dear friend is to us a strange and refreshing sight."

At Midsummer, two of his pupils (Lord Spencer Compton and Mr. Sitwell) left us.

We went, now four in number, for a three weeks' tour in the North. We spent at York the day (June 28, 1838) on which Queen Victoria was crowned; then to Knaresborough and Skipton by Bolton Abbey, seeing Walham Cave and Gordale Scar; to Kirby Lonsdale and Kendal, and thence to the Lakes. In returning, we spent two days at Maryport and came by Halifax and Sheffield. The Sonnets numbered lv.—lviii. ("Poems," page 183) were written in this tour.

It should also be recorded that whilst spending a day or two at Windermere we walked to Rydal Mount, to call on William Wordsworth. Most unfortunately he was not at home[5], having only some half-hour previously left by coach for Keswick to call on Southey. Mrs. Wordsworth was

---

[5] See page 116.

most kind to us, and showed us over the grounds. A short poem entitled, "Rydal Mount, June, 1838," refers to this visit. ("Poems," page 136.)

The autumn of 1838 found him with only three pupils, Messrs. Dickinson, Bastard, and Wynne. The Infant School-room at Wymeswold was begun in earnest, and was completed in February, 1839. It turned out to be a more costly work than was at first expected; and in order to clear it from debt, a bazaar on a large scale was held at Wymeswold in the autumn of 1840.

He says in his journal :—

"*Oct.* 7.—I must record my thankfulness at having been preserved to enter my twenty-ninth year.

"My domestic comforts have been yearly increasing. Three nets are woven round my heart, and in all these I am indeed happy. My health is on the whole good, my only ailment of any consequence being an unpleasant faintness during my Sunday morning's duty. I am enabled to do three services on the Sunday without serious inconvenience, the more bodily exercise I take the better I find myself.

"Of my intellectual state I fear I have not much to say that is favourable. I feel the total want of any intellectual society, or of stimulus to thought; this affects me considerably. Books are poor substitutes for the stir of thought and discussion to which I had formerly been accustomed. But amidst this I feel that the faculty itself is not impaired. I can grasp a subject when under a certain degree of intellectual excitement, and enter into it as deeply as ever."

In the Christmas of 1838-9 we went for a week or two to visit his father at Aston Sandford Rectory, whither he had removed from Ampton. The lyrical Poem, "The Dead," and Sonnet lxxxvi. were now written ("Poems," pp. 243. 199).

At the beginning of 1839 Henry Alford acceded to a request of Mr. Dearden, Nottingham, bookseller, and undertook to edit a monthly magazine, "Dearden's Miscellany," from January 1839 to June 1840. It occupied many of his spare moments and was the cause of his making frequent journeys to Nottingham; this, however, was a healthful and pleasing variety from the routine of his home-life. His principal contributions to "Dearden's Miscellany" were a series of articles entitled "Chapters on Poetry and Poets." The first division of these articles, called "The Poets of Ancient Greece," was afterwards published in a separate volume, and dedicated to his former schoolmaster, Mr. Allen, of Ilminster. He also published in "Dearden" for the first time "Muchelnay Abbey," and many of the Poems which were subsequently included in the third edition of his Poems; and he wrote articles in the Miscellany on three of our modern poets—Cowper, Wordsworth, and Byron.

It was in acknowledgment of one of these articles, which he sent to William Wordsworth, that he received the following letter from the poet:—

"*Ambleside, Feb.* 21, 1840.

"My dear Sir,—Pray excuse my having been some little time in your debt. I could plead many things in extenuation, the chief that old one of the state of my eyes, which never leaves me at liberty either to read or write a tenth part as much as I could wish, and as otherwise I ought to do.

"It cannot but be highly gratifying to me to learn that my writings are prized so highly by a poet and critic of your powers. The essay upon them which you have so kindly sent me seems well qualified to promote your views in writing it. I was particularly pleased with your distinction between religion in poetry and versified religion.

"For my own part, I have been averse to frequent mention of the mysteries of Christian faith; not from a want of a due sense of their momentous nature, but the contrary.

"I felt it far too deeply to venture on handling the subject as familiarly as many scruple not to do. I am far from blaming them, but let them not blame me, nor turn from my companionship on that account.

"Besides general reasons for diffidence in treating subjects of Holy Writ, I have some especial ones. I might err in points of faith, and I should not deem my mistakes less to be deprecated because they were expressed in metre. Even Milton, in my humble judgment, has erred, and grievously; and what poet could hope to atone for his misapprehensions in the way in which that mighty mind has done? I am not at all desirous that any one should write an elaborate critique on my Poems. There is no call for it. If they be from above, they will do their own work in course of time; if not, they will perish as they ought. But scarcely a week passes in which I do not receive grateful acknowledgments of the good they have done to the minds of the several writers.

"They speak of the relief they have received from them under affliction and in grief, and of the calmness and elevation of spirit which the Poems either give or assist them in attaining. As these benefits are not without a traceable bearing upon the good of the immortal soul, the sooner perhaps they are pointed out and illustrated in a work like yours the better. Pray excuse my talking so much about myself, your letter and critique called me to the subject. But I assure you it would have been more grateful to me to acknowledge the debt we owe you in this house, where we have read your Poems with no common pleasure. Your "Abbot of Munchelnaye" also makes me curious to hear more of him.

"But I must conclude. I am truly sorry to have missed you when you and Mrs. Alford called at Rydal. Mrs. Wordsworth unites with me in kind regards to you both, and believe me, my dear sir,

"Faithfully yours,

"WILLIAM WORDSWORTH."

In the summer of 1839, we visited Heale; and from thence made a tour round Devonshire and part of Cornwall, in the course of which Sonnet lxxxv. ("Poems," p.199) was written.

The following reflections occur in his journal, dated

"*Aug.* 7.—Physical employment has of late usurped too

much with me the place of mental, which must not be. My garden and greenhouse have occupied much of my time, to the benefit certainly of my health, but not of my intellectual well-being. I begin to feel a want of resource which is the sure accompaniment of mental idleness.

"We are just returned from a tour round Devonshire and part of Cornwall, and a visit to Charmouth and Heale, which we have enjoyed as far as bad weather would allow; having resumed my home-duties, I must begin some course of study too long neglected. In my own library are many books which I have never sufficiently looked into.

"Besides all this and much more, German must be taken up again, and persevered in thoroughly. It strikes me that the best study for it will be to read chapters in the Polyglot Bible, marking down all the words I do not know.

"Will the 'School of the Heart' do to make into a larger poem, such as Book I. 'Love;' Book II. 'Truth;' Book III. 'Beauty;' keeping Book I. as at present, writing Book II. now, and keeping Book III. for hereafter? Of this I have thought much; also of a Poem on the truth of things, to be called 'The Mask.'"

The vacation which followed Christmas, 1839, was spent at Wymeswold. The new year was remarkable for many parochial gatherings. There was a festive opening of the Infant School. There was a presentation from the parishioners of a piece of plate to the vicar; and on the other hand, the vicar placed in the church a new organ, the wooden front of which had been carved not unskilfully by his own hand. It may be mentioned here that when the church was placed in 1844 in the hands of Mr. A. W. Pugin, for restoration, this piece of carving was of course discarded. It lay in disgrace for several years in a workshop. On our removal to the Deanery, Canterbury, where a lofty room had to be furnished for the occasional reception of an honoured guest, this despised specimen of handicraft was used for fourteen years as a suitable decoration for a bedstead.

Perhaps the best record of many of his thoughts and feelings at this time is to be found in various articles which he wrote in "Dearden's Miscellany;" a book which must be unknown to most of the readers of this volume. His characteristic delight in the beauties of nature, the interest with which he watched the political events of the time, and his sympathy even at this early period with those who cared for the education of the people, and the improvement of the English Version of the Bible, are shown in the following extracts:—

September and October.

"With no months have we sweeter recollections bound up than with September and October. Then come those rich mellow days, when the morning lawns are bathed in lavish dew, and the far-stretching fields are white with the gossamer; when the sportman's gun cracks sharp over the level ground or is repeated from the woods; when you may bask in the full hot sun, and in an instant taste the coming winter in the icy cool of the nearest shade; when those grand and heavenly colours which autumn only knows, descend upon our trees, so that our gardens and hedgerows are one blaze of purple and gold; and when the gorgeous sunset overtakes us in our ramble, prelude to the now lengthening and welcome evening, beginning to be gladdened by the cheerful and flickering fire. For occasional moments of intense existence, when being is condensed into pleasure—for sudden scent of violet, or first outbreak of unlooked for melody—spring may bear the palm; summer with its long rambles, and its hours of unfailing daylight may hoard up treasures which our winter fancies may feed on; but for actual enjoyment, constant quiet, and healing to the soul, commend us to autumn. And not only do the sunny and gladsome days of this time delight us; but there is that in the autumn storm, loud and blustering though it be, which especially suits our habits of thought. A storm in spring, what disappointment and contrariety does it bring with it—the fresh bud bitten or snapped—the new leaves blackened—the hopes of nature defeated; but a storm in autumn brings no disappointment—the fading flowers bow their heads and yield; their time is come, the trees send to strew the path of the fierce reveller their myriads of willing leaves. Nature bears her part in the uproar, and stern winter brings up his tempest stores for more and ruder havock. Reader, the spring is to sing and read of; the summer to long for, and long for, and sometimes it comes; the winter to invent employments for, and love them when invented; but, depend upon it, the autumn is the season really to enjoy."

Autumn Night.

"We have surely experienced the most extraordinary season on record. Still do the flaunting dahlias toss their heads over our garden walls, and lobelias, geraniums, and myrtles are yet in lingering bloom. When will that mighty potentate Jack Frost sweep away these sickly remains of the summer, and bring us the season's work at the season's time? The nights, when we should have had the heavens full of meteors, prove failures. But why are we murmuring, who are writing under the brightest moon which our land of mists ever beheld? We might, indeed, outnight Jessica herself in singing of 'such a night as this.' Never saw we 'heaven's queen' so purely dazzling bright. The smallest print is clear and distinct as at noon-day. The scattered and sere leaves on yon bank of elms are each one brought out into strong relief from the dark stems behind. Not a star is visible, though the heavens are clear. Such a moon we remember when journeying a long night[6] through the level rice-grounds in the North of Italy, with its long line of glitter reflected from their inundated surface, and the line of unearthly snow-clad Alps stretching away into dim vastness beneath the hoary light; but in England never before. Yet what does all this avail with a falling barometer, and the prospect ever dismal of 'a wet day to-morrow'?"

Review of 1829—1839.

"We have past another decade of the nineteenth century—

---

6 See page 111.

an eventful one at least. Its first year was marked by mourning in the palaces of England. Hardly had it passed before the wild cry of liberty sounded across our Channel, and the Bourbons fell from the throne of France. Shortly subsequent was the great change in the predominance of political parties in England, pregnant itself with changes still greater: shortly followed by transient reigns of terror in Nottingham and in Bristol, and resulting in the accomplishment of the plan of Parliamentary Reform, so long agitated by its framers. As if in answer to the tocsin of reform, the flames of destruction broke out in our ancient halls of council, and swept away the relics of ages. We are at least to have a new house for our new Parliament. Soon the shades gather round another of our line of kings, but not before, by the merciful care of Providence, we were secured, in our time of stir and change, from the coils and intrigues of an interregnum arising from the minority of the heiress. We had but lately been rejoicing for her arrival at legal maturity, when our beloved princess was summoned to wear the crown, and she who was the darling of our hopes became the Queen of our realms. Not unaccompanied has this last change been by other like events elsewhere. Haughty Austria has bowed the head in death; the fading lustre of Turkey has lost its one remaining bright star, and seems nearing its western obscurity. To the man of study the signs of the time are not unapparent. Intercourse is facilitated, both by locomotion and correspondence. Never at any time were the components of the human race brought into such close connexion. Many are running to and fro, and knowledge is being increased. Returning to our domestic concerns, let us express a fervent hope that another such period may not pass without education truly national being established by the State, and working for good among the English people. Prussia is before us; Switzerland is before us; France is before us; there is no record of any people on earth so highly civilized, so abounding in arts and comforts, and so grossly, generally ignorant as the

English. One thing seems to us most clear, that before another ten years have past, we shall be reaping, either the benefits of national education, or the consequences of the want of it."

Education.

"While the Education question is pending, we would express our opinion, in hopes that some may be induced to take it up and forward it; that some well organized system of inspection would be, at the present time, the fairest and most feasible way of meeting the difficulties which beset the subject. Government should not so much establish, as endeavour to right what is established. In the present state of toleration and liberty, no general system will ever succeed; but it strikes us that much good might be effected by School Commissioners of each denomination, who might inspect, report, recommend grants, or their discontinuance, as in each case should seem fit. If these were to be the agents of a Central Board fairly chosen, and to be the ultimate referees in each case, we think the system might be worked—and we see not how else."

Revision.

"It is necessary that something should be done to rectify the errors in our English Version of the Holy Scriptures. That those errors are few we are ready and thankful to acknowledge; but that there are some of great importance, even so great as to destroy to English readers the sense of the passage, every Greek scholar will acknowledge. And if so, why should they not be altered by authority? We would not go the length of altering antiquated, or even coarse expressions;—let the venerable aspect of antiquity, even with its rust and unseemliness, continue to hang about the thing of all others which most we honour; but we would say, let all absolute misapprehensions and blunders of the translation be corrected fearlessly and at once."

CHAPTER IV.

1840–1847.

VISITATION SERMON—CORRESPONDENCE WITH MISS E. MOTT—APPOINTED HULSEAN LECTURER AT CAMBRIDGE, AND EXAMINER IN LOGIC IN THE UNIVERSITY OF LONDON—TOUR IN FRANCE—DEATH OF YOUNGEST SON—NEW VICARAGE BUILT—RESTORATION OF WYMESWOLD CHURCH BEGUN—NATIONAL SCHOOL-ROOM BUILT—COMPILES A LARGER HYMN BOOK FOR WYMESWOLD, AND PUBLISHES A VOLUME OF SERMONS—VISITS BONN.

IN this spring his poem on the Marriage of Queen Victoria (Feb. 10, 1840) was written; and later in the year three other poems, Sonnet lxxviii., "The National Prayer," and "The Dirge of the Passing Year," were composed ("Poems," pp. 195, 244, 246). The 7th of May was the birth-day of his third child and first son, who was christened with the name of Ambrose.

In the summer of 1840 he was called upon to preach the sermon at Melton Mowbray, at the primary Visitation of Dr. Davys, Bishop of the diocese. The text was from Ezekiel xxxiii. 7, and his subject "The Clergy watchmen unto the people." The following extracts will show that he held thus early the same views, which he frequently stated in later years, regarding the position of a clergyman among his own parishioners generally, and especially towards such of them as do not conform to the Church:—

"Having fallen on the predicted times when 'men shall heap teachers unto themselves,' our own sacred appointment is in danger of being confounded with that of those who are self-elected or chosen by their congregations to the ministerial duties. Now, holding as we do, that no doctrine is to be insisted on as necessary to salvation, which may not be clearly proved by the Word of God; and constituting our ministers the exponents of doctrine, subject to this test, we must yet remember that we are widely distinguished from our Dissenting fellow-countrymen in believing the ministerial appointment to be outwardly and visibly not of man, but of God; that is, entrusted to His servants the bishops, who are, if not by direct ecclesiastical lineage, yet, which is more important, by continuation of official action, the successors of those to whom our Lord in His parting words committed the power of ordination: 'For He breathed on them, and said, Receive ye the Holy Ghost,' and added a clause empowering them to dispense the same Spirit, 'As My Father hath sent Me, even so send I you.' It is our duty, then, to stand as watchmen against this error so extensively pervading society, to vindicate our office and mission, and those Sacraments, which, by virtue of it, we are empowered to administer. While we adhere in all unalterable points to the spirit of the formularies of our Book of Common Prayer, we must remember that, when they were drawn up, the present state of things was not contemplated; and that therefore (I press the point no farther) it is no justification of a harsh, intolerant spirit, to maintain that it is in accordance with such expressions as occur on the subject in those formularies. These expressions will not indeed bear such an application, the present case not being then supposed; and had our Reformers lived among the various Protestant bodies now existing there is little doubt that their language would have been that of the Apostle, 'Grace be with all them that love our Lord Jesus Christ in sincerity.' For this portion of our flock are, however unreasonably, opposed to the words and counsels of man, and given to think slightingly of what they conceive to be human appointments. As from God, then, let us speak to them according to their own acceptation of the Word, and whether they will hear or forbear, testify unto them, 'Thus saith the Lord.' Our position then will be impregnable, even in their own estimation,

They are at least occasional attendants on our ministry, and I may venture to say that by our strict adherence to the text and tenor of Scripture will our success among them be measured. Above all, should we be anxious to retain our hold upon them by being constant comforters in their hours of distress, and attendants by their beds of sickness and death."

It was in this year that he began a correspondence with a lady, which must be noticed at some length, as it occupied no inconsiderable portion of his time, and in its effect was beneficial not only to herself, but also to his household and parish. And here it might be remarked that while he was very far from desiring to be referred to and consulted by strangers, yet whenever a genuine case of perplexity or distress, whether of a religious kind or not, was made known to him, he spared no time or pains to make himself thoroughly well acquainted with its difficulties, and his advice was generally marked by sound judgment, and always by tender consideration for the person who consulted him. Another, and a larger class of persons, more particularly in later years, sought from him aid of a different kind; and if to the former class he was ready to give counsel, to the latter he was still more ready with pecuniary help, a large portion of which was unknown, even to those who were nearest to him, till after his death. The difficulties which caused Miss Eliza Mott to become acquainted with him in 1840 were entirely of a religious character. She was brought up by her parents, who lived at Loughborough, as a Unitarian. But doubts arose in her inquiring mind as to the correctness of much that she had been taught. Peculiar circumstances made it unadvisable that she should seek the counsel of the clergyman of the parish in which she lived.

Curiosity led her in 1839 to be present at the visitation of the Bishop of Lincoln, when the whole solemnity and particularly the Bishop's address left on her mind a favourable impression of the teaching of the Church. Next year, having heard some report of the sermons of the Vicar of Wymeswold, she took the opportunity of his preaching at Loughborough on October 7 to go as a hearer. His sermon (which was on the text Jeremiah ix. 23, and is included in a volume of sermons published in 1850) had the effect of moving her to lay her case before him. Several letters were exchanged. His answers to her questions tended to confirm her faith. He directed her in her study of religious books, and with the assent of her parents baptized her in the spring of 1841. She was remarkably disinterested and unselfish, and nothing could exceed her devotion to him whom she regarded as her spiritual father, and to all persons beloved by or connected with him. One or two remarks from her letters to him will show how she appreciated him.

FROM MISS ELIZA MOTT.

" *Nov.*, 1840.

" This correspondence must be a tax to you, to me it is indeed a treasure. I cannot but think the Lord directed me to you; for I had been longing for an adviser, and had almost despaired of finding one, when the idea came into my mind of applying to you. Only the Lord and my own soul know, how often you have been made to me a visible token and reminder of His mercy."

On one of his birthdays, she writes :—

"All the happiness, and all the good that birthday thoughts can bring, I wish for you, dear friend, the strengthening of sorrow, the heightening of joy: for well I know that both are mingled in your heart, and indeed in every Christian soul that has in good earnest entered upon the battle-field of life, and advanced any distance upon its thorny way. You know how sincerely the old saying comes from me, 'Many, many happy returns of this day;' happy notwithstanding all the trials and the blights, and the seeming griefs of our mortal state; yea, happy in one sense through these: and who should more sincerely desire all this, than she who through your instrumentality has been placed within that covenant, and upon that narrow way, which year by year becomes more real, more delightful to her soul? God ever bless you, my beloved friend and father in Christ, is indeed my earnest prayer."

The following extracts are selected from some of his numerous letters to her:—

To MISS E. MOTT.

"*Wymeswold, Oct.* 16, 1840.

"I hasten to give an answer to your letter, knowing that your mind will be relieved by it, and feeling deeply anxious that you should obtain the spiritual assistance which you need. My first answer can however be only preliminary, as there are difficulties in the course which you propose, of which perhaps you may not be aware. I could not consistently with the uniform understanding among the clergy (and which I think is most desirable to uphold except in extreme cases) visit you as a clergyman, without the knowledge and permission of the minister of your parish; nor I think if this difficulty were removed, would it be well I should, considering all circumstances. The course left open, which with God's blessing I might follow, is that of correspondence, which I think might be more effectual than personal intercourse; inasmuch as you would have all I might be able to say on record, and might refer to it again if you wished. This course I am willing to adopt, under one condition, which, from what you say I apprehend would not be a difficult one to fulfil, namely that your father is aware of the circumstances, and gives his approval. I cannot but rejoice that you have been led to see the truth, and sincerely pray, that should any correspondence take place between us, you may be confirmed and established in the faith."

The following passages are in answer to her inquiries respecting, 1. Baptism by Immersion; 2. The writings of Dr. Channing; 3. The Mystery of the Trinity; 4. The (so-called) ignorance of the Son (Mark xiii. 32); 5. The alleged inability of some persons to believe; 6. The inheritance of the earth by the meek (Matt. v. 5).

"1. Your difficulty about immersion in baptism being the true mode of administering baptism will, I think, be removed when I remind you of two things, first that immersion is the way prescribed by the Church of England, and that any one may claim it who wishes; second, that we have evidence of the use of sprinkling even in the Apostolic age, and the word 'baptize' itself fairly translated according to the usage of the Greek language includes the meaning of aspersing or sprinkling. When St. Peter (Acts x.) was with Cornelius and his party, he said, 'Can any man forbid water that these should be baptized?' and clearly implied that the water was to be brought in, or administered, and not the converts taken to the water. Again, he seems to allude to baptism when he speaks of obedience and sprinkling of the blood of Jesus Christ (1 Peter i. 2). But this is so trivial a matter that the minutest balance of usage on the part of Christ's Church, one way or the other, would suffice to turn me either way. At Milan where they retain many customs from St. Ambrose's time, not common to the rest of the Roman Catholic Church, they immerse three times, thus, 'I baptize thee in the name of the Father (1), and of the Son (2), and of the Holy Ghost (3).'"

"2. I have no doubt the clever writings of Dr. Channing would stagger your convictions, but you should remember, that you and he do not start from the same point, and therefore how much eloquence soever he may expend on his argument, it does not touch yours. He starts on the supposition that human nature can renew itself; you on the fact, that human nature is lost and helpless. He sees no divine interference necessary, you feel that without it none could be saved. He acknowledges not the ruin brought in by the *first* Adam, and therefore cannot have any idea of the life and purity introduced into our nature, by the glorious indwelling of the *second*—even the eternal Son of God. He cannot interpret the Bible on his hypothesis, and therefore is obliged to cut and carve it to his liking, pronouncing some part spurious, and giving proportions of authority as he pleases to its portions; you, on the contrary, find it all light and consistency, and need no such trimming and dubious process. . . . Our foundations entirely differ; he laying human nature as his foundation, and bringing in Jesus Christ how he can. I, on the contrary, believing that other foundation can no man lay than that is laid, which is Jesus Christ, and that in

Him the Father's pleasure is to gather together all things in heaven and earth."

"3. As to the Trinity, you must bear in mind that this so formidable word means no more than Threeness, and that when we speak of the Doctrine of the Trinity, we mean no more than the eternal coexistence and coequality of God our Creator, Redeemer, and Sanctifier; with this doctrine you have the Atonement, for the Atonement is the eternal decree of God the Father, in His free and unmerited love, declared and acted out by God the Son, and sealed to our hearts by the indwelling and blessed teaching and work of God the Holy Spirit. And, on the other hand, if you hold the Atonement you must hold the Trinity, for what should devise Redemption but Almighty power, what should effect it but Almighty love, what should teach it but Almighty wisdom? And all these are continued in a wonderful way in every particular of our Redemption, strictly one and the same Almighty God. Pardon me if I endeavour to correct your expression, 'The perplexity of the Trinity,' and to express my own conviction, that without it, all is perplexed and confused. What we argue for is not the term, but the great and essential thing signified by it. And as to its pointing to heresy, for what other end were St. John's Gospel and his first Epistle written, except to point to heresy? Why should we shrink from pointing to heresy wherever it occurs, and maintaining the great bulwarks of our faith, and stand against it on all occasions? I shall be ready to go deeper into this subject whenever you wish to renew it."

"4. There is no difficulty in Mark xiii. 32, for there is no doubt that the Lord Jesus Christ in His mediatorial office, is even now in His glorified state inferior to the Father; and that He shall not be complete till all His people, His members, His elect, be gathered in, when this His mediatorial office will be laid down, and God will be all in all. His intercessory work in heaven implies this, for why intercede except with a superior? Apply this to the text in hand, and you will at once see that the difficulty has vanished, as Christ is the anointed Head of the Church, the Mediator between God and man. He has laid aside His glory, emptied Himself of it, as St. Paul says."

"5. The mistake is, they set about to conceive, and comprehend, and understand; whereas no such exercises of the mind are required of us in receiving the Gospel of Christ, the great duty of a humble believer is to believe. We believe a thousand things every day of our own lives which we do not understand. Is it likely that the spiritual world will be simpler and less difficult than the natural? If I have reason to believe the Bible comes from God, then what the Bible says, I believe, though my poor contemptible understanding should not be able to pierce any distance into the darkness in which God's ways are enwrapt to us mortals. And I do find and do believe that the resurrection of the body (of what else can there be a resurrection? the soul never goes into the grave) is and was the great doctrine which Christ rose to prove, which the Apostles preached, and which we believe in common with God's holy Catholic Church for 1800 years, every where, and at all times."

"6. Do they not? Has the proud, selfish, illiberal man any real enjoyment of God's blessings, whatever he may have? Do they possess any charms for the spirit of bondage wherein the slaves of this world's pride are bound? Thus far for the primary sense of the text. But I believe it to have a further and more glorious sense, viz. that the meek, humble, despised servants of the Lord shall possess the new and glorified earth in the blessed future state of which we read such glowing descriptions in the Book of God; the inheritance is theirs. With regard to your own spiritual feelings let me counsel you not to expect too much. You will have a struggle, and the more light breaks in on you the better you will see your enemy; this is the meaning of your appearing so sinful to yourself. And remember that it is not only the prayer of excitement which is the prayer of faith; sometimes the dullest and coldest prayers are the most profitable, and the most excitable ones bring the least fruit. As to speaking to others, yours is a very trying situation, and you are yet, remember, but a novice, so to speak. Remember that those are not the deepest streams which make most sound. I, perhaps, undervalue too much what usually passes for religious talk; there is seldom reality about it; it is as far as possible from the true communion of saints. Oh, may you be kept firm and unwavering in the faith! The way to this is to live upon the faith, not to think of it as matter of question and controversy, not to regard your faith as 'views,' as one often hears it called, but as the food of your soul. The way to believe the Godhead of Christ is to be in continual receipt of grace from Him as God. The way to believe the Personality and Godhead of the Spirit is to be under the teaching of the Spirit day by day. Oh, may you be thus practically assured, and doubts will fall powerless on you! I have tried to give you the sword of the Spirit, which is the Word of God. Add to it the shield of faith, whereby you may quench all the fiery darts of the wicked, and for an helmet the hope of salvation. Read that glorious description of our Christian warfare and armour in Eph. vi. 10—20, and let your heart glow with desire to be full and complete in the service of Christ. I do most fervently hope and pray that all clouds and uncertainties may be cleared off from your spiritual sight as far as is good for you. You cannot too often remember that as we walk by faith and not by sight, it will even be good for us to be in doubt about some things, for where there is no uncertainty there is no trust. When all is clear there is no waiting for the manifestation of the sons of God. At the same time we know whom we have believed, and are persuaded that He is able to keep that which we have committed to Him against that day. May you ever have this knowledge!"

After this correspondence had continued some months the following letter was written to her previous to her baptism:—

"I have arranged it all with ——— about your baptism in Wymeswold Church. Let me remind you (not as though you did not know it, but that you may realize it the better) that you are about to dedicate yourself to Christ as your Lord and Master; to rely upon Him as your Saviour, and to serve Him in purity of thought and self-denial and deadness to sin all your life; and if this seems a difficult thing, do not forget that He giveth His Holy Spirit to them that ask Him, and that this Spirit helpeth our infirmities. Therefore, you have before you a life of prayer and a fight of faith. For many reasons your course is not likely to be one without stumbling-blocks and struggles; therefore your religion should be to you the more real, the more heartfelt, the more decided. Love is the best remedy for doubt, and humble reliance for ungrounded fear. If you feel that you love, adore, and trust wholly in the Lord Jesus Christ, your faith will be proof against all mere speculations, doubts, and suggestions. I assure you, as far as my knowledge extends I shall ever be ready and willing to satisfy you on any question which may arise in your mind, and so far from regarding it as a favour conferred on you, I cannot be thankful enough that it pleases God to make me instrumental in any way in bringing you to the truth as it is in Jesus. May you continue steadfast to the end, grounded and settled in the faith, even till you enter into His glory!"

Henry Alford's time was now sufficiently occupied by his pupils, the parish, and his literary works. The seclusion of Wymeswold had been a matter of regret, inasmuch as it separated him from the refined and intellectual society so dear to a person of his temperament and acquirements. That regret was very much mitigated by our acquaintance, which gradually became intimate, with our neighbours, Mr. Smith Wright[1] and his wife, the Dowager Lady Sitwell, of Rempstone Hall, about two miles from Wymeswold. Our intercourse with them was of the most delightful and useful character, and their kindness and hospitality, which extended to our family and the pupils, and their liberal assistance in parochial works were such as can never be forgotten. Their house was the resort of visitors who had won for themselves a name among the literary or political men of the day. And in late years it was a pleasure to us to trace back to our

[1] His nephew, Mr. Ichabod Charles Wright, is well-known as the translator of Dante.

casual intercourse with such persons at Rempstone Hall many acts of kindness shown to us from quarters whence we had no sufficient reason to expect it.

It might have been about this time that he met at dinner there the late Bishop Blomfield. The fact is vividly impressed on my memory by a circumstance. When my husband came home I was told he had asked the Bishop of London to walk over and see Wymeswold Church, which, though not then restored, was not without points of interest. Next morning, about ten o'clock, just as he was beginning the work of the day with his pupils, we were taken by surprise by the bishop, who came with some of his young people to see the church, and remarked in his quick way, 'He was an early man, and liked a good walk.'

In 1841 Henry Alford was appointed Hulsean Lecturer in the University of Cambridge. The subject of his lecture was "The consistency of the Divine conduct in revealing the Doctrine of Redemption." The appointment was continued for two years, and two volumes of lectures were published.

JOURNAL.

"It may be, that not yet, but at some future time, I feel persuaded, that I shall be able to bring myself to undertake and carry through a long and earnest poem on the great subjects which now agitate the inner and more serious thoughts of the better part of mankind. For this end much is wanting, my spirit must be more thoroughly imbued than it is now with the thoughts, and the tone of the great masters of poetry and of poetic prose. A complete reading of the works of Milton and Jeremy Taylor seems to be requisite; that I may sink deep into the 'harping symphonies of the one, and learn to weave the fancy's web with something of the happy skill of the other.' A careful re-perusal of Wordsworth is necessary. The 'Guesses at Truth' of Archdeacon Hare, I have found very suggestive of earnest thought on the highest subjects.

"Nor should I leave unread the various publications of the present day touching the great question of Church and State. Gladstone pleases me as much as any of the authors now writing. There is much food for earnest thought in the Tracts for the Times (I have not read them thoroughly, except Tract No. XC.). There can be no doubt that years hence many of their present positions will be left far behind by themselves and their successors, nor can I see how they can have any rest for the sole of their feet till they arrive within the stronghold of Rome. As to all the opponents of the Tracts which I have seen, their spirit is so unchristian, their ignorance so truly barbarous, and their theological systems so discontinuous and inconsistent with themselves, that I have never been able to read many pages of their writings without indignation; one honourable exception I may make in favour of Maurice's 'Kingdom of Christ,' with which however I have still some fault to find.

"Of all the opponents of the Oxford Tracts ——— is the vainest and the most objectionable. The fallacies on which he proceeds are not founded in error of judgment or deficiency of the understanding, but in obliquity of the moral sense. To all this the preparation for my next set of Hulsean Lectures may be rendered in some measure subservient. Would that my life, desultory as I am sensible it has been, may have been a gathering here and there for some such great work, and that my powers and attention as I advance may concentrate. I am deeply conscious of a want of earnestness and reality about my opinions—a want of self-discipline—an indolence and dispersiveness about my efforts, which render me far other than I might be if I would.

"There is also a continual morbid looking for promotion which is quite unworthy of one who feels any resources within himself; why cannot I act as I profess, and leave all this to Him who knows what is my proper station and employment? These things seem to me to betoken deep faults somewhere, and I see the effects of them on my temper and intercourse with others. The head and the heart both require discipline and correction."

This spring a pupil is remembered as a most agreeable accession to our household. This was Mr. Charles Buxton, the son and the biographer of Sir T. F. Buxton. He afterwards wcn distinction in the House of Commons. His death at an early age is announced while this memoir is in preparation. In the summer we, and one of his pupils, Mr. Burnett, went to Switzerland for a few weeks, leaving his parish in the charge of his brother-in-law, the Rev. S. Alford (now Rector of Upper Helmsley), who had been ordained in the preceding April.

In the spring of 1842, he took a tour into Derbyshire with his four pupils, Messrs. Pepys, Wilbraham, Nicholson, and H. F. Hallam: a reference will be found subsequently where the early death of Mr. Hallam is mentioned. In the summer we went to Somersetshire and Charmouth, returning home by London. About this time he was appointed Examiner in Logic and Moral and Intellectual Philosophy in the University of London, an office in which he continued to work for many years; and in the autumn of this year, he became a candidate for the Head Mastership of the newly-established College of Marlborough, but retired before the election took place.

In January 1843 we paid a short visit to Aston Sandford, where his father then lived as rector of the parish, and on the following May 8th, our fourth child and second boy Clement was born, a babe only lent for a short time. Our family circle had now reached its fullest expansion, too soon to be contracted. A few months later, he wrote the poem inscribed "To Alice, Mary, Ambrose, and Clement, from their father in the flesh, and elder brother in Christ" ("Poems" p. 249).

In the summer and autumn he gave much time to superintending the building of the new vicarage, and the laying out of the garden, both which were planned by himself. He visited France accompanied only by his friend C. Merivale. It was almost the first occasion on which we had been separated since our marriage; but the graphic letters which he sent home, went far to make up for the parting.

To his boy he prints a letter from Saumur:—

"*July* 20.

"MY DEAR LITTLE AMBROSE,—You cannot yet read this

yourself, but you must ask dear mamma, or Alice, or Mary to read it to you, and then you must keep it till you can read it; for it is the first letter you have ever had. I am a long way off, my dear little boy, but you see I do not forget you; but I pray for you every day, that you may be kept in good health, and may be a good little boy to dear mamma, who is so kind to you. My darling boy, I hope I shall see you soon.

"Your loving father."

From Rouen he writes to his wife:—

"*July.*

"God bless you, and grant that the bond which unites us may daily become more firm till it is for ever made sure in His heavenly kingdom. With such thoughts do I begin my day's accounts. My first business is to the post for letters, the exile's food, even more necessary than breakfast. [Then a long description of Rouen and its churches with pen-and-ink sketches of windows.] The Norman style in England gave place to the Early English, that to the Decorated, the summit of Gothic beauty.

"This journey has put me back ten years. I could hardly have believed how much I should feel during an absence of three weeks. There is no occurrence in my life which I cannot place in the scheme of Providence, as overruling my lot, and I think this present journey will pack in well in its place. It has shown me what I have at home, and how I ought to value it; and in giving me fresh strength and vigour for future exertion, has, I hope, shown me how well worth making that exertion is, for you and our four dear children. God has given me you to check me in my occasional self-will, and I am fully persuaded He has arranged all things for my benefit, that I am in His hands, and that He has His work to do with me. Multitudes of love for you and the dear children; I will write to them."

In the spring of 1844 he was preparing a larger Hymn Book for the use of his parishioners. "A Collection of Psalms and Hymns, adapted for Sundays and Holidays throughout the Year, and Prose Hymns pointed for Chanting." The Harvest Hymn ("Poems," p. 314), which afterwards became one of the most popular of his poems, was first published in this collection.

The following lines, written about this time at the request of a lady, show his power of composition in a less serious strain:—

"I'm to write in an album, but what shall I write?
My brain is not fertile, my wits are not bright!
I cannot spin cobwebs to catch fleeting hours,
I cannot draw cottages, ladies, and flowers.
I can copy from books, but then, I suppose,
You'll disdain to put up with what every one knows.

"I have, it is true, a stray thought now and then,
Which run to my fingers, and ask for a pen:
The sight of a cloud, a bird, or a flower,
Brings tears for a moment, and joy for an hour;
But somehow, whenever an album's in sight,
I may try as I will, but naught can I write.

"Accept, then my wish as a contribution
From minds of a different constitution,
Who carry their brain in their fingers' ends,
And write sonnets impromptu to please their friends.
I'm like a young miss, when I'm call'd on to sing,
A wayward and shy and untractable thing."

That spring was a sickly season. Influenza was prevalent in the village of Wymeswold: and in our home I alone was exempt from illness. Our eldest daughter was laid up with typhoid fever, and her life was in danger for some weeks; all the rest of the household suffered from influenza, and in our youngest child Clement, this was accompanied first by inflammation of the lungs, and at last by water in the brain. Previously we had regarded him as a healthy, bright-spirited babe, but he had not strength to bear up under this attack, and after a few weeks' illness he died on Easter Monday, 8th April, 1844. It was the first opening made by death in our happy circle. His father thus announced the bereavement to my brother, Walter Alford (now Vicar of Drayton):—

"*Easter Monday.*

"You doubtless heard of the serious illness of our dear little Clement, and the last account was a favourable one; but on Thursday last a relapse came on, which brought on effusion of the brain, and at half-past twelve to-day the dear babe fell asleep in Jesus, to our bitter loss, but his own unutterable gain. Amidst our sorrow at present, we cannot but feel that there is no part of our earthly career on which we shall look with such unmixed joy, as the short course of this blessed infant. He now sings praises in heaven, and sees Him whom not having seen we love. You know well what these trials are, and we need not bespeak your sympathy or your prayers, indeed our cup of sorrow is mingled with every blessing. We have kind Christian pupils, and affectionate servants, and then the triumph of having one dear child safe landed in glory. Is not all this enough to comfort the heart, even of bereaved parents? And I assure you, that tears of sorrow have not been the only ones which I have had this day."

To his friend E. T. Vaughan he writes, May 4th :—

"Many thanks for your kind letter of friendly Christian sympathy. Our sorrow has been great, but we have had many bright points to cheer us, and to keep any thing like gloom away from our hearts. I never saw a child (certainly none of our own), who seemed so completely to wear his baptismal purity fresh and unsullied. He was all smiles and happiness. The affliction has done us good; we used to look on our prosperity, and tremble to think what God would do with us, we had felt our hearts hardened in spite of ourselves. We knew it, and lamented it, but this has opened the fresh fountains again. Oh that they never may be closed, but flow forth for the good of our dear people!"

His feelings on this subject were also expressed in three Poems—one, entitled "First Sunday after Easter, 1844" ("Poems," p. 252); another, April, 1844 ("Poems," p. 142), both which were written immediately after the event; and a third, entitled "Faith" ("Poems," p. 253), composed somewhat later; and amongst his papers were found the following thoughts, dated, "First Sunday after Trinity :"—

"Dear child, now thou wouldst have been playing with the bright summer flowers, and trying thy first steps on the soft turf, and gladdening us with new sounds of childish love. But my own sweet Clement, thou art reposing on the immortal flowers of Paradise, or stepping joyously along the crystal pavement. But my own sweet angel child thou hast learnt the new song which thy poor father knoweth not, or but lisps like a babe! Watch round me if thou mayest, dear Clement, stand by and wipe the soil of sin from thy father's spirit, even as I stood over thee on the Lord's Day at midnight, nine weeks ago, and wiped the sweat from thy brow. Blessed Jesus, hold my own babe to Thy bosom, for he is with Thee in Paradise."

In after-years this beloved child was commemorated by a stained glass window in the restored church at Wymeswold, and by another in the south transept of the choir of Canterbury Cathedral.

It may be that he felt it a relief to sorrow, to throw himself with more than usual ardour into his work, for he describes himself at this period as "living in the continual hurry and tear of labour and fatigue. I hardly know what it is quietly to sit down and look on the blessings with which God has surrounded me."

In the summer the new vicarage was ready for the reception of his family and his pupils, and it became our residence accordingly. It was in a nice airy situation, and much more convenient in many respects than our small hired house, and afforded more room for pupils. By increasing the number of pupils he intended to get the necessary money for a scheme which was now in earnest beginning to shape itself, namely the restoration of Wymeswold Church. The feelings with which he resolved to undertake this great work, are expressed in his own Poem, entitled, "Wednesday in Easter Week, 1844" ("Poems," p. 251).

The following statement of the condition of the fabric at this time is abridged from his "History of Wymeswold Church:"—"The Parish Church of St. Mary's, Wymeswold, presented the appearance of a venerable building disguised by decay and disfigurement. Beginning with the west end the stranger observed a rich Early Perpendicular tower flanked by massive buttresses, whose various stages were surmounted by crocketted gablets. The pinnacles, however, which once finished these, were gone; and worse than this, a magnificent spire, the pride of the country round, had disappeared. The tower, seen over the trees in which the little town is embosomed, led the stranger rather to expect a ruined abbey than a parish church. He would find, however, on nearer approach, that the tower was not the oldest nor the worst part of the building. The arches of the nave bear the impress of the early part of the 14th century. Their design and relative position is unexceptionable, but their workmanship harsh and clumsy. The windows, with few exceptions, had been despoiled of their tracery and fitted with upright munnions of brick, on each side of which the skill of the parish glaziers had been displayed in torturing panes of glass into all forms but the right one in laborious attempts at Gothic effect. The chancel was the latest in date, as it was the best in stability, of the various parts of the building. The roofs were unfortunately in a lamentable state of decay, far too much so to admit of any part of them being replaced. The porches were great curiosities. That on the south side was a massive stone cavern, built for convenience, in all ages and of no style. That on the north had once been a richly-carved wooden porch with a steep roof. This latter had, however, disappeared, leaving the moulded timber arch alone to record what had been. As the wood decayed the sides had been patched with brick, or boulders, or whatever each successive churchwarden could best spare from his stack-yard. I doubt whether the country could furnish two less comely or more grotesque entrances to a parish church. On preparing to enter the church from the west the first thing worthy of notice was the fine Early Perpendicular doorway, of a kind not uncommon in towers of this date in Leicestershire. This goodly portal, now the main entrance to the church, was, however, then only the door to a kind of pig-sty, or worse, dark and filthy, the receptacle of coal, and firing, and rubbish of all kinds. Having made his escape from this place into the church, the stranger found himself under the shadows of a vast and hideous gallery, by which the beautiful tower-arch was entirely blocked from view. Part of the nave and chancel were occupied by examples, of about the usual deformity, of the long, the square, and the polygonal deal pew. Facing all ways, and enclosed in boxes of all heights, the congregation were placed in every position of advantage for observing the dress or habits of their neighbours, and of disadvantage for concentrating their attention upon any one subject or employment. The *pulpit, reading-desk,* and *clerk's desk,* placed after the usual Pelion, Ossa, and Olympus fashion, were of the faintly carved and uninteresting character commonly called Jacobæan: the former being surmounted by a massive sounding-board, which, by the laws of reflection, might concentrate the minister's voice over a very small audience close under the pulpit, but could never disperse it to the ends of the church. The font was a rude and plain modern stone basin, on an equally plain stone pillar, and might contain from two to three quarts of water. The church was lighted by tallow dips stuck on sticks, which were inserted in holes bored in the top rails of the pews. These were usually in all progressive degrees of filth and leaning all ways. Such a church as this, in all its decay, filth, and unseemliness, could not but prove to the parish a heavy source of expense from time to time in necessary but wholly unavailing repairs, and a subject of grief to those among the parishioners who had been taught to believe that, although the LORD dwelleth not in temples made with hands, yet His service and His House of Prayer ought to be honoured and provided for in a comely and decent manner." At this time the parish was so distracted by divisions in religion that it was "impossible to collect a rate even for the common purposes of the annual expense of public worship." The vicar, therefore, in a paper which was sent to every parishioner, offered to undertake the needful repairs, and pay for them by voluntary contributions.

Amongst other schemes to raise money for this restoration one was an advertisement in the *Times.* Two of the answers must be recorded.

"An offering to the Lord for the restoration of Wymeswold Church, from Mary, a penitent, 2*s.* 6*d.*"

"*Mexico, Dec.* 30, 1844.—Rev. Sir,—Having seen in the *Times* a communication from you respecting the intended repairs of the church of Wymeswold, I take the liberty of asking you to put my name down for that purpose for 5*l.* I am in no way connected with your part of the country, but I could not read without much interest the truly Christian appeal you have made in favour of the sacred edifice entrusted to your care. Will you be good enough to call me in your list C. B.?"

A. W. Pugin was the architect chosen, and no man could have done his work better. The building of his new vicarage and the restoration of his church were both connected with our first domestic trials. Our summer holiday this year was spent in the Isle of Wight. The newly published "Life of Dr. Arnold" was read at this time, and it gave rise to the following reflections, which I find in his common-place book:—

"*Aug.* 24.—I have just finished reading Dr. Arnold's Life, and do trust that the very vivid feelings of delight with which I have contemplated his character may produce some lasting fruit in the reformation of my own idle and desultory life. Though I differ widely from him on many most important points, yet I intensely admire his earnestness of character and real devotion to one object. I seem to myself to be here at thirty-four, frittering my time away in a hundred little matters, and doing no real substantial good to any body. Why so? Day by day I have time and spirit and energy, but all are uncentred. My task of editing the Greek Testament flags from my unreadiness to buckle to work again after a long interval of building and superintending; and then the work itself is almost hopelessly long and tedious. I believe my first exertion will be to write a volume of Sermons on the reality of the Christian's life, addressed to the various bodies amongst us, e.g. to the Baptists—to the Dissenters in general—to Low and High Churchmen; or again a volume of Sermons on the reality of the Christian life, on the unity of the Church, on Christian practice; each of these subjects seem to me well to deserve treatment, and from my own circumstances and bent of mind I believe I could treat most of them so as to be listened to.

Soon after our return home he received another mark of the favourable opinion which Bishop Kaye, of Lincoln, held of him. The Diocese of Fredericton was about to be created; and the Bishop being a member of the Colonial Bishoprics Council, by whose efforts the endowment was provided, wrote to ascertain whether Henry Alford was willing to become the first Bishop of the new See. On this subject he writes to his father:—

"*Wymeswold Vicarage, Sept.* 6.

"I wish to consult you, and all who are able to give me advice, on a most important subject.

"The Bishop of Lincoln has offered me the Bishopric of New Brunswick. It only occurred last night, so that I have as yet made no inquiries, which of course will be my first business. If inclination only were to guide us in these matters, I should have declined previous to all inquiry. My studies, tastes, and predilections are all in favour of England, and I myself imagine I am unfitted for Colonial labours. Then there are the usual reasons for not quitting home augmented in my case by my just having entered this house and enfeebled my present resources by what I have expended on it, and by what I have engaged to expend on our Parish Church. But if the matter be a leading of God's Providence, a call from Christ to take up the cross and follow Him, I can sacrifice these things, and undertake the life of a Missionary (for such I apprehend it is) in a distant Colony. As soon as I hear more particulars, I will write again. Meantime let me have your first impressions of the matter, which often are very valuable."

To Eliza Mott he wrote on this subject:—

"I told you about a matter which at present occupies much of our thoughts. You will think of, and pray for us also. This is a glorious field of work, but my question is, Is it the field which God has prepared for me to work in?"

After mature consideration, and by the advice of friends, the office was declined, and eventually Dr. Medley was chosen to be the first Bishop of Fredericton.

On New-year's day, 1845, daily Morning Service was begun in Wymeswold Church, then about half completed.

In the summer of 1845 he went with his wife and children to London, and whilst he remained there to perform his duty as Examiner in the University of London, he sent them to visit relations in Somersetshire. Their journey was interrupted by an accident on the line, near Slough. The carriage in which they were, became detached from the train, and rolled down an embankment, turning twice over in its descent. Providentially no passenger was seriously injured, and after a delay of two hours, they went on their journey. Though a letter was sent to him from Slough describing their escape, he did not rest without going after them the same evening to Taunton, and so satisfying himself as to their safety. He thus refers to the accident in two letters, the first written as he was on a railway journey between Rugby and Leicester to his wife, June 27:—

"The more I think of you and the dear children being spared, the more merciful it seems. When we have gone full speed to-day, I have thought how almost impossible it would be, to be upset and not crushed to pieces. The line is so rough, I may well say excuse this scrawl."

To Eliza Mott at the same time:—

"It is indeed a source of most heartfelt thankfulness, that my dear wife and children have been preserved from death, and not only that, but restored to me unhurt and unterrified, as I found them at Taunton. I thought the other day, when standing over my blessed Clement's grave, that I might be mourning over them all but for God's mercy."

I may be allowed to insert a letter which at this time he wrote from Wymeswold to his boy Ambrose, at Taunton. The letter is written in Roman characters, such as a child of five years old would be capable of reading:—

"DEAREST BOY,—I must write a letter to you before I leave home. The rain is falling fast, and the clouds are as black as ink, and the wind is making such a noise. All the hay is wet through. The nursery is papered, and looks very nice indeed.

"The plants are in flower, and the bird is singing. The rabbits and the bantams are very well, there are two young ducks, only two. I was so glad to hear from dear mamma that you were a good boy. Do not forget, Ambrose, that you are God's child, and our blessed Saviour loves you, so you must be very good to mamma, and very kind to every one, and to Alice and Mary, and pray to God always that you may continue His child as long as you live, and lie in His bosom when you die. I hope, if God brings me safely, that I shall soon see my darling boy again. Give my kind love to dear mamma, and Alice, and Mary, and all,

"Your loving Father, dear Boy."

In the autumn he obeyed an urgent summons to go to Weston-super-Mare, where his father had been suddenly seized by an illness so severe, that his life was at one time despaired of. With that sorrowful prospect before him he wrote thus to his wife :—

"I write to prepare you, in case any thing should occur to detain me, or otherwise cross our present plans. Thus has it pleased God to mingle affliction in our cup at a time when we least expected it. But I am persuaded such disappointments are good for us. I feel it a blessed thing to be cast into the hands of God more sensibly, than in my forgetfulness I am apt to feel myself. May we so live together in all holy devotion and obedience to our Blessed Lord, that we may watch one another's beds of sickness or death, when it is His will, without distrust or fear."

The design of writing a Commentary on the Greek Testament, began about this time to assume a definite shape. He has been heard to say, that the notion first entered his mind after he had taken his degree, and was suggested by a sermon which he heard at Cambridge. It was mentioned to a publisher, who encouraged him to proceed with it, and he then calculated that the work would occupy two thin octavo volumes, and would be complete in a year. The purpose, though not acted on, was not forgotten. In March, 1843, he wrote in a letter to his friend C. Merivale :—

"I have undertaken an edition of the Greek Testament, which at the very least will occupy me a twelvemonths' incessant labour."

And again in December, 1845, he wrote to another College friend, the present Archbishop Trench, then Professor of Divinity at King's College, London :—

"Will you give me a little help towards the work which I have, I suppose, now finally undertaken, that of editing the Greek Testament, by furnishing me with a few hints as to what sort of a book it is that you at King's College want. I will tell you what I think of; I propose to adopt in the main the text of Lachmann and Buttmann, and to give the greater part of their various readings. In the margin I mean to give references, not to subject-matter (except in the case of quotations from the Old Testament, which will be distinguished by small capitals) but to Hellenistic constructions and usages of words; thus forming a very useful body of references to the student, which has never before been collected in the same form; then in the notes my idea is to make my commentary rather referential and suggestive than complete in itself: just give me your impression on these points. I mean to point out sources of Biblical information rather than expand the information itself: but then such a plan has its disadvantages, and I have some doubts on this head, on which I require counsel.

"As to the sources whence I may draw my annotations, I am afraid I am somewhat at a loss. My knowledge of the German commentators is but scanty. Olshausen I have, and like what I have read of him better than any other modern commentator; pray tell me what place he holds in the esteem of learned men? I found the translation of Hug very useful to myself when studying the Greek Testament, and have thought of making considerable use of his remarks. The usual German helps, such as Wahl and Winer, I have and use; if you can suggest to me any others, I shall readily adopt them. The work is a most important one and seems to me more and more to require not only extensive acquaintance with books, but above all that sound and discriminating wisdom, which learning may be the secondary means of obtaining, but which we can only believe to be the gift of that good Spirit who leads into all truth. Pray do not let me be troublesome to you, but if you should have a spare hour to bestow, let me have what you can spare on the above points."

While the restoration of Wymeswold Church was steadily going on, a daily morning service was kept up in one part or other of the church throughout 1845. On New Year's day, 1846, he tried the experiment of daily morning and evening service, but this was not long continued, in consequence of the paucity of the congregation. In Easter-week, 1846, Wymeswold Church was opened, and there was a series of ten sermons on the general subject of "The Conformity of the Christian to the Resurrection of Christ:" the first two and the last two were preached by the Vicar; the others by the Rev. J. H. Hamilton, then Vicar of Sheepshed; the Rev. T. Hill, Canon of Lichfield and Vicar of Chesterfield; the Rev. G. E. Gillett, Rural Dean, and Rector of Waltham-on-the-Wolds; the Rev. R. Blunt (now Dalby), Vicar of Belton; the Rev. R. Meek, Rector of Sutton St. Michael; the Rev. W. Selwyn, Prebendary of Ely, and Rector of Branstone.

The total cost of the restoration, excluding the work in the church which Trinity College undertook, was about 3500*l.* A full account of all that was done was published in a thin quarto volume profusely illustrated, and entitled "A History and Description of Wymeswold Church."

Referring to one of the sermons preached by the Vicar, a contemporary Notice states:—

"We shall never forget what a striking impression his sermon made; it was Easter-day, his text was Phil. iii. 10. After alluding to the joyful event which that day celebrated, as well as to the interesting occasion on which they were met together, he then begged the prayers of the congregation for the blessing of God upon the series of religious

INTERIOR OF WYMESWOLD CHURCH, RESTORED: LOOKING WEST

To face page 146

services by which they were about to celebrate the restoration of the Church, and lest it should be supposed that this request was made merely as a matter of course, he paused for a few minutes while his hearers commended the work to the Holy Spirit."

In the summer of 1846 he went to the Tyrol, accompanied by two of his pupils, Messrs. Holland[2] and Wright[3]; they left England on June 14. The following extracts are taken from numerous letters then written to his wife:—

"It is well worth a journey from England to see Nuremburg; the houses are all sorts of grotesque shapes, and in a church in which we have been, there is most splendid painted glass. I have chatted with German peasants, and nursed and played with German children, and come to the conclusion that they are the very best people on the earth, contrasting most favourably with their neighbours (il ne faut pas le dire à la Bonne[4]). It is dull between Ratisbon and Nuremburg, but we pass over a range of hills which forms the backbone of Europe, the Maine going into the Rhine on one side of it, and the Regen and Latten into the Danube on the other. We started on foot for the Lake of Halstadt through a most grand valley. The village of Halstadt is perched about like bird's-nests on the rocks. Berchtesgarden we saw, and the Königssee, which is exceedingly wild and solitary. We took a great walk over the Malnitzer Taneur; it was very, very steep, but full of beautiful flowers of all colours. A serious loss awaited me, for on arriving at the bottom I found my stick[5] minus the bottom joint, including my pens, ink, sealing-wax and pencils. . . . . .

"We were now in Illyria, where they have the drollest affair by way of carriage I ever saw. A very low, primitive

---

[2] Minister of Quebec Chapel, and son of Sir Henry Holland.

[3] Son of I. C. Wright, Esq., the translator of Dante.

[4] Referring to a French nurse at Wymeswold.

[5] This useful walking-stick was made specially for him according to his own directions. Besides the articles named it held in the upper part of the stick his money and dressing materials. It is now in the possession of the Rev. T. Scott Huxley, of Canterbury.

kind of cart, covered with sheepskins, no springs, the travellers in the cart, and the man sitting on the front bar; and this thing tearing along up and down hills like precipices, jolting in the most laughable and least terrible manner. To-day we have crossed the Ampezzo, and are now in Italy. . . . . .

"Of all places I ever saw, Venice is the least disappointing. A most glorious and extraordinary view, a city on the sea; we were rowed by gondoliers, who sing stanzas of poetry in clear melodious voices. San Marco is a most wonderful building, thoroughly un-European, and yet entirely Christian; every bit of the walls, roof, and floor is mosaic, gilt ground, inlaid with very small stones. The richness of the marbles and inlaying is almost incredible. There are many hundred pillars of precious marbles, some unique in the world. The whole effect is sombre and very fine. The architecture is Byzantine and mosque-like. Venice is like fairy-land, so unusual, so still, and yet so full of life and animation. . . . .

"I grieve to say that in all the Roman Catholic churches, in which we have been, much levity and irreverence prevail among the clergy and assistants, even in the most solemn mysteries of our religion, and when they believe our blessed Lord to be materially and bodily present. I only wish poor —— could have come out with me this summer, and seen the clergy of the Roman Catholic Church where they have not our sharp English eyes upon them. On Torcello, near Venice, on an island, there is an old cathedral of the ninth century, all over mosaics, some of which evidently furnished Dante with ideas for his 'Inferno.' . . . . .

"Verona lies on the swiftly-running Adige, at the foot of hills crowned with castles and vineyards. The chief object there is the magnificent amphitheatre. I am writing in the train, on the road between Morbegno and Sondrio, on the Stelvio; from Verona we came to Brescia, passing by the Lago di Garda, by far the most beautiful of the Italian lakes. We crossed the lake to Sirmio, the famous villa of Catullus, one of the sweetest of the Roman poets. There is a very beautiful little piece of his about Sirmio, which I translate for your benefit." . . . .

Several beautiful letters to his children, and the Lyrical Poem "On the Saltzburg Chimes" ["Poems," p. 258] were written at this time.

It was early in the summer of 1846 that an event occurred which continued for several months to cost him much anxiety and trouble. A pupil, whose agreeable manners and earnest piety endeared him to all the family in which he was a sojourner, left Wymeswold in 1845 for Cambridge, visited us at Easter 1846, when the restored church (to which he was a contributor) was opened, and very soon afterwards professed himself a member of the Church of Rome. Certain circumstances connected with the conversion were discussed with much heat in the newspapers, and there were some persons who spoke of Henry Alford as culpably negligent in that he did not suspect what was passing in the mind of his pupil, and did not so effectually counteract the influence by which he was moved, as to prevent the consummation which occurred at Cambridge. The following extracts from my husband's letters to his father refer to this pupil, and to the strictures which were a consequence of his act. He tells his father "he was very wavering when he came to visit us at Easter, and I had several long and serious talks with him, and vainly hoped I had removed his doubts. I have thought it right to return his subscription to our church."

In November 8 he writes :—

"The truth of the matter about —— is, my confidence in his soundness and attachment to the Church of England led me to give him too free an exeat to places and persons which it is now sought to mix up with his apostasy. I am perfectly sure that, had he fallen into a different set at Cambridge, these matters would never have left an influence on his mind other than what he professed at the time, viz. increased attachment to the Protestant faith. I need not waste paper in proving to you, my dearest father, that I have never held any of the doctrines which have been ascribed to me; I have never even thoroughly read 'Tracts for the Times,' except No. 90, which every body reads, and one other on Prophecy."

He writes to Eliza Mott:—

"I feel quite easy about it. My whole writing and preaching have been in direct antagonism to Romish error, and all who know me know this. That I have given the Roman Catholics too much external encouragement for the times to bear has been the effect of a liberality which those who most blame me for it have always been the first to recommend. We must have more of the serpent and less of the dove in future. Strangely enough, yesterday's post brought me a letter from a clergyman with a whole budget of thanks for my 'Dissuasive[6]' having, by the blessing of God, been the means of reclaiming a young person just on the point of 'going over.' I believe very great caution is necessary. I am disposed to draw in; I freely acknowledge it. I have not altered, but the times have. Would you blame the traveller for wrapping his cloak around him in the storm?"

Some time afterwards a meeting took place between Henry Alford and his former pupil, now a priest in the Church of Rome, and he thus describes the interview in a letter to his wife:—

"—— and I had a luncheon together and a two hours' talk about the whole matter. I am very glad this has been so, for it has given me the opportunity of healing wounds and removing misapprehensions which, although kept in the background by his affection for me, were evidently still existing. We also had much talk about the Church of Rome and our different but now perfectly intelligible positions—his that of traditional sacramental transmission of Christianity; mine that of individual guidance by the Holy Spirit, the promise of the covenant irrespective of any external form of Church. Certainly no two could be more opposite, and no two more without hope of any ap-

---

[6] "An Earnest Dissuasive from joining the Communion of the Church of Rome."

proximation. He is the same kind, earnest fellow as ever, full of energy and affection."

About this time he went to London in the discharge of his duty as Examiner in the University of London at Somerset House. A letter written from thence expresses his feeling with regard to the controversy respecting the appointment of Dr. Hampden to the See of Hereford, by which the Church was then agitated. An amusing incident is related in the same letter which arose out of the youthful appearance of the Examiner.

To his Wife.

"Don't take your Hampden views from ———. You see that the Bishops of Lincoln, Oxford, and Salisbury have declared themselves satisfied with Dr. Hampden. On the whole, from what has passed on the matter altogether, and the stir which has been made about no one exactly knows what, though I think the appointment not a judicious one, I am now glad that it has been made, and I should be ready to declare my opinion if required.

"There are four candidates at Somerset House. On my entering the room one of them said, 'A fellow aspirant, I presume?' on which I replied with all my disposable dignity, 'No, sir, the Examiner.' The unfortunate individual has been apologizing ever since, and looks firmly convinced that I shall pluck him for contumacy."

This autumn some persons with whom he was not closely acquainted came to live at Wymeswold, who, not being members of the Church of England, intended, from the motive of personal attachment, to join in the services at Wymeswold Church. Being urged by a common friend to exert his influence to induce his new parishioners to make more distinct profession of separation from their former community and of adhesion to the Church, he wrote on this subject as follows:—

"The exact shaping out of the course to be pursued with them has already occupied my anxious thoughts, and will do so yet. You must make every allowance for me, and not suppose that want of progress indicates want of zeal. I am no controversialist; indeed, of all people to persuade those who differ with me I am one of the very worst, apt to say more or less than I mean, apt to lose my temper in debate, and make the better appear the worse side; for this reason I always studiously avoid debating religious differences. I can only sow the seed; and the blessing, and more than that the harrowing and working the seed in, must come from above."

Another of his parishioners, to whom he was attached by many pursuits and tastes which they had in common, took offence from some supposed neglect which, if not imaginary on one side, was certainly unintentional on the other. As soon as this feeling showed itself he attempted (and not in vain) to remove it by the following letter :—

"*Dec.* 27, 1846.

"I cannot refrain from writing a line to tell you what great grief your letter has caused us. I do assure you most sincerely and solemnly that there never has been in the mind of either of us any feeling towards you and your wife but that of love and respect; and it has been a cause of much regret to us that we could not succeed in making this apparent to you. Why, my dear sir, should we cast off one another who have been placed by Providence in the same parish, with the same labour of love to assist in, and in great measure the same tastes and pursuits? I do assure you the misunderstanding is wholly unfounded in any feeling or act of ours. Let me implore you to reconsider the matter with those kindly feelings to which this season above all others gives rise. There is nothing I would not do, nothing I would not submit to, rather than be on ill terms with a neighbour; and in consequence I shall not relax my efforts, but redouble them, to hold with you that kindly and familiar intercourse which ought to subsist between us. May all the choicest blessings of this blessed season rest upon you, your wife, and your little ones!"

It was at the end of this year, 1846, that he published for the first time a volume of Sermons. It was a small octavo volume of 125 pages, containing fifteen sermons, entitled "Plain Village Sermons on the Lord's Prayer and the Beatitudes." It was published by Dearden, of Nottingham, and in the preface it is stated that most of the sermons had previously appeared in a series entitled "The Nottingham Church Tracts."

A journal records that at this time he was "working hard with six pupils and Greek Testament; studying various readings of St. Matthew and St. Mark; rode to Hathern and talked with Mr. Phillipps[7] on prophecy." On Feb. 23 he writes: "Read a paper before the Nottingham Mechanics' Institute. Was mercifully preserved from death, my horse having fallen with me in my way to Nottingham." The accident thus simply recorded entailed some troublesome and annoying consequences; and his conduct at the time illustrates the quiet determination which was a feature in his character. He was about six miles on the road from Wymeswold, when the horse which had been recently bought, and was not a sure-footed animal, stumbled on some loose stones, and threw his rider over his head. Though much shaken, bruised, and disfigured, especially about the face and head, he persisted in his intention to give his lecture, and accomplished it notwithstanding the pain. After first having recourse to a druggist in the town who by the help of bandages and plaister made him less unfit to appear before an audience, as a newspaper truly stated—"Mr. Alford, although in much bodily suffering and no little disfigurement, rather than disappoint the assembled audience, most kindly gave his intended lecture." He was compelled to put himself under medical treatment for several days afterwards, and his face bore a mark of the accident for the rest of his life.

His pupils were a constant object of solicitude to him, and he watched over the development of their dispositions and minds, strengthening them with advice whenever it seemed likely to be useful, and taking note of every influence under

7 The well-known Rector of Hathern, whose life was recorded by his daughter, "Recollections of the Ministry of E. T. M. Phillipps," 1862. He died in the summer of 1859.

which they might fall, with that conscientious carefulness which seemed to belong to a father rather than to a tutor who was ready to share the liveliest recreation with his pupils. The two following letters are instances of this trait in his character :—

TO A PUPIL.

"I assure you that it will give me very great pleasure to be of what use I can to you in deciding the very important matter which you have already referred to me. It is one on which I had some idea you were not quite settled, and was thinking of talking it over with you. I mean the important subject whether you should take Holy Orders. This is a matter in which you should, after mature deliberation, be guided mainly by the promptings of your own conscience, guided, as I am sure it will be, by the Holy Spirit, who never leaves a sincere and honest mind to come to a wrong decision; and to assist your deliberations, perhaps, I may be able to offer one or two suggestions. First, your desire of doing good as a clergyman is a great thing really. You will have the means, and the will is not deficient, does not this of itself constitute a powerful motive? Secondly, you seem rather to overrate the sacrifices of society, &c., required of you. I see no reason why you should not do what you propose, provided you do not fall into habits of self-indulgence and forgetfulness of your profession and duties. Thirdly, what will you be or do if not in Orders? What sort of a life do you propose to yourself? This should (although it must not decide the question) be taken into account. Will it be satisfactory to you to have shrunk from a life of usefulness and high example for good, merely for the sake of indulgence and the love of society? Fourthly, your views respecting situation, &c., will alter as you advance onward in life. You are now young, and such things present themselves in a very different light a few years later. Fifthly, may not this question be deferred till you have passed through the University? The studies which you will there go through will have done no harm, nay, even good to you as a layman; and at twenty-one or twenty-two your mind will be more matured and better able to form a judgment on its own future course. Sixthly, do not suppose from what I have said that I have been urging on you the entering Holy Orders. I should not feel justified in doing this to any one. It is a point which must be decided by a higher counsel than the advice of any man, which must be sought and found within yourself. If you go to Oxford, I own to you I see no plan but this, that you should leave me and fairly go to a regular Oxford tutor, and not lose any time in doing so. And in deciding this do not take your own wishes or associations too much into account. It will be a matter of duty which should overweigh all minor considerations. Least of all bestow a thought on me or mine. Pray hold yourself perfectly free from all thoughts, except what may be most for your own real advantage. I shall be happy to give you all the assistance in my power in making inquiries for such a suitable tutor. Meantime, do not suppose that I grudge time or trouble in assisting you all I can to form so important a determination as this is for you, being no less than the whole course and bent of your life's work. I assure you nothing gives me more unfeigned pleasure than to think that I may have been the means of any of my pupils finding themselves more usefully or more comfortably placed by means of my advice. This will especially be the case with you, towards whom I have now for some years entertained feelings of regard and affection, and have never found them misplaced."

The next letter was addressed to a gentleman who at this time was living in constant and peculiar intercourse with the pupils and ourselves:—

"I am sure you will excuse my addressing a few lines to you on a subject which has of late given me much anxiety, and on which I have more than once thought of speaking to you, but have determined rather on committing to paper what I had to say as the safer method. You can, I think, hardly be aware how often in conversation you are found the commender and apologist of the practices of Romanism as distinguished from those of the reformed Protestant Church of England. If this occurred in private conversation with myself I should lament it for your own sake, and endeavour to persuade you otherwise, from the deep and growing sense which I have of the vital importance of the principles of the Reformation to the very existence of spiritual religion among us. But the presence of my pupils and children somewhat alters the case and renders it quite necessary that I should endeavour to persuade you not only by argument on the subjects themselves, but by begging you if possible to suppress such advocacy before them. I assure you I have more than once trembled for the impression which some remarks you have made might leave on their minds; for such remarks are not easily answered; they leave on their side all that is strong and outward by which the young are mostly attracted, and the deeper truths whereby they are answered take but slight hold on their young and ardent minds. Might I venture on a word of counsel to you, it would be to endeavour in your reading and sermons at present, at least, to fix your attention on the great verities of our faith as revealed in Scripture, and rather abstain from the exclusive consideration of the outward means whereby these truths are to be conveyed to mankind. I am persuaded such a course would be most useful both to the people and yourself."

With the design of becoming better qualified to edit the Greek Testament, he went this summer to Bonn for a month, and there reading with a German tutor, and limiting himself as much as possible to German society, he acquired a mastery over that language which, notwithstanding repeated attempts previously in England, he had failed to acquire, and which gave him for the rest of his life easy access to the vast stores of theological learning which German industry has accumulated.

Before leaving England he wrote in his journal:—"Daily the importance of the work which I have undertaken grows before me. Oh that I were able to give my whole time and strength to it! I shall see this vacation what may be done if I devote my whole attention to a thing; and I have besides the work of various readings and references to many German Commentaries to read through before my notes can assume any thing like form and completeness."

During his absence he wrote to his wife at Heale letters so minute and descriptive that they have the appearance of being intended for publication. A few extracts from these will be given:—

"*Dover, Ship Hotel, June* 26.

"I mean to keep, during my present absence from you, a sort of journal which my copying-book will allow me to write in duplicate, and to transmit one copy to you: and as I can carry the said book in my pocket, and as no ink is required, I can write at any time and under any circumstances, which will be very pleasant. Here we have the full moon in all her majesty reflected on the rippling sea. I, after tea, walked on the beach and watched the waves as they drew their slow weight down the glittering shingle. It is quite one of my nights to be remembered. I can fancy you looking out through the flickering leaves of the great Turkey oak at Heale. I enclose the dear children three flowers, picked off the top of Shakspeare's Cliff. Find them the famous passage in King Lear, and read it to them."

"*Steamer between Dover and Ostend, June* 27.

"It is a most lovely evening; the sea as smooth as a pond, and the cliffs of old England glittering in the distance with the evening sun. What a wonderful land this is that we are leaving! What a mighty portion of the human race is behind those white cliffs! How many true, and noble, and pious hearts are beating beneath that calm and dappled sky! And then, again, what a struggle between power and weakness, misery and energy, poverty and wealth, is daily carried on in that land! It seems like the laboratory—the workshop of all that is great and new in this our race. And who can tell what future destiny awaits its people? whether to fall as other empires have fallen, overgrown, bloated, full of luxury and pride, or to purge off its prejudices and selfishness and run a course of usefulness and glory yet unconceived. He only knows in whose hands are the kingdoms of the earth.

"*Cologne, June* 28.

"The cathedral has advanced, and so have I; for I cannot regard it with any complacency, as being destined for a temple of false worship and fables. Let us hope for better days and a happier destiny for those who, with true laudable toil, are striving to rear a temple worthy of God's worship. I long for the pure truths of spiritual freedom to echo through these magnificent vaults. They may bar their doors as they will, but, under God, knowledge and education will overthrow popery. I think so at home, but I am sure of it here: only let us beware of sham education. God grant that this election in England may be productive of great results; not by sending to Parliament foolish anti-popery delegates; but by choosing intelligent, honest men, who, with the Bible in their souls, loyalty in their hearts, independence in their minds, will refuse to make pledges when asked, and be brave enough to change their opinions when convinced.

"*Bonn, June* 29.

"Arrived safe and sound at the scene of my next four weeks' sojourn, thank God. I have seen the most lovely sight, after wandering through several streets, which I had half forgotten. I at last came on the river, and the whole reach of the Drachenfels was lying bright and glittering in the reflection of the new moon, with the Seven Mountains rising at the end of it. It was a sight worth all the journey to see. I have taken lodgings three pair of stairs up, commanding the view over the Rhine and Seven Mountains on one side, and the town and cathedral on the other. In my next I will enclose a letter to one or other of the dear children. I wish I had Alice out here; I think she would enjoy it. Pray thank them for their letter. It is St. Peter's Day. How I wish the English Church would take some very decided step to sever itself for good and all from the semi-pagan Church of Rome, and then we should be in no fear of keeping our commemoration days. Certainly the Germans are a better behaved people than the English. There is more real good-breeding among them; every one seems to be aware of the rights, and to respect the feelings of every one else. When will proud insulated England throw off her self-imposed code of pride and ignorance, and learn that God has made all men, and we are all brethren of the same great family? Never till she does will she or her children be happy. I have just bought the German of Bunsen's book, 'The Church of the Future,' which, you remember, pleased me so much at home.

"*June* 30.—Last night old Scholz paid me a visit. He has been good enough to engage a German tutor for me, M. Wolter, a student of the University here. It is very odd for me to be entirely in a strange place, without a soul whom I know, or who knows me. I can't say I dislike it for a change, inasmuch as all changes, unaccompanied by positive mischief, do one good, but I should not like it continually. I can fancy something of what banishment must be, but, dearest, don't think me solitary or unhappy, thank God, with so many blessings and resources I cannot be either of these. Indeed, as I said, I enjoy a little solitude if it be only to think of all that He has given me.

"*July* 3.—I have just returned from witnessing a very pretty and characteristic sight, a torch-light procession, which the town and University had prepared, to greet on their return a body of singers, who had gone from Bonn to a great musical concert at Ghent, and had borne away the prize from all the others there. The procession was accompanied by a band and flags and torches. As they came into the town, the effect on the buildings and trees was very striking. They went into the Münster Platz, where there is a statue of Beethoven (who was born and died there), and which was decorated with flowers, and lighted up. Then the singers sung one of Beethoven's pieces, and then the torch procession went round the town and dispersed. The effect of the cathedral lighted up by the torches was very striking.

"If you should fall in with the speech of Mr. Sheil, in which he makes a sort of funeral oration on O'Connell, you should read it: it is a very fine piece of oratory, not true however, but that is no matter.

"*Sunday Afternoon, July* 4.—I am writing this in a most lovely spot on the hills between Bonn and Godesberg, after attending the German Protestant service, and afterwards in the same Church the English Service, and receiving the Holy Communion.

"The spot where I am sitting is one of the best points of view. A German family have come here also, the little girls are picking whortleberries, and bringing them to their mamma. I wish they were two certain little girls and a little boy whom I know, and the mamma, my own dear Fanny; but it is not so, and yet I am very happy and thankful. On one side of me is the whole flat plain traversed by the Rhine, bordered by a line of wooded hills, like Sedgmoor [in Somersetshire, near Heale], only the plain is larger, the hills about the same height. In the horizon is the spire and large unfinished cathedral of Cologne. I can see by glimpses the Rhine all the way from Cologne to Bonn, and villages and churches dappling its banks; then comes Bonn about four miles off, glittering in the hot sun, and all the houses on the opposite bank of the river reflected in the still water. To the right the Sieben Gebirge rise out of the Rhine. From here I cannot see the water, but the whole seven ending with the Drachenfels, are stretched out before me. Then on this side of the river is the conical wooded hill, topped by the ruins of Godesberg, which I dare say you remember: it is altogether a lovely sight, and one calculated to carry on, and fix the feelings of love and joy which this morning communion has left on my mind. Were you also at the Communion to-day?

"10 *o'clock, Eve.*—I have returned from my walk not at all tired, and I have had a good supper. I heard some Englishmen talking German, and I gathered from their talk, one came from Yorkshire. I asked him whether he knew Archdeacon Wilberforce. Judge my surprise at his answer, 'I am Archdeacon Wilberforce!' He is come here to learn German. A little man, very like his father.

"*July* 7.—I have made the acquaintance of four professors; two I met last night at the house of Mr. Glover, a clergyman here, who kindly invited me there, Professor Hässe, and Professor Dorner, the latter one of the first men in Germany, very lively and animated in his talk, and very deep and intense in spiritual life and feeling; he has succeeded Nitzsch, whose name you probably know, as the greatest of the German Protestants. The other two Professors are Arndt (a delightful old man), and Welcken. But I am stealing this out of working time, so adieu, I will describe them hereafter. I work ten hours a day on German. I send you a piece of poetry, the production of a 'Truant Hour' this week. I think you will like it, it is the only piece I have written for more than a year:—

"The golden stars keep watch," &c.[8]

"*July* 18.—I shall leave this place with regret, having spent many profitable hours with my books, and met with every civility and kindness.

"Yesterday the first load of wheat entered Bonn from the present harvest. It was decorated with flags, and had a band of music on it, and the following lines inscribed on it [the German given], i. e. in English:—

"He who clothes the lilies and birds of the field,
Hath granted our land this abundance to yield;
Now the usurers mourn, that the famine is o'er,
And bread again gladdens the heart of the poor.

"The abundance here is really astonishing. I was told to-day the harvest is expected to be three times the average quantity, and the grapes even more than that. I understand that in England also, every thing is very prosperous. How can we be thankful enough to the Giver of all good who has thus answered (so far at least) our prayers!

"*July* 22.—I must now conclude my last letter. Yesterday I called by appointment on Professor Scholz, to see his cabinet of curiosities, and spent three hours with him, and was very much interested by his various and curious collections of copper-plates, wood-cuts, memorials, manuscripts, and every conceivable thing, which he has brought from the East and

---

[8] "Poems," p. 259.

all parts of the world, where he has been in search of manuscripts of the Scriptures. I have just had a visit from old Professor Arndt, a glorious old fellow of nearly eighty, who was the object of Buonaparte's persecutions in 1807. He is the author of the famous song,—

'Was ist des Deutschen Vaterland?'

and as lively and active, and full of spirit as a youth of twenty. Last year he swam across the Rhine; he talks very loud, and is full of all sorts of information and good-humour. I don't know when I have seen such a striking old man[9].

"I have worked harder, and lived cheaper here than I anticipated. I hope I have facility enough now to read slowly all the commentaries which I want. In spirits I have never drooped, as I have had too much to do. When tired of my German work I have taken up my journal, having the satisfaction, that I was recording what would be hereafter interesting to myself, and that I was writing to my dear ones in England. If God will, and I can afford it, I should much like to repeat it next year with you and the dear children."

The course of his next year was however ordered otherwise. In that year of revolutions (1848), few summer tourists, if any, ventured to visit the Continent. France, after prolonged internal struggles, became a Republic under Louis Napoleon. Louis Philippe, the Emperor of Austria, the King of Prussia, and the Pope, fled from their capitals. Paris was for four months in a state of siege, and there was fighting in Milan, Naples, and Messina, Berlin, Munich, Vienna, Prague, and Madrid. Wars raged between Austria and Sardinia, Denmark and Prussia. Our own country was disquieted by the Chartist Demonstration of April 10, on Kennington Common, and by acts of sedition in Ireland. In such a year travelling abroad was out of the question, and his vacations were spent as we shall see, in visits to the West of England, a short tour in Wales, and in the North of Devonshire.

---

[9] He was born in the same year as Napoleon, 1769: and died in 1860.

CHAPTER V.

1847—1851.

GIVES UP PUPILS—PUBLISHES ANOTHER VOLUME OF SERMONS—PUBLISHES THE FIRST VOLUME OF GREEK TESTAMENT—CANDIDATE FOR THE REGIUS PROFESSORSHIP OF DIVINITY, CAMBRIDGE—DEATH OF HIS ELDEST SON.

AFTER his return from Bonn and the extension of his acquaintance with German commentators, the magnitude of the work which he had undertaken grew upon him. Happy and useful as his life was at Wymeswold he could not but perceive that the combined occupations of a tutor and a parish clergyman were scarcely compatible with the work of a commentator on the entire New Testament. He therefore made an effort to obtain a change of situation, whereby without forsaking the active ministerial life which was of all the most congenial to him, he might devote the time now absorbed in tutorial work to the composition of his Commentary. With this view he wrote to Bishop Pepys of Worcester (whose son was one of his pupils at Wymeswold) the following letter; to which the Bishop, probably from want of a suitable opportunity, did not then give the desired answer, but which is inserted here as a faithful description of his views at this time:—

TO THE BISHOP OF WORCESTER.

"I have been now for some years employed on an edition of the Greek Testament for the use of students in the Universities; and am earnestly endeavouring, by devoting all my energies to the work, to produce an edition more worthy of the present state of Biblical criticism than any which we now have. The work is one of Herculean labour, comprising as it does, on my plan, no less than a thorough digest of various readings founded on the present improved collations of the principal MSS.; an entirely new collection of references not to the subject-matter, but to verbal and constructional usage, and copious English notes exegetical and philological. It necessitates a thorough acquaintance with what has been done both here and in Germany of late years, and collateral reading of various kinds. With the progress of the work an increasing wish has possessed my mind to devote myself wholly to it; and indeed I see no reasonable prospect of completing it unless I can do so.

"My present circumstances however wholly preclude this. I may be excused mentioning that since my residence here I have felt the wants of the parish to be so pressing as to wholly prevent my accumulating money. The church twelve years ago was tumbling down; there were no schools, or none worthy the name; no habitable parsonage. These are all now provided for, and I don't know which way to turn. I am most unwilling to give up that to which I look as the work of my life, and for which I do believe that the course of my studies has in some measure fitted me; and yet I now feel that I am hindered in carrying it on, when perhaps that hindrance might be relieved by the kindness of some of those who have taken an interest in me and my pursuits. I am deeply interested in the work, and desire no reward but being spared to complete it."

This appeal was responded to afterwards as we shall see, but meantime he had to plod on at Wymeswold for six more years.

Soon after writing to the Bishop he was a visitor at Hartlebury Castle, as will appear in the following letter to his wife, dated from Heale, where he spent part of his Christmas vacation:—

"Here I am in the very room which you so long inhabited in childhood and youth, which I remember as your nursery under all sorts of circumstances in days long gone by, by the same blazing fire at which we have played many a Christmas game. Well, God be praised for all His mercies since. It is really delightful to see Eliza Foster in her nice country home as blooming as ever, with her simple and interesting way of speaking and laughing, and all drawn out and brightened by the newly-found treasure which lies quietly looking up in her affectionate face; it is a sight to make one weep for joy as it has done me.

"I found it cold at Hartlebury Castle, where I have been staying for a few days with the Bishop of Worcester. It is rather a curious house, an old castle battered down by Cromwell, and rebuilt at the Restoration in a sort of sham-everything kind of style, but very substantial, and with very good rooms. The present Bishop has done much to it, and it is now, he says, the best episcopal residence in England."

The death about the close of the year of a sister-in-law, Mrs. Burford Norman, in her first confinement, called forth these reflections:—

"My dear sister Harriet is buried to-day; the brightest moon is now shining on her grave at the east end of the chancel of Curry Rivell church. She was a bright, joyous creature, the delight of all who knew her, and a notable example of the loving spirit which is in Christ. She is basking in the sunshine of the Divine presence; she is with my dear absent babe and my fond mother, all in glory and joy, with no speck of care, nor fear of blighting frosts to come. May I and mine join them there for the dear sake of our Redeemer—would that the blessed day were come!"

A short poem beginning—

> "Oh for one word of that Almighty voice[1],"

was written at this time.

In the same vacation he went to see the tomb of his friend, Arthur Hallam, at Clevedon, which he thus describes:—

"*Jan.* 4, 1848.—Came here by rail; most lovely day, beautiful situation and sea-view. Visited Arthur Hallam's tomb. The village is on a high promontory looking over the Channel

---

[1] "Poems," p. 143.

to the Welsh coast; balmy air and clear sky, and all the houses and churches in Wales glittering in the sunshine. A veil of cloud resting on the tops of the Welsh mountains. Sea as smooth as a lake; a sight and day to be remembered, and recorded to my dear ones at home."

Whilst thus enjoying his short emancipation from domestic work he was not unmindful of a relation who in sadness of spirit had sought a change of scene in his home. Octavia Alford, one of his sisters-in-law, was naturally of a melancholy disposition, and was a constant sufferer from organic disease. Whilst visiting her sister at Taunton he wrote to her the following letter, which seems to have answered its purpose of consolation most effectually; for when she died, twelve years afterwards, it was found in her pocket-book carefully preserved, and bearing marks of frequent perusal.

TO MISS OCTAVIA ALFORD.

"I am spending a quiet evening alone, and feel disposed, partly from the subject of my morning's sermon, partly from a resolve I had made, to write to you. I have been setting before the people here that gracious promise and exhortation of our dear Redeemer, 'Come unto Me, all that labour and are heavy laden, and I will give you rest.'

"I have thought much of you, my dear sister, in connexion with this subject. You have your burden to bear, and your own heart knows the weight of it. He has laid it on you who spoke those gracious words; and He has laid it on, that you might come to Him, that you might in child-like simplicity of heart cast that burden upon Him, and He will give you rest. Yes, doubt not; as surely as you in simple faith and reliance throw yourself and all you have and desire into the hands of Jesus, so surely shall you find your burden lightened and your heart cheered. And in doing this go out of all human systems, all forms and all ordinances into the immediate contemplation of that divine and loving Saviour as He is now in heaven pleading and feeling for you. Can He break His own promise? Surely not, and you shall find rest unto your soul by this simple act of faith, in laying yourself into His hands. Commune with Him Himself, in all His eternal loveliness, the perfect Man; in all His eternal power, the perfect God; and your spirit shall be the abode of His Spirit, and perfect peace shall be the result.

"Forgive me, dear sister, for presuming thus to address you. I felt instigated to do so. Something said, Is there not one weary and heavy laden to whom such a message might be blessed, and are there not yet a few minutes in which it might be delivered?

"I hope I shall find you when I come home. Do not trouble yourself to answer this, as I know writing tries you. God bless you, now and ever."

His journal records in the beginning of 1848 his undertaking a larger and more distinct share in the education of his three children, to whom he now began to assign two hours, from five to seven every evening. Leaving their other lessons to the kind and judicious care of Miss Mott, who at this time constantly resided as a friend in the Vicarage, he himself instructed them in arithmetic, Euclid, the elements of natural science as contained in Joyce's "Dialogues," and the Latin Grammar. He was also particularly attentive to the development of their bodily powers; and a room was elaborately fitted up for the practice of gymnastics, in which he was frequently their teacher.

His wish for a change of situation, which prompted the letter to the Bishop of Worcester, became known to his parishioners: to one of them he wrote early in 1848:—

"I am determined, as soon as an opportunity offers itself, to leave Wymeswold. Something has been done here, and very much more than I had any right to expect, still I firmly believe and am persuaded that my work here is done. It is well known that when a clergyman has made extensive alterations in his parish he works at a disadvantage, he has stirred up ill-will, or provoked coldness among many of his people; he has passed through brick and mortar, and bears the stain upon him; he has been mixed in tangled worldly business, and is distrusted; and therefore a successor has greatly the advantage over him, who enters on his labours with all men's fair wishes, and no reason for making enemies save what lies in his own work itself."

In March, 1848, he received an address signed by above five hundred parishioners who "had heard with great surprise and regret that he was seriously entertaining the thought of resigning" the living; and they "anxiously and seriously entreated" him to recall his determination. In his reply he acknowledged having thought that their spiritual interests might now be confided with advantage to other hands than his own; but he said that the kindness of the address removed that feeling, and he now felt it his duty to comply with their request, and "not cast aside so important an instrument of usefulness as the good will of five hundred parishioners."

After this the thought of removing seems to have passed away from his mind, at least for a time; and he again settled down to his various duties at Wymeswold. Among these his pastoral work called for much thought, for it was his habit to enter thoroughly into individual cases. Some portion of it was necessarily entrusted to his curate, and he took great pains to secure colleagues of congenial spirit with himself. Each soul was treated distinctly as a part of the charge committed him. Though naturally disposed to be reserved and shy, he did not seclude himself from personal intercourse with any of his parishioners if it might be profitable to them. Privately as well as publicly his gentle and winning sympathy was ready to be offered to each one who sought it, whether in joy or sorrow. Nor did he omit to take any suitable opportunity that presented itself to him either to correct or to encourage those whom he desired to see walking in the way of godliness.

The following letters will illustrate the method which he pursued in his pastoral work. The first was written to a youth who had occupied a subordinate post in the parish school, and who had quarrelled with his immediate superior:—

"I thought it would be a kindness to you to write to you on the subject of your letter to the National School master.

I must say I was very much grieved at seeing it; I thought your Christian education would have prevented you from ever using such language to any fellow-creature, as you have been foolish enough to address to him. I am sadly afraid from the spirit and tone of your letter, that you have fallen into bad company, and that they are leading you astray. I will give you an example of this; you say, 'Do you think I will ever do a service or a kindness to one who has used me thus? No, I never will.' Now let me ask you, is this the language of one who reads his Bible and knows that Christ has commanded us to love our enemies, to do good to those who despitefully use us? Oh, Joseph, think of this, and let it show you how foolishly you have acted. I consider ——— has been very kind to you; he has let you off several payments he might have charged you with, and you ought to be very thankful to him, instead of being induced by evil-minded persons where you are, to try and blacken his character. I write this as your best friend, to endeavour to persuade you better. You are young and inexperienced, and depend upon it if you go on thus you will get into great trouble before long; do think of what I have said to you, and above all of what you have learned and read in the Holy Scriptures, and may God give you a better mind for Christ's sake. Your affectionate Minister."

The next was written to a girl, who, having been brought up in the parish school and confirmed at Wymeswold, had gone out to domestic service.

"I have received two letters from you, and have been very much pleased with them. I am sorry to hear you are not so well again. I was afraid that you would not be able to undertake a place so soon after your illness; you have been wonderfully raised up as it is, and you should be very thankful to your gracious Father and God who has brought you out of the jaws of death almost to health and strength again. You must never forget that you are the Lord's child, and bought with Christ's most precious blood; be sure to endeavour to adorn the doctrine of God your Saviour in all things, by meekness and patience, by faith and hope, by prayer and praise, by humility and holiness. Think on yourself as one for whom Christ has died, how precious must such a one be to Him, and how earnestly should you strive to keep that robe of His spotless righteousness with which His grace has clothed you. I am writing this to you as being a child of God, which I hope and trust you are, and will continue; if you fall away to this wretched world, God's promises and His inheritance will cease to be yours, and what a thing that would be. I shall never cease praying for you that you may endure unto the end, and be found among the elect of the Lord, at His glorious coming to take His kingdom. God bless you, and give you a large measure of His Holy Spirit.

"I am, your affectionate Minister, and brother in the Lord."

The next was written to an experienced brother clergyman, whom he asks to help him in seeking for a curate. It was evidently written after he had been disappointed by the conduct of one whose work at Wymeswold was not altogether beneficial to the parish.

"I want him to teach and preach Jesus Christ, and not the Church; and to be fully prepared to recognize the pious Dissenter as a brother in Christ, and as much a member of the Church as ourselves. If you know of such a man, it will be a real kindness to put me in communication with him. I would add, I cannot from the nature of the case work actively with my curate. Some little experience in parochial work is desirable; a very young man would not suit me. Above all, he should be a man of peace, who will quietly do his own work and not breed strife."

The next refers to a rather unusual incident. A parishioner notoriously culpable for his inadequate discharge of certain official duties received a private remonstrance from his pastor, the force of which he attempted to evade by angrily retaliating with a charge of negligence. In the course of the day the following was sent to him by his vicar:—

"Regarding my own pastoral deficiencies, I heartily thank you. I am deeply aware that I am not 'sufficient for these things,' and only wish my place were better filled. At the same time, the deficiencies of one man do not excuse another. Let us both strive and pray that we may be found diligent in our business, fervent in spirit, serving the Lord our God, and do our best to live in charity and peace with one another and with all men.

"Believe me, your affectionate Minister and friend."

Another parishioner, after long withdrawing himself from the Holy Communion, wrote to ask permission to accompany his wife to the Lord's table, and then to go away without partaking himself of the Lord's Supper. There were sufficient reasons to surmise that the cause of his extraordinary proposal was the consciousness of cherishing enmity. The following letter, written to him by his vicar, had the desired effect:—

"The only hindrance which the Church recognizes, or which I can conceive to a man's receiving the Holy Communion in such cases, is the existence of vindictive feelings in his own bosom. The conduct of others, it will be plain to you, cannot affect a man in his estimate of the duty of communicating. Believing this proposition to be self-evident, it certainly strikes me that to attend and not to partake would be to make an open profession at the Lord's table of being actuated by vindictive feelings, a thing which I am sure would be very far from your intention and frame of mind. I just state the matter as it strikes me, and as I am sure it would strike any indifferent person qualified to form a judgment. Hoping you will find in this and all other cases guidance from the Spirit of wisdom and love,

"Affectionately yours, my dear friend."

In the summer of 1848 he left Wymeswold for the purpose of officiating at the wedding of his brother-in-law, Mr. S. S. Alford, in the neighbourhood of Liverpool, and afterwards went to spend a few days in North Wales. A few descriptive extracts from his journal will be read with interest:—

"At Carnarvon the castle, where Edward II. was born, is very striking. From thence I went in a carriage to Llanberris. On mounting a hill and looking back, the whole of

Anglesea is seen, the heights of Holyhead in the distance, and the town and castle of Carnarvon beneath one's feet.

"Soon the mountains are approached, and the road descends to the Lake of Llanberris. My first view of this was very striking. The lake is discovered suddenly, the red light of the sunset was clothing the hills and rocks with rosy tints, and the top of Snowdon was hidden in a bright illuminated cloud. The mountain scenery far surpasses any thing I had imagined, and is certainly much superior to the English lakes. We started with a guide the next day for Snowdon. The ascent was easy for some distance, by-and-by very steep. The top was hidden in clouds and rain all the time we were there, and consequently we saw nothing; but the savage grandeur of the summit far surpasses any mountain I have ever seen. Vast black masses of spiral rock compose it, through which the path winds.

"On descending, imagining we must be content with the grandeur of the summit itself, a sudden exclamation from the guide directed our attention to the Lake of Llanberris, seen through a gap in the clouds. From this time the view was most magnificent; one bright place after another appeared, and finally the whole curtain of clouds drew up and revealed the various surrounding mountain passes. I never in any of my tours saw a mountain scene so picturesquely beautiful as the pass of Llanberris, glittering in the sun like silver, every rock distinctly marked, the white streams and waterfalls threading the little defiles, and the intense green of the valley below."

Returning to Wymeswold after his brief journey in Wales, he took his wife and children, and their friend Miss Mott, to spend a summer holiday on the north coast of Devonshire.

The lodging which they occupied at Linton was near a bridge across the Lynn, and the window of their sitting-room looked down upon the stream. In the dry season, when they arrived, the supply of water was scanty, and the incessant noise made by the shallow stream in its course through its rocky channel to the sea became an annoyance to the family. One morning they were struck by the perfect stillness of the river, the cause of which proved to be the advance of the spring-tide up the mouth of the stream. It is one of the many indications of his habit of observing and recording all natural phenomena that he made use of this incident eight years afterwards, when, preaching in London a sermon on church-building[2], he wished to illustrate (after quoting) the well-known saying of Dr. Chalmers on "the expulsive power of a new affection," and he thus refers to our morning's surprise at Linton:—

"I remember once, during the summer weeks, fixing our lodging on the sea-coast close to the roar of a torrent, which chafed beneath our windows. Morning, noon, and night it was the same. Conversation and reading required exertion, and before long we grew thoroughly weary of the incessant din around us. But one morning we awoke and all was still. The spring-tide had come up the water-course and flooded out the noisy torrent. You might have toiled long to silence that unceasing roar; you might have removed stone after stone and smoothed the channel, but the next rains would have brought down more; no amount of labour and expense would ever have produced the effect which the fulness of the ocean produced that morning. And so it is with our vast and neglected districts, seething in profligacy and wrong, sending up to heaven their unceasing cry of iniquity and excess. You may remove a mischief here, and may smooth a rough place there; but the turmoil will return as loud as ever. Nothing but the great deep of God's mercies will ever suffice to flood out this tumult of sin."

A small work of his was published about this time under the title of "Four Lectures on the Influence of the Fifth Commandment as the great Moral Principle of Love of Country and Obedience to constituted Authorities." The history of this publication is told in a letter which he wrote to his father:—

"I have a little piece of good news to tell you which I know

---

[2] See "Quebec Chapel Sermons," Vol. V. on "Christian Doctrine," p. 241. Sermon 16.

will give you pleasure. Some gentlemen connected with the City of London School last winter proposed a prize to be written for in the shape of four lectures on the Fifth Commandment, showing that the divine command therein contained was the basis of social and patriotic affections. These lectures employed my leisure time last Christmas whilst visiting you, and working at all sorts of odd times and whilst travelling. The decision has been made, and I am the successful candidate. The premium is £80. I kept my intention entirely to myself."

The editor of the "English Review" having inserted in that periodical an article "On Tendencies towards the Subversion of Faith," drew forth a somewhat severe pamphlet from Archdeacon Hare, entitled "Thou shalt not bear false witness against thy neighbour;" in which, amongst other things, the Archdeacon entered into a warm commendation of Olshausen's "Commentary," and expatiated on the benefit which English clergymen might derive from studying German theology. The Archdeacon sent in the spring of 1849 a copy of his pamphlet to my husband, and received the following letter in acknowledgment of it:—

"I return you my best thanks for your interesting and important pamphlet. I had just taken up the 'English Review' during a morning's call at a friend's house, and had seen in a few minutes enough to show that an answer was required. . . . . . I do hope your answer may preserve many earnest minds from being misled. . . . . . As regards myself, I am fully prepared, however unworthy, to cast in my lot among those who are digging in the soil of Scripture for the precious truth that lies beneath; and I cannot feel grateful enough to those German writers who have done so much of the heaviest earthwork before me—some, I own, in the wrong direction and leading only to disappointment; but some also in the right one, and that one untried before. I have been painfully struck as I have advanced in my work with the dishonesty of our English commentators in concealing difficulties, or solving them in a manner which must be even to themselves unsatisfactory. I am now deep in St. John, in which I find the most valuable helps to be Lücke's 'Commentary' and De Wette's 'Handbuch.' I hope my first volume may be in the press by Midsummer. The work is one which I should not have undertaken had I at first known the amount of labour required; but whatever may be the amount of good done to others, I never can regret having been led to undertake it, as it has been the means of emancipating and strengthening my own faith."

A young friend, whom he knew intimately, and to whom he was much attached, applied to him about the spring of 1849 for advice on the question of entering into Holy Orders. His answer, which was very full, was as follows:—

"Many thanks for your kind and welcome letter, which I will try to answer as well as I am able. I will reply first to your first inquiry. I should certainly say that a constant desire to enter the ministry, provided it be not as a life of ease or a life of affluence, but with a serious view to the performance of its duties, quite answers to the call of the Holy Spirit intended by the Church in her Ordination Service. I acted on this in my own case, and should not scruple to advise you, if the desire should continue, to do the same. As regards the second question, I do not myself hold any such thing as Apostolic Succession or a derivation of authority by virtue of which we are ministers of Christ. I see no warrant for such a belief in Scripture, and think it to be contrary to the spirit of the Lord's promise that He will be with His Church always, not by delegation or succession, but by His Holy Spirit even to the end of the world. If I derive my official authority through a stream of human hands, then I do not derive it immediately from the Lord Himself, as I firmly believe to be the case. It may be a fact, and an interesting one, that our orders are traceable to Apostolic Succession; but it is the same kind of interest as attaches to a venerable building, or any thing else ancient, not therefore one whit the better for its purpose, but only more venerable. But then you may say how differs the Church from a sect? This question I answer on entirely different grounds, viz. from consideration of the duty of unity among Christians and the sinfulness of those who break that unity needlessly. By unity I do not mean conformity; nor by breaking unity do I mean having a different form of Church government—but by unity I mean unity of spirit, true charity, and Christian love; and by the breach of it, the kind of hatred which modern English dissenters show to the Church of this land. With regard to conformity, I should endeavour to judge fairly of the objections which the sects have, and see whether they are sufficient to justify their position. Certainly not, I should say in the case of Wesleyans, Baptists, &c. Then if not, their separation is unchristian; in fact, as every one knows, the majority of separatists just split from us because they want, in the natural vanity of the human heart, to set up for themselves, and are averse to any obedience to constituted authorities. With Quakers and some few others I believe the case to be different; then they come under the former head, and all Christian kindness and absence of hostility ought to be manifested mutually. You will see that my ground is what would be called by many that of unlimited private judgment. I own it, but I look on it in a very different light. I view it as the Scriptural ground of churchmanship, which represents to us no undeviating form of government nor universal pattern of Church ministry, but tells us that the Holy Spirit shall guide into truth, those who walk in love and seek His guidance. In Christ Jesus Episcopacy is nothing, and non-Episcopacy is nothing, but the new creature; and in whatever way the spiritual temple of the Lord may be best reared under the various circumstances which His providence has appointed, in that way would I humbly acquiesce, whether Episcopacy or Presbytery, or whatever else it be called. I find my own place and office in the Church of England. She appeals to the written Word, and gives me therefore the great warrant that I am in the way of the Spirit, whose witness that Word is; and she oppresses no man's conscience, but sends us to God's Word to see whether these things are so. If she did the contrary, if she oppressed the conscience, commanded me to adore baker's bread, or bow to the day's work of a stonemason, I would as unscrupulously leave her and become a dissenter as I now gladly adhere to, and minister in her communion. I think I have now answered your questions, I am afraid not satisfactorily, but as well as I could. Do write again, and never scruple to ask or impart any thing which you think requisite.

"P.S.—What I said about leaving the Church of England, is *only* to be understood as referring to the extreme case of her commanding what God forbids. Remember this; for I believe otherwise all dissent to be in its nature wrong."

As a further illustration of his opinion on the questions of the right of private judgment and of Church authority, the following letter is added here. The name of the person to whom it was addressed has not been preserved:—

"I cannot hold that the voice of God's (visible, audible) Church from the beginning, even if able to be ascertained, has power to declare the sense of Scripture in any such way that we can collect that sense from it. I find in the course of my critical labours that the Fathers, even when unanimous, were often beyond doubt wrong from the imperfection of critical research in their day, or the prevalence of inadequate methods of interpretation. If the Lord by His Spirit is now with us, guiding us into all truth, why should we be dependent on the sense given to His Word ages ago, and not free to discover it for ourselves? I have always deprecated and held off from party in the Church, claiming for myself to follow, in humble dependence on divine guidance, that which may seem to my own judgment, and in subjection to authority, to be right. Thus I have been classed among all parties in turn by those who have not known me, and at the very time that I was on one side accused of Romanizing tendencies, I was being shown up by a Nottingham paper for Liberalism and Low Churchmanship on account of my support of a Mechanics' Institute there.

"I believe that there are persons looking above their system, and living by faith on the Son of God Himself, constituting that great family, one of a city and two of a tribe, who shall be the Lord's at His coming. And with all such persons, whenever I find them, I am desirous and ready to unite

N

on the common ground of Jesus Christ and Him crucified, reserving for proper times spiritual opposition to the errors of the system. I rejoice that we can look out of and above all outward Church systems to our dear Saviour, who is to us the source of all life, and in whom we stand accepted before God. May we be gathered unto Him in the day of His glorious coming; may we have preached and laboured for the truth as it is in Jesus, and have abundant seals to our ministry!"

In the summer of 1849 he carried into effect a resolution which he had long been forming, being led to it principally by the increasing work connected with his Commentary on the Greek Testament. His journal, on June 9, contains this entry, "Pupils left for ever. After seventeen years myself a pupil, and seventeen years chained to pupils, at last free! However, much to be thankful for."

Since he took his degree he had had not less than sixty pupils; many of them have been mentioned by name in this Memoir. Three of them are now in the House of Peers, five or six are or were in the House of Commons, twelve became clergymen, and nearly as many barristers. It was not without regret that this step was taken; its effect was the loss of some agreeable society, and a diminution of income which created a little difficulty; but it left him more at leisure for study and for the education of his children, to which he now regularly devoted more time.

In the same month in which he parted from his last pupils he took his two youngest children, Mary and Ambrose, for a visit to their grandfather at Tonbridge, to which a very short trip to France was added. In his journal he says:—

"*June* 12.—Lionized Mary and Ambrose in town, then to Tonbridge with them; on 26th took them from Tonbridge to Folkestone, and crossed over to Boulogne and on to Amiens by rail, and saw the cathedral; magnificent, pure Gothic. 27th. Cathedral again, walked round the town, very hot; returned to Boulogne, and walked up the cliffs to the Napoleon column. 28th. Beautiful bathe on the sands with the children; off for Folkestone at three; some Hungarian refugees on board."

On his return to Wymeswold he was fully employed in seeing through the press the first volume of his Greek Testament and a volume of Sermons. The latter of these works was published by subscription "in the hope of diminishing the author's somewhat heavy share of various necessary parochial works undertaken at Wymeswold." It included twenty-three sermons [3]. In the following letter to his father he refers to these works:—

"I have been busy this week getting ready for the press my volume of Sermons, and have sent off about half of it to the publishers; so that I have now abundance of press work going on. My Greek Testament is approaching its completion, we are printing John vii., and have six or seven more sheets to complete. I hope by October 25 to be *in manibus hominum;* and then comes the struggle with I expect almost every party, and party organ in the country. . . . . . So that it will be well if the English Church does not cast off her recreant son, and put my book into an *Index expurgatorius,* thickening up the gloom of the approaching November, not, however, without brighter spots of consciousness that I have humbly and earnestly laboured at God's Word, in God's strength, and of hope that those few among us who really are students of Scripture may give me quarter, and regard my book as a contribution, however humble, to the understanding of it."

The first volume of his Greek Testament was published in November. Perhaps the truest estimate of the labour which it cost him would be formed by comparing it with the editions of Valpy, Bloomfield, and Burton, which preceded it. It differed from these not only in the unsparing pains of which nearly every line bore testimony, but in the originality and comprehensiveness of its plan. It offered to ordinary English theological students the results of the labours of Lachmann and (to some extent) of Tischendorf on the text, and a new digest of various readings; it supplied a new body of marginal references intended to illustrate not the subject-matter of the

[3] Six of the sermons in this book were never preached, one of these contains many original remarks on Funeral Pomp, on the text Genesis iii. 19.

text, but verbal and idiomatic usages. In the Prolegomena and the Commentary it opened, almost for the first time to the English reader, the stores of learning which had been accumulated in Germany by more than one generation of critics. No previous editor of the Greek Testament had been so conversant as he was with the vernacular language in which those stores were deposited. At the end of this Memoir will be found some estimate by able and friendly scholars not only of the intellectual powers which he brought to his task, but also of the effect of his Greek Testament as a whole in increasing the Biblical knowledge of his contemporaries. I will only add now that the first edition of the first volume was the fruit of assiduous labour for three or four years; that it contained about 750 pages, which were increased to upwards of 1000 in succeeding editions, and that the principles on which the text was arranged and the conclusions arrived at in some of the notes were modified in later editions. It was not till more than a year after its publication that it became the subject of elaborate criticism in the leading quarterly periodicals. Soon after it came out he wrote to his father :—

"In the 'Morning Post' there is a long and most favourable review of my Greek Testament, speaking of it in the highest terms; in short, calculated to do it and me much good."

Early in 1850 we were invited to visit Belvoir Castle, which was a seat of princely hospitality to a very extensive neighbourhood. The visit was an agreeable relaxation to him in the midst of his work, as will appear from the following letter written to me from thence—

"I do indeed wish you had managed to have come here. We have a party of thirty, the star of whom is Madame Sontag, who has just been singing so as fairly to make the tears run down my cheeks; then there is Elliot Warburton[4]

[4] Two of the distinguished persons mentioned in this letter were connected with signal calamities. The husband of Madame Sontag, Count Rossi, was barbarously murdered in Rome, Nov. 15, 1848; and Mr. Warburton perished in the conflagration of the "Amazon," near the Scilly Islands, January, 1852.

and his wife; and to-day Mr. Disraeli and his wife are coming, and the rest are mostly members of the numerous family of Manners. And here, who do you think I find located as domestic chaplain, living here all the year round? No other than my old school-fellow at Ilminster, Philip Mules.

"Every thing is done in the most princely way here. The Duke's band in uniform play us in to dinner, and at intervals during dinner, and after dinner they come and sing glees, &c. Then at ten o'clock they play in the great hall, and go on till half-past twelve, when they are dismissed. My room is a long way up one of the towers, a very nice comfortable room, but nothing splendid. At half-past nine there are prayers in the chapel, and breakfast at half-past ten. It is altogether a strange and pleasant visit. I have not been idle; on my way here I read a whole work of Tertullian, and before dinner yesterday went on with my last sermon.

"I find I am fortunate, for they only began living in state the day before yesterday; they only do so when the house is full."

The appointment of Dr. Ollivant to the Bishopric of Llandaff, in 1849, left a vacancy in the Regius Professorship in Cambridge, and Henry Alford was one of the candidates for the chair. With a view to this, he took his B.D. degree in November, 1849, having preached before the University as an exercise for the degree, a Sermon "On the Inspiration of the Holy Scriptures." Throughout January, 1850, he describes himself as "preparing for my examination for the Regius Professorship which, however, I have no chance of getting. God will do for the best I doubt not;" and on February 14th he read in the schools at Cambridge a Prælectio on the Authorship and Address of the Epistle to the Ephesians. He received on the 16th a telegram announcing that the choice of the Electors had fallen on Dr. Jeremie (afterwards Dean of Lincoln).

In the beginning of April he mentions meeting at Rempstone Hall, Mr. I. C. Wright. "Much talk with him about Homer; I agreed to do the Odyssey, and next day began it."

When his translation was published ten years afterwards, it was dedicated to this friend.

A family trip from Wymeswold to Somersetshire and the coast of North Devonshire was planned for this summer. It was destined to be darkened by the sudden death of Ambrose our only boy, then in his eleventh year. No foreshadow whatever of this great affliction fell on us when we left home full of bright expectations. Two extracts from letters to his father will show how my beloved husband looked forward to this journey, and how the early part of it was spent:—

TO THE REV. H. ALFORD, SENIOR.

"We leave home on the 29th July and hope to get six weeks clear at the sea. My Greek Testament goes on but slowly; I am writing notes on the Acts, and find plenty of difficulties to grapple with. At the sea I shall have nothing but references and routine work.

"Poor Sir Robert Peel[5]! it seems a melancholy end for a public man, and just now very mysterious, but God knows what is best."

This was written also to his father from our lodgings, Carey Arms, Babbicombe—

"*August* 16.

"We are much pleased with our lodgings and the very beautiful spot where we are staying; it is a fine bracing air, and a great contrast to Torquay. The bathing is delightful, the sea as clear as glass, one can scarcely tell on looking down on it where the sea-water begins. It is a little bay full of rocks, and the children and I have built a table and a seat of smooth pebbles, where I do my Greek Testament the whole morning, and manage to get through a good deal of work till two, our dinner-time. After dinner we wander far and wide, and make expeditions to Torquay. About seven we return to tea, and from eight to nine I read aloud 'Paradise Lost' to them, which we have set ourselves to finish

---

[5] Died July 2.

whilst we are here. From our window we can see full forty miles of coast from hence to Portland; so you see we are enjoying ourselves, and, we hope, laying in a stock of health for new home duties. At odd times I pursue a work which I have been at for some months at leisure hours, dressing, travelling, &c., and which suits the sea very well, namely, translating the Odyssey. I portion out twenty lines a day for my task, and have found much enjoyment from it, not allowing it to interfere with the Greek Testament hours. I have done about 2200 lines, four Books. I allow two years for the work suggested to me by Wright, who is doing the Iliad."

These calm and happy days were brought abruptly to an end by the alarming illness which preceded our dear child's death on August 31. It was not till just after that day that his father entered in his journal a few short but precious memoranda of the incidents which marked the last days of Ambrose's life here. He writes:—

"*Aug.* 22.—Mr. and Mrs. C. Merivale came to see us; went about the cliffs and to Anstey's Cove; she had a donkey, which dear Amby led.

"*Aug.* 23.—All went to the Torquay regatta. Very hot; dear Amby enjoyed it much, and we were all very happy. *Les derniers jours de bonheur.*

"*Aug.* 24.—Walked to Watcombe with our dearest boy—our last walk.

"*Aug.* 25.—Went to church all together,—the next time will be in the kingdom of God; delightful talk in the evening; the last memorable Sunday.

"*Aug.* 26.—Dear Amby not well. Alice, Mary, and I went to Exeter to see the Merivales; in the evening dear Amby no better.

"*Aug.* 27.—Dear Amby no better; went to Torquay and got him some medicine.

"*Aug.* 28.—Amby no better; sent for Mr. Bradstreet of Marychurch. He feared peritonitis.

"*Aug.* 29.—The dear child a trifle better. The girls and I saw the Teignmouth regatta from the cliffs.

"*Aug.* 30.—Amby had a better night; we had prayers in his room. He dictated a letter to George (the servant whom we left at Wymeswold) about his pets at home. We three went to Torquay to get him various nice things, but he could scarcely notice them; his appetite was gone, and at night he was in great pain.

"*Aug.* 31.—Bad night, hands and feet cold, pulse very low; we tried mustard poultice and a hot bath for the dear child, but all to no purpose—he gradually sunk and at six died.

"The Lord's will be done! The purest and happiest spirit, the joy of our hearts and the desire of our eyes! May this make me a wiser and better man as it has a sadder one. I trust these events will soon lose much of their sadness, for the day is fast approaching when we shall be with our two dear ones, where there is no more parting, no more sorrow."

Of all the sorrows which my husband knew in his life, none, I think, made so deep an impression on him, or so often came back to his recollection as this. In a paper written and published nearly twenty years afterwards[6], he describes a scene which to those of us who survive is not an imaginary one, but a reminiscence of that last day in August.

"You remember when we last entered such a chamber; and on that little press-bed in the corner by the window lay all we cared for; in that room we scarce dared breathe; even grief was lulled, and all was solemnized without a feeling beyond. We stood all four round his dying bed, with the sunset from the western sea filling the room with rosy light: and we watched till the dear features lost meaning and their lines stiffened; and then I pressed down the eyelids, and we left mamma with him, and we three went out bewildered, and sat down on the beach, and I said, Where is he now? I have it all before me—indeed that lovely bit of water-colour by Philip Mitchell which hangs there[7] would bring it before me, could I ever forget it. The sun had gone down and had left in the lower sky

---

[6] "Sunday Magazine," "Fireside Homilies," No. ii., December, 1868, and No. viii., August, 1869.

[7] Deanery, Canterbury.

a few lines of dull red, and under them the sea looked a pale ghastly blue (so it seemed to me), and the sky above was clear, but as yet without a star. And there was not a sound, not a breath, not a ripple. All seemed to speak of a presence gone. He had been about those rocks, and on that beach, and cleaving those waters—and now?"

Immediately after the death he wrote the following letters:—

To his Brother-in-law, the Rev. Walter Alford.

"I write with a very heavy heart to announce to you sad news. Our dear little Ambrose, after a few days' severe illness, has been taken from us, and is now, we believe, with his Saviour in glory. It has been a very severe stroke to us, but we have been sustained by knowing that God has done it for the dear boy's and our good, and to bring us together for ever with Him. But I write not only to announce the news, but to you, as the dear boy's godfather, to ask you a great favour. I propose to bury him at Wymeswold, by his brother, leaving Fanny and the girls at Taunton, and go up with the dear boy's remains. But on all accounts it is not well that I should go alone, and of all our friends down here you seem both by feeling and by office, to be the one to whom I feel drawn to ask to accompany me."

To his Father, the Rev. Henry Alford.

"We have been graciously supported, and are enabled to see that God's will is best for us. Our dearest boy is safe; and in this perilous age, when men's faith and honesty are sorely tried, it is no small consolation to think of this. It is a very heavy stroke, and we can at present hardly believe it, but its full meaning has yet to come to us. It is very, very kind of you and Bradley to think of coming with us, and it would be a great comfort, but are you equal to the journey? I am quite equal to the journey with Walter; don't injure your precious health by coming with us on my account, we had not calculated on it. . . . The trial was required, and will do no harm, translating the dear boy from faith to sight, and ourselves, I would fain hope, from weak faith to strong, helping him forward all the way, and us part of it."

TO THE DOWAGER LADY SITWELL.

"I little thought when I wrote to you on Friday that I should have to follow that letter by one bearing such heavy tidings as I have now to announce. It has pleased Him whose ways are not ours to take from us our dearest Ambrose. His apparently light illness which I mentioned in my last, turned to acute and most rapid inflammation of the bowels, which defied all medical skill, and at six o'clock on Saturday evening the dear boy left us. . . . . We are going before we return to Wymeswold to my father's at Tonbridge, to seek comfort from the one person on earth whom I have ever found to administer it most effectually. You knew our dear boy, indeed he won every body's heart by his openness and engaging words and ways. I thought you would like to hear from ourselves some account of his removal.

"We all request your sympathy and prayers."

TO THE REV. H. FEARON, RECTOR OF LOUGHBOROUGH.

"I know, my dear Mr. Fearon, you are interested in us and ours, and therefore include you in the list of my friends to whom I have to announce the sad news of the death of our dearest and only boy. We only knew of his danger about an hour before. We had very few parting words, but those very sweet, it seemed like a dream. He died very peacefully: so we have lost his happy voice and his bright promise from amongst us—a sad trial, but not, we hope, beyond the power of faith to see through in course of time."

The burial of Ambrose took place at Wymeswold[8] on September 5; and shortly afterwards he wrote thus to his friend the Rev. Edward Vaughan, at that time vicar of St. Martin's, Leicester:—

"Thank you for your very kind and brotherly letter which reached me at Wymeswold on Friday. There we took our

[8] A memorial window was placed in Wymeswold Church, near the one put up to his young brother six years before, and also a stained glass window was placed in the south transept of Canterbury Cathedral.

dear boy's remains, laying them by his brother at the north-west angle of the tower. It has indeed been a most heavy, unexpected stroke, but tempered with much mercy. He was taken just at a crisis of his young life, when the noble qualities of the home-bred boy were beginning to pour their clear stream into the turbid river, whether to purify or to be corrupted was an anxious and long inquiry. All this we have been spared, and we have left us one of the brightest examples of the fruits of divine grace in early years. I never saw in any one such a stern unbending love of truth and justice, so tender and scrupulous a conscience. Whatever Ambrose said he did."

It was not unnatural that he should communicate the feelings which now oppressed him to his old friend and tutor the Rev. John Bickersteth, which he did in the following letter:—

"I have to thank you in common with very many of my kind friends for writing to console us in our grief. We have been abundantly blessed with comfort in knowing that our dearest boy was taken from the trials of a distracted and evil age, to be in full fruition of heavenly knowledge and light. As for ourselves, though it was very hard to bear at first, we have become persuaded that it was lovingly as well as wisely done. He was always a very strong healthy boy, even to the last; and we were not aware of any danger till about an hour before his death. . . . . He went off at last most rapidly; wished us good-bye; said 'Yes' when I asked him if he should like to join his departed brother in heaven; just a short prayer, and that was all, there was no time for more. Never did child or man live in a clearer light of truth than dearest Ambrose. From childhood he was inflexibly conscientious, just, and self-denying. It was often no easy matter to get a promise from him; but when once given it was inviolate. Every thing that he had he shared with his sisters and us, and many times, if not enough in quantity to share, he put it by, and refused to enjoy it. His great pursuit was natural history, and especially ornithology, in which he was really a wonderful proficient for his age. Next to his Bible, White's 'Selborne' was his favourite book. He has written himself several little books descriptive of the habits and history of such birds as had come under his own notice. In book learning he was no prodigy, but rather a dunce, but more from preoccupation with busy thoughts than from any deficiency. If it had pleased God to spare him he would have made an honest, useful Christian man. But He has taken him from the toil and struggle and uncertainty of this world to ripen in heaven. May we be found worthy to join our dear boy where he is gone, and to witness the everlasting bloom through eternity of the bright bud removed from us here before the clear stream of his boyish life had mingled with the turbid waters of this world!"

Our friend and former neighbour, the Rev. J. H. Hamilton (now Canon of Rochester), had undertaken in our absence this summer from Wymeswold to be the occupant of the vicarage, and to take charge of the parish. My husband wrote to him the following letter:—

"Heale House.

"I am so glad that you were providentially led to take up your abode at Wymeswold this summer for our relief and comfort. We both feel much your kindness and Christian sympathy with us. God bless you and Mrs. Hamilton for it, and keep long and always from your lips the draught which we are drinking to the dregs. I must join my thanks with my wife's for the sermon which we received yesterday. Like every thing else connected with our dear boy, it has given us a consolation under our great affliction, now pressing on us even more heavily than at first.

"We are at present spending a few days at our childhood's home, a large old house in one of the beautiful sites in the county of Somerset. Every thing here is sombre and solemn. The house is one of the last century, and part of it no one knows how many centuries before. The timber is vast and untrimmed, the boughs waving before and scraping the windows, the front looking up a decayed avenue of chestnuts yearly despoiled of some of their companions, at the end of which is a tall column erected by the great Lord Chatham to the memory of Sir William Pynsent, who bequeathed him the estate of Burton Pynsent, all now gone to ruin, the title extinct, the house fallen down, the garden a wilderness; add to all this that my wife's father, the head of our family, is paralyzed and helpless, waiting his dismissal. In this place we have all grown up and played our childish games, and now it is the centre and resort of the widely scattered members of a family numbering twelve married couples and thirty grandchildren, besides brothers and sisters of the last generation—in all numbering sixty-two persons. Is it not a place strangely in harmony with our present feelings? 'This is not your rest,' is written on every mouldering stone of the old house, and to add to all, dear Ambrose was here full of life and spirits only a month ago! But I shall weary you with the loquaciousness of grief."

To his Brother-in-law, Mr. S. S. Alford.

"It will give me great pleasure to stand godfather to your dear little babe. I have no scruple to undertake that relation where the parents live in the fear of God and seem likely to exercise that authority over their children, which is necessary in order to bring them up in His nurture and admonition. Our sorrow is indeed very heavy, almost more than flesh and blood can bear; but thanks be to God, we are not overwhelmed by it: we know that He doeth all things well, that He has taken our dear child from much trial and peril of faith and conscience in these dangerous days. Still, we have lost all his sweet words and ways, and promise for this life, and the prospect of his sustaining our age,—but we are not broken down, only very sad."

After our return to Wymeswold, in November, he wrote thus to his father:—

"We are now in the midst of the haunts of our dear lost boy (lost to us at least for the present). It seems to me as if I had only been playing at the loss before, but as if the reality was come now. . . . .

"Our thoughts have been much turned of late to the eternal state. Half our children are there, and where the treasure is, there will the heart be also. The fact of our dear children having wrestled with and overcome death by Christ and entered into His rest, seems to have practically disarmed death of his terrors, and shown us how to die."

TO THE REV. C. MERIVALE.

"We found it a great trial at first, and Fanny was in very low spirits for some time. She is now certainly better, and the soothing effects which you so justly ascribe to home are beginning to tell on her. As I anticipated, the fact of his image being ever before us has become a pleasant thing instead of a mournful one.

"Death has been busy this autumn among our friends. ——'s eldest daughter, a playfellow of dearest Ambrose, has just died at Rome. Henry Hallam's death you have doubtless heard of. Poor Mr. Hallam, how he has been again and again called on to drain the cup of suffering!

"Our best love to your wife; it forms an additional tie to her and you that you were the last of our friends who saw him; that your and her impression of him reached up to ten days before his death."

TO THE DOWAGER LADY SITWELL.

"*Nov.* 11, 1850.

"We were much grieved to see in the 'Times' yesterday the death of dear Kythe; and knowing how much you must be afflicted by it, I felt disposed to write to you and say how deeply we feel for you and sympathize with —— and yourself. It is a solemn thought, that of the four happy children round our luncheon-table on Easter-day, two have now entered the eternal state! I find myself the greatest comfort in reflecting that my dear boy has attained by a shorter and more merciful way the perfection after which we amidst many errors and sorrows are still painfully striving. The dear children who have been taken before us who now live, have been, I am persuaded, saved more than common trials and temptations, to judge by the thickening symptoms of the coming age. It threatens to be one of severe individual sifting of faith and conscience, of much family disruption for the truth's sake, and, I fear, of growing disregard to the holy laws of simplicity and ingenuousness. From all these evils our beloved ones are for ever delivered, summoned away in the midst of their first fresh faith and open-heartedness, full of truth and joy and love. I have found, too, that the fact of our dear children having wrestled with and overcome death seems more than ever to remove all terror from the prospect of our own struggle with him. To think that those cherished ones, from whom we carefully fenced off every rough blast, whom we led by the hand in every thorny path, have by themselves gone through the dark valley; that those weapons of which we had only begun to teach them the use have now been successfully wielded by their little hands, and their victory gained before it has come to our turn to prove them. These thoughts seem to show us the meaning of the wonderful expression, 'More than conquerors.' If they could struggle and overcome, much more we, with so much more knowledge and experience. No doubt our fight will be harder: the world has wrapped itself more closely round our hearts, and our experience has been not only of the spiritual, but of the temporal also. But let our faith not fail in Him who has conquered death, and I doubt not that He who now leads our dear children in the green pastures of eternal joy, will in His own time make perfect His strength in our weakness, and show us that all deep afflictions have been in reality our best and greatest blessings."

The following letter was written on another sorrowful occasion. Mr. H. F. Hallam, a pupil (see p. 134) of my husband, died in Siena, in Italy, on Oct. 25. A brief memoir of this promising young man was prepared for private circulation, and his former tutor was asked to contribute some information. His reply was as follows:—

To F. Lushington, Esq.

"No apology was required for your note respecting Henry Hallam. On our return from a long and very bitter absence from home (you have probably heard of our bereavement), the first thing on our drawing-room table was a slip of paper with his name, and an expression of regret that he did not find us at home. A few days after we saw his death in the paper. He was with me so short a time, and our intercourse since then has been necessarily so very slight, that I feel quite inadequate in his case to the sacred task of describing the dead. When he came to me I looked on him with great interest for his brother's sake, and soon learned that he was himself worthy of being the brother of such a man. He was with me only two months, hardly time to thaw the reserve natural alike to both of us. Once during that time my four pupils and myself took a walking excursion into Derbyshire, which he seemed much to enjoy. Those two days let me more into his character than any other intercourse which we had: but as we ever disparage by comparison with a model which we believe unapproachable (at least, not more than once approachable in our own experience), so I fancied I found less grasp of generalizing thought, less though no mean share of that sweetness of bearing in argument and rebuke which in Arthur was something almost more than human; still my recollections of him during that week are those of a very lovely character, full, if time had been given to me to explore them, of treasures of no ordinary kind. As regards our scholastic work, I can speak with more precision. Mr. Hallam wished that he should devote the short time here to practising accuracy of translation into English, and the formation of a good style of severe composition. For this purpose our principal work was translating the speeches of Thucydides. This he did with much care and precision, giving admirable readings of those knotty periods into nervous, and at the same time elegant English, and weighing most carefully any alterations suggested by me, weighing and digesting previous to adoption into agreement with his own style and cadence.

"We have felt very deeply for poor Mr. Hallam; pray tell him so, for we know by sad experience that the assurance of sympathy is of itself a comfort of some kind, and that *οὐ σοὶ μόνῳ*, though a poor consolation, is yet sometimes found to be one."

Our own cloud had not yet passed away; its shadow appears in the following letter:—

To the Rev. J. H. Moultrie.

"Many thanks for your poem, just read. I should hardly be disposed to rank the character of the Virgin as high as you have done; for, reasoning from recorded facts to unrecorded ones, I think it probable that trials from *οἱ ἴδιοι*, in the closer sense, were a part of the sufferings of our Divine Lord. Where she does appear, it is as a faithful, holy woman; not, however, exempt from waywardness and folly. If you ever see Vol. i. of my Greek Testament, you will find a note, Matt. xiii. 55, in which I have argued, as I am fully convinced, that *οἱ ἀδελφοὶ τοῦ Κυρίου* were actually brothers, sons of Joseph and Mary. . . .

"It always gives a poet, like a parent, pleasure to hear of his children. You will be interested to hear that, under our very severe bereavement this summer of a very dear and only boy, your little poem of the 'The Three Sons was one of the things which we read oftenest, and felt most comforting to us."

The following letter, referring chiefly to the volume of the Greek Testament on which he was then engaged, was written to a distinguished scholar, the Rev. Dr. S. Davidson, Professor in the Lancashire Independent College, Manchester:—

"My second volume will be yet a considerable time before it is ready for the press at all. The work is so very heavy, that I must allow two years at least, if spared and in health, before I can hope to be in print. As yet I have done (1) the text and various readings, which will, however, want revising, I fancy, on the appearance next spring of Dr. Tregelles' Greek Testament; (2) the marginal references, which are very laborious and important, especially in doubtful epistles, as a running comment on the diction. In compiling these I have to search into the entire Hellenistic usage of every word. They will be much more systematic and more copious than in Vol. i. Of these, I have completed as far as the end of Ephesians, and hope by hard work to get them done by December 31. The work is getting easier towards the end, as I always pencil onwards, referring back to references already verified, and thus have not to verify again. Of notes I have written hardly any, only about five chapters of the Acts. I have given up every thing else to devote myself entirely to the work, turning over my parish to a curate, seeing that, if I am to do it, it must be the work of my life. I get about seven hours a day at it.

"I find it just now an admirable consolation under deep affliction, the removal of my only surviving son, a fine, promising boy of ten years old. It is a great comfort to have the best of employments to beguile my sorrow.

"Your account of your progress interested me much. I should be at present quite unfit to talk over the difficulties, not having yet grappled with them in earnest. In January I hope to attack the Acts, and perhaps (D.V.) by March either St. James or Romans. Should you not be out by then, I shall feel very much obliged by the loan of your sheets: they will be certain to add much to my *apparatus exegeticus*. Besides their intrinsic value, we have indeed thorny ground to go over, and great need of a sound mind, a spiritual understanding, and a constant use of good English honesty, to shun on every occasion the *ambages theologicæ* which have been the disgrace for ages of our divinity. . . . Those who really value the Scriptures, and know why they value them, should understand each other, and stand side by side in the conflict which is coming.

"Your friend and fellow-worker in the Lord."

The next letter is written to a correspondent in America:—

"Thank you for your kindness in sending me a copy of the 'Christian Examiner,' containing a notice of my poems. It is indeed refreshing to find that my strains have awakened an echo on the other side of the broad Atlantic. I know that you are a people eminently poetical, and look for great fruits from you at some future day; but indeed you are far from idle at present. You have in my opinion decidedly the advantage of us now as to freshness and vividness of poetical life and imagery. There is rising in England, from the class of educated mechanics now happily increasing, a genuine school of poetic excellence; but the old classical poetry is wearing out. Tennyson is our only poet of high powers. Wordsworth being of course reckoned a little gone by, though still happily spared to us. And poems do not sell in England; we are all too busy, all at work, and no play, and are in consequence 'dull boys.' I fear I must reckon myself among this number, for my poetical flights seem to have been long ago tamed down. I have written very little of late years.

"It has, however, been from want of leisure not of inclination. I have been engaged for some years on an edition of the Greek Testament, which will be the work of my life. The first volume, containing the four Gospels, was published last November, and I am now working hard at the remainder. When I tell you that I am employed for eight or nine hours every day on my theological labours, you will see that not much time or strength is left for work of any other kind."

In the following letter, dated 25th December, to the Rev. J. Cunningham, editor of the "Christian Observer," he refers to another criticism:—

"I have only this day seen the letter in your December number, headed Alford's 'Prolegomena:' in consequence, this letter will, I fear, be too late for your January number. . . .

"I am persuaded we are on the eve of a great struggle for the inspiration of the Holy Scriptures. In this contest it will be most essential, for the cause of truth, that we should be at least as well armed as our adversaries; every difficulty must be thoroughly opened, solved honestly and fairly, if capable of solution, or shown and confessed to be incapable. There must be no ignoring, no healing over of difficulties, as has been too much the case in past time. In God's word, as in God's works, we must be humble and adoring, but at the same time truthful towards the bringing about this important end. I have cast in my humble contribution, with fervent prayers, that the God of faith may bless it; in doing this, I expect to encounter no small share of opposition and misunderstanding. I have no sympathy whatever with rationalism; one of my great objects is to deal thoroughly and truthfully with the word of God, that I may, if it please Him, furnish to our students of Scripture fitting weapons for the coming struggle with infidelity."

The Christmas of this year was, to us, shorn of much of its ordinary gladness. He wrote thus on December 23, to a former pupil:—

TO THE HON. CHARLES SPRING RICE [9].

"Many thanks, my dear Spring Rice, for your welcome letter, which arrived, during the dearth of letters at Christmas, much like cold water to a thirsty soul. Our home is much changed since we lost the merry voice of our dear boy. In 1849, when I gave up pupils, we had been living in too happy a state for this world, and I sometimes used to think it could not last. Well, we must all bear sorrow; and it will be well for us if it comes in a shape unmixed with any regrets, except for our own loss, as this of ours does. I sometimes sigh over my distance from libraries for my work, and masters for my girls."

His journal contains the following reflections at the end of this year, and the beginning of 1851:—

"My darling Ambrose, a noble boy of ten years of age, has left us for the land of the leal. Sad indeed was our parting; a few short hours our only notice; the last scene, clouded by partial delirium, but clear at the end. He died by the bright blue sea of Devon, August 31, and was buried by the side of our dear little Clement. I have only my two sweet girls left me to stay my declining years and those of their mother. They are, thank God, well able and well willing to do it.

"I have translated half the 'Odyssey,' and I am going on

[9] Who died 1870.

with it, I hope, ere long. I am also preparing an article for the 'Edinburgh,' on Conybeare and Howson's 'St. Paul,' and some poems for an American publisher, who is going to bring out an edition of my poems.

"I have, by God's mercy, been enabled to look forward to suffering and death as nothing to be dreaded, and to eternity as a glorious entrance on my final and more exalted state. May my gracious God protect me through this year, and help me in my great work for His glory; or if He pleases to cut it short (and in this as in all things His will be done in me), may He take me to His safe keeping among those who sleep in Jesus, where my two dearest boys are already. And may He bring me with Him at the day of His appearing. Amen."

CHAPTER VI.

1851—1853.

LETTERS CONCERNING THE GREEK TESTAMENT—THREE MONTHS' RESIDENCE IN LONDON—DEATH OF HIS FATHER—REMOVAL TO LONDON AS MINISTER OF QUEBEC CHAPEL.

IN the early part of this year he published, at a small price, a selection from his poems, and took the opportunity to insert a new one, "Lacrymæ Paternæ" ("Poems," p. 145). Some of the thoughts in it are also expressed in the following letter :—

TO MISS E. MOTT.

"*Wymeswold Vicarage, April*, 1851.

"You may imagine, as spring comes on, and the flowers open and the merry birds begin to sing, that he who was the most joyous of the whole at such times is more than ever in our thoughts. It seems now as if nature wanted some one to love her; to-day his little wren has been singing in the rose branches over my window, fluttering its tiny wings and pouring out its clear shrill song, just as it did last year when I called him from his lessons to hear it. I shall never forget it. For some moments he stood with his hand in mine, eagerly listening and watching the little bird, his bright blue eyes glistening with intense delight; then, scarcely daring to turn for fear of alarming the wren, he whispered, 'Oh! papa, how beautiful;' and it inspired the dear boy with his first and last simple strain of poetry. One more lamb is safe for ever from the roaring lion; one precious opening flower in all its brilliant hues untarnished. We feel that we are fast going to join him, and our endeavour must be to hold on our way, earnestly and cheerfully, by divine grace, looking to Jesus for the few days which remain."

The following letters are selected from many which he wrote about this time with reference to his work on the Greek Testament, and as showing the spirit in which he was carrying on that work. Among those which are not inserted is one to Mr. James Smith, of Jordan Hill, who had written on the voyage and shipwreck of St. Paul, in which, while discussing some details of interpretation, he acknowledges his very deep obligations to Mr. Smith.

To the Rev. R. C. Trench.

"*April* 12, 1851.

"Many thanks for your kind present and the letter which accompanies it. It comes the more acceptably just now that I have this morning brought St. Paul to Rome, and hope, after a week's holiday at Easter, to begin the Romans. I have arranged with Rivington to have two more volumes; I found one utterly impracticable. I suppose I probably know all there is to be consulted (I mean the names of the books, not their contents as yet) on the Romans; but if you have heard of any thing new, do let me know.

"We have, indeed, been very heavily weighed down by our great sorrow. Our darling boy was one of the most unlikely, humanly speaking, to have been thus taken off; full of robust health and strength, a complete child of nature . . . so that you see the very return of spring, the birds with their nests, bring a pang to us; but the retrospect of his course is very bright and happy, and fills us with thankfulness that we have been permitted to be the parents of such a child. The character by which the villagers and strangers in general knew him, was his generosity and love of truth and justice. Not a boy brought him a bird's egg but was paid punctually and conscientiously; and he never saw an act of injustice without using all his influence to stop it. . . . I string together these few particulars because I know you can feel for us. We are very well, and beginning to breathe freely again; but we are not what we were. I feel now longing for the day when tears will be wiped from every eye. My work has been a great support to me."

TO THE REV. C. MERIVALE.

"*Wymeswold Vicarage.*

"I am glad to hear that we are interweaving Christian matters. Just now we are working not far off each other, not above a century apart[1]; for I am writing notes on the beginning of the Acts. I have found (or rather been found by, for he came here to seek me out) a most efficient censor of my geography, &c., in Mr. Howson[2]; his book also helps me. Did I tell you the booksellers have agreed to three volumes; the same to be published as soon as ready? I hope this may be by next Christmas, or not much after. I do the Acts at about three chapters in a fortnight, I mean notes only; and I suppose the Romans, Corinthians, &c., will take about the same time, the collateral work in the Acts balancing the difficulty in the others.

* * * * * *

"I hope a second edition of Vol. i. may soon be wanted, as the text is a very lame affair in the first edition.

"You see I had no article in the January 'Edinburgh;' I wonder when it is coming. 'The Christian Observer' has reviewed me in January, on the whole favourably: 'By far the best edition of the Gospels which has appeared in this country,' &c.

---

[1] It is perhaps unnecessary to remind the reader that the earlier volumes of Dr. Merivale's "History of the Romans under the Empire," had already appeared, while his college friend was now tracing the history of that Apostle who stood at Cæsar's judgment-seat.

[2] Afterwards Dean of Chester.

"The editor was good enough to offer me a few pages next month to explain some things in the review if I liked, so I have written him a letter.

"My 'Odyssey' appears not unlikely eventually, if it can ever be praised enough, to make its appearance as a gay book, under the artistic auspices of Mr. G. Scharf, with whom I have lately made acquaintance. . . .

"Can you tell me this—when Claudius presented Herod Agrippa with Judæa and Samaria, which were before parts of the province of Syria, what was done about the military forces stationed there? Did the Romans evacuate the district? Hardly I think, for if so how would the new king have raised the necessary men at once to garrison the town? If the Roman garrison remained, on what footing were they? What was the practice, and what are our authorities? I ask because it is of some interest to me to know whether by any possibility Cornelius and his devout soldiers can have remained at Cæsarea over the death of Agrippa, and by any chance have been Luke's authority for his narrative of that event."

To B. H. Norman, Esq. (a brother-in-law).

"You are a man who has an eye-dispensary, can you throw any light on the following:—'Saul could not see for the brightness of that light,' Acts xxii. 11; and when Ananias laid his hands upon him, 'there fell from his eyes, as it had been scales,' Acts ix. 18. Now, of course, the case was miraculous, no doubt about this. But is there any thing physically analogous to the circumstances described? When men are blinded by excessive light, what takes place physically?

"Would the eye suppurate, and a scale form over it, or the eye be glued up? Saul's eye-lids by the way were not glued up, for Acts ix. 8, 'When his eyes were opened, he saw no man.' What I want to know is, does the sacred text, connecting the blindness owing to excessive light with the falling of the scales, describe any known ophthalmic phenomenon; or is the latter detail to be understood of something supernatural representing rather than attending the recovery of sight?"

TO DR. TISCHENDORF.

"I feel myself to be under such great obligations to you in the Digest of various readings in my second volume of the Greek Testament, that I cannot forbear from writing to you this private acknowledgment, in addition to the public one which I shall make in my Prolegomena. I enclose a specimen, from which you will see what my obligations to you have been.

"The nature and extent of these, as well as those to Lachmann and others I shall fully state, as indeed I did, though it escaped your notice in my first volume. The enclosed will show you that the whole critical construction of my second volume is different from that of Vol. i., which was a crude and ill-digested production. A second edition of it is now called for, which, if my health and strength suffice, I shall make uniform with Vol. ii. Will you be so kind as to state in your answer, how I may convey to you the two volumes when published, which I hope may be by October next?

"Your much obliged and humble fellow-labourer."

TO JOHN RUSKIN, ESQ.

"Concerning *sheepfolds*, one mistake has been made by our translators, and generally in the rendering of a most important passage, John x. 16, *καὶ γενήσεται μία ποίμνη, εἷς ποιμήν*, 'and there shall be one *flock*, one Shepherd:' not 'one *fold*,' which is *αὐλή* just before; the distinction is one of some moment, as the verse is much used by the Procrusteans in arguing for their 'spatia iniqua' of outward uniformity. You will, I know, excuse my addressing you as long ago a literary—now a theological acquaintance. I do so on account of the thorough sympathy which I feel with your tract, and because I thought, from one or two expressions in it, that you had not noticed the above."

To Dr. Kitto.

"Thank you for your intention of reviewing me: every discussion of such a subject, whether favourably or unfavourably to me personally, must be good. Apathy to Biblical research is our great enemy. I only hope all the Reviews will deal with me before I go to press with the second edition, that I may get as many hints as possible for improvement. I get more and more dissatisfied with the book as it is, and I am continually making resolutions respecting the second edition."

The Brief of the Pope creating a Roman Catholic Hierarchy in England was published at the end of September, 1850, and was followed in November by Lord John Russell's famous "Durham Letter." The Ecclesiastical Titles Bill was introduced into the House of Commons on February 7, and on the 22nd the Russell Ministry retired from office, though only for ten days. These events by which the whole kingdom was kept for several weeks in a state of agitation, are referred to in the following letter:—

To his Father.

"How very remarkable it is that the Pope, who could not keep himself on his seat, should be able to throw such a hand-grenade into England as to upset the Government and throw all sorts of difficulties in the way of a new one! That God may bring good out of it I do not doubt. I deprecate all revival of intolerance, but think it well to show his Holiness, that it requires two to play at dividing all England into dioceses. I am not sorry that abundance of unmistakable protestations have been sent up from the land. The High Churchmen have certainly done service in their day, but their proceedings have not been wise, and I am not sorry they should have a check."

He was one of the multitude who went to London in May,

1851, to see the Great Exhibition in Hyde Park. His impressions of that wonderful spectacle are recorded in the following letter :—

TO HIS WIFE.

"*May* 18.

"It far surpasses any idea you can get by reading; and indeed, all one can say after the bewilderment of one day's view is, that this earth never saw any thing like it before, and perhaps never may again. I must leave all particulars till we meet. I was within a few yards of Prince Albert, who was walking about inspecting things just like any body else, only with a little space kept round. The Queen was walking with the Prince of Prussia, and Prince Albert with the Princess of Prussia; they were talking German. The Archbishop, many Bishops, and the old Duke were there. I remained all day, and just had time to run through the greater part of it, and arranged a definite plan of four days, for us and the girls to see it thoroughly.

"At the Literary Fund dinner I heard Alison give an energetic speech. . . . Thackeray a capital one. I sat next to, and became acquainted with Stanley, the biographer of Arnold. At the Royal Academy there are some good pictures; a striking one of Landseer's, the Duke of Wellington on the Field of Waterloo."

The plan announced above he carried into effect, by bringing his wife and children on June 16, to London, where we spent thirteen days. A few brief notes which he made at this time, record our visits from Haverstock Hill to the Exhibition on the 19th, 20th; 23rd, "65,000 persons there;" 24th, "nearly 70,000 present:" to Hampton Court; to the National Gallery, and "a very beautiful moving diorama of the Holy Land; to the House of Lords and Westminster Abbey. In the intervals he carried on his work at Somerset House as Examiner in Logic; and on the two Sundays he preached in Trinity Church (St. Pancras), at Bedford

Chapel, and at St. Michael's, Chester Square. On the 30th, he took us back to Wymeswold, though some duty at Somerset House compelled him to return to London the same evening.

He went again to London to preach a sermon for the Scripture Readers' Society, in St. Michael's Church, Chester Square, on July 13th. On the following Monday, he saw the article in the "Christian Remembrancer," No. 73, for July, 1851, on the first volume of his Greek Testament, which had now been a year and eight months before the public. His only observation on reading it was, "Very bitter and severe, but not I think damaging." The next day he wrote an answer to the "Christian Remembrancer" in the "Guardian;" and soon afterwards he published a pamphlet of fifty-five pages, "Audi alteram partem: a Reply to an Article in the Christian Remembrancer." That the article contained useful suggestions, of which he subsequently availed himself, he was ready to acknowledge. But no one who has read it will be surprised at the terms in which immediately after reading it, he describes it in a letter to his father from Wymeswold, July 18th.

"I saw in London the article in the 'Christian Remembrancer.' It is, as I suspect, intended to demolish me entirely. The grand charge is that of compiling from German sources, which in the advertisement of my book I proposed to do. They announce it as a grand discovery, parade the passages in parallel columns, and denounce me as a convicted felon. They are very severe on a few disputed points of scholarship, and point out a few carefully-culled inaccuracies as specimens of the book. I have sent a few lines of explanation of the charges of compiling to the High Church weekly paper, the 'Guardian,' as likely to meet the eye of the same readers as the review. The article will not do much harm. . . .

"The 'Edinburgh' article is much better: very faint in praise, but friendly in spirit, pointing out various defects and inaccuracies, and differing in many points open to debate. The general aspect of the paper is to make people think that it is a laborious and praiseworthy work ill executed, so that I fear neither article will do much for the book; but, at all events, this will add to its notoriety, and thus do it service. It is said that to be well abused is the next best thing to being well praised, and I am sure that for an author it is the better thing, inducing more caution and self-distrust than the other."

To a friend who expressed fear for the effect of such criticism on him, he wrote:—

"I beg to assure you I am alive and well, and happy and of a good conscience, notwithstanding the charges made against me."

His reply was adverted to two years afterwards, July, 1853, by the "Christian Remembrancer," in an article on the second volume. The least justifiable charge of the reviewer, viz. that of a design to conceal his obligations to Continental critics, was not reiterated. The improved system on which the text was arranged in the second volume was acknowledged, while credit for it was claimed, not unfairly, as due to the reviewer. If, on the one hand, it may be said that his prediction that the book would be cleared away to make room for a better has not been justified by the experience of the last twenty years, it must, on the other hand, be acknowledged that his anticipation that the first volume would lead to greater and more mature efforts in the field of sacred exegesis, was fulfilled; though, perhaps, in a quarter where it was not looked for, by the readiness with which the author so severely criticized, adopted every suggestion of his critics which appeared to him likely to conduce to the great end of his labour—the more accurate knowledge and deeper understanding of the Word of God.

He thus records, in a letter to his father, the only notice which the "Remembrancer" took of his pamphlet at the time of its publication:—

"The 'Christian Remembrancer' this month has taken notice of my answer very laconically, among their short notices of books at the end of their review, thus:—'That

Mr. Alford should be dissatisfied with our article on him, is natural; that he should reply to it in a pamphlet, is reasonable; that he should write with courtesy and in a Christian spirit, is creditable.' "

During the remainder of this year he continued to work at Wymeswold, for many hours daily, on the second volume of his Greek Testament; although neither that nor the cares of his parish, and of his daughters' education, were allowed so entirely to absorb his mind as to prevent his attention being given occasionally to mechanical inventions, to manual work in his garden and greenhouse, and to the political questions of the day. He wrote this autumn a short article in the "Christian Observer" on Paget's "Unity and Order of St. Paul's Epistles." In December, though he was working very hard to complete the second volume of the Greek Testament before Christmas, he went to Loughborough to examine a school, and to deliver a lecture on "The Poets of the Last Century." His sermon on December 28 is recorded by a hearer to have been very striking:—

"He always has a special sermon for the last Sunday in the year. He mentioned the events of the last year, the Papal Aggression, the Exhibition, and the French Revolution."

Early in January, 1852, our friend, Miss Mott, came to spend with us at Wymeswold the last weeks of her single life. She was married to the Rev. John Martin, on January 20, in the same church where my husband had christened her elevens year previously. In the same month he was cheered by receiving from his publishers the welcome tidings that a second edition of the first volume of his Greek Testament was called for.

About this time his friends appear to have begun to appreciate more highly his power as a lecturer. His first lecture was delivered under unfortunate circumstances in February, 1847 (see page 153); and I have a list of more than twenty lectures which he composed between 1851 and 1869, and delivered, many of them again and again, in various places. His favourite lecture at this period was "Saul of Tarsus," first delivered at Loughborough, 1851, subsequently in Nottingham, Leicester, &c., &c., and London. It was published in the "Exeter Hall Lectures" for the year 1855, and it formed the basis of an article which he wrote in the "Edinburgh Review" in January, 1853. His lectures on "The Queen's English" gradually grew into a small volume, which he published in 1863.

His lectures on "The Prose Writers of the 17th Century," "The Intelligent Study of the Holy Scriptures," "True and False Guides," "English Descriptive Poetry," "Christianity of the Future," &c., were published. Others, on Music, Sound, Athens, "Paradise Lost," Scenery, Canterbury Cathedral; a Short Sketch of Sepulchral Tombs, from Rachel's Tomb down to the present day, illustrated by Brasses, &c., &c.; Astronomy, the Greek Drama, the MSS. of the Greek Testament, &c., &c., were not published.

Besides these lectures—most of which, if not all, were written—he used frequently to invite his parishioners to a simple evening lecture, generally on some scientific subject. Notices of these parish lectures were lithographed by himself, and sent out.

About this time he conceived a project of writing a poem, entitled "Jerusalem, the Holy City," in twelve books. This was the origin of the lines which appear in his "Poems," p. 323, under the title of "A Fragment of a long-pondered Poem."

He determined to take his daughters to town this year for the improvement of their education, especially by attending the lectures at Queen's College, Harley Street; and he wrote accordingly to his father:—

"I have made all the arrangements to have my house occupied and parish attended to during our three months' absence in London; for the more convenience in point of distance I have taken lodgings in Welbeck Street, not far from Queen's College, where our girls will go daily."

About a fortnight after reaching London he seems, from the following letter to his father, to have preached at Quebec Chapel for the first time:—

"I preached last Sunday (May 9) in the morning at Quebec Chapel, the resort of Portman Square people; a fashionable congregation, with a staff of professional singers in the gallery. In the evening I preached at Hamilton's[3].

"I attended yesterday morning a great meeting at Exeter Hall in favour of the retention of the Crystal Palace on its present site, and heard good speeches from Lords Shaftesbury and Harrowby, the Duke of Argyll, Mr. Hume, and Dr. Cumming, and its projector, Paxton. From the enthusiasm shown, and the names of those who have offered themselves as trustees and guarantors, headed by the Duke of Devonshire and Lord Carlisle, I should think there is now a fair prospect of its preservation. I gave a lecture on the Prose Writers of the Seventeenth Century, to Mr. Gurney's Literary Institution. A London audience is so different from rural ones, the very faces are encouraging from their intelligence and sympathy. I received a card from Lord Rosse, inviting me to the soirée of the Royal Society. I suppose this is owing to my position as Examiner."

During our stay in London, which lasted till July 8, he had access to many books which he was unable to consult at Wymeswold; he renewed many old friendships, and enjoyed extended intercourse with literary people.

Not long after our return, a German lady, Miss Von Stadlinger, came to be an inmate in our home to superintend the education of our daughters. The change from the excitement of London to our quiet parsonage was great, but not unpleasant. He thus mentions it in his journal:—

"*July* 10.—We have returned home after our three months' sojourn in town. Mercies as ever have been abundant. We live in our own pretty parsonage, which, with our garden, is all our own making. I have a study which is a perfect hermitage, filled with every *αὐτάρκεια* imaginable. Our rooms are full of memorials of pleasant tours and happy times gone by, and we have a nice green-

---

[3] The Rev. J. H. Hamilton, then incumbent of St. Michael's, Chester Square.

house opening to our drawing-room, which furnishes us with employment in unfavourable weather, and where I can literally sit under my own vine and my own fig-tree; but all this is nothing to our higher and holier comforts and joys. I have, by God's mercy, and I may speak for my dearest Fanny too, been enabled to lay hold on the anchor of the soul sure and steadfast; and, therefore, to look forward to suffering and death as nothing to be dreaded, and to eternity as a glorious entrance on my final and more exalted state. O, praise be to God who has given me this hope, now that I am passing the prime of life and looking down the valley of years."

Not long after our return he went with his young brother, Bradley Alford, for a short tour in Wales. Not the most pleasing part of their experience is recorded in the following lines which he sent in a letter to our eldest daughter:—

"*Llanberris, August* 3.

"If you ask me to put together,
Some account of this morning's weather,
I will try; but if I should fail
'Tis not for want of rain and hail:
For at this moment the rain is pouring,
Rushing and shooting, and hissing and roaring;
First against the window dashing,
Then on the roads, and glass-plat plashing;
And all the torrents are raising a cry,
To make up for so many weeks of dry;
Racing and plunging their leap to take,
Into the rain-drop mother lake.
Above, the clouds in grey procession
Of all the mountains have got possession,
Save, where some rock, more bold than the rest,
Looks from the mist with its great black crest,
Or waterfall flies from crag to crag,
Like petrified lightning with fork and jag.

* * * * *

"We are sitting quite uncertain
Staring beneath the window curtain,
Sitting and walking as we list,
Missing the view, and viewing the mist—
For, alas! the horrible rain,
Has begun to patter again:
And the wind, which this morning long
From the south was blowing strong,
As if we weren't sufficiently drown'd,
To due north has shifted round;
And the clouds, instead of bidding good-bye,
Again drive over, again let fly;
To be continued, unless weather vary,
Another day in a letter to Mary."

About this time he wrote the lyrical poem, "De Profundis" ("Poems," p. 263).

In the autumn of 1852, while he was carrying the second volume of the Greek Testament through the press, and writing for the "Edinburgh Review" an article on Conybeare and Howson's "Life of St. Paul," he received a summons to Tonbridge, where his father, now in his seventy-first year, was lying on a bed of sickness from which he never rose. Immediately after arriving at Tonbridge he wrote as follows:—

To his Wife.

"As soon as I came my father said to me, 'You see, Henry, God is taking down this earthly tabernacle, but He is doing it gently.'

"I went to Tonbridge Wells to get him some comforts. I thought of our going to Torquay for Amby's little things on that last sad Friday.

"I cannot leave my father, as they could not possibly go on without me; both my father and mother wish to have me here to refer to and consult with; this arrangement will, of course, be a self-denial to me, in cutting me off so much from my happy home and from you, but I feel it must be so at present. I give you a long list of books to send, for I must go on with my work; the publishers are waiting for me. Alice can help you in packing, Mary in selecting, and Miss Von Stadlinger with the German books. You must please make all the cuttings this year, and soon in case of frost. I send you a plan of the beds. The choice geraniums are where I have dotted my plan. Whilst giving you these directions, I have fancied myself in the pure air of my own dear home, with all your faces beaming on me, but my present post is by the bed of my dear father, to lift his emaciated form and watch his faintest whispers for help; and I am content it should be so. Mine has been, as you say, no ordinary father, and no ordinary man, and every thing that I can do shall be done, to ease and comfort him in his last moments.

"So the old Duke is gone at last[4], one of the greatest of this world's men. I told my father of it, but he was too ill to heed it."

A page in the sheet which contained the above letter was reserved for his younger daughter, then troubled with some trifling ailment, to whom he wrote as follows:—

"I hope by this time the ache in its upward progress has got far beyond the head, and is in fact in its way to the zenith. Did it touch the little curls by the way? You will see in mamma's part all about dear grandpapa. He is, I fear, very ill, and will not, to all appearance, be spared to us much longer; but he is very patient and cheerful, and speaks of his death quite as calmly as we should speak of a journey to London. This is the state of mind, my own dear child, in which we should ever be as regards death, steady in faith and hope, knowing that the Lord Jesus Christ has been in the dark valley before us, and there are now no terrors there.

"I have been writing multitudes of letters. You will both like much 'Uncle Tom's Cabin.' You must put all the tears in a bottle for me when I come. You will find plenty of bottles in a cupboard near the servant's room. Adieu, mein Liebchen. Pray give my respects to the Fräulein, and many kisses to Alice."

The next letter shows the increasing weakness of the patient. It contains also a reference to an offer (which sprung out of the recent visit to London) to place him in the Incumbency of Quebec Chapel:—

"Dr. S. Thompson says there is no hope at all. I could not leave him, and the nurse likes me to be near, so I have been the greater part of the day in his room correcting the last sheet of my second volume. He asked me how my second volume was going on, I told him I was then correcting the last sheet. As he had begun to speak, I put in a word respecting a difficulty of my own, namely, the offer of the Incumbency of Quebec Chapel in London.

---

4 The Duke of Wellington died on Sept. 12.

His opinion was that I ought not to lose sight of it, but keep it in view, and, if possible, eventually accept it. . . .

"I am nearly worn out; but any thing for him, if we could keep his valued life a few weeks longer, but I fear not. His will be done, and God will bring good out of it, glory to Himself, and everlasting bliss to that dear one whose every breath we are watching, believing it may introduce the final change."

His father died on the 22nd September, and I received the following letter from my husband:—

"*September* 22.

"It is over. Our dear father is just gone, and so peacefully, that we did not know when. His last moments were very sweet and glorious, not a doubt, not a cloud ever disturbed the serenity of his faith. When I came to his bed-side for the last time he said, 'I cannot see,' then added, 'So much the rather Thou shine inward[5];' and then, 'I hail every symptom.'

"These were his last words; dear blessed saint, he now is in glory with all our dear ones who have gone before, and one of the cloud of witnesses. O may we have grace to follow, and lay aside every weight, and look to Jesus as he did. He was a holy and humble servant of God, if ever such a one was seen: the friend, adviser, and counsellor, and example of us all, whose quiet feeling, unerring judgment, and loving spirit made him powerful for good even where others had no power.

"I feel very sad. I have lost my best and earliest friend and adviser, perhaps the only person in the world who understood me, and could feel with me—now I must bear up alone; but I am willing, if God sees it good for me, and I have no doubt it is. You will, I know, help me and the dear girls, give them my very best love, and tell Miss S. all, she has an impressible heart, and it may do her good as well as us."

---

[5] "Paradise Lost," Book iii., near the beginning.

After the funeral, which took place at Curry Rivell, on September 29, he thus wrote to his stepmother on the same day from Heale House :—

"All has gone on as you proposed, and as you and my dearest father would have wished. It was exactly two o'clock as we went from Curry Church to the grave. He is laid by the corner of the schoolroom, close to Walter's little boy; 'Till He come[6].' Now, my dearest mother, let us support and cheer one another along what remains of our appointed way, till we join him at rest. I believe we thoroughly understand one another, and feel for one another. Whenever you feel disposed to write to me, you know what delight it will give me to receive an answer, and I shall look for your letters as I did for his; and whenever you would like to see me, just say so, and I will make it a point of duty to come."

The following letters to his two daughters were written a few days afterwards while he was yet in Somersetshire. They may serve to show how carefully he took every suitable occasion to draw out for his children the lessons which God teaches us by the events of our life:—

"Men talk of victories over kingdoms and nations; but depend upon it, in the end, it will be found that no victories have been so glorious as men's victories over themselves. Our characters lie very deep, and can only be changed by the continual seeking of grace through life. But you have Jesus to help you, and His throne of grace ever open all day long for you to lift up your heart to Him for strength. . . . .

"I know I sometimes speak harsh words to you, dearest, but I should not do so; we must try to bear one another's burdens, and make allowances for one another. I love you, my darling child, very, very dearly. Yours were the first bright little eyes that ever looked on me with that look which none but one's own flesh and blood can give. Yours the first prattling tongue that ever called me papa. God

---

[6] The words which he wished put on his tomb.

bless you, my own child, and strengthen your good resolutions. Your letter made my eyes overflow with tears. May we be a blessing to one another, and dear mamma and our beloved Mary in this life, and be united to our sainted ones in a glorious eternity."

"Thank you, my child, for the fervent affection which you express, and I know you feel for me. I trust I shall ever return it, and be spared to guide your mind and your course through the days of youth, and see you settled in the world. If you are a child of God by faith in Christ, as dear grandpapa was, it will not matter whether death comes early or late to you, it will only be a removal to a higher and happier state, not really any thing dreadful or to be afraid of. I only wish, dear child, that when you stand over my death-bed, as I hope you may, you may see as calm and as peaceful a departure as his was. In order to this, let us live in God's faith and fear, and in holy love with each other, and do His will with all our might whilst there is time.

"I have not a Wymeswold hymn-book with me; but you must do for the best. I think 'Lo He comes' will do for one hymn; the tune is Helmsley, which you can soon learn. Or you might play 'Sicilian Mariners;' but I have no doubt you will manage somehow[7].

"I have been all day making my funeral sermon for dear grandpapa, which I preach at Curry, on Sunday morning. The text is 1 Peter i. 5, 'Kept by the power of God through faith unto salvation.' It was a very favourite text of his. There is a great deal in the sermon about him. I only hope I shall be able to deliver it with a firm voice. But God can give me strength to do so, and I am sure it will do good. Give my best love to mamma and Alice, and a little slice to Miss S."

The quiet but not inactive life which we led at Wymes-

---

7 The organ in Wymeswold Church was played by an amateur residing in the parish; but for many years, before this gentleman came into the parish, the Vicar himself played the organ. His younger daughter sometimes took his place as on the above occasion.

wold in the early part of 1853, will be best described by giving a few extracts from his journal. Such details will not be without their interest to any readers who take pleasure in observing how entirely he rejoiced in doing with all his heart the diversified work which lay immediately before him, while yet he did not fail to try any opening into that sphere of more extended usefulness towards which he was led.

"1853. *Jan.* 1.—I commend myself, and all mine, and all I do or design, to my gracious Father's care during this year. Whatever I do, may I do it with my might; may I live to His glory; and if I am to die this year, may I die in His fear and enter into His rest. Keep me, O Lord, entirely regardless of men's opinions, free from ambition, willing to fill 'little space, so Thou be glorified.'

"I could wish, if possible, before my strength fails, to be placed in some situation where I may preach to the intellectual and educated.

"On the other hand, I want to finish my Greek Testament; and what place so good as this, where I have uninterrupted leisure and healthy air; but my dear father on his death-bed wished me to get to London, that I might be the means of serving the great Head of the Church more effectually, by being known and employed to the greatest advantage in the service of my Lord and Master.

"*Jan.* 6.—We all five went to the Strutts at Kingston, and had a most pleasant visit there. Such a pretty sight in the morning to see her with all her little tribe about her, chanting the Psalms at the organ in the hall before breakfast. I played on the organ afterwards. Mrs. Strutt[8] read us afterwards some of Mr. Senior's 'Diary in Ireland[9]:' awful accounts of things there when the agents do their duty. These holiday visits do good; not only do they enlarge acquaintance, always a good thing in this sulky world, but they give home duties a relish, and refresh literary resolutions.

---

[8] Now Lady Belper.

[9] Mr. N. W. Senior's Journals have now been published.

"*Jan.* 10.—Worked very hard in the morning at my Greek Testament; in the afternoon planted roses in the dear girls' gardens, and in the evening dined at Rempstone: met there a lady, said to be the best singer, rider, and swimmer in Scotland. Copied Burgon's poem on the Duke's funeral for Lady Sitwell. Read an article in the 'Quarterly,' demolishing Disraeli and his government. At night wrote to Rivington to send a copy of Vol. ii. of my Greek Testament to Bunsen.

"*Jan.* 16.—Received by post the new 'Edinburgh,' with my article on 'Conybeare and Howson's St. Paul' in it. May each advance be accompanied with more endeavour to humble and improve myself, and to do good!

"*Jan.* 18.—Read an article in the 'Edinburgh' on 'Cathedral Reform.' I agreed in the main with it. It seems to me that they are gradually narrowing the ground for learned men in the Church of England, and by consequence lowering the general standard of the clergy, and the learning will pass to the Dissenters.

"Received some packets of my dear father's letters. I must soon set about my labour of love, the Memoir of him; but when or how to do it I know not, my time is so occupied. Wrote to the 'Critic,' among other things, offering to write notices of theological or poetical works.

"*Jan.* 22.—All the morning very busy correcting proofs; then helped the girls with their gardens, and planned some alterations behind the laurel bank. Got a very nice letter from Edward Elliott, my father's old friend, offering me a copy of his 'Horæ Apocalypticæ.'

"*Jan.* 23.—Sunday morning, preached from 'God said, Let there be light;' in the evening, from Rev. xxi. 3, 4, to comfort poor Miss Von Stadlinger, who had lost her sister. I spoke much of the glories of the new earth, when all beautiful things shall not fade, when the desert shall rejoice and blossom as a rose. O Lord, hasten this happy day! Read hymns to them, and I played some tunes on the harp, and spent, I hope, a profitable day.

"*Jan.* 31.—Went to Leicester to hear Sir H. Halford

lecture on 'The Republic of Plato.' Much sparring about Plato and Greek music. Slept at Vaughan's[1], and had a chat with him about my Greek Testament.

"*Feb.* 3.—Correcting proof-sheets all the morning, then to Rugby to lecture. Dined at Moultrie's. Mrs. Moultrie showed me some very beautiful lines which her husband had lately written to his eldest daughter, also some others called 'Anticipation' and 'Experience.' Read to her some of Mrs. Browning's things, 'To Flush, my Dog' and 'The Cry of the Children.'

"*Feb.* 6.—Heard from Rivington, agreeing to publish my English Testament. Heard also from Mr. Field, of Boston, with scraps from the American papers criticizing favourably the Boston edition of my poems.

"*Feb.* 11.—Busy preparing specimen sheets of my proposed English Testament.

"Afternoon, stayed in and tried experiments with glass and sand for my lecture on 'Sound' at Loughborough next week. Heard of a letter written about me and Wymeswold Church. . . . . So troubles increase as we go on; but I feel quite in heart to bear up against them, thank God, and would not do any one harm for all the pleasure it would give them.

"*March* 4.—Preparing to give a lecture on 'Athens;' wrote to Merivale and Mr. Scharf about it. Copying, with some trouble, Wordsworth's picture of 'Athens Restored,' in the frontispiece of his book. My picture must be as large as I can make it. Fanny and I worked very hard about it, and she made a map for me. My only time is late at night.

"*March* 5.—Saw in the 'Times' an advertisement of the Classical Examinership [in the London University] held by Jerrard. Offered myself as candidate.

"*March* 7.—My lecture on 'Athens' went off better than I expected. Heard of my election to my old Examinership, and consequently not to the classical one. Thus ends another

[1] Then Vicar of St. Martin's, Leicester.

scheme. I seem doomed to disappointment in every prospect of more extended action in this world. May I learn to disregard such rebuffs, and strive to do actively and well what lies before me! Finished my critique on 'Hymnology' this evening. Merivale tells me that Smith, the editor of the 'Dictionary of Antiquities,' is elected Examiner."

In the previous year some overtures had been made to him with reference to the incumbency of Quebec Chapel, which was in the gift of his friend, the Rev. J. H. Gurney. Reverting to this, he wrote, April 11:—

To the Rev. J. H. Gurney.

"I wish to say a few words to you on your proposal last summer about Quebec Chapel. Many reasons have set me very seriously reviewing your proposal, and I have at length determined, should it still be open, and should I be enabled to do so consistently with common financial prudence, to accept your offer; but don't let me for a moment stand in the way of any of your plans. I would rather withdraw the proposal altogether, should you consider it best."

Whilst the contingency of thus entering on a London life was under consideration, I felt quite reluctant to abandon our home at Wymeswold, and encounter a future the advantages of which I was scarcely competent to appreciate. My sentiments were well known to my husband, and he took the trouble to state his own views in writing as follows:—

"I feel deeply my work at Wymeswold is done; it has been the work of a pioneer. I have been the means of preparing and working for what is to come; but, like all others who do this, I am not the man to continue it.

"Untoward circumstances have thrown me into false positions; and now that my Greek Testament withdraws me from the parish, I have, and must have to the people in general, the aspect of an idle shepherd, letting others do his work; and after eighteen years, as the generation grows up which knows not Joseph, this must infallibly get worse and worse. As to my Greek Testament, when the second edition comes out, I shall have arrived at a period of my work which will require more than any before that I should have access to public libraries. The work must go on slower, but I trust it will be better done, and I shall seek out the men who have worked on the same subject. As to yourself . . .

"As to the dear girls, the change would be a most important one, with two sides to it I own; but in my mind the advantages vastly preponderating. As to myself, on the most favourable human calculation, half my ministerial course is run; not I would hope its best, its most vigorous half. Is it not time to make a break? time to endeavour to put my talents to the best account for my Master's service? time to enter upon that sphere of active duty which shall be the great field of exertion of my life. I want to be in and among the throng, doing God's work; to be telling from a recognized position among them, and not as a mere charity-lion, home truths to minds cultivated like mine own. I feel the power, sometimes I can use it. But going to be stared at, as a comet, effectually damps all holy energies, and I shall never use it aright or effectually, till I stand on my own watch-tower as Christ's messenger, and speak His truth because it is my duty to do so.

"As for preferment, I fairly tell you I do not care two straws about it; but a high sphere of usefulness I own is tempting to me, and it has appeared to me, that this place is the path by which God Himself is leading me to such a sphere. Then even more serious thoughts come in, suppose a little self-denial is required in my new position, suppose the green fields, and the stores the garden yields are not so acceptable, suppose what annoyances the imagination will, is there not a far weightier consideration over-balancing all these? When I look at the great throne set, and the books open, then all doubts vanish in a moment, and I am resolved to work while it is day.

"First trust me, which I only mention first because it is in this matter the necessary inlet to the other, and next trust God; if we take up this plan determined to serve Him, not neglecting common prudence, but at the same time, in a humble self-sacrificing spirit, He will bring us safe through, never doubt it; so let me have at least your sympathy. Eve wept over her flowers, Eve's daughter can do no less. Eve's son will have hard work to get up a dry parting; but sure I am of one thing, heaven's flowers will bloom the sweeter for it. God bless thee, and strengthen us for God's work, whether here or there, for Christ's sake."

Writing at this time a letter of congratulation to his early friend, Edward Bickersteth, recently advanced to the Archdeaconry of Buckingham, he says with reference to his own work:—

"*April* 14.

"I am more hopelessly than ever working like a horse at the mill, furnishing a daily portion of copy to the printers of my second edition of Vol. i., which I hope to make a far better book than the first edition. I sent you Vol. ii. I am glad to say it is selling exceedingly well.

"I am projecting an English edition for ordinary readers, with a text of my own as well as the received text. I do so want to furnish during this short life, which is slipping away from under me, some solid contribution to the better understanding of God's Word among us. The conviction was very painfully forced on me while engaged on Vol. ii., that the mere English reader cannot, and never does, understand the Apostle's arguments in Romans, or the First and Second Epistles to the Corinthians. The translators did not appreciate the importance of connecting particles: *γὰρ*, 'therefore;' *οὖν*, 'but;' and *ἀλλὰ*, 'for,'—these and the like renderings were not likely to clear up passages otherwise obscure. Salvation we trust and know our people get from the present version, under God's blessing, but one would like them to be made as wise unto salvation as the case admits of."

At length all obstacles were overcome, and our migration to London was decided on. He wrote to me from London on May 9:—

"It is just settled about Quebec Chapel. I shall have

400*l*. a year fixed. I am trying to get a house in Upper Hamilton Terrace, St. John's Wood. Just been to the Water Colour Exhibition, which is a great treat to me. Yesterday I preached in St. Michael's, Chester Square. I had been reading Schleiermacher's sermon on the Christian's reward with Miss Von Stadlinger, to prepare me for my sermon.

"I find the Bishop of London does not object to me, so now all is right."

On the next Sunday (Whitsun Day, May 15) the following entry was made in his journal at Wymeswold:—

"Evening with my dear ones after preaching twice. I more and more love and enjoy their company; and now the prospect of our change seems to have still more endeared them to me, to think that I should be taking them from so pleasant and happy a home into the great whirlpool of London for my sake. O Lord, bless them with Thy richest blessings, and unite us after this life in the happy world to come with our dear boys, for Christ's sake!"

The following letter, written on June 5 from Heale House to his younger daughter, will show the intimacy almost on a footing of equality which he sought to maintain between himself and his children:—

"I got your nice loving letter on my arrival here yesterday, and was much amused and pleased with the facetiæ therein contained. God bless thee, mine own child, and return all thy kindness and love for me a hundred-fold into thine own dear bosom! How blessed a thing it is when one desire, one love, one set of thoughts animate our hearts, to please and serve each other and Christ, and help each other onward in the way to the heavenly country! and I do trust such is the case with my darling child and me, we seem so completely united, and to understand each other so well.

"May God's grace be given abundantly to you and dear Alice, to guard you from all the temptations of the life which is now opening on you! May we be kept as a Christian family without any difference or coldness to each other, and each be the means of good to the rest, as long as we are spared together here! I feel and know that I am often wayward and hasty to dear Alice and you, and that my manner and words discourage and grieve you. This is very sinful in me; and when you see it, you see that your father on earth is not like your Father in heaven, on whose brow there is never a frown, who never is wayward or hasty. Forgive it, and do not let it discourage you, dearest children. Pray for me, and I will strive to be gentle and loving at all times, and to reprove not with temper, but with equity and mildness."

About the end of June we went for a short tour in Wales, and on our return at Bedgelert he received a letter from Bishop Pepys, of Worcester, most kindly offering him the vicarage of Grimley with Hallow, and the post of Examining Chaplain. Had such a post been within his option at an earlier period (see page 163), it might have changed the current of his life. But the decision had now been made, and we were to move to London. Once, indeed, before our removal he went to town to preach at Quebec Chapel. The contrast between it and the church at Wymeswold struck him forcibly. He wrote:—

"I have been preaching at Quebec Chapel. What a poor place the chapel is, compared to my own beautiful church where my best energies have been spent to make it what it is! O Lord, make my ministry there the means of saving souls and of glorifying Thee, through Jesus Christ our Lord!"

A suggestion was made to him from more than one quarter, to the effect that he should retain the living of Wymeswold, together with the incumbency of Quebec Chapel. To this he replied, after referring to legal obstacles:—

"I have a decided objection to pluralities myself; where a man's duty is, there should be his residence, and one cure of souls is enough for one man."

As the time of our removal drew nigh, bringing with it an increasing load of small cares, my husband's health suffered severely. One of his anxieties was ended by a confirmation, which was held in our church at Wymeswold on July 25.

His daughters were among the candidates, and I insert here a letter which he wrote to them from London on May 8, with a view to this important event in their lives :—

"*Chester Square, May* 8.

"It has come into my mind this Sunday afternoon to write to you on the subject of your approaching confirmation. I do indeed rejoice, my darlings, that God has put it into your hearts to desire to be confirmed, and that He has in His providence directed the Bishop to choose our own parish to confirm in. There, where you were first dedicated to Christ, will you of your own accord renew your dedication to Him. For this is, dear children, a dedication of yourselves to God, not such a dedication as to require your retirement from social duties and pleasures and relations; this would be to fly from temptation, which we are never expected to do, and which is but a poor and cowardly act for a soldier of Christ; but such as to devote yourselves, your social and private lives, your pleasures and duties and pursuits, your sorrows and joys, your affections and hopes to Him who hath loved you and given Himself for you. I hope and trust, my dear girls, that you are ready and anxious to do this. It is a blessed opportunity to give your young loving hearts to Christ, with all their many interests and prospects. Dear children, you know not what sorrows and temptations, what trials you have before you. Depend upon it you will want divine grace for all; much prayer of the heart, much inward and real conflict in Christ's strength : and now you will be laying the foundation for this conflict, enlisting yourselves, of your own act and word, under Christ's banner, to serve Him as your Captain. You know, my dearest girls, that we have brought you up somewhat differently from most children, with freedom of intercourse and Christian liberty and broadness of principle, such as few girls are taught, or accustomed to practise. Now is your time to show the advantage of this in your own characters, to become more intelligent, more sound-hearted, more mature Christians. For it is with a view to your higher and eternal good that all this has been done; not merely from caprice or opinion as to your worldly interests, but because we thought in God's sight that it was right so to bring you up, and to teach you things which other girls are not taught, that you might serve Christ better. I shall hope, at home and while we are in Wales, to say much more to you on this subject; meantime, do let me entreat you both to make it a subject of prayer to God. Pray to Him to enable you to see it in its proper light, as a bright and joyful thing to give yourselves to Him. Pray to Him to give you a desire to glorify Him in your lives. Pray to Him to guard you now in the midst of the temptations which beset the lives of all young women, and which will specially beset you both in London where we are going. And as regards the Lord's Supper, it will be one of the happiest moments of my life, when I see my own two darling girls coming with the assembled church to that refreshing ordinance. May you indeed be partakers by faith of the realities of Christ, and be one body with Him and His people, and cleansed from all sin by His blood! You have each peculiar difficulties to struggle against. . . . . Thus, my darlings, I have spent a pleasant hour in Christian converse with you on this important and delightful occasion which is coming. Receive, as I know you will, kindly and thankfully these overflowings of a father's full heart for your spiritual and temporal welfare. Half our little band is already with the Lord, let us ever be so living as hoping to join them where they are. They are one with Christ in glory, let us be one with Him and them in faith and hope and purity, living by one blessed spirit. Many and sweet are our comforts here, deep and blessed our love for each other, and what will our joy and love be when our circle is again completed, father and mother, brothers and sisters, in a glorious eternity."

Our friend Mrs. Martin (formerly Miss Mott) came to Wymeswold, and was present at the confirmation of her young friends. The following entries occur in his journal:—

"*July* 28.—Eliza Martin is come to be present at our

dear girls' confirmation; she is much changed, and evidently, I fear, in a consumption, but so cheerful and resigned.

"There were twenty-four at the confirmation and our two girls. God bless them, and make them His dear children. I felt very fluttering and not well all day.

"*Aug.* 15—Memorable day on which my two dear girls came to the Lord's table with us; thank Him for all His mercies respecting them.

"In the evening preached the first of a series of farewell sermons, on Original Sin; much fluttering again and giddy; getting somewhat anxious about myself, but I must trust in Him who has my life in His hands."

A letter written on August 15th to the Rev. E. T. Vaughan, refers to his last sermons to his rural flock:—

"I began last night a course of farewell sermons here; first, Original Sin; the next I propose taking the Atonement, then Justification by Faith, and Sanctification of the Spirit, &c.

"I have not been by any means well lately; I believe the cause was the occurrence of three anxieties, my father's matters, my own plans, and my book. I trust, with great care in diet, I am mending. Our dear girls joined us at the Lord's table yesterday."

His illness, however, continued, and he could not preach without difficulty. Some account of his last sermon was given in a local paper to the following effect:—

"On Sunday, September 25, the Rev. H. Alford preached in the morning on the words of our Saviour, 'The harvest is the end of the world,' and alluded to his separation from his flock, which was about to take place. In the evening Mr. Alford took for his text, 'The grace of our Lord Jesus Christ be with you all. Amen.' He said he had selected this passage, being the last verse in the Bible, and this being the last occasion on which he should address them as their minister. He pointed out what the nature of the grace here alluded to means, its application, and the effect upon the life and conduct in general. He wished to apply the subject more particularly to his own flock, although he observed many strangers present, and if he spoke with earnestness and plainness, he hoped he should be borne with. He would address them as a dying man to dying men. He then addressed the young, and invoked the grace here spoken of to accompany them throughout their pilgrimage in the present evil world; he warned those of mature age, and in forcible language spoke to the aged. The rich and the poor were the next divisions of his subject, believers and unbelievers, the two great classes of mankind, and of every congregation. Churchmen and Dissenters were severally addressed, communicants and non-communicants; absentees, those who never enter a place of worship except on some public occasion. The duties of parents and children were next pointed out, then those of masters and servants.

"He lamented the many divisions which existed in the parish, and hoped that after he had been removed from them a better state of things would exist. Having preached for upwards of an hour, he prayed that the grace of our Lord Jesus Christ might rest on them all."

It will be inferred from an expression in the foregoing sermon, and indeed from other passages which have been conscientiously preserved in this Memoir, that there were among his parishioners at Wymeswold some few to whom their Vicar's method of doing what he believed to be his duty was less acceptable than to the rest. But whatever alienation existed at any time of his residence there, was extremely limited both in its extent and duration. Numerous testimonies of the affection of his people generally were received both at the time of his quitting the parish and on subsequent occasions. And I may mention here the last spontaneous manifestation of the general feeling. Soon after the news of his death reached Wymeswold, the parishioners placed a painted east window in the south aisle of their church as a memorial of the pastor for whom their love was not extinguished by a separation of eighteen years. The foregoing account of that portion of his life which was spent at Wymeswold, may be appropriately ended by the two following letters which I have recently received, the first from his former pupil, the Rev. W. H. Gurney, now Rector of North

Runcton; the second from Archdeacon Fearon, who was his neighbour at Loughborough.

"*North Runcton Rectory, Sept.* 6, 1871.

"MY DEAR MRS. ALFORD,—I could have much to say about your husband, if only I had the power of saying it in a way that would be worthy of him, or of what he was to me as a most wise and tender friend and guide in the best things, and at a most important time of my life. But, independently of my own feelings for and about him, I am sure, in looking back, that the time I was at Wymeswold was a very important one in his own mental and spiritual history from 1843 to 1845. The restoration of the church, which he undertook and carried through as hardly any one else in England at that time did, or could have done, was of great interest not only in itself, and in the complete and perfect way in which it was done, but as indicating the then condition of his own mind and feelings, perhaps, rather than teaching in religious matters; and certainly the power and effect of his preaching never was greater (though afterwards it was much more widely spread) than during those years that I was with you at Wymeswold. Those extemporary sermons of his (three every Sunday, I think, there used to be) were wonderful, and the impression they made can surely never be lost by those who heard them.

"Among my many pleasant recollections of that time is that of the expeditions which some of us often took with him on Saturdays, seeing and examining the churches in the neighbourhood. I learnt a great deal from him, which has been a great pleasure since, in the way of knowledge of architecture and antiquities; and besides this, the expeditions themselves were such fun—and I always thought he enjoyed them as much as we did—and the small adventures which used to arise in the course of them. How well I remember, in particular, going with him and John Morris one Easter holiday (when I had not gone home as usual, for some reason), a tour of three or four days to see the Lincolnshire churches, and spending one whole day at Lincoln, and almost the whole of it in that glorious cathedral! How we all did enjoy it, and how full of energy and brightness he was all through the time! Those were bright days indeed, and have left their brightness, and something better than mere brightness behind them.

"No doubt that trying episode of ———'s going over to Rome will be very carefully treated in any account there may be of your dear husband's life. I am quite sure there never was any thing in his teaching then, or at any other time, which tended in the slightest degree to Romanism. The utmost that could be said in that direction is, that his taste and genius were often offended by the carelessness and want of reverence in the Low Church school at that time, and that his sympathies were in a great measure repelled from that school. But I am sure that his warm friendship, e. g. with Mr. Phillipps, of Hathern, was quite enough to show the real agreement that he had with the Evangelicals in all sound and Scriptural doctrine.

"I can only add, my dear Mrs. Alford, that as I grew older I more and more valued my intercourse with him, and more and more felt the great privilege of having for my most intimate friend one whose powers were so great and varied, and all used first for the glory of God and the building up of Christ's Church in the knowledge of His Word, and then for the great help and comfort of all who came to him for advice or help. Certainly the variety of his powers was very remarkable. In small things as well as great this was shown: every thing he did was done well, and done in a way that showed the man of genius as well as of ability.

"You have seen or heard, I dare say, of the death[2] of my cousin, Charles Buxton, one of the old Wymeswold pupils, and one who truly valued the dear Dean in every way. Poor Charles's death is a great loss both to his own family and to many others besides.

"Most truly yours,

"W. H. Gurney."

---

[2] See page 133.

"*Loughborough Rectory, Sept.* 7, 1871.

"MY DEAR MRS. ALFORD,—It seems a long time ago since you and your dear husband left Wymeswold, to embark on a London life, and encounter the labour and anxiety of the Quebec Chapel ministry. I wish that I could respond with greater fulness to your request that I would recall some of the incidents of his early career when we were neighbours; but the lives of both of us were then so much occupied with our parishes, and his with the addition of his Greek Testament labours, that we had little leisure for that occasional intercourse which was always to me most agreeable as well as instructive.

"When I first knew him he had just finished the restoration of his church, and was encountering the obloquy of having very High Church tendencies, under which reproach in those days every clergyman was likely to suffer who ventured to make up for a century of neglect which our predecessors had permitted of their sacred buildings. Wymeswold was one of the first churches in this part of the country which were brought under the hand of those skilful ecclesiastical architects who, until about thirty or forty years ago, were almost unknown in England. It must be that length of time ago that the restoration of Wymeswold church was taken in hand. I was in the church a few days ago, and could not but think of the discouragements and difficulties, both moral and pecuniary, which had to be surmounted before such a work (which, by-the-bye, has stood admirably) could have been completed. I never knew what portions of the expense were defrayed by local subscriptions, but it was always understood that it took Alford many years to recover from the sacrifices which his zeal and public spirit had impelled him to make. To him was left the satisfaction of having set in his own neighbourhood an example which has since been so extensively followed every where, that an unrestored church is now rather the exception than the rule. All honour to those who were the pioneers!

"The advantage of your husband's proximity to my parish I frequently found in his ready willingness to 'come over and help us' when we wanted an address to a working man's institute, or a lecture to a literary society, or a penny reading, on any subject which his varied accomplishments embraced. His readiness of speech and good humour made him a most valuable coadjutor on all such occasions; and he used to say, 'If I can once get a laugh out of them I shall do.' This he did effectually even in dry subjects such as acoustics, when I remember, after maintaining that every substance in nature was capable of emitting a musical sound, he added, with gravity, 'To be sure, you can't get much of a note out of a blanket.' One day, at a meeting on some educational matter, after we had all been lamenting in our solemn speeches the difficulty not only of teaching our school children, but of bringing them into any habit of subordination whatever, and keeping them from the most mischievous tricks, he refreshed our party by naively assuring us of the consolation which he had always felt in the old schoolmaster's apophthegm, 'After all, sir, boys is boys.'

"I need not tell you of the effect of his preaching. There is a common opinion, in which I do not agree, that a good plain sermon is equally acceptable to poor and rich, learned and unlearned. Those who so imagine have, perhaps, little idea of what is most grateful to the poor man's ear. He delights in platitudes at which those who sit before him in soft raiment can scarcely repress a smile. Repetitions are dear to him, without which an idea does not make its way to his mind. Now, to a cultivated person nothing is more wearisome than to hear the same thought put over and over again into slightly different words; especially if those words be accompanied by a string of Scripture texts, to the applicability of which he has a most indulgent indifference.

"But if any man could make his sermons attractive and edifying to persons of very different acquirements, the late Dean had that power. At the same time, I think his sermons were more suited for the atmosphere of Quebec Chapel and Canterbury Cathedral than of Wymeswold Church. How, indeed, could it be otherwise with a mind overflowing with theological learning, of which some congregations would perceive the proofs continually cropping out, and would thoroughly appreciate, while they would be entirely lost upon less educated people? One quality his sermons always possessed, suited alike to all hearers—the most impressive seriousness. His deep voice, his reverential manner, gave a solemnity to all he said, which could not but impress itself upon the congregation. You were not likely to indulge in any levity of thought when Alford was preaching; so thoroughly did he make you feel that the preacher was deeply conscious, and that his hearers ought to be, of the importance of the subject in which they were engaged, and the magnitude of the interests which it involved.

"Nothing, in fact, could be more striking than the contrast between the immovable seriousness of his demeanour when engaged in sacred duties, and his liveliness and elasticity when these duties were discharged. When our church at Loughborough was reopened he was one of the preachers, and immediately after the service was concluded some of my principal parishioners came to my house and asked me if I thought he would allow his sermon (which was an admirable one) to be printed. It had been extempore, and I knew he would not be able to recall it. But I desired them to speak to him about it. It was a weekday, and (must I confess the truth?) they found the distinguished preacher on the lawn in the midst of a large party of ladies, as earnestly engaged in a croquet game as if interests depended upon it as great as those which he had just so successfully advocated. Whatever he did he did with a will, and this, I think, was the great secret of his literary and ecclesiastical life.

"If it be said of him, as it has been, that in the course of his lifetime he passed through every phase of doctrine, or, at least, ecclesiastical opinion, it may be replied, so did the world. Until the last half-century all the earnest-minded of religious men held the opinions commonly known as Evangelical. In these, inherited from his father, he was no doubt brought up; nor did he ever, as I conceive, forsake the salient opinions held by that school. But he added to them other most important elements of Christian faith and worship, which the Low Church system had altogether ignored. But what was of more consequence, he hesitated not in later life to hold out the hand of Christian fellowship to the great bodies of Nonconformists, with whom it is for every reason desirable that we should endeavour to act for those numerous objects which we hold in common. Thus did the Dean manifest not only the tolerant spirit which becomes a Christian minister, but the far-sightedness which recognizes comprehensiveness as a first necessity of a National Church. Let not, then, that be considered inconsistent which was rather the natural development of thought both in theological and ecclesiastical subjects, and to which, indeed, he himself largely contributed.

"It is needless for me to say to you, my dear Mrs. Alford, with what affectionate esteem I shall ever regard your husband's memory. Your daughters, who have now made you a grandmother, were little girls when I first knew you all, and your house was a pattern of domestic happiness and duty, an example to your pretty village of what a clergyman's household ought to be.

"The pleasure which your subsequent visits have given sufficiently show in what esteem you are still held; and indeed I think some of his parishioners did not sufficiently appreciate your husband until they felt the loss they had sustained by his removal from them. He is now removed from us all, but let us indulge the hope and the belief that it is not for ever, and with that prayer for you, I will conclude.

"Believe me, always your affectionate friend,

"HENRY FEARON."

CHAPTER VII.

1853—1857.

LONDON WORK—CRIMEAN WAR—TOUR TO THE PYRENEES—CONTROVERSY ON THE SABBATH QUESTION—TOUR IN SCOTLAND—REVISION OF PART OF THE AUTHORIZED VERSION OF THE NEW TESTAMENT—APPOINTED TO THE DEANERY OF CANTERBURY.

WE left Wymeswold on September 26, 1853. Our new home, 6, Upper Hamilton Terrace, St. John's Wood, was a semi-detached house, with a garden behind of sufficient size to afford us some recreation in the cultivation of our favourite flowers. The quietness of its situation was favourable to literary work, and the distance from Quebec Chapel (less than two miles) was not too great for a walk. Here we remained until our removal in June, 1857, to Canterbury.

His habit at this time was to rise about six in the morning, light his own fire in the study, and work there till one o'clock. I believe that an hour before breakfast was frequently assigned to the composition of sermons, and the rest of the morning to the Greek Testament; and in the afternoon he usually walked into town, visited the members of his congregation, went among the poor inhabitants of his district, though the care of them chiefly devolved on his curate, and occasionally attended committees, &c. If no engagement took him from home in the evening, and no unusual pressure of work compelled him to spend that time in his study, it was given to reading aloud to us.

Quebec Chapel is so called from the street in which it is situated, which was probably built about 1759, when the heroic death of General Wolfe was a recent national glory. It was a proprietary chapel, and its special distinction for many years was the attractive presence of a band of eminent professional singers. The lease of the chapel was purchased by the Rev. J. H. Gurney, Rector of St. Mary's, Bryanston Square, in whose large parish the chapel was situated, a man of remarkable generosity, truthfulness, and zeal. At considerable cost to himself he determined to place a portion of his parishioners under the pastoral care of a minister of their own, and to offer to the fashionable congregation who found it convenient to attend Quebec Chapel, something which might be not less attractive than elaborate music, and more effective in winning souls, and elevating the standard of religious attainments in the higher rank of life.

Mr. Gurney was not disappointed in the result of his experiment, as may be shown by the following letter which he wrote to my husband soon after the beginning of his ministry at Quebec Chapel:—

From the Rev. J. H. Gurney.

"That I should have acquired the disposal of Quebec Chapel, have found you, brought you there, is a chain of circumstances in which we cannot help recognizing a divine hand and purpose; and I look to your coming to Quebec Chapel as one of the happiest events in my ministerial life. If I were taken away speedily, among the thanksgivings of my death-bed, would be one most fervently offered, that I had been enabled to place a younger and abler man where he is likely to do so much good among my neighbours and parishioners. Glad I am of an opportunity of bringing you and such a post together. I shall be deeply thankful that a large portion of my flock, whom I could never before reach, have had the benefit of your ministrations for a time."

Two letters which my husband wrote to his intimate friend, the Rev. E. T. Vaughan, in the course of 1854, will show how from his own point of view he regarded his work in Quebec Chapel:—

"*Upper Hamilton Terrace, March* 12.

"Very welcome was the sight of your dear old handwriting, among a basket full of letters last night on my return from Plymouth, where I have been spending a week lecturing, to the great amendment of my health, which was getting jaded by London work. Since I last saw you I have had a winter of real trial among the poor of my district.

"You kindly inquire about my work, or works. My pulpit and district work is much to my liking. The Chapel is full, and the people seem attached, and kind and liberal in contributing to every good work. My morning congregation is, of course, *the* congregation, and for them I write my sermons, having begun with the year. But the afternoon congregation is the one which I love best, being my own child. It has increased from absolutely nothing to within a hundred or two of the morning. To them I do not preach but expound the Gospels; in fact expand my Greek Testament notes, a sort of thing in which, as you may imagine, I delight much. My district work is very interesting, and when our schools are once set on foot will be much more so. My situation, you must know, is no sinecure. I find it difficult to get time for my Greek Testament work amongst its duties. My mornings are uninterrupted, and I can then count on three or four clear hours, but my evenings I am obliged to give to sermon writing. I am going on Wednesday week, by old Mr. Cunningham's request, to preach at Harrow. Fanny and I dine and sleep at his house the night before; it will be an interesting occasion, as he tells me the boys are to come to church."

TO THE REV. E. T. VAUGHAN.

"*October* 15, 1854.

"I have never once regretted the step which brought me here; may I look on it as one of God's most signal mercies to me? It is a real joy to feel that I am able, in my present post, to be doing the Lord's work in a way congenial to my daily labours and studies. If you could look in on my afternoon congregation you would find me dealing forth to them something of which Stier's 'Reden Jesu' will give you the best idea, a mixture of comment and sermon, in which I greatly delight, and which I do hope is telling for good on some, who may do good to others. My morning sermons are collected in a little volume, which I forget whether I sent to you or not. If I have not done so, tell me, and I will immediately forward one to you. We really have some very nice people here, people amongst whom I think real good may be done by quietly pushing on the real thing, the root and ground of the matter, keeping clear of all party names and phrases. May God prosper my work for their good and His glory.

"As to study work, I am now vigorously at work at Vol. iii., just in the Galatians. I have an Edinburgh article in brewing, on the new version of some of the Epistles which the American Bible Union have put forth. I mean to go into the subject generally, the expediency of revision, how to be done, &c. At the same time I have an Exeter Hall lecture on the stocks, 'On the Intelligent Study of the Scriptures,' in which, among other matters more within the reach of the whole audience, I wish to give a stimulus to the Greek Testament classes just now beginning in the 'Christian Young Men's Society.'

"Once so many notes tripped backwards and forwards between us:—the longer I live the more I feel there is no friend like an old friend. No letter now-a-days ought altogether to omit mention of the solemn events which are passing around us.

"How wonderfully God has been dealing with us this year! Several of my people have been thrown into distress and mourning [1] by the recent conflict."

When he had been a few months at Quebec Chapel, Messrs. Rivington undertook to publish the sermons which he preached there. The first volume of his "Quebec Sermons" was accordingly published in the autumn. It contained

---

1 The battle of the Alma was fought on September 20th, 1854.

twenty-five sermons preached in the first half of the year. It was followed in due course by six other volumes[2].

While he was preparing the third volume of his Greek Testament, which was published in 1855, he was encouraged by a demand in May, 1854, for a second edition of his second volume.

This year he composed a Memoir of his father, the Rev. H. Alford, a volume of 259 octavo pages. It was intended for, and at first was limited to private circulation among the numerous members and friends of our family. This year was marked by the death, on March 22, of my father, the Rev. S. Alford, of Heale House. We were present with twenty-two other members of his family at the funeral at Curry Rivell. This is described in the following letter from my husband.

TO THE REV. J. H. HAMILTON.

"Though we had for some years been expecting my uncle's death, it came very unexpectedly at last; it is the end of our young lives, the taking the key-stone out of the family arch, the removal of the last apparent barrier between ourselves and the unseen world: last week we were one family, now we are thirteen families, twenty-five sons and daughters, thirty-eight grandchildren,—the whole family about seventy-eight, a mourner for each year he was old."

Though this event had the effect of secluding us from much general intercourse with the increasing circle of our acquaintance, my husband decided on giving us the opportunity of seeing the most remarkable spectacle of the season. On the 10th of June we went to the opening of the Crystal Palace at Sydenham, which he describes as "A magnificent sight, such as neither of us ever saw before, nor are likely to see again. The Queen, &c., &c., young King of Portugal, and all the grandees, and 1600 performers, Hallelujah Chorus. This world will never see such another sight." On the 29th

[2] A complete list of his works arranged in the order of their publication will be found in the Appendix at the end of this volume.

of the same month he records, "went with Lady Sitwell to the Harrow Speeches; Prince Albert and the Prince of Wales there, and all sorts of grandees; saw many old friends."

This summer our usual vacation was spent in the West of England. A few notes from his journal record its progress:—

"*Aug.* 7. Left London at nine by the express to Trowbridge; by fly to Winkfield, where we explored the old place; then to Farley Castle, by Tellisford to Westbury.

"*Aug.* 8.—After breakfast to Steeple Ashton, and looked up the old place, my father's first curacy; then over the hills, by the White Horse, to Frome and Wells.

"*Aug.* 9—Showed them the cathedral; to Glastonbury, and returned to Wells; then to Wookey, by Cheddar to Axbridge.

"*Aug.* 10—After breakfast to Cheddar Cliffs, where we spent a very pleasant morning, and then saw Banwell, and on by rail to Yatton.

"*Aug.* 11—To Brockley Combe, and Wraxall. The latter very much altered since my father and I lived there. The house pulled down. Got to Heale in the evening, perhaps our last visit to the dear old place.

"*Aug.* 12—After breakfast corrected proofs in the summer-house; heard of dear Eliza Martin's death,—so one goes after another; may I be ready when my time comes! O Lord, grant it for Christ's sake; read much of my uncle's journals, very nice Christian spirit and reflections.

"*Aug.* 14.—Heard from my curate that cholera is in our district; only one case as yet near Quebec Chapel. If it spreads I shall return. O Lord, if it be Thy will, preserve me and mine safe, and be merciful to my poor people.

"*Aug.* 17.—The whole five sisters met, and their belongings, &c. Sixteen at dinner: afterwards went to the top of the monument, and in the evening walked to Burton.

"*Aug.* 21.—After breakfast, in Tom's trap, with Brad to Ilminster; saw the church, &c., and dined at Mr. Allen's; he much broken in health. We went over Heron Hill, and I saw my name, H. A., 1826, on one of the trees. We went on to Charmouth in the evening; next day strolled on the beach and picked up fossils.

"*Aug.* 27.—Dr. Wolff preached at Curry; strange reading. Sermon rather striking on the Lord's Prayer.

"*Sept.* 1.—Went from Taunton, in a van, to a picnic to Castle Neroche. Lovely day, enjoyed it much. All planted now with wood. Last time I was there, 1825, not a tree.

"*Sept.* 6.—Correcting proof-sheets of my father's Memoir. Called at Oaklands, and on Mary Young, just the same as she was twenty years ago.

"*Sept.* 7.—Off to Bristol, bad accounts of the cholera, but not in our district. Glorious day, all but cloudless sunshine.

"As I was passing Brean Down [3], on the rail, I saw a dark shadow resting on the bare side of the hill; seeking its cause, I saw a little cloud, bright as light, floating in the clear blue above. Thus is it with our sorrow, it is dark and cheerless here on earth; but look above, and you shall see it to be but a shadow of His brightness, whose name is Love.

"*Sept.* 9.—Started in a steamer for Chepstow, thence to Tintern by Wine Cliff, returned in the evening. Letter from Mr. G. C. Lewis, accepting my article for the 'Edinburgh' for April next. From Bristol, 15th, we all four went for a day to Blaise Castle, to visit Mr.[4] and Mrs. Harford. In the morning we walked about the grounds and had some music. In the evening I expounded to them 1 Cor. xv.

"*Sept.* 23.—Returned to town.

"*Sept.* 25.—Saw a cholera patient.

"*Sept.* 28.—Went to the Young Men's Christian Association.

"*Sept.* 30.—Mr. Tarlton engaged me to lecture at Exeter Hall on 'The Intelligent Study of the Scriptures.'

"*Oct.* 3.—Begun Vol. iii. of my Greek Testament. May God prosper it, and spare me to finish it, if it be His will.

The death of our dear friend, Eliza Martin, which is

---

[3] This incident is mentioned in a sermon preached in Quebec Chapel a few weeks afterwards. Vol. ii. page 144, "Quebec Chapel Sermons."

[4] J. S. Harford, author of "The Life of Michael Angelo," in two volumes.

recorded above, took place at Dawlish. Previous to her marriage in 1852 she had shown signs of consumption. The beginning of the disease was traced to exposure to inclement weather and fatiguing work, during a visitation of cholera in 1851, when she was at Liverpool, where she voluntarily undertook and discharged, with perhaps too great zeal, the duties of a district visitor in connexion with the church of St. Martin. Notwithstanding all that medical skill, and the incessant attention of her husband could do for her, she sank gradually under the disease. We were about to return from our tour to visit her on her death-bed, when we received a message informing us that we could not arrive in time. We felt our parting from her as from a friend, whose ardent devotion, unselfishness, pure and lofty motives, never failed to encourage and cheer all who were included in her circle of acquaintance.

The vicissitudes of the Crimean War were watched by all classes with the deepest interest. My husband's journal records, that "on April 26, fast day for the war, we collected 231*l.* at the three services at Quebec Chapel." On October 1, the day the news of the battle of the Alma arrived, he preached a thanksgiving sermon for the harvest, and in a note referred to this event[5]. The short poem entitled "A Crimean Thought" ("Poems," p. 153), was written about this time.

Three weeks later, October 22, he records:—

"Preached at Quebec Chapel from 'Thy will be done in earth, as it is in heaven.' Mr. and Mrs. Bracebridge at church, and Mr. Nightingale; they spoke to me about making some prayers for the nurses who go out to attend the wounded in the Crimea. Mr. and Mrs. Bracebridge and Miss Nightingale go out to-morrow. I sent the prayers to Mrs. Bracebridge. O may God bless my unworthy work!" And two days afterwards he attended a meeting to raise a fund for supporting Chaplains at the seat of war.

---

[5] "Quebec Chapel Sermons," vol. ii. page 110.

A sermon which he preached, November 19, on "Render, therefore, unto Cæsar the things which are Cæsar's, and unto God the things that are God's" (Matt. xxii. 21 [6]), made such an impression on his hearers, that he was requested to print it for circulation among the troops in the Crimea.

The following letter relates to a subject which often engaged his thoughts—the imperfect acquaintance of the educated classes with the text of the New Testament. He made many efforts to procure a general acknowledgment of this defect, and to remove it. The plan was never fully carried out which was broached in this letter. The gentleman to whom it was addressed was a graduate of St. John's College, Cambridge, who had long been engaged in educational work at Bristol.

TO JOHN PRICE, ESQ.

"*June* 12, 1854.

"I have been thinking over a subject on which we had some conversation, the possibility of doing something for the study of the New Testament in Greek here in London; the object seems to me more and more important, and I do think some movement in the direction might be made. A scheme has struck me on which I should much like to hear what you say; I have not yet broached it to any one else. It has struck me that an institution, or association, or society, might be formed for the promotion of the study of the New Testament in the original Greek. The work of such an institution would be to open classes and give lectures on the Greek Testament to persons of various proficiency, in the first place. If it could be established and prosper, I think it might aim higher and assume more of the character of a learned society, making research and giving papers to be read at its meetings. But this latter is a mere offshoot from my present scheme. I wish you would

6 "Quebec Chapel Sermons," vol. ii. pp. 194, 263.

kindly give me your impression of such a project. Of its usefulness I have not the shadow of a doubt, and its practicability might soon be ascertained. If I move in it, my next step would be to distribute privately a few circulars among persons who may be supposed interested in the object, to ascertain their opinions and get their advice. After that, a private meeting might be held, and a more extensive canvass organized; and when we had provided a sufficient array of names, we might in some shape come before the public. I am not given to castle-building, but it does seem to me that great good might be done in this way by diffusing the knowledge of the Greek Testament."

He endeavoured, not without some ultimate success, to suggest a step towards carrying out his views in a lecture which he thus records in his journal. It will be seen further on in the Memoir that classes of this character were established in connexion with Quebec Chapel, and in connexion with the Young Men's Association, although no distinct institution was ever founded:—

"*Dec.* 19.—We all went to Exeter Hall. My lecture on 'The Intelligent Study of the Scriptures' went off well; voice, thank God, held out fairly. I only hope it may issue in an effort for knowing God's Word better."

At the end of the year he made this entry in his journal:—

"*Dec.* 1854.—This year has been an eventful one to myself, as well as in a public point of view. In it, it has pleased God to bring me into a prominent post of duty and usefulness which is full of promise for good. My great work has been, it is true, somewhat delayed by this, but a greater work is, I would fain hope, being carried on amongst my people and by lectures. I am employed in putting forward the study and knowledge of God's word amongst various classes of persons. I would go about this work cautiously, not in the eager spirit of a partisan, but as working surely for God. I believe I am soon to have a Greek class in the Young Men's Christian Association, and I think there will be no great difficulty in getting one among my own people.

"My second volume of 'Sermons' is in the press, the first

having sold well. May I make them an instrument for good. During the next year I must give attention to reading if I would keep up the efficacy of my preaching. Δοξά τῷ Θεῷ."

The beginning of 1855 was a season of unusual severity. Great distress among the poor included in the Quebec district, occasioned proportionate efforts by their clergyman and his congregation to alleviate their sufferings. About the same time my husband found himself involved in additional secular business in consequence of the death of my mother, who soon followed to the grave her husband, the Rev. S. Alford, of Heale House. In my husband's early days she had been as a mother to him during his long and frequent visits to Heale House, and she was beloved by him for that reason, as well as for the remarkable unselfishness and amiability of her character.

Early in the spring of this year it became known to him that some of his friends had spontaneously applied in his behalf for the Rectory of All Souls', Marylebone, which was vacant, and in the gift of the Crown. Shortly afterwards he received from the Lord Chancellor Cranworth the offer of the lucrative living of Tydd St. Mary's, Lincoln, which, if he had accepted it, would have removed him from that access to books and intercourse with scholars which were essential to his Biblical studies. He briefly describes in his journal his visit to the Lord Chancellor on this occasion:—" When I asked to see his lordship, the servant said his master was engaged. I then said, 'I am not come to ask for any thing, but to refuse something offered.' 'O, sir, then I am sure he will see you,' was the reply."

The Lord Chancellor was an occasional attendant at the services in Quebec Chapel. But my husband had no acquaintance with him until they met half a year afterwards under the hospitable roof of Lord Cranworth's brother-in-law, Sir Culling Eardley, at Belvedere, near Erith.

These incidents in some degree caused us to feel unsettled in our home: and he wrote thus to his friend, the Rev. E. T. Vaughan, with reference to the Rectory of All Souls':—

"*May* 2, 1855.—I have been a long time answering your kind letter because I wanted to tell you about a matter which has kept me in some uncertainty now for nearly six weeks; to-day I have heard of its decision, and in a way of which I am very glad. The matter is this: Mr. Baring is resigning the Rectory of All Souls', and I was pointed out by various persons as his successor. For some time I doubted very much about accepting it, but at length I determined on many grounds if offered to go there. I need not detail all my reasons to you, but you will readily imagine some of them. Quebec Chapel is, I feel, more and more a dangerous position for one's own inner life, the sort of soldier-of-fortune character of it would corrupt an angel with pride; and it sadly wants the ballast of a parish to keep down its holder. But I have heard they cease to think of me, on account of my Greek Testament and because of my work at Quebec Chapel, so I have the prospect now of going on in peace with my Vol. iii., for the sake of which I should have regretted the change. And I have the far greater satisfaction of feeling that He who fixes the bounds of our habitation, has thus allotted me my place in which to work for Him. May I be able, if it be His will, to finish my work before the night comes."

My husband's attention, however, was not diverted from his ordinary work, and he continued to take a special interest in the efforts which were made by Lord Shaftesbury and others for sending out well qualified nurses to the seat of war in the Crimea.

Early in this year he received from the Rev. C. J. Ellicott (now Bishop of Gloucester and Bristol), a copy of his Commentary on the Epistle to the Galatians. This present, warmly acknowledged by my husband at the time as from a fellow-labourer in the elucidation of the sacred text, led first to an interview, and then to a friendship which lasted unbroken for sixteen years.

The work and anxieties of the summer[7] began to tell on

---

7 Just before leaving London, his journal says, "Went to Maidenhead with Mr. Gurney's schools, our Quebec children being included, 960; beautiful day; all returned in safety."

my husband's health, and he formed the project of a family tour to the Pyrenees. He amused himself with preparing for it by reading and making extracts of various authors, from the time of Strabo downwards, who refer to the places which he intended to visit. We left London at the end of July, a party of five (for my husband's young brother, Mr. B. H. Alford, just matriculated at Cambridge, went with us), and though the tour was marked by two adverse events, loss of health to one of the party, and a robbery, it was always remembered as one of the happiest of our vacations. My husband wrote a careful journal of considerable length, some extracts from which may be of interest:—

"We took with us to read on the spot 'The Subaltern,' that most interesting little book written some thirty years ago by the Chaplain-General of the Forces [Rev. G. R. Gleig], who, when a young man, was in the campaign in the Pyrenees 1813—1814.

"Got to Paris exactly twelve hours from London. After coffee sallied out to Place de la Concorde; beautiful as ever, nay more so, under the brightest rays of a clear moon; from the Pont de la Concorde, a lovely scene up the river, the moon on the water, the dark mass of the Tuileries on the left, and the dome of the Institute on the right, while in the distance the towers of Notre Dame rose faintly bright against the sky, a view never to be forgotten. Louis Napoleon has much improved and beautified Paris, and it is nowhere more visible than here, where vast masses of new buildings are rising, all in an imposing and grand style. . . . . On our way to Orleans we saw the castle of Malliéry on a peaked hill to the right.

"We ascended the cathedral at Orleans. The view extensive over the flat valley of the Loire; saw in the distance Notre Dame de Clery, where Louis XI. carried on his superstitions and was buried. To Blois through vineyards, with occasional glimpses of the Loire.

"From Blois we went to the Château of Chambord, dull drive through many avenues of poplars and over sandy plains; at last the towers of the old château came into view at the end of a dusty road over a heath. The château is very interesting, as being in the style of the old palaces of France—a huge central tower carrying a double staircase, flanked by round corner towers in every direction: inside are the devices of several kings, Francis I. with his salamander, Henry II. with the crescent of Diana de Poitiers, &c. . . . . The old castle at Blois, since I last saw it in 1843 with Merivale, has been to my mind altogether spoilt, by being restored to its old state of splendour by Louis Philippe. . . . . From Tours we went to Plessis, the scene of much of 'Quentin Durward:' not much of the old castle remaining; we saw the prison of Cardinal de Balue in the garden. To Poitiers, through a rich but uninteresting country. The place is finely situated on a high hill, promenades on the ramparts. The cathedral, Notre Dame de Poitiers, is very curious indeed, earliest Byzantine, full of quaint sculptures. Left Poitiers at half-past five for Angoulême; a striking approach, situated like Poitiers on a hill, surrounded by a deep valley containing the Charente. At Angoulême is the curious Romanesque grotto of St. Agbard, also a castle. On our way to Bordeaux we saw several old châteaux, and the famous iron-wire suspension bridge here thrown over the Dordogne. The sight of Bordeaux, lighted up along its immense length by the lights reflected in its river, very striking. Spent Sunday, August 5th, at Bordeaux. The cathedral is a fine building, built by the English in Edward III.'s time. We were too late for the high mass, but saw a low mass, the service utterly without meaning to the poor wretched people; enjoyed our 'reasonable service' in our own room very much, afterwards; then to the Protestant Church service, where we heard some very simple catechizing by the pastor, the greatest possible contrast to the service in the cathedral. We walked out in the evening, and saw all manner of amusements going on in the Jardin Publique: this solution of the Sunday question will not do in England, but solved it must be some day.

"Next day we took a carriage, and went about to see the

town; cathedral interesting. We mounted the Tour de Pey Berland to get a bird's-eye view of the town. In the vaults under it we saw many human bodies, which, from some property in the air or the stone, have remained in perfect preservation. Horrid sight.

"Saw the large wine-vaults of M. Cuzol et Fils, to whom Mr. Wace, of Baker Street, had given me a card. After dinner we took a boat and rowed down to Lormont, on the other side. Walked up a hill, and from a garden, belonging to some people who civilly let us pass through their house for the purpose, got a glorious view of the Garonne and confluence of the Dordogne, with the sunset glow on the water. We did not reach the city till long after dark. Beautiful approach; lights twinkling in the river.

"Left next day by train at six. Ride very extraordinary through the Landes; wild, uncultivated heath, with large pools of water. Saw some peasants on stilts knitting. The dreariest place I ever saw; black sand ankle deep, and almost a natural horizon in all directions. As soon as we reached Bayonne we got into an omnibus for Biarritz, up and down hills of straight road, but interesting country; fine trees and clustering vines. At last we took a turn, and came down on the blue Bay of Biscay, tumbling in foaming waves on a wild, fantastic coast. The sands were full of bathers in costumes of bright colours.

"I sketched the rocks and the Emperor's château, and we returned to Bayonne in time for the *table-d'hôte*, and in the evening walked up to the citadel, and saw the spot of the famous passage of the Adour by the Duke of Wellington, and where the sortie of infamous memory by the French took place [on April 14, 1814: see Alison's 'History of Europe,' vol. xviii. p. 280]. The view is very interesting. South-east the lower spurs of the Pyrenees reach down towards the sea; south lies the town, with its bridges and churches; south-west the Adour, rich in remembrances to an Englishman.

"We started next morning for St. Sebastian, passing St. Jean de Luz, on to the Bidassoa, with Fontarabia on the

Spanish side, and Hendaye on the French side. This I sketched, also the heights of St. Marcial, looking up the Bidassoa from Behobie, and that curious land-locked harbour at Passages.

"St. Sebastian is a very singular place, with very narrow streets and high houses. It has been entirely rebuilt since 1813 [see Alison, vol. xvi. chap. 77]. It is grandly situated at the foot of the high hill on which the citadel is built. We went with our landlord to see the grand breach where, in 1813, the city was first entered more than forty years ago, just about this time of the year, and where so many of our countrymen fell. We saw the tombs of several of our officers half way up the hill, which I sketched on the spot. [See "Quebec Chapel Sermons," vol. iii. page 292.]

"At Pau we saw the castle in which Henry IV. was born, redecorated by Louis Philippe. After Pau we went to Eaux Chaudes, a curious little group of houses, presided over by the manager of the baths. The journey was very interesting, gradually more and more hilly, with vineyards and flowers.

"After Sévigac we got a grand view of the Val d'Ossau. The gorge leading to Eaux Chaudes is very fine, a torrent tumbling below the road. The road from Eaux Chaudes to Gabas is most striking. First, boxwood, firs, rocks, and cascades; then widening, higher mountains, firs in patches, and snow above.

"Next day, there being a fête at Laruns, we could get no horses; so we went to the fête, and saw young men and women, in the brightest costumes, dancing in the market-place to a monotonous tune played on a zittern. I took a sketch of the scene, and took down the tune.

"Started at six next morning on horses for Cauterets, through the gorge, and up the bare mountain. Weather glorious. Over the Col de Tortes; very steep. Some boys with sheep's milk met us at the top. We walked down the steepest part; it was most lovely, with oxlips close to the snow, and gentians, auriculas, saxifrage, &c. We crossed the Col d'Arrens, then on to Val d'Arzun, and a bit of level road just as we came to Cauterets. Eleven hours on horseback: a hard day for us all.

"Next morning we started for Pont d'Espagne. Very fine indeed. At the Cascade La Cerex a most lovely rainbow we saw; then under the Vignauale, a first-rate mountain, with its glaciers; and that melancholy little lake, Lac de Gaube[8].

"*Sunday, Aug.* 19.—Came here (Luz) yesterday from Cauterets down the gorge to Pierrefitte, then up a gorge to this place. . . . Service in our room, then strolled to St. Sauveur, and wrote half a sermon sitting on some rocks. Off at six next morning for Gavarnie on horseback. We came soon to a curious double bridge; it then got finer and finer. High mountains on each side of the gorge. At Gedres the clouds cleared as we approached Gavarnie, where we breakfasted in a châlet, and then to see the very glorious cascade—wonderful, far finer than the Staubbach; no words can describe its magnificence. We got a glimpse of the Brêche de Roland. . . . Barèges is a wretched place. We went along the torrent of the Bastan, a desolate valley, and at the foot of the Tourmalat turned to the left, and climbed the Pic du Midi de Bigorre; stiff work for the horses, and rather perilous. Splendid view at the top, where we lunched. The Pyrenean mountains are inferior to the Alps. We walked down, but mounted our horses to cross the Tourmalat. Some of our party were not well, and at Grip we were very glad to have a carriage to take us to Bagnères de Bigorre, where we stayed a day to rest ourselves; and then on, up the valley of the Adour, to Arreau, a village approached by zigzags. Thence we had splendid views, and watched a storm gathering over the Maladetta, and at eight got to Luchon."

[The whole party halted at Luchon on account of my illness, and we did not quit the place till September 10. In

---

[8] A small lake, about two miles and a half in circumference, said to be the largest in the Pyrenees. He calls this lake melancholy, because near the châlet, on a rock, is a white marble monument to the memory of Mr. and Mrs. Patterson, a young barrister and his wife, who in 1831 were drowned here on their wedding tour, having gone alone on the lake in a boat. It was some time before their bodies were found. See a poem of Lord Houghton's on this subject, called, "A Tragedy of the Lac de Gaube in the Pyrenees."

the interval, however, many little expeditions were made, as appears by the following notes.]

"*Aug.* 24.—Three of us on horseback back to the Val de Lys; very beautiful valley, rich in forests, and at the head a grand snowy mountain with glaciers.

"*Aug.* 30.—To the Lac d'Oo, and reached it, but we had a storm of rain; the way there very striking; wooded valley, with torrents; the cascade fine, but no adjuncts.

"*Aug.* 31.—Part of the way up Super Bagnères on foot; a very fine ramble; we got ferns, and caught a large yellow-black lizard [now in the possession of Dr. Mitchinson, of Canterbury].

"*Sept.* 1.—Walked to Montauban; saw the garden and cascades; petty and artificial, but pretty. The Dean and Mrs. Milman, Sir Henry and Lady Holland, are here.

"*Sunday, Sept.* 9.—To the English service. I preached in the morning from Matt. x. 32, 33, and Mr. Milman intoned. Afternoon I did the whole service. A most violent thunderstorm.

"*Sept.* 10.—Left with much regret, yet glad to get away. Stopped to dine at St. Bertrand de Comminges, where there is a most curious old cathedral."

[Here is a gap in the journal which I must supply. On the 10th we slept at a small inn without unpacking our luggage, which was strapped behind our carriage. Next day (11th) we passed through St. Gaudens, where we stopped to dine. Long after dark we reached Toulouse, which was illuminated on account of the fall of Sebastopol. Great was our dismay, when we ordered our luggage to be sent up, to find that all our money had been stolen. A hole had been made in my husband's knapsack, and it had been emptied. Happily for us, the money was in circular notes which, of course, were of no use to the thieves[9].

"*Sept.* 12.—Awakened at five by infinite clatter of market women in the place outside. At eight went to the Capitole

---

[9] Nearly every thing they had stolen from us was found some months afterwards in the thieves' house, and restored to us in London.

about my unfortunate luggage. Went to the Palais de Justice, and there saw commissaires, and was questioned by the Procureur Impériale.

"Coutoir, the banker (most kindly, though I was a perfect stranger, and without a passport, for the thieves had taken it), immediately let me have 20*l.* in French money, and advised me to telegraph to my London banker, Barnett and Hoare, which I did, and in six hours an answer came.

"Toulouse is an old town, for the most part irregularly built; streets narrow, and houses high. We saw in the Capitole the throne-room where Napoleon and Josephine held their levées, and the Duke of Wellington afterwards; and we saw, too, the court where the Duke de Montmorency was beheaded by order of Richelieu. A short distance from Toulouse we saw the Obelisk to commemorate the battle. After leaving the department of Haute Garonne, and entering that of Aude, a miserable difference for the worst in the roads. We did not reach Carcassonne till late. The stars are beautiful in this southern climate. I noticed that the Great Bear was much lower than it ever is in England. Carcassonne is a very curious old town. The fortifications of several different periods running round the top of a wooded hill; a fine old church, pure Byzantine; choir flamboyant, with some fine painted glass. There was a curious well, into which the Visigoths were said to have thrown their treasures.

"The country beyond Carcassonne began soon to alter, and put on a more southern character; olives soon made their appearance, and the grapes were ripe; then the road became arid and dusty; low hills, bare and rocky, approached the road, and this scenery continued till we came near Narbonne. It is impossible to imagine a bleaker situation than that of Narbonne as approached from the west; the whole country is whitened with dust—olives, grapes, figs—all as if powdered with flour. The cathedral at Beziers is the scene of the slaughter of the Albigenses. There is a striking view from the terrace in front; a rich plain, full of vines and olives, stretching to the Cevennes mountains, beautifully dappled with the morning sun and shades. . . . As we came near Montpelier some beautiful views of the blue Mediterranean. We saw here first the grapes being trodden out by men with naked feet. Splendid sunset, colours more brilliant and distinct than I ever remember having seen them, except perhaps at Venice.

"*Sept.* 16.—Sunday at Montpelier. Heard the day is set apart throughout France for a great *jour de fête,* on account of the taking of Sebastopol. We had service in our room, and went out in the evening to see the illuminations. Next day by train to Nismes, where we saw the Amphitheatre and Maison Carrée. It is difficult to describe the interesting points of these splendid remains; the Amphitheatre is perfect in circumference, here and there broken and ruined in detail, but still in good preservation enough to have accommodated 30,000 persons at a bull-fight. Within, all the fittings-up are still in a great measure perfect; the whole is a vast monument of that wonderful people with whom 'panem et circenses' was the secret of colonial as of urban government. From the Amphitheatre we went to the Maison Carrée, whose beauty must be seen for any idea to be formed of it: it is indeed an exquisite gem, never to be forgotten. There is among the old paths in the public gardens, a very interesting round temple of Diana. The antiquities at Arles are on a much larger scale than those at Nismes, but not in such good preservation. The cathedral has a beautiful porch, and an exquisite cloister; transition from Classic to Christian architecture. At Avignon we went to the Hotel Palais Royal, the same house in which Marshal Brune was assassinated. In the cathedral is a very curious portico, almost like a pagan temple.

"At Orange we saw the Arch of Triumph spanning the road, probably built to celebrate a victory over some allies of Hannibal in the second Punic War. The theatre here is a vast and most interesting ruin. We mounted the hill in which it is excavated, and saw an exquisite view from the top; the plain of the Rhone, for many miles fertile, and dappled with towers and houses; to the east, the lower spurs of the Alps. The colour and character of the landscape surpassed any thing I had ever anticipated.

"Next day to see the Pont du Gard, crossing the two branches of the Rhone, magnificent views over the valley of the Rhone—yellow vineyards, grey olives, and rocks sloping down to the valley, a few dark cypresses spire up among the vines, and like landmarks give distance to the foreground. The valley itself is all luxuriance and richness, full of timber and divided by the full glittering Rhone; beyond are the lower spurs of the Alps, bright and distinct against the sky, and over all the delicious climate pencilling and painting all objects with its clear pearly atmosphere; as we mount higher, Avignon itself comes out from behind a hill all reflected in the glassy stream.

"The Pont du Gard is 120 feet above the stream. The sun came out as we sat looking at the bridge and lit it up with a warm yellow colour, which, with the blue sky behind, produced a lovely effect. Early next morning to Vaucluse. The fountain is in a dark cleft of some bare limestone hills much resembling the Mendip chain. The water in the stream is the brightest and clearest I ever saw: vivid green; every pebble at whatever depth clearly seen, and every leaf of the water-plants as distinctly. As we advanced the water tumbles over large loose rocks, then one part of it and another comes to its source, rushing out from under the rocks on each side until the whole at this season of the year is exhausted, and nothing is left but a chaos of large rocks covered with black dry moss, very strange. Under a huge limestone rock is a great cavernous opening, above which grow two or three wild fig-trees, marking the spot to which the waters reach in winter when they tumble in a cascade over the black rocks. Then we made our way back, and collected many roots of the beautiful maiden-hair fern.

"On our route to Lyons the most interesting points were the Château of Mornas, whence the Baron des Audrets made his Catholic prisoners leap the famous Pont St. Esprit, the longest stone bridge in the world; Pierrelatte, with its isolated rock; Viviers, a cathedral on a rock over the Rhone, and its town clustering round it. Montelimart, the metropolis of the silk-worm district, Livron and Loriol, one on each side of the Drome, up which is seen the majestic mass of La Roche Courbe, and other grand mountains, bounded on the east by large dark limestone cliffs, serried by yellow water-courses. Thus we passed Vienne, and thus we approached the lights of Lyons twinkling far up in the sky.

"At Lyons we mounted the 580 steps of Notre Dame des Fourvières, whence a magnificent view of the city and the river for many miles; the mountains of Switzerland, Italy, Auvergne, Dauphiné, and the Jura. From Lyons, through Dijon and Sens, to Fontainebleau, which Fanny and I saw last in 1837. Louis Philippe has half spoilt it by restoring the faded old rooms, and Louis Napoleon has removed one of the most interesting things in it—the table on which Napoleon I. signed his abdication; however, we were much struck with the old place, and had a nice drive in the forest. The rocks are like those at Tonbridge Wells; in some parts very fine trees: one oak, called 'Le Bouquet du Roi,' eighty feet of straight stem before it branches off. . .

"At Paris I found I was placarded to preach at the Oratoire on Sunday. Spent our time in sight-seeing. We thoroughly examined the Louvre, and I was much struck by the excellent classification and arrangement there. To the Exposition to see the pictures—some of the best pictures at present in Europe. . . . . England cuts but a very sorry figure, in my opinion, except in portraits. On Sunday 30th, at eight, went to help at the early communion at the Oratoire. Then finishing my sermon[1], which I preached at two. It was a thanksgiving-day for the fall of Sebastopol. Good congregation. Collection for the widows and orphans of those who had been killed. October 3rd.—Home, thank God. A very

[1] The text was St. Luke xiv. 11. The sermon was printed in "Quebec Chapel Sermons," vol. vii. No. 18.

rough passage. Did not reach Hamilton Terrace till after one o'clock."

After our return, the last three months of the year were spent in ordinary work. He was engaged in writing the Commentary on the Epistle to the Ephesians and Colossians included in the third volume of the Greek Testament, and in seeing through the press the third edition of the first volume. His journal records a party at which he met "Mr. Ruskin, very interesting and original;" a perusal of "'Maude;' very remarkable poem, but it is a pity that Tennyson does not labour at something greater;" his lecture in Exeter Hall on St. Paul; his going to Windsor Castle as one of the deputation who presented an address to Victor Emmanuel, King of Sardinia; and his attending a meeting under the auspices of the Society for the Propagation of the Gospel, at which it was resolved to build a Memorial Church at Constantinople.

At the end of the year his closing reflection is:—"Of many mercies this year, the chief has been the sparing my darling wife's life in her serious illness, and so far restoring her precious sight. 'Praise the Lord, O my soul, and all that is within me praise His holy name.'"

The first half of 1856 passed without any unusual incident. His journal shows that he was engaged in his Commentary on the Pastoral Epistles of St. Paul, and the first edition of the third volume was completed before the end of July. All the sermons contained in the third volume of his "Quebec Chapel Sermons" were composed and printed within the same period. Amongst them is included one (Sermon xxii., On the Perils of Unlawful Gain) which attracted considerable notice at the time, and was printed separately.

During this time he gave much attention to the concerns of a reformatory. His journal records his pleasure in meeting several persons of intellectual distinction at the hospitable houses of members of his congregation: as Mr. Hallam, at Mr. C. Buxton's; Lord Elgin and Lord Dufferin, at the Duke of Argyll's; Lord Stanhope, at Mr. Caldwell's, &c.

Soon after the Proclamation (April 2) of peace between

Russia and the Western powers, he preached a thanksgiving sermon (Vol. iii. Sermon xxiii.), and the collections on that day in Quebec Chapel amounted to 253*l*. for the Memorial Church at Constantinople.

Early in June he went with the Cambridge "Deputation to Buckingham Palace to the Queen with an address on the Peace. Her answer was read beautifully; great crowd, and most undignified squeeze in the presence."

He continued his habitual attendance on the Committees of the Society for the Propagation of the Gospel, and of the Foreign Translation Fund of the Society for Promoting Christian Knowledge. Besides ordinary work in connexion with Quebec Chapel, he gave much attention to a singing class and to a class of ladies whom he instructed in the rudiments of Greek, with a view to their becoming able to read the New Testament in the original language. In the course of a year he carried them through some chapters of St. John's Gospel, explaining every word grammatically. This class met every Wednesday afternoon in the vestry of Quebec Chapel. I may here mention that when he left London in 1857, he was presented by the members of this class with a time-piece of red Devonshire marble, two bronze vases and a dog, which he acknowledged in the following letter to Mrs. Manning, one of the givers.

"Pray let me convey through you my most hearty thanks to my kind Hellenistic friends for their very beautiful present. I ought to be well up in my tenses, with a clock to mark time, two urns to bury it in, and a dog to keep watch over it. I assure you all four shall adorn my chimney-piece in the Deanery Library. I only should like to assemble my class again in front of it, and give them another dose of Greek in our mellow Kentish air. Once more, dear friends, with very pleasant recollections of the past both aorist and perfect, lively sympathy with the present, best wishes for the future, and earnest prayers for the second future, I heartily thank you all,

"Yours, in the bonds of lasting remembrance,

"HENRY ALFORD."

There was also a young men's class which studied under his direction with the same object. They met every Friday evening in Aldersgate Street; from them also he received a handsome and useful present when we left London.

Early in 1856 he was forced to enter on a personal controversy. He records in February his attendance at "a meeting of clergy about opening the Crystal Palace and Public Galleries on Sundays: J. H. Gurney made a noble speech." The proposal for such opening of places of amusement was opposed by the speakers on different grounds, according to their views of the obligation of the fourth commandment. To correct misrepresentations of his own opinion he printed two letters to J. Sperling, Esq., on the Lord's Day Question. In the first he thus states his view of the Lord's Day, which he declines to call the Sabbath. "The Lord's Day is an ordinance of the Christian Church, which has gradually grown up from Apostolic usage, and is binding on Christian men as a matter of religious order and humane provision for rest and for worship; but it has absolutely nothing to do with the Paradisaical Sabbath: and to maintain their identity is, in my view, not only indicative of ignorance of the constitution of man in Christ, but absolutely anti-Christian in tendency."

In the second letter he refers to a newspaper which had accused him of ministering disingenuously at the Communion Table when he read the Fourth Commandment, and had pronounced him "unfit to remain in the Church of England." He answers,—

"I utterly deny the charge of disingenuousness. I read the Ten Commandments in the sense in which I consider all Christian ministers must read them—in their Christian sense, as necessarily interpreted for us by the light of Christ's Gospel, which has not destroyed but fulfilled them, deepening their meaning and binding on us more solemnly the eternal truths which they enforce, while at the same time it has removed from them all mere local and temporary references."

And he supports his view by quotations from the Church Catechism, the Confession of Augsburg, Luther's Commentary on Galatians, Calvin's Institutes, Cranmer, Becon, Thorndike, and Jeremy Taylor. The article in which he was thus accused was full of personal vituperation, being one of a series by which (as he was informed by a trustworthy person) it was intended by the proprietors of the newspaper to "write him down." He comments on this in language which perhaps might apply in some degree to other publications besides that at which it was levelled. "It is the deliberate conviction of the writer, founded on long experience of hearts embittered, love between good men chilled, ungrounded suspicion sown, and mischief occasioned by slander and falsehood in parishes and families, that this paper has done and is doing more to hinder the spread among us of 'the mind which was in Christ,' and the progress of His work, than all the infidel publications of our time put together. Their evil influence, sad as it is, affects for the most part those without; its evil influence is exerted over those who are Christians in heart and life." He goes on to invite men of piety in the Evangelical party to put forth a manly expression of their opinions respecting the course followed by the newspaper, or, "better still, let the paper cease from its present practices and learn to write in truth and love, then would all good men hail it, whether they agreed with or differed from its peculiar sentiments, as a fellow-worker in God's cause and a furtherer, instead of a hinderer of those things which are true and lovely and of good report." His fearless reply had at least one good effect: it was followed by a cessation of the series of personal articles.

A good illustration of his way of spending Sunday, amid the difficult circumstances of an Italian tour, is afforded by a passage in his "Letters from Abroad," pp. 184—187, written in 1864.

About the end of March he spent a week among old friends at the Rectory of Loughborough and in its neighbourhood.

His principal recreation was a sojourn for two months in Scotland, whither we went in July 28th. Our retreat was a little cottage at the side of a hill near Pitlochrie, Perth. "The first Sunday," he says, "was very wet; so we had in the poor people round, and gave them a service after their own fashion, singing too, there being one of their hymn books in the cottage. This service I continued all the time I stayed there, and every Sunday (being asked by Lord Effingham) we all went to Pitlochrie, and I gave the English in the neighbourhood an English Episcopal Service. So I have not much rest in that way in Scotland."

"*Aug.* 27.—Made an expedition to see Balmoral from Braemar with Miss Leycester and Mrs. Hare and her son. We four went in a dog-cart drawn by two piebald ponies, who did not like the new bridge as we approached Balmoral, and darted off at a furious pace, and we were very nearly having an accident close to Her Majesty's Lodge. Most happily, Mrs. Hare's coachman and the people at the lodge made a line across the road and stopped the little spirited things. Balmoral is a large, imposing mass of buildings: we took several sketches. On September 22nd we left our cottage, and after seeing Taymouth Castle, Glencoe, Oban, &c., returned by Inverary, Loch Tyne, Loch Katrine, and the Trossachs, to the Macnaughtens at Invertrossachs, where we spent a few most pleasant days; and home by Stirling and Edinburgh, making an expedition to Roslin Chapel, which is very beautiful."

The following letter was written whilst we were in Scotland to our intimate and valued friend Mrs. Speir (afterwards Mrs. Manning), authoress of a well-known book on Ancient India.

"*Dunfallandy, Pitlochrie, Aug.* 6, 1856.

"Many thanks for your letter received yesterday; the weather has been perfectly tropical since we have been here, and the days are so long, that there is no end of strolling, and sitting out of doors; we spent a day in sight-seeing in Edinburgh; from Perth we took a drive to see the view from

Moncrieff Hill, which is very fine; at Dunkeld, we saw highland games which were going on. All the world in kilts, plenty of kneeology, and that in Presbyterian Scotland. We went over the Duke of Athol's grounds; very pretty, most luxuriant timber, which I had not expected so far north. They took us to see a waterfall, for which we should not have turned our heads in passing last summer in the Pyrenees. On Thursday we came on here; ours is the merest little cottage, the whole house, chimneys and all, would go into a Portman Square drawing-room. It is literally 'In my cottage near a wood,' under a great heather-clad glen-intersected hill, itself on a grassy knoll, commanding a view up and down the vale of the Tummel for many miles. Here we are as quiet as we please, walking, fishing (without any result except pleasant explorations as yet); we have been up to Killiecrankie, to Tummel Bridge, a very lovely and at last wild ridge. Fanny sketches all day, I occasionally, as leisure serves, as I am correcting proof-sheets. We are all very well and enjoying ourselves vastly; the air is very fine here, at least it provokes immense consumption of oat-cakes and Scotch broth, and smells of all manner of mountain flowers. Your pictorial apparatus is in constant use, not yet by me, but I mean to attack it in a few days."

To the same lady he wrote, a few weeks later, when the weather had changed, a poetical letter, which is to be found in his "Poems," p. 330.

The following letter was written from Scotland to the Rev. H. Fearon, Rector of Loughborough, in answer to an invitation:—

"*September* 4.

"It would give me great pleasure to spend a few days with you, and rub up our social sympathies among our old friends, not excepting the clan Kingston, of whose Chief, I trust it may still be said, Στρύττ αὐτὸν καλέουσι θεοὶ ἄνδρες δέ Βέλπερ.

"Well, here we are in a very pretty place in the valley of Strath of the Tummel, just below the Pass of Killiecrankie, where, you remember, Claverhouse fell. We might have plenty of amusement in glen and hill and lake, were we not persecuted by the most execrable weather, clouds, rain, and wind every day. We went last week to Braemar and Balmoral; it is a fine wild country, possessing nothing to be called a mountain to one who has been to North Wales, say nothing of the Alps and Pyrenees;—they are all mere upland hills."

On our return to London, he began the Fourth and last Volume of his Commentary on the Greek Testament, beginning with the Epistle to the Hebrews and ending with Revelation. At the same time he entered, in conjunction with four clerical friends, on the work of revising certain books of the Authorized Version of the New Testament. The Rev. W. G. Humphry, Vicar of St. Martin's in the Fields, who took part in this work, has kindly written the following account of it.

"The Rev. Nugent Wade[1], who for many years has acted and still, as you know, acts as Secretary to our Clerical Club, has fortunately preserved a record of the conversation in which the work of the 'Five Clergymen' took its origin. The entry made by him in his journal of the proceedings of the club is as follows:—

"'May 7, 1856, the club met at Cook's; and all were present, viz. Hawkins, Kempe, Howarth, Maurice, Ayre, Hamilton, Humphry, Alford, Brookfield, Wordsworth, and Wade. The question of the desirableness of a new translation of the Scriptures was discussed. The objections to any move at the present time were considered. Mr. Humphry suggested that a revised translation might be made by six of the ablest scholars of each University acting in concert; that such a publication would be highly beneficial, at all events to the clergy, and would be a safe mode of ventilating the subject; in this opinion all concurred. The subject was again discussed at the next monthly conference held at Kempe's, on the 5th of June.'

"The project which had been thus set on foot, was warmly taken up by Ernest Hawkins, who laboured heartily for its

[1] Now Canon of Bristol.

accomplishment. He obtained the co-operation of the two Oxford members of the confraternity, Dr. Moberly, and Dr. Barrow; while Alford secured the willing adhesion of Ellicott. And on further consideration it was thought best in such a tentative undertaking to limit our number to five.

"The first union of the little brotherhood took place on the 19th of June, at St. Martin's Vicarage, where the subsequent meetings were usually held.

"The mode of proceeding was as follows:—each of the four independently of the others, made his suggestions on a prescribed number of verses, and sent a copy of them on a certain day to each of his colleagues. This interchange was repeated at weekly or fortnightly intervals for several months, until we were able to meet together, and devote a few days to the joint consideration of that portion of the sacred text which had been already considered by us separately.

"Ernest Hawkins was a frequent assessor at our deliberations; and though he modestly declined to give an opinion on questions of scholarship, he was useful as peculiarly sensitive to the English idiom and rhythm. He did much also by his constant good humour, and by the interest which he took in the work, to enliven our long discussions, and lighten our toil.

"The first publication, the revised version of St. John, with a preface, appeared in the spring of 1857. It was followed by the Romans, with a preface, December, 1857. The two Epistles to the Corinthians, with a preface, December, 1858; and the Epistles to the Galatians, Ephesians, Philippians, and Colossians, May, 1861. The second edition of the Gospel of St. John, and the Romans appeared without alteration; and a third edition of the Gospel carefully revised in 1863. I need hardly tell you that Alford was a most delightful fellow-worker and gained the affection of us all. Thoroughly versed in the subject, he was not in the least disposed to dogmatize, or press his own opinion unduly; he was quick in catching and appreciating the suggestions and arguments of others, even when they were at variance with his own. Though our work did not attract a very large share of attention from the public in general, it was favourably received by those who were competent to judge of it, and if by its conservative character it allayed the apprehensions of many persons, and disappointed the expectations of a few, it fully answered its purpose in contributing to prepare the way for the more comprehensive scheme of Biblical revision which is now in progress.

"With regard to his part in initiating in 1870 the present undertaking, others, *e.g.* the Bishop of Gloucester and Bristol and the Dean of Westminster, would be able to tell you much more than I can, as I was only invited to join when the preliminary stage had been passed. While the matter was under discussion in the Lower House of Convocation, Alford took an active part in advocating the admission of the Nonconformists of all denominations to a participation in the work; and a speech which he made in that behalf was described, even by those who did not agree with him, as one of the most eloquent, touching, and effective addresses that had been heard in the Jerusalem Chamber.

"As a member of the Company formed for the revision of the English New Testament, his opinion on difficult points of criticism, interpretation, and rendering, was always received with interest and respect; but it seemed to me that in general he kept himself in the back-ground, as if he felt that his suggestions were sufficiently before us in his revised version of the New Testament published in 1869: a copy of which he presented to every member of the company.

"The book remains, but makes us feel continually how much we have lost in the man."

It was his practice, as has been already mentioned, to preach twice every Sunday at Quebec Chapel. His morning's sermons were carefully written, and seven volumes of them are published under the title of "Quebec Chapel Sermons," which convey the best representation of his method and style of preaching. But the afternoon was appropriated to an extempore expository lecture on some portion of Scripture. For this he entered the pulpit with a single sheet of notes, and Theile and Stier's edition of the New Testament in Latin, Greek, German, and English. Having thus, in the course of about a year and a half, gone through St. John's Gospel in order, he began in the winter of 1856 to explain the Acts of the Apostles. In accordance with a suggestion of some of his hearers, he tried the experiment of procuring a short-hand writer to take down the afternoon lectures as they were delivered. I believe he was not himself perfectly satisfied with the result. But the afternoon discourses preached between November, 1856, and Spring, 1857, were printed in a volume, entitled "Homilies on the First Ten Chapters of the Acts of the Apostles." The afternoon lectures were regarded by many persons as the most peculiar feature of his ministry at Quebec Chapel. A friend, B. Shaw, Esq., who was no unfrequent hearer, has thus recorded his recollection of them :—

"During the time that Dean Alford was Minister of Quebec Chapel, though I had the happiness of knowing him in private, I had not often the opportunity of attending his ministrations. When I did so it was at the afternoon service, when he was accustomed to deliver what might be described as an exegetical lecture, embracing (for instance) the whole context of a passage in the Acts, and going somewhat fully into its connexion and argument. Critical questions were often handled, though only as far as the subject in hand fairly demanded. This kind of preaching was then a novelty, though it has since become less uncommon. However, it was at that time a very attractive thing to find a first-rate preacher in the afternoon of Sunday: as in other churches, the principal second service was on Sunday evening.

"The consequence of all this was, that the Sunday afternoon congregation of Quebec Chapel was of a high order; members of Parliament, eminent lawyers, and other representatives of the intellectual classes were always to be found there. To such men the careful study of a definite, but not fragmentary, portion of the New Testament which was presented to them was certainly an interesting thing. Escaping from the ordinary routine of the pulpit, it invited them to verify what was said by the conscientious study of the chapter for themselves. This was, probably in many cases, no small gain. But this was not all. There was a freshness and candour about the whole that was very attractive. There are some men who are possessed of great ability, much learning, considerable intellectual acuteness, but who irresistibly convey the idea that they hold a brief for orthodoxy, and are bound to argue in the interest of their client. It is very eloquent, but it does not suggest the idea that the speaker has ever put himself in the position of his antagonist or fairly weighed both sides. He concedes nothing, he allows nothing to be doubtful, he is prepared to defend every point equally.

"It was not so with Dean Alford: as I have said, his mind was liberal and candid. He could give up what was untenable, while maintaining with the most entire conviction what his own mind had verified for itself. I am inclined to think that herein, and in his severe style, unburdened by any weight of useless ornamentation, lay much of his power with the class of minds of which I have been speaking.

"It was known, too, that he was a careful scholar and a diligent student. Men went to him as one who could render a reason, and who was not likely to rely on a mistranslation in the authorized version, either because he had not looked at his Greek Testament before he went into the pulpit, or because he would not have detected the error, if he had.

"These are the traits that suggest themselves to my memory. I speak only of what I witnessed. Of his pastoral care, of his more practical and spiritual ministrations, others no doubt, who were members of his flock, will speak.

"I heard only occasional specimens of his exegetical afternoon lectures. I cannot doubt that it was a useful form of preaching, at all events, at one of the services.

"His character in private at this time (as always, as far as I have been able to form a judgment of it) was marked, as it appeared to me, strongly by three qualities—earnestness, for his religion was no mere theory; manliness, for it never degenerated into sentimentalism; energy, for it abhorred all idleness of mind or body: his grasp of the truth he held was very tenacious. As to this, perhaps, I may add one word, though it belongs to a later period. About a year before his death, walking with him at Canterbury, I spoke of the sceptical doubts which are trying the faith of so many in this day. I well remember that he seemed almost surprised that I spoke of them so seriously, as if they had any danger for God-fearing men, and said, with a quiet simplicity, 'Well, I have never felt tempted to go from my anchorage.' I do not think I saw him more than once afterwards."

The following letter was addressed to a young colleague, and is introduced to show how anxious he was that the poor included in his district should be treated with the utmost kindness and patience:—

"I am afraid you will think me very unreasonable in what I am going to say, but fairness requires that I should say it notwithstanding. It is, that your letter, just received, is to my mind by no means satisfactory as to the delinquency of some of the parties. ———'s case I still must think a very hard one. Grant all you say, I cannot think it made out; still less, can I conclude that they should be condemned for not bearing false witness against their neighbours. You allude to ———'s opinion of them being bad: I may almost reply, did you ever hear him give a good opinion of a poor person? I found this so constant that I altogether at last abstained from consulting him: there was an air of triumph and persecution and self-consciousness about the man that disgusted me extremely.

"Let me give you one friendly caution. It is a tempting path to seem to see more sharply than others, and many men win their way by establishing this character; but I doubt whether it is one which becomes us as Christian ministers. Some of the faults you mention are such as kind rebuke and pastoral watching might serve to turn into occasions of repentance. Why not try this path instead of giving up the culprits at once as wretched, abandoned people? Let me tell you, the opinion which I formed of them, I did not first form; I received it from my predecessor in the district, who doubtless had his own grounds, as I had mine."

At the beginning of 1857 he writes thus in his journal:—

"Another year opens upon me. O my God and Redeemer, sanctify me to Thy service during it, or such part of it as Thou art pleased to keep me here in the flesh! Bless my work in my study, in my pulpit, in my district, in my family, in society, in the world. Give me grace to think less of myself, to be indifferent to men's estimate of me, and more thoroughly and earnestly to do Thy work wherever I am. Give me prudence and self-restraint to behave wisely among men, and to be useful in counsel to those about me. May I be diligent, remembering that life is wearing away, and that daylight is short in which Thy work must be done. Bless my darlings at home, my own dear companion, and my two beloved girls. Keep them in safety and health if it please Thee; at all events, keep them in Thy faith and fear, and them and me in holy unity and love. Thus, living or dying, working or resting, waking or sleeping, we shall be safe; for we shall be Thine, and Thou in Thy good time wilt take us to be with Thee and with our dear ones, who are in bliss under the shadow of Thy wings and in the light of Thy glorious face. Do it, my Saviour, for Thine own sake!"

The first two months of the year 1857 he carried on his usual work with so much energy that his health was affected, and he found it necessary to consult his friend Sir H. Holland.

In the beginning of March he went for a few days to Taunton, where he delivered a lecture on "The Pulpit Eloquence of the Seventeenth Century." The day after his return (March 6), whilst we were all receiving some instruction in water-colour drawing from Mr. Leitch, jun., in Hamilton Terrace, a letter came to him from Lord Palmerston proposing to nominate him to the Deanery of Canterbury. Some slight intimation of the possibility of such an appointment had been received from Mr. A. Kinnaird, whom he met at a friend's house the preceding evening; but it was a surprise and a great pleasure to us all.

Our first visit to Canterbury took place on March 9th, but more than three months elapsed before we finally left our home in London on June 19th.

Those few weeks were full of excitement. There were the visits to Canterbury, as when, on April 19th, "Read in and did all the morning and afternoon services. Lovely day: enjoyed it much, from the contrast in quiet to London. No sound but birds and bells." And again, on May 29th, "Preached for the first time at Canterbury an accession sermon." There were not a few additions in London to his ordinary occupations there, as when, on May 3rd, he preached at St. Paul's Cathedral at the Festival of the Sons of the Clergy (see "Sermons," vol. vii. page 261). And again, June 7th, Trinity Sunday, he preached "at St. Paul's, at the Bishop of London's Ordination." And in the following week he went, June 10th, "to the state dinner at Lambeth," at which the Archbishop of Canterbury is wont to entertain the Stewards and Preacher of the Festival of the Sons of the Clergy; and on June 11th to dine with the Bishop of London, Dr. Tait [whose acquaintance he had made just ten years previously as a guest at Rempstone Hall]; 16th, to dine at the Mansion House. He also began on June 7th his farewell sermons (vol. vii. p. 306) to his congregation at Quebec Chapel.

A letter written in April to his friend, the Rev. C. Merivale, gives a lively description of his induction into the decanal seat at Canterbury:—

"Your congratulations on my completion as Dean put me in mind how often I have intended to sit down and scribble you an account of all that has been done, but have not been able: how I was led in by Canons; how Harrison neither forgot nor mumbled his Latin collect, which he put up for me in placing me in the stall; how I was taken to the Prior's stone seat in the Chapter-house, and there swore a monstrous long oath without, as I believe, any false quantities (which flit about a man on such occasions); and how the Canons, one and all, came and bowed obedience to me, hereafter to be proved. Harrison is really an acquisition to one's acquaintance—a ripe, though somewhat stiff scholar, and a nice, friendly Christian fellow. Mrs. H. and her husband have both shown us all imaginable kindness.

"All this coming unexpectedly over and above parish work has overdone me, and I sadly want change; so I am off on Easter Monday for South Wales, to Glasbury, near Hay, where a brother-in-law of mine has a curacy. There I spend a week, and make my way to Canterbury on Saturday to read in on Sunday. On Easter Monday Mrs. Lyall leaves the Deanery, and on the following week is her sale, so that I shall be fairly in possession in May.

"This, as you may suppose, has suspended the Greek Testament, but I hope to get to work again in October or before with redoubled vigour. Poor ———'s has indeed been a melancholy course. We must now be expecting almost yearly thinning off; and indeed one's own summons begins to assume a reality in the future, and to occupy a place in one's thoughts which it never did before."

The following letter, written about the same time to his aged aunt, Mrs. Freeman, mentions one of the first plans which he formed to increase the usefulness of his new office:—

"*Upper Hamilton Terrace.*

"I am sure you will be glad to hear that Lord Palmerston has offered me the Deanery of Canterbury, and I have accepted it. I have every reason to be thankful for this gracious arrangement, for my work here was getting very hard, and I must soon have made some change; whereas now, please God, I can finish my Greek Testament with much more leisure and quiet. There is much to be done at Canterbury. At present the Dean only preaches three times a year!—and there is but one sermon each Sunday. My first care will be to establish an afternoon sermon, which I shall take myself when in residence. I have been much overdone for the last few weeks, what with this new matter, and all the Lent and Easter work coming after it.

"I send you [vol. vii.] my last volume of Quebec Sermons. I have not printed any volume in which I have had more my heart and my prayers—may God bless it, and may it be used for His glory.

"Last autumn I went to the West, to attend my sister's funeral, it has been indeed an afflicting and mysterious dispensation. Six little helpless children are left without a mother. Our meeting was even cheerful; it seemed as if death had lost its sting to us all: may it prove to be so in the hour which shall try us all!"

It is due to some members of the congregation of Quebec Chapel to say that a proposal was made by them for presenting some kind of Testimonial from the congregation to their Minister on his removal. But it came accidentally to his knowledge at an early stage, and in deference to an expression of his wishes, the proposal was abandoned.

Among the numerous letters of congratulation which he received, perhaps none was more gratifying to him than the following from Archbishop Sumner:—

"*Lambeth, March 9.*

"My dear Sir,—I did not venture to express my satisfaction at your appointment to Canterbury till I had ascertained the fact without danger of writing prematurely; but allow me now to add, that it has given me much gratification to know that you are to be the head of my Cathedral Church, and that my metropolis is to have the advantage of your talents, and my clergy your example.

"I am, my dear Sir, very faithfully yours,

"J. B. Cantuar."

His old acquaintance the Bishop of Ripon (Dr. Bickersteth) said on the same occasion:—

"It seems the very post for which you are fitted, and in the occupation of it abundant leisure will be afforded for the prosecution of the studies which you pursue with so much advantage to others. May God bless you in your new sphere!

"R. Ripon."

Mr. (now Bishop) Ellicott said:—

"You have indeed borne the heat and burden of the day, and borne it bravely, and now comes suitably and appropriately your present reward."

His friend and old pupil, Mr. W. H. Gurney, wrote:—

"It is delightful to think of you in a place you are so fitted for; the only drawback seems to be that you will have to leave London and give up Quebec Chapel; however, you have done a great work there, and one you will look back upon with thankfulness as well as pleasure."

CHAPTER VIII.

1857–1860.

Work at Canterbury—Tour in Germany—The Evangelical Alliance at Berlin—Tour in the West of Scotland—Visits the West of England—Bishop Mackenzie's Farewell Service at Canterbury—Last Volume of the Greek Testament.

THE new duties on which he now entered as Dean were very different from the daily cares of a pastor of a large rural parish, and from the excitements which belong to the life of a minister of a congregation in the metropolis. Still he continued to apply himself to those Biblical studies which he regarded as the principal work assigned to him by the Great Taskmaster, amidst other duties belonging to the positions which he filled. From the time of our arrival at Canterbury he began to attend as a rule, the meetings of the Ecclesiastical Commission of which he was an official member. At some seasons this required a weekly journey to London; and it gave him an opportunity of transacting many matters of business connected with his various occupations. Another office, which also belonged to his position as Dean, was perhaps somewhat more congenial to his character. He was an official member—indeed, next after the Prolocutor, the senior member—of the Lower House of Convocation of the Province of Canterbury. He took at all times an interest in its proceedings; and on such occasions as the debate on the Revision of the Authorized Version of the Bible, he was one of the prominent speakers.

T

Two brief entries from his journal and an extract from a letter to his wife from town, whither he had been summoned to preach a funeral sermon, afford a specimen of his occupation in the first month at Canterbury.

"*July* 13.—Cathedral service in the morning—nice walk with the dear girls to St. Stephen's—glorious weather; sat in the Deanery garden in the evening; what shall I render to the Lord for all His mercies to me!

"*July* 17.—Very busy arranging my library, my newly bound books are come—settled about work to be done whilst we are away on our German tour—made calls, felt low and poorly, but how wrong in me—got some iodine for my hand, which I hurt in packing my books."

TO HIS WIFE.

"*July* 26.

"I steal a few moments after an interesting and trying day. I preached from John xiv. 1—4. I did not prepare but spoke extempore, and was enabled to do so with effect, I trust; at least, I felt very much what I said, which is, I suppose, the best test of preaching with effect.

"In the afternoon I went to Quebec Chapel; how natural the ugly old place looked; I felt much addressing my old flock, and spoke to them about their old minister.

"*July* 27.—What would you like by way of sketch-book for our German tour? I have got a large book, and a little one for scraps. I have one brief hour to rush about, getting the passport viséed for Austria, Belgium, Bavaria, and France."

For some time past we had felt a little anxiety about the health of our eldest daughter: and this led him to effect a costly and permanent improvement in the Deanery, by laying down hot-water pipes on each storey.

During the first few weeks his ordinary studies were partially intermitted, and he applied himself to storing his own mind and his children's with information connected with a long projected Continental tour, in which he designed to visit that part of Germany which is connected with most of the events in the life of Martin Luther, to increase his knowledge of the Continental picture-galleries, to compare the beauties of the three great rivers—the Rhine, Danube, and Elbe—and to be present at the conference of the Evangelical Alliance, which was held this year at Berlin. His journal, and a letter to his brother, Mr. B. H. Alford, record the incidents of this tour.

"*August* 3.—From Canterbury to Valenciennes through Calais and Lille. To Namur and Dinant, sketched the church before breakfast. On to St. Hubert and Luxemburg—long reaches of road bordered by poplars. . . . . To St. Goar, up the Schweizerthal, where Fanny and I walked up twenty years ago. To Frankfort, Bamberg, and Nuremberg; saw the churches with more pleasure than ever, having my three dearest ones with me; here we spent Sunday. Then on to Stutgard and Munich, where we saw the Pinakothek collections and the Glyptothek, &c. At the Pinakothek we had a very narrow escape,—a large wooden shutter fell from the roof on the spot where we had just been standing; thank God for this.

"Next day we saw the Bavarian Statue, and had a drive in the English garden—but Mary was not well, and we found the place unhealthy, as Sir Henry Holland had told us."

To Mr. B. H. Alford.

"*Munich, August* 23.

"Here we are in Munich, and a wonderful place it is; we went from Namur to Luxemburg because it seemed to promise well; and Stanley told me that Luxemburg was exceedingly well worth seeing, very like Jerusalem. We got to Namur by rail, thence to Dinant, a very curious place on the Meuse, under rocks; thence by *voiture* to St. Hubert to sleep, in the middle of the Forest of Ardennes, most interesting; thence by *malle-poste* to Arlon, next day to Dinant, and on to Luxemburg by carriage in the evening. Next morning to Treves; very interesting, glorious Roman remains; the Basilica, now a Protestant church, and Porta

Nigra, baths. Then, alas! no water in the Moselle; five steamers laid up at the old Roman bridge, and we were forced to post to Coblentz. Nuremberg is by far the most interesting place I have ever seen, full of middle-age remains, and quaint works of art. The house of Albert Durer, Hans Sachs, Peter Fischer, Veit Stoss, Adam Kraft, &c. Nearly all the people are Protestants. We heard two capital sermons in the two charming old churches on Sunday last. Augsburg is a quaint old place, its Confessional, &c. Then to Ulm, with its grand and vast cathedral, Protestant. We went then to Stutgard, to see the Von Stadlingers, and spent two very pleasant days there, and came on here last night. To-day we have seen the Glyptothek, the Pinakothek, and I know not what besides. If you ever come to this part of Germany don't fail to mark the pictures of Luther, by Lucas Cranach, with their dates. I have already seen four all dated, they form four most interesting comments on his history."

JOURNAL (*continued*).

"After Munich we went to Frabertsheim, Berchtesgarten, and Salzburg, taking on our way the Königsee, splendid morning, the Watzmann most grand with the setting tints on it. Made several sketches. Here last in 1846, with Holland and Wright; to Ischl, and across the Lake to Hallstadt for Sunday, and then on to Lintz and Vienna.

"The Danube is dull after Lintz, but it becomes soon beautiful again, flowing through deep ravines, with several old castles on the heights. At Vienna we went to the Volksgarten and heard Strauss's band, a most curious sight, and such gay dresses. We saw St. Stephen's, a grand cathedral, the spire surpasses any I had ever seen. In the Imperial vaults we saw Maria Theresa's coffin, &c., &c., and in another place the hearts of the Emperors.

"We spent Sunday at Prague, and had service in our room. Afterwards we went to see the Hradschin, and saw the tombs of the Bohemian Kings, passing over the wonderful bridge.

"On our way to Dresden, we stopped to see the pretty district called the Saxon Switzerland; saw the Kuhestall, and then on by steamer to Dresden, where we stayed a few days, and spent many hours at the Gallery looking at the glorious pictures. The Madonna del Sisto is here, also Correggio's Notte and several *chef-d'œuvres;* we left Dresden with regret; at Berlin all the hotels were full, and we were obliged to take lodgings.

"On 12th September, we went to the Garrison Church to the Conference, we had an account of Protestantism in various lands, the King, Frederick William IV., was there. Afterwards I went to a gathering of German members, and met Hoffman.

"*Sept.* 13, *Sunday.*—At nine a.m. we all went to the Hôtel de Russie, where about 150 English Christians of all denominations received the communion together; no form except the reading the words of institution, a thing I should imagine without parallel in the history of the Church.

"*Sept.* 14.—To the Picture-Gallery with the Eardleys and Dr. Waagen.

"*Sept.* 15.—To Charlottenburg, and then to the Conference, and in the evening to Sir Culling Eardley's Jews' Meeting at their hotel.

"*Sept.* 16.—Called on Bunsen, and had a long talk about the Revision; then to the Picture-Gallery again, and to a Concert of Sacred Music at the Cathedral afterwards.

"*Sept.* 17.—Last day at Berlin; we all went to hear the end. The King and Queen were there. I gave thanks to the King and the Germans on behalf of the English. The hymn at the end was very fine. Then we all went to a Moravian Church, to receive the Communion together, most interesting; the words were said in three languages.

"*Sept.* 18.—To Potsdam and on to Wittemberg, to the latter place with many English. The Hotel was so full, we were obliged to sleep—Fanny and the girls in the salle, and I in the billiard-room.

"Here we saw Luther's, Melancthon's, and the Electors John and Frederick's tombs; then we went to Luther's house and saw various relics of him, also the oak which stands where he burnt the Pope's Bull.

"At Leipzig they were preparing for the fair; we drove to see the field of battle.

"At Naumburg is a remarkable cathedral. At Erfurt we saw Luther's cell, and where he went through all his anguish of mind.

"We took a guide at Eisenach to show us the Wartburg, which we got to in a carriage up a winding steep path; a most striking place.

"After that we went to the Anna Thal, a deep narrow glen, mossy and cool, hollowed out by the water, quite unique in its way; then through the narrow Thal and back to Eisenach, and from thence by rail to Cassel. Here we saw in their gallery some fine Rembrandts and Vandykes, and went to see Wilhelmshöhe, where are artificial rocks and cascades, and all sorts of princely follies.

"From thence we went to Marburg and Weilburg, and joined the Rhine at Coblentz, and on to Bonn and Cologne, where we found the cathedral wonderfully got on since we last saw it.

"We got home on the 30th by Brussels."

On our return to Canterbury, we found that the act at Berlin had been the subject of severe censure in some religious papers, and had created considerable distrust in the minds of many friends to whom he was sincerely attached.

In order to escape misrepresentation he drew up a statement of the facts as they occurred; and subsequently he wrote an explanatory letter to the Rev. Dr. (now Bishop) Moberly, both which are here inserted.

"*Deanery, Canterbury, Oct.* 25.

"I have set down the following particulars respecting

the part which I took in the Sunday Morning Communion at Berlin, for the information of those of my private friends who have made inquiries respecting the facts. I have felt this to be preferable, on many accounts, to inserting any statement in the public papers. Such statement would be sure to involve me in controversy, for which I have neither time nor inclination; add to which that it is exceedingly difficult to word a statement so carefully as to escape all possibility of misunderstanding or of wresting so as to be misunderstood, and after all the public journal is not the place exactly where a Christian minister should give an account of, or vindicate his actions.

"The facts were these: it had been announced that on Sunday, September 13th, at nine, the English Christians present at Berlin to attend the Conference would receive the Holy Communion together, how, or at what hands, was not stated.

"I and my family went as recipients, and as such I had taken my place in the room (the large saloon in the Hôtel de Russie). After a few minutes, some one whom I did not then know, asked whether I would assist in distributing the elements, adding that it was intended merely to read 1 Cor. xi. 23—26, and distribute the bread and wine in silence—such being the only ground on which all would meet in the celebration. To the granting of such a request I did not, and do not see, that my position in the Church of England formed any obstacle. I at once acceded, and when the time came I distributed the bread, in silence, to one row of persons, out of the four into which the assemblage was divided.

"I do not expect to carry all my friends' approval with me, but I only beg them to believe that in doing what I did, I was actuated by no leaning whatever towards nonconformity, but simply by a conscientious belief that we are not justified in refusing to communicate with any who are believers in the Lord Jesus. The occasion was altogether of an exceptional kind: the method adopted was the only practicable one in the exigencies of the case. The act of communion was doubly important, seeing that the high Lutheran party kept aloof from, and denounced the Conference on the ground of their own peculiar sacramental views. It was repeated on a larger basis to the members of the whole Conference, German, French, Italian, English, and others, on the concluding evening. I was there also present, but as a recipient only. This took place in the Moravian Church lent for that purpose.

"I have thus stated the facts, and though I am prepared if necessary to vindicate my consistency in detail, I will add no more at present, but leave my statement to speak for itself."

TO THE REV. DR. MOBERLY.

"With regard to what happened at Berlin, I have no hesitation in saying that, had I borne in mind the wording of the 27th Canon[1], I should have hesitated before I consented to the request that was unexpectedly made to me, to take part in the distribution of the elements. I will also add, that had I known the pain which my so taking part would give to yourself and many other Christian friends whose judgment I highly value, I should have declined that request, and confined myself to simple participation; for by this latter the principle would have been asserted, which I consider myself bound to maintain, and which it was so especially important to vindicate on that occasion, viz. that we are not justified in refusing Christian communion in common with those who believe in the Lord Jesus Christ, and give proof of loving Him in sincerity."

The Archbishop of Canterbury, in a letter acknowledging a presentation copy of a volume of sermons, took occasion to express his opinion on the whole subject in the following manner:—

"*Addington, Dec.* 5.

"MY DEAR SIR,—I have to thank you for the new Volume issued from your prolific pen, and cannot help feeling glad

---

[1] "No minister, when he celebrateth the Communion, shall wittingly administer the same to any but to such as kneel, under pain of suspension; nor, under the like pain, to any that refuse to be present at public prayers according to the orders of the Church of England," &c., &c.

that you are not to be so largely drawn upon hereafter, though I see no signs of exhaustion have hitherto appeared.

"I must take this opportunity of saying how much I have resented the bigotry and uncharitableness which the Berlin communion has excited. It is very right that at home we should keep out of *canon* shot, but widely as the range has been extended of late years, I never before heard that it could be stretched across the Channel.

"Very faithfully yours,

"J. B. CANTUAR."

On All Saints' Day (Nov. 1) when the cathedral regulations require the Dean to perform the service, he began the practice of intoning his part, thus using his peculiarly clear and musical voice in the service of Him who gave it. On the same day he preached a sermon, "The great multitude which no man can number," which is sometimes spoken of as one of the most eloquent of his compositions [2], ending with these personal remarks. "And now, brethren, still keeping our eyes on that glorious and triumphant multitude, let us ask ourselves how it stands with us here present, as to our hope, our claim, one day to be among them. And first it is an individual matter of which I speak. Many are its relations, wide-spreading its duties and its influences; but in its issue every one of us stands alone. Alone must we wage God's battles in our inmost soul; alone must we repent and seek for grace; alone must we die; and every one of us must give an account of himself to God. 'No man may deliver his brother, nor make agreement unto God for him: for it cost more to redeem their souls; so that he must let that alone for ever, yea, though he live long, and see not the grave.' Let the question then be put *by* each one of us, be put *to* each one of us. My brother, my sister, art thou in the way to join this blessed company? Dost thou believe on the Son

---

[2] It was printed separately,

of God? I mean not as a fact in history, convincing thy mind, falling short of thy heart: but I mean as thine own personal Saviour and Master, and atonement before God? Hast thou taken by faith of that blood of His, which in symbol was sprinkled on thee on thy baptism, and hast thou with thy will and with thy might sprinkled it anew on thy soul, trusting to it for forgiveness, for acceptance; standing in its power before God, and in its power pleasing God—growing in grace and doing battle for God day by day? Art thou cleansing thy robe in that blood? Art thou becoming more holy, more pure, more useful, a brighter example indeed, in word, in temper? O search and see. If this be not so, then is thy faith dead, bearing no fruits: if it be not so, take heed that thou be not accounting the blood of the covenant wherewith thou wast sanctified an unholy thing; take heed that thou be not doing despite to the spirit of grace. O brethren, I deeply feel that, as it is a very solemn thing for any man to search himself with these questions, so it is a still more solemn thing for us of this cathedral body, dwelling as we do in the midst of the full privilege of daily Christian worship, of weekly participation of the Supper of the Lord. On us, my reverend brethren, as leading the band; on you, who are privileged by your calling to sound the high praises of God in this stately temple; yea, even on the youngest and least who daily lifts up his voice in that choir, and on the members of our families who assemble here, and the very door-keepers in the house of God, on all and each of us will the account fall heavy indeed, if our daily worship becomes a dead form to us, our sacred duties mere routine; nay, if we learn not, believe not, practise not, more and better than others. If our place be not higher than theirs, assuredly it must be far lower; for to whom much is given, of them will much be required. Let us not shrink from the lot of all God's people nor refuse God's own way to His kingdom of glory. Each one for himself, young and old, high and low, must repent and believe; for each there is but one way of pardon and acceptance, but one admission to that triumphant company. That way and that admission is righteousness; not our own, but the Lord's; put on us by faith in Him, wrought in us by obedience to Him."

When Christmas came he gave a children's party, which afterwards developed into an annual entertainment at the Deanery to the choristers and other young people, where he always contributed by his own exertions the largest portion of the evening's amusement.

A little before Christmas, in a letter in which he invites his friend the Rev. E. T. Vaughan to pay him a visit, he describes his way of life at Canterbury:

TO THE REV. E. T. VAUGHAN.

"*Deanery, Dec.* 4.

"I live in hopes that we may prevail on you to bring all your family here some day, to see us in our new and somewhat capacious abode. This climate is peculiar, quite *sui generis*, moist, but with very little rain, mild but not relaxing; we read now for instance of frost and snow in some parts of England, here we have had none, and our nasturtiums and calceolarias are still in full bloom.

"You wish to know about our proceedings. We returned from Germany, where we made the complete round, seeing all the great cities except the northern ones of Dantzic and Hamburg, about October 1. We had the good Archbishop with us for a week, and since then we have been busily employed, I at my book, working at the Hebrews. I find this a very good place for work, interruptions are very few, and one's head is clear and fit for grappling with tough questions in a way which it never was in London. But with all this advantage, I am now only just concluding Hebrews vii.; it is a *verbosa et grandis Epistola*, and Bleek has done it so thoroughly, that to do much less than he has done seems like shirking the work.

"You will be interested to hear, that after having long fought the battle of the afternoon sermon, I have to-day carried it. I hope when once begun it may become an institution ἐς ἀεί."

He writes in the beginning of 1858 :—

"*Jan.* 2.—If other years have all begun with mercies, what shall I say of this one ? of this at the opening of which I find myself in the possession of that which I have so long wished and prayed for, a place of rest, where I may in peace and free from distracting occupations complete my work on God's word. He has, indeed, been very gracious to me, and I only hope I may ever bear in mind my increasing obligation to devote myself in all simplicity and earnestness to His work.

"I am now in the Hebrews, chapter ix., having been interrupted half a year by the event which brought me here. Several interruptions are before me. I preach at Cambridge in February. I am, thank God, in good order for work, and days here are for the most part uninterrupted days. This spring I hope good progress will be made in my work. My Cathedral sermon begins at Easter: 'O praise the Lord, O my soul; and all that is within me, praise His holy name.'"

The year was not eventful. His journal records a brief visit to London.

"*Jan.* 25.—Princess Royal married to Prince Frederick of Prussia. After the morning service in the Cathedral, Canterbury, I went off to London and saw the bride and bridegroom leave Buckingham Palace for Windsor; God bless them! then went to Sir C. Eardley's. Next day lectured at Exeter Hall 'On Pulpit Eloquence of the Seventeenth Century.'"

In the next month he went to Cambridge, to preach at St. Mary's a course of four sermons on the "Parable of the Sower," which was published in a small volume. He was the guest of Dr. Whewell, then Master of Trinity, whom he thus mentions in a letter :—

"The Master and I breakfast every day *tête-à-tête*. I have only to start a subject, and off he goes for five minutes, till he has said all he has to say, and then I start another."

In the course of his sojourn at Cambridge he visited a place with which he had been very familiar, Ampton Rectory, he says :—

"*Feb.* 20.—Slept in my old room, went to see the clerk's wife, aged ninety! The schoolmaster and his wife are both dead; walked to the Wadgate cottages, and through all the old haunts.

"Years upon years have fled, and once again
I tread these long accustomed paths; yon screen
Of leaf-deserted limes, as heretofore,
Veils the keen starlight: as before the clock
Tells with shrill note the warning of the hours.
But where are they whose faces lit this home,
Whose tones yet vibrate, turn where'er I will?
Where all the flock whose steps my youthfnl staff
Essay'd to guide? cold, cold, and silent all.
Some here, some laid afar, where western gales
Temper this freezing air. Thou solemn court
Of God's own Temple, paved with heaving graves."

He also visited friends in Leicestershire and Norfolk, and returned to Canterbury on March 1st. Here he began on April 11th the practice, which he took so much pains to establish, of preaching in the Cathedral on Sunday afternoon. An incident which occurred after the second of these services, affords an instance of the facility with which he could preach an extemporary sermon.

"*2nd Sunday after Easter, April* 18.—In the afternoon concluded my History of Balaam. Whilst walking in the nave of the Cathedral with the girls, I was summoned by a messenger from Mr. Lee Warner's people to say by some accident they were waiting in the church, but no clergyman came. Harrison and I went immediately. He read prayers, and I preached; but, finding no Bible or Prayer Book in the pulpit, I gave out my text—1 Peter ii. last verse—being the Epistle for the day."

The following letter, written in May, to his friend Dr. Merivale, gives a good insight into his occupations:—

"*Deanery, May* 3.

"Thank you for your promise of a new volume. I hope you may live to give us several more. I always remember Milton, who began 'Paradise Lost' at fifty, and blind. I cannot be at the Literary Fund, having an engagement at Canterbury that evening; but I come up next morning, and give the first of four lectures at Queen's College on the

Greek Drama. I shall be to be heard of at the Athenæum between ten and one.

"In the evening I return to Canterbury. I suppose you have heard of our vacant canonry[3]. The appointment which was made was much to Lord Derby's credit. Chesshyre is the best clergyman in Canterbury, and has been the means of rebuilding several churches and stimulating charities all over the city; his health, poor man, is the one drawback.

"We have now got the afternoon sermon in the Cathedral fairly launched.

"As to plans, we go to town for a week, then to Somersetshire. As soon as the Trinity Examination is over, my brother joins me in the West, and we both of us go to the Land's End[4]. We return to Canterbury on the 24th June for our Midsummer audit. I find the place agree with us very well, I am much better than in London. My work goes on steadily; I finished the Hebrews last week, and am now well in St. James; I hope I may get to the beginning of the Apocalypse by Christmas, and then I shall go to press, leaving next year for the joint work of the Apocalypse and printing."

This summer the Archæological Society held a meeting at Canterbury, and on this occasion, as well as on another which soon followed, the meeting of the Diocesan Society, he was enabled to contribute materially to the hospitable reception of visitors by entertainments at the Deanery.

Bishop Cotton, of Calcutta, also visited Canterbury, and the last Sunday he was in England was spent there, before embarking for his diocese.

Many improvements were made this autumn in the garden. On the top of the massive old city wall, which bounded one side of it, a pleasant grape-walk was constructed, and a conservatory and hot-house were built.

---

[3] Vacant by the transfer of the Rev. A. P. Stanley to Oxford as Canon of Christ Church and Regius Professor of Ecclesiastical History.

[4] Whilst the Dean was on this tour, he returned to Canterbury every Saturday in order to preach the afternoon sermon on each Sunday.

The autumn was also marked by our first visit to Archbishop Sumner, then a hale old man of eighty, at Addington.

His reflections at the close of the year are :—

"This has been my first full year at my Deanery. I hope something has been done, but it is indeed trifling in comparison with what remains. The afternoon sermon has been established, and, as far as attendance goes, is successful. Would that it may have produced some effect for good! I and mine have, thank God, been preserved in safety and comparative health; but I am much troubled by flutterings and occasional palpitations, and I cannot exert myself without bringing it on.

"As to my work, I have this day sent to press the first sheets of Vol. iv. I have written during the year upwards of 400 pages of notes, from the middle of Hebrews to the end of Jude. I am engaged in a new edition of Vol. i. with my secretary Grafton; and Hake, my other secretary, corrects the press. I am engaged in Dr. Smith's "Biblical Dictionary," and in revising with my four colleagues. During this year we have done and published the Corinthians, and are now engaged in Galatians. On the whole, need I say that it has been a year of mercies? God is, I hope, clearing the way before me here to do much good in course of time: the limit at present seems to be my own physical strength."

The next entry in his journal refers to a project which was never carried into effect :—

"Talking over with my dear ones the plan of a special evening service on Fridays in the nave of the cathedral."

In 1859 he was occupied in seeing through the press the First Part of Vol. iv. of the Greek Testament, and in composing the Second Part. He visited London to confer with his colleagues in the revision of the Authorized Version of the Epistle to the Romans, and also to preach at Westminster Abbey, Whitehall, and St. Paul's. He also visited the Archbishop of Canterbury at Lambeth, as appears from the date of the following entry in his journal :—

"*Lambeth, Sexagesima.*—Assisted the Archbishop in the Communion service, and in laying hands on the priests.

"At seven to St. Paul's, where I preached on the Gospel. The people, I saw, could not hear me at first, and were leaving; then I half shouted and half intoned, it seemed, to half the human race: most striking sight, and opportunity for good. May God bless what I said!"

This spring he went to Oxford and Cambridge to preach, taking his Doctor's degree at Cambridge. His favourite recreation at this time was sketching. Having previously received a few lessons from Mr. Leitch, he made some considerable progress by his own unaided and persevering efforts; and, as we shall see, he subsequently received instruction from Mr. Burrell Smith.

Two poems came from his pen: the first entitled "How we buried him" ("Poems," p. 267), commemorating the Rev. J. W. Chesshyre, the recently-appointed Canon. The Dean visited him repeatedly in his sickness, and when death released him from his sufferings preached a sermon on February 6th in his memory, and two days afterwards officiated at his funeral in St. Martin's churchyard. The lines dedicated to the memory of our son Ambrose (*Filio Desideratissimo*, "Poems," p. 332) were now written, and on May 7th his journal records that the two memorial windows to our two darling boys, Ambrose and Clement, were put up in the south transept of Canterbury Cathedral.

His brother, Mr. B. H. Alford, was at this time travelling with his mother on the Continent; and from Rome he sent to Canterbury an interesting account of his tour, and (what was certainly not less valued) the notes of a collation of certain texts in the ancient Vatican manuscript, known to scholars as B. The two following letters were written to him by the Dean:—

"*Deanery, Canterbury, April* 13.

"Many thanks for your letters, which we have read with great interest. I especially followed you about the glorious old place as well as my '*demissa per aures*' will keep up with your '*oculis subjecta fidelibus*' at every step. All the bad passions connected with envy come boiling up in me. I especially envied you that day's walk about the Mons Sacer and its neighbourhood.

"We are all especially anxious about war, which some say is inevitable; while others, again, do not believe in it. To-day is a little more pacific in the *Times*, Austria seeming to come into the Congress idea; but, on the other hand, it is announced that our troops which were going to India are countermanded, which does not look well. I hope you will escape it all, and indeed we too: it would be a horrible thing in Europe just now. My best love to *La Madre*. What a treasure you must find her historical knowledge!

"*May* 27.—A thousand thanks for the MS., which arrived safe, and just in time to be used for the sheet containing the passage. Only fancy, it is the fifth century, and I fear must decide the fate of verses 43, 44 of Luke xxii. I will not fail to write as soon as the rest arrives. Permission seems to be easier than it once was, for Tregelles says in his letter he supposes it will be impossible to get leave to collate. It is said that Tischendorf has discovered in the Mount Sinai Convent an entire copy of the Scriptures (Greek) of the fourth century. What a revolution it will work in our critical texts!

"Your journals and letters have much interested us. I only wish I were with you. I suppose now I shall never see Rome. Fighting seems now to have begun in earnest. Of course, you have heard of Montebello, and our last accounts say that firing was going on when they left; so we shall probably hear soon of a battle. Are you as much enraptured with Naples as every one else? I seem to know every bit of it from my father's journal, which I used to study as a boy.

"Our Chapter is reduced to the smallest possible state of decrepitude. For the next few Sundays all rests upon me, the two sermons and everything."

The months of July and August were spent in a family tour, in which the west of Scotland was our principal object, and several cathedrals were visited in the way. A letter to his friend, the Rev. E. T. Vaughan, and a few extracts from his journal, will describe this:—

"After a long year of work Biblical and homiletical, we are off at the end of this month (D.V.) for six weeks to Scotland, making one week of cathedrals by our way. I have been working very hard of late, and feel the want of a holiday. I find it difficult to get away here, especially in the crippled state of the Chapter, four out of six of our canons being away ill. I have just now the whole cathedral duty upon me, five sermons in eight days."

Extracts from JOURNAL.

"*July* 11.—Awfully hot, 90° in shade; off to Ely, calcined, 6000 excursionists added fuel at Shoreditch Station; to Thompson's [now Master of Trinity], where, met at dinner the Dean, Mrs. Goodwin, and Mrs. Peacock: service on the whole good. At twelve to Norwich.

"*July* 13.—By Lynn to the Deanery, Peterborough, Dean Saunders and large family most kind; service very passably done, precincts very nice.

"*July* 14.—To Lincoln by Boston, Jeremie [late Dean of Lincoln] had us to breakfast, lunch, and dinner, and had expected us. Service good, Mendelssohn's Te Deum. We went round the cathedral by moonlight.

"*July* 16.—By Retford to York, three hours there, then on to Durham: disappointed with the outside of the cathedral, but glorious in situation, most glorious.

"*July* 17.—Sunday service very nicely done: dined with the old Bishop of Exeter [Canon in residence], who was most kind[5] and pleasant.

"*July* 18.—Left Durham at five. To Berwick, then on to Melrose and saw the abbey; Abbotsford and Dryburgh, and on to Edinburgh in the evening.

"*July* 20.—Left Edinburgh amid mist and rain, by Stirling to Dunfermline; then to Kinross, and in a boat on Lochleven, and saw and sketched the castle and Queen Mary's rooms.

---

[5] See p. 91.

"*July* 21.—At twelve reached St. Andrew's; out to see the ruins immediately, and after dinner began sketching a part of the cathedral; very noble and striking; most interesting place.

"*July* 22.—Sketching before breakfast, and at eleven to Aberdeen; a fine city, but by reason of the uniform granite without any light or shade, very monotonous and uninteresting.

"*July* 23.—By rail to Keith, Elgin, and Inverness, where spent our Sunday.

"*July* 24.—Very simple service and fair sermon both times; thought of my flock at Canterbury.

"*July* 25.—Up at half-past five to go by steamer on the Caledonian Canal to Invermoriston. First saw the Falls of Foyers; very little water, but very fine situation. Landed and found we could not go on to-day. Sketched some falls at a bridge and lost my sketching umbrella; it was blown into the stream.

"*July* 26.—Off for Cluny Inn in an open phaeton driven by the landlord, rain part of the way; most beautiful drive, never saw such colours or mountains, took several sketches.

"*July* 27.—Most blustering night; our inn a very homely little place, the only house for miles, and mountains all round it; we started in rain but it cleared off when we reached Sheil Inn, and we got a lovely view of Loch Duich, thence crossing Dornie Ferry to Balmacarra opposite the Island of Skye.

"*July* 28.—Off in a phaeton to Strome Ferry, very beautiful; nice view of Loch Duich; fine but somewhat dreary drive to Auchnasheen, past several lochs, then by two nice locks to Loch Maree.

"*July* 29.—Drew before breakfast; weather improving, in a dog-cart on the south shore of the lake, most lovely in every point of view, whether as seen from Kinlochewe, with its many promontories, and one of its islands, or from any part of the eleven miles of coast; the south side contains almost every variety of shore scenery, now clothed to the water with birch-wood, now like the Trosachs or Undercliff, now rocky with the remains of the primeval pine forest perched on all the heights, now grassy, now a bare arid waste of jumbled rocks and banks of blossoming heather and heath. The islands are very beautiful on this loch. I should like to come with Burrell Smith for a few days and sketch all day.

"*July* 30.—Got to Jean Town, where we spend Sunday; a most lovely day for crossing Loch Torridon, but we were weather bound at Jean Town.

"*Aug.* 2.—Then to Kyle Akin and across to Skye, where weather again persecuted us.

"*Aug.* 3.—We went from Sligachan in rain, and over the Cuchullin Hills to Loch Cornisk.

"*Aug.* 6.—Saturday, from Portree we set off in a dog-cart for Quiraing; very tedious ride, horrid road; tremendous climb at Quiraing, but very striking place, gigantic columns; saw the coast opposite as far as Cape Wrath.

"*Aug.* 7.—Sunday at Portree, witnessed a most curious sight, the Free Kirk Sacrament, 2000 persons sitting all day in a field opposite our window. We had our service, after a nice walk and talk, under a rock overlooking the Bay of Portree.

"We had a calm, pleasant day to go by steamer from Skye to Oban, but a most unfortunate day (11th), for our expedition to Iona and Staffa. It was so rough we could not land at Staffa, but the captain to compensate took us round the island. At Iona more and better ruins than I had imagined, and most interesting; after a good deal of the Atlantic roll, got into smooth water in the Sound of Mull, fine evening, wrote and drew.

"*Aug.* 12.—From Oban by Crinan Canal (such part as is not destroyed), by Kyles of Bute to Glasgow, fine city and most beautiful cathedral, crypt first rate. On Sunday streets densely crowded; A.M. we went to Caird's Church, an energetic preacher.

"*Aug.* 15.—For four days to Arran, but such wretched weather; however, I managed to sketch the fallen rocks, Glen Sannox, &c. We got home by Carlisle, Hereford, and

Gloucester, seeing each cathedral and attending the service in each."

Soon after our return he was engaged in a correspondence with a gentleman whose indignation was excited by a figure of St. Mildred, introduced in a stained-glass window which had been recently placed in the Cathedral.

The following reply to the objector is here printed, partly because it may gratify some readers to know how highly the Dean appreciated the employment of artistic skill in beautifying the House of God, and in appealing to religious feelings:—

"*Sept.* 11.

"Will you allow me to suggest that one link is wanting in your remark? You infer that because we in a series of historical windows introduce the figure of Mildred, we therefore accredit her fictitious miracles, surely this will at once appear to you on reflection to be unreasonable. I may say, in answer, that I do not see any reason why characters historically connected with our Church and land should not be commemorated in our Cathedral, whatever fables the Papists may have chosen to attach to their names. You will infer from this there is no intention of altering the windows in question. One word in your letter induces me to trouble you with a line without loss of time. You speak of 'Public Correspondence.' I hope I am not to understand by this that you intend to publish what has passed between us. While ready at all proper times, and to proper persons, to give full account of all I do and say, I must distinctly withhold my consent to the publication of letters written by me in a private capacity. In my opinion, one of the reasons which has contributed as much as any to the mischief which you wish to prevent, has been the unhappy thirst of notoriety fostered by a half-educated press, which has induced every one who has a say to say, to rush into the provincial papers with his *ex-parte* statement. With regard to the matter itself, I regret that I cannot take your view of it. It seems to me, and I speak not vaguely, but from much experience in this unhappy matter, that exaggerated acuteness in scenting out Popery in titles and decorations, and such like trifles tends to feed the evil, and to turn many a weak mind in the wrong direction, when such thoughts otherwise never would have entered it; it is not by these things that Popery is spread, the poison lies far deeper.

"At the risk of being troublesome, I cannot help closing our correspondence by a protest against what appears to me the very extraordinary theory of your last letter on our Protestant standing; viz. that of ignoring and repudiating the Church of Christ in this land during the darkness of Popery. I cannot accept such a view for one moment. God had a work in this land during the whole of that time, and that work forms part of our history, and is rightly claimed by our Reformed Church. And the titles of saints who lived during that time are adopted by us in very many cases entirely without regard to the fabulous tales which have been attached to the bearers. We commonly speak of St. Augustine, St. Anselm, St. Mildred, St. Alban, and believing them to have been good Christian persons in dark times, and the only mischief which I can conceive likely to come of doing so is, when men's titles are made matters of importance by taking offence at them. It is this gnat-straining which, in my experience, has done half the mischief."

Two or three extracts from his journal may close the account of this year:—

"*Oct.* 7.—My forty-ninth birthday; a solemn thing to come in sight of fifty. How thankful I ought to be to my gracious God for having spared me so long; may my remaining days be better spent to His glory than any yet.

"*Oct.* 11.—Busy making a small cloister leading to the Cathedral from my private door.

"*Oct.* 21.—To town to consult the Alexandrian MS. in the British Museum about εὐφροσυνην in Ps. xv. 11, &c. [Acts ii. 28.] Home by 4.30.

"*Oct.* 26.—Poor Charles Hodge drowned in the 'Royal Charter,' the cousin so mixed up with our early days."

The Rev. C. Hodge was a distant cousin, who, being an

orphan, was a frequent visitor at Heale House in early life. The health of his wife led to a visit to Australia; whence he was returning in the "Royal Charter," when he shared the fate of the passengers in that vessel, which was wrecked in Red Wharf Bay, Anglesey, and went down three hours after striking. Only thirty-nine passengers were saved out of 498. Mr. Charles Hodge's body was never found. A local newspaper records how his last hours were spent in preparing his fellow-sufferers for the awful future which lay before them[6].

In the next month some unusual visitors came to the Precincts.

"*Nov.* 1.—Showed one hundred soldiers over the Cathedral. Anniversary of the Soldiers' Institute. The Chaplain-General and I addressed them on the occasion."

Other entries record his progress in finishing the sketches which he brought from Scotland, and in composing the last volume of his Notes on the Greek Testament.

Ending with—

"*Dec.* 31.—Read aloud to them in the evening the year's summary in the *Times*, and the memoir of Lord Macaulay [who died 30th]. Thanks be to my God who has brought me in safety to the end of another year. May it not rise up in judgment against me!"

The first week of 1860 was spent in a visit to the Rev. C. J. (now Bishop) Ellicott, who then resided at Cambridge. In those pleasant days we were far from anticipating the dangerous accident which befell our host soon afterwards. My husband made an appointment to meet him in London on February 20th, but on arriving at King's College, he heard of the distressing accident which nearly deprived the future Bishop of life, the train in which he was travelling from

---

[6] In the midst of the most heartrending scenes the Rev. C. Hodge (Vicar of East Retford) endeavoured to calm them and begged them to join with him in prayer: many of the passengers were happy at that dread hour to commit themselves to the care of their heavenly Father, and participate fervently in the service: his countenance was the only one that was calm and unruffled amid scenes which baffle all efforts to describe.

Cambridge to London was upset; some passengers were killed, and others more or less severely injured. My husband's first thoughts are recorded in his journal, and in a letter to his younger daughter at Canterbury.

"*Feb.* 20.—Went to town by appointment to meet Ellicott—heard of his most sad accident. What a useful career cut off, so dear and good a man crushed! God's ways are indeed mysterious; arranged to take his King's College lectures for him."

"Your heart will bleed when you read the enclosed. Oh, is it not sad that such a life should be sacrificed?

"The loss to me will be more than I can describe, a brother in my life's labour. I am sure you will weep with and for me; there may yet be a ray of hope, but I confess I have none. I really have thought of nothing else. He went up by an earlier train than usual to be photographed for his pupils. 'His vanity,' he said, 'after all did it.' I saw his father, and arranged to take his lectures for him till Easter."

In his journals he records many journeys "To London to take Divinity Lectures at King's College. Large class of men, two hours of it."

He was now drawing near to the completion of his work of eighteen years.

"*Feb.* 17.—Finished the Apocalypse, and with it the work I began in December, 1842; but much remains to be done in writing Prolegomena and correcting notes."

At this time he was obliged to consult his friend Sir H. Holland, having some troublesome symptoms in his head, the effect of over-work. But it was not till May that he left Canterbury for a few days, when he went on the Archbishop's invitation to Lambeth. His journal records a characteristic act of Archbishop Sumner.

"*May* 5.—Staying at Lambeth.

"*May* 6.—Preached at Westminster Abbey from John xvi. 8—11. Next morning the good old Archbishop got up to see me off by the express train, and sent me in his own carriage up Constitution Hill to the Great Western."

From thence he went for a few days into Somersetshire,

preached at the completion of the restoration of Curry Rivell church, and gave a lecture at Taunton on Canterbury Cathedral. After his return he gave at Canterbury his first lecture on the "Queen's English." In July the Agricultural Meeting was held in Canterbury, in which he took much interest, and whilst it lasted kept open house.

On the 14th of July we went for a family tour in the West; his chief amusement was sketching; and he wrote two or three short poems, namely, "Here, midway perch'd between the sea and sky" (p. 333) and "The Land's End" (p. 334). We spent Sunday, 15th, at Exeter; the places which we visited were Bideford, Clovelly, Bude, reaching Tintagel on Saturday and spending Sunday there, having made acquaintance with the Vicar, Rev. R. B. Kinsman, who showed us the remains of the Castle, &c. Then southward to Falmouth and Lizard, &c.

"*July* 25.—To Kynance Cove, as beautiful as ever; took and finished a sketch on the spot; next day to Penolver Point, where I finished a sketch on a ledge of a rock in a fearful place over Belidden Cove; then all along the cliff paths by Landewednack Cove to Cadgwith, back in a boat seeing and sketching Dolor Hugo (see "Letters from Abroad," chapter v. p. 161, 2nd ed.).

"*July* 27.—Sketching towards Kynance Cove; Alice and I went down to the beach, where Philp's picture, which we have, was painted.

"*July* 30.—To Mullion Cove, most striking and glorious place, even more so than Kynance, if not so pretty, grand jumble of rocks of a grand size; to Gunwalloe, Helston, and Penzance, seeing and sketching St. Michael's Mount,—

"Where the great vision of the guarded mount[7]."

"*July* 31.—To St. Burian's[8], where we have engaged lodgings for a week at a farm-house called Bowcastle.

"*Aug.* 1.—To Logan Stone, and on to Porth Kernow, where we sketched, lunched, and picked up shells.

---

[7] Milton's "Lycidas," line 161. [8] See p. 1.

"*Aug.* 2.—Walked from Tol Peer, Penrith, to Land's End, and lunched in a cove at Mill Bay.

"*Aug.* 5—8.—At St. Just, helped Rev. J. H. Hadow on Sunday, thence we saw Cape Cornwall, Botallack Mine, Gurnand's Head, St. Ives, and had a most pleasant time with the Hadows.

"*Aug.* 9.—Off by train to Plymouth, crossing the wonderful bridge at Saltash; found all the Hutchinsons well at Government House.

"*Aug.* 10.—To the Dockyard with General H., and in his boat after lunch with Mrs. H., and the party to the Breakwater; next day to see Mount Edgecumbe."

The following letter to his brother, Mr. B. H. Alford, was written in the early part of this tour:—

"*Bowcastle, St. Burian's, July* 31.

"We have had a splendid week at the Lizard; a week ago we came to Lizard town from Falmouth by a much prettier way than you and I did that evening when we went down to the Lion's Den and looked about. We went to the same spot to sketch in the morning, and in the afternoon to Kynance Cove, where I sketched again; after breakfast on Thursday we went to Penolver Point, and over the cliffs to Cadgwith, back in a boat by Dolor Hugo, and passing Ravens Hugo to Landewednack, and next morning on the cliffs towards Kynance, and in the evening to Polpeer Beach, poking about and sketching. On Saturday we migrate to St. Just, where on Sunday I preach for Hadow, and remain there till Thursday, when we are due at Plymouth."

On October 2 Canterbury was again the resort of many visitors on a different occasion. Archdeacon C. F. Mackenzie came to Canterbury to bid farewell to as many of his friends and well-wishers as could meet him there, and the Cathedral was used for the service on that occasion. Six years previously Mr. Mackenzie had given up the quiet and honourable occupation of tutor in his college at Cambridge, to undertake the rough work of a Colonial Missionary in Natal; and now, when the example and exhortations of the African explorer, Dr. Livingstone, had led to the formation of the Universities' Central Africa Mission, Archdeacon Mackenzie complied with the request that he would lead the new Mission to its work, How nobly he laboured and died in the Missionary field has been related by his biographer, Bishop Goodwin. His farewell at Canterbury was a memorable occasion. The Missionary College of St. Augustine was filled with guests and visitors. The Bishop of Oxford (Dr. Wilberforce) preached an eloquent and touching sermon in the Cathedral. No token of sympathy which could have warmed the hearts of the departing Missionaries was wanting. My husband's journal states:—

"*Oct.* 1.—Prepared Apocalypse before breakfast; then arranged some flowers; then with my secretaries, Hake and Grafton; at half-past one to the Mayor's, to sit to Mr. Papworth for my bust; a walk then to the station, to meet the Bishops of Oxford and Chichester, the Dean of Ely (now Bishop of Carlisle), Mrs. Goodwin, Archdeacon Mackenzie, &c. They and many more dined at the Deanery, and all the world in the evening.

"*Oct.* 2.—Very busy making arrangements in the Cathedral. At ten Archdeacon Mackenzie planted a Wellingtonia Gigantea in the Deanery garden. Service at 10.30; very full; 500 Communicants, and 400*l.* collected. Lunch at St. Augustine's; 300. Speeches."

A few days afterwards we heard of the sudden death of my sister Octavia by epilepsy. She has been previously mentioned (p. 166). It was, as my husband's journal states, "a merciful end to the dark prospects which seemed crowding round her. She was quite prepared for her sudden summons." His entry at the end of the year is:—

"*Dec.* 31.—Mr. G. Richmond breakfasted with us a few days ago. Showed him all the Deanery pictures, and took him to see the Dark Chapel. I have been skating: I have not put on skates for ten years. Busy about arrangements for our *Masque*, and church, &c.

"I am now writing with the ten midnight bells ringing in 1861. God be praised for all the mercies of another happy year, in which I have been enabled to finish my Greek Testament, the work of eighteen years. May He grant that future years, if I am spared to see any, may be spent more to His praise! If I am to live, keep me with Thee; if I am to die, take me to Thee."

CHAPTER IX.

1861—1862.

MASQUE OF "THE SEASONS"—FIRST VISIT TO ROME—PREACHES BEFORE THE QUEEN—CATHEDRAL REPAIRS—AUTUMN AT THE LAKES—TRANSLATION OF THE ODYSSEY PUBLISHED—DEATH OF THE PRINCE CONSORT—VISIT TO NICE—TOUR IN SWITZERLAND—DEATH OF ARCHBISHOP SUMNER, AND ENTHRONEMENT OF ARCHBISHOP LONGLEY.

ON the first day of the new year 1861 our ordinary choristers' evening party was diversified by an entertainment which called into unusual exercise the versatile talents of the host. "THE SEASONS: a Masque" ("Poems," pp. 355—361) was "presented" before as numerous a company as the Deanery could accommodate, a principal part in the performance (the character of Father Christmas) being undertaken by the Dean, who had written all the songs and choruses, and composed all the music. He says in his journal:—

"*Jan.* 1.—Our *Masque* went off well. Words and music both mine; 104 guests. We had a Christmas-tree and presents. All seemed pleased."

The employments of the next few days are curiously contrasted with that bright scene:—

"*Jan.* 2.—Last proof of the Apocalypse.

"*Jan.* 3.—Looking over papers for Cambridge Middle Class Examination. A regular stiff lot: 284 candidates.

"Went with Robertson in the afternoon to see the old columns from the Reculvers Church, which have been given to the Dean and Chapter."

On January 21st we went for two days to the Bishop of London's (Dr. Tait) at Fulham, and on the 30th he had the pleasure of receiving from Rivington the first copy of the last volume of his Greek Testament. No doubt this was before his mind on the next day, when he wrote, in a short letter from Folkestone to me: "It has pleased God to enable me to finish my work of many years. I hope and trust He may have more work for me to do for Him; if not, it would be with me *nunc dimittis*—life has been quite as long as I could expect."

In the beginning of the year, as well as some weeks previously, he gave many spare hours to preparing for a long-intended visit to Rome. He says, "Preparing for my visit to Rome. Reading Milman's 'Latin Christianity,' and cut out Burgon's Roman letters from the *Guardian* to take with us"

Soon after we went, in 1853, to reside in St. John's Wood, London, we became acquainted with the Rev. W. T. Bullock, then an Assistant Secretary of the Society for the Propagation of the Gospel, who lived in Hamilton Terrace, near us, and it was agreed between my husband and him that they should visit Rome together. Various engagements on both sides prevented the design being carried out for three years; but the convenient time came in 1861, and they left London together early on the morning of February 1st, with the intention of returning at the end of four weeks. I shall allow, as usual, my husband's letters to tell the story of one of the most delightful tours which he has recorded:—

TO HIS WIFE.

"*Hôtel de Louvre, Paris, Feb.* 1.

"Here we are, all safe. We had a pleasant passage; not smooth, far otherwise; and so, breakfasting on French rolls and English chops (both in a marine sense), we at length found ourselves 'half-seas over,' and soon after at Calais. This is the grandest place I ever saw by way of an hotel, and so comfortable."

To his Daughter Alice.

"*Lyons, Feb.* 3.

"Here we are; came last night, and have been all day here. We left Paris in a brilliant mild morning, after a walk to see what has been done of late years. Numerous changes have been made, so that you would hardly know some parts of Paris again. As we got farther south it got colder and colder, and the patches of snow and ice became larger, and in the deep cuttings the water which ought to run down the sides was frozen in solid columns all sorts of fantastic shapes. This morning we found out the English Church. What we heard by way of sermon I leave you to surmise by the enclosed note, which the clergyman sent to me during the singing[1]. Service being over, we explored the old Church of St. Martin Amay, where the martyrs were imprisoned; then we mounted the Fourvière by a different way from one which we took before; thence down to the cathedral, where we witnessed vespers, and heard a sermon. During vespers they sung our 104th Psalm tune (Handel's). Afterwards there was a grand procession of the Sacrament, held up by a Bishop under a canopy, followed by all the cathedral body. The effect was very striking; and if one could believe what they believe, I have no doubt very solemn. Then followed the sermon, a very interesting one, with much action, from Matt. v. 48. The preacher introduced all sorts of anecdotes about St. Bernard, St. Thomas Aquinas and his sister, St. François de Sales, Frederick the Great, Madame Maintenon, Madame la Vallière, &c. To-morrow at 7.30 we start for Marseilles.

To his Daughter Mary.

"*Marseilles, Feb.* 4.

"That little face at the carriage-door at the station, that

1 "I am suffering from sore throat and will take it as a great favour if you will kindly preach."

In those days the English Church Service was performed at Lyons under discouraging circumstances. On this occasion the Dean assented to the request from the unknown clergyman officiating which reached him in the interval between the Litany and the Communion Service, and preached an extemporary sermon on the Gospel for the day.

kiss of the hand, that form becoming tinier as we steamed away, these were the last of thee, something like these may be the first of thee again, an it please God. Well, to my work: up to last night was sent to Alice from Lyons. Up at six, and to breakfast with what appetite we might, the omnibus, baggage, and salle d'attente, &c. as usual: fog and cold as yesterday, ice and snow and frozen falls of water on either side of the line; but soon after Vienne we dashed out of a cutting into the sunshine, and have had ever since the most beautiful spring day. You can imagine Avignon. Mount Ventoux looked with a brilliant snowy top over a bank of clouds, and the distant Alps were glorious. After Arles all was new: the queer descent of the Crau, the Etangs, or Salt Lakes, and, finally, Marseilles itself, a very large and remarkable city. We walked up to Notre Dame de la Garde, where is the celebrated view of the city and the Mediterranean, and a truly striking view it is; inland lies Marseilles spread out round an irregular bay, and backed by a range of odd jagged mountains, and the other side the expanse of the Mediterranean with two or three rocky islands in the middle distance, not blue this evening, for though very calm and warm it is overclouded, but clear and smooth even to reflecting the boats sailing in it. Hence we saw the sun slip into bed through a chink in the clouds, with his crimson dressing-gown on.

"So now we are fairly in for it; and whether we are to have as calm a night as it is evening, or whether, as I rather suspect, this calm is only a prelude to a brisk wind,—to-night and to-morrow, and to-morrow night, we shall spend on the broad sea, with our safety in His hand who rules the waters, and many thoughts and prayers from three dear souls at Canterbury, and from others as dear to my companion in London: and now, fare thee well. Only think, very likely the Trenches and their daughter will join us at Rome next week."

TO HIS WIFE.

"*Feb.* 5.

"Between the Gulf of Genoa and Corsica I am going to

write you a sea letter: given the deep blue Mediterranean all round, calm, but with a ripple, and many a twinkling dimple just making it a living thing; the most lovely of June days, pure blue sky with light fleecy clouds lying still in packs; the Alps fading into mist, very glorious, early in the morning, as I saw them lit up by the newly-risen sun; Corsica coming plainly into sight.

"*Civita Vecchia, Feb.* 6.—Here at last, thank God, after such a night. On rounding the north end of Corsica, all was changed, the sea 'wrought and was tempestuous,' the sun set fiery red, and all night has been one continued storm."

To his Wife.

"*Hôtel de Londres, Rome, Feb.* 7.

"Here we are in Rome; what does and what does not that word carry with it? the capital of heathen dominion, the capital of worldly Christianity, the metropolis of the world; all these titles meet in this one most wonderful place, and make the moment when one first walks abroad, and looks on its thousand monuments of each of these facts, almost the event of one's historical life. We have been to the Mausoleum of Augustus, where all the early Emperors were buried, now a comic theatre! to the castle of St. Angelo (once the Mausoleum of Hadrian). Over his bridge, the Pons Ælius, and so on to St. Peter's. Nothing can be more disappointing than the first sight of it. In the general effect it is certainly wanting, but the effects of particular parts are most astonishing. From St. Peter's we went up to the Janiculum, whence is a very fine view of Rome, and where Tasso died and is buried. Then down again, and up by the City flour-mills, built up a steep ascent, and driven by the water which comes from the Fountain of Paul V. The fountain is very striking, one of the best in this city of waters; the water comes from the Lake Bracciano, thirty miles distant, brought by Pope Paul V. Close to the fountain is the Church of St. Pietro in Montorio, from the front of which is the view of Rome in the little print on my study chimney-piece; this view is magnificent, the whole city, ancient and modern, with its domes and towers and its seven hills, the Tiber winding beneath, and beyond the Alban Hills to the right, and to the left the Apennines; the tops covered with snow and the sides glittering like silver in the sun. Thence down and through the region of the Trastevere (beyond the Tiber), where the people retain more of the characteristics of old Rome than anywhere else. We then crossed the Ponte Sisto, having first seen a remarkable fine old church, Santa Maria in Trastevere. Then to the Pantheon, (as we could not get in, more of this hereafter,) then home; but the impossible thing now at Rome is to cross the Corso, as it is the height of the Carnival, and all the houses are hung with flags and red cloth, and fitted with balconies full of masked people, who throw white-washed pebbles at everybody below.

"At five o'clock each evening the horse-race takes place of horses *sans* riders, and the cannon of St. Angelo fires, and all is over. I am tired, having walked eight miles by my pedometer. Thermometer outside our window at half-past eleven, 52°.

"*Feb.* 8.—To deliver our letters of introduction at the Vatican; no end of trouble up and down long flights of stairs, and, after all, found no one whom we wanted; then back on the other side of the Tiber, and making our way through the Ghetto, the Jews' Quarter, to the island on the Tiber. As we were crossing the bridge two or three red carriages came by, and a gay one with six horses—and in this sat Pio Nono, with one hand stretched out blessing as he went; this was luck; then we struck into some of his Holiness's filthiest alleys through the Ghetto, stopping in the fish-market to see the Portico of Octavia, a massive remain of the time of Augustus. Then to the island of the Tiber; the so-called Temple of Venus; the arch beneath it is the wonderful Cloaca Maxima, or main sewer of Rome, constructed by Tarquinius Priscus; the Temple of Fortuna Virilis; the Arch of Janus, erected by Septimius Severus; the Forum, with its never-dying interests; then mounted the Capitol[2]. Saw the Church of Ara Cœli and the Mamertine Prison, where Jugurtha was starved; then home fagged out. A sirocco blowing.

"*Feb.* 9.—To-day has been a delightful day of comparative rest after the fatigues and sirocco of yesterday. At ten with our friends, the Misses Baily, in their carriage to a service at St. Peter's for the repose of the soul of some mediæval Pope, I could not tell whom. The singing was tolerable; the music as to character and composition atrocious. The interior of St. Peter's grows upon us more every time we go there. After this we went to see the tombs on the Appian and Latin Ways, through the Forum, and by the Circus Maximus, past the church erected to mark the spot where St. Peter (so says the legend), when flying from persecution, met our Lord, and asked Him, 'Domine, quo vadis?' ('Lord, whither goest Thou?') to which our Lord replied, 'Vado ad Romam iterum crucifigi' ('I go to Rome to be again crucified'); on which the Apostle went back and submitted himself. On from thence to the Tomb of the Scipios, and a very interesting little Columbarium, so called from being full of little pigeon-holes in which in little marble boxes the burnt bones are deposited. Thence to the famous Tomb of Cecilia Metella, like a huge drum of massive stone; then on and on for miles through a street of tombs large and small, and unnamed and unknown heaps of old Roman masonry, most striking and solemn. The Via Appia runs on a ridge in the Campagna, commanding a view of wonderful beauty over the Campagna itself, with the aqueducts running across it in two or three directions; and, beyond, the glorious mountains, gleaming to-day like molten silver in the rich sun and shade of a windy, showery day. On our way back we turned across a field into the old Via Latina, and there we saw the sight of the day. The present Pope has been making many excavations since 1859, and has made some very beautiful and interesting discoveries. They consist

[2] Not the tower, which is hopelessly shut to all.

mainly of painted tombs, sepulchral chambers, vaulted with the most exquisite Arabesque patterns and figures.

"*Sunday, Feb.* 10.—Went to the English Church (nearly 700). Service and singing fair; and Mr. Woodward, the chaplain, preached an able sermon. After church we went across the Pincian Hill to Overbeck's studio near Sta. Maria Maggiore, on the Viminal. Overbeck shows his pictures himself, and explained to us some beautiful outlines which he is making of the Seven Sacraments. Then we returned by the Baths of Diocletian, part of which was made into a church by Michael Angelo, now call Sta. Maria degli Angeli, and is one of the finest in Rome. This church contains the tomb of Salvator Rosa. Sunday is very well kept in Rome: shops shut, no post, no carnival.

"*Monday, Feb.* 11.—To the Sistine Chapel to see the famous frescoes of Michael Angelo, which much surpassed my expectations; they are described in Murray and Kugler, so I will not waste time in doing so again.

"*Tuesday, Feb.* 12.—Determined to take a country walk, so off we started. Out by the Porta Pia, along the Via Nomentana, past the church and catacombs (yet to be seen) of St. Agnese, and on and on and on, sometimes deviating into the fields to examine a ruin and pick wild anemones and geraniums now just coming into flower. About four miles from Rome we came upon the Anio, and even the Ponte Lomentano, a queer old bridge with a tower at each end (the old Pons Nomentanus). Just beyond rises the Mons Sacer, a little green hill of tufa, with several promontories quite large enough to hold the plebs of old Rome; from it are fine views of the Apennines and Alban Hills. Here we lunched, and I took a sketch, the last materially curtailed (excuse the pun) by the approach in the distance of a great sheepdog. We returned by the same Via Nomentana as far as St. Agnese, then struck off at right angles by the road leading to Porta Salara (you can trace our walk on the map of the Campagna I bought at Miss Webb's sale), and in descending from the Villa Ludovisi came upon a wall quite matted with maiden-hair fern.

"*Ash-Wednesday, Feb.* 13.—To the Sistine Chapel in the Vatican to see the Pope distribute ashes to the Cardinals. The little Princes of Naples were there. Then to the museum in the Capitol; there we went through the various halls and galleries of statues. The Gladiator, Antinous, Faun, Girl playing with a Dove and frightened by a Serpent, the Doves drinking from a vase, the very one which is described by Pliny, &c. Then to St. John Lateran; the old parts of this great Basilica, 'the first church in Rome and the World.' The gem of this noble church, indeed almost the most beautiful thing I have seen in Rome, is the old cloister belonging to the first Basilica, with pillars of spiral alabaster worked between the spires with old Byzantine mosaic, of which there is also an entablature over the arches in beautiful patterns. Near here is the Lateran Museum, which consists wholly of tombs and inscriptions found in the Catacombs, numbers of most interesting sarcophagi with Christian bas-reliefs."

TO THE REV. W. H. GURNEY.

"*Rome, Hôtel de Londres, Piazza di Spagna, Feb.* 13, 1861.

"I came here last week, having fairly finished and published my last volume, thinking I had fairly earned a holiday, and wishing to spend it in this city of the world, which I had never seen; and I must say everything has very much surpassed my expectations. The place is really endless in interest of all kinds, classical, ecclesiastical, mediæval, artistic, political; as a city, as a piece of scenery; in society, in solitude; every hill has its charming view, every street its romance; the very people are pictures; the pictures and statues are living people; the great temptation is, I want to bring away photographs of the whole place and its treasures."

TO HIS DAUGHTER ALICE.

"Well, little dark-eyed maid, and how wags the world with you? with me right pleasantly; Rome is not Heaven, nay indeed, it is far enough from it just now, Heaven knows! but as to climate and scenery it is as near it as any place can be; the weather now is such as we should call glorious in England, the last week in May; buds bursting, birds singing, all the gardens and vineyards full of almond-trees in full bloom, and every bank sweet with enormous violets; from my bedroom I see up the Trinità steps, the front of the church and the houses on the Pincian silver in the moonlight; but alas! no more visiting the Coliseum by moonlight, things are in a very odd state here! . . . .

"The King of Naples is still here, and walks and rides as if nothing had happened, very foolish, and calculated to excite the people; but I hope I am not saying too much to pass the post-office, for I don't want you to lose this; the upshot of my visit here is, we must all come together. You have no idea of the enjoyment here, the habits are far more English than in any other foreign places; English bread, and good lodgings and carriages, and the place so full of all kinds of interest; we must think about it, and try and bring it about, and meantime be reading for it. Well, it is a quarter to one, and I am well tired. God bless you, my own child, and bring us again to our own home in peace and safety! so hopes and prays your loving father."

TO CANON ROBERTSON.

"I, God willing, return to Canterbury by Palm Sunday, to bear the burden, if not the heat of Passion and Eastertide.

"Now for tidings; we have seen a great deal, or rather become aware how much there is to see, for, as you know, the thing is endless; 'omnia vici olim; verti et nunc omnia vinco' is true without the 'verti.' I don't suppose any man ever thoroughly saw Rome. I have been doing a stroke of work, five mornings at the Codex Vaticanus; I went twice over the doubtful passages and fac-similised most of the important various readings."

TO HIS WIFE.

"*Feb.* 14.

"An ever-memorable day; set off at nine for Old Rome by the pouring fountain of Trevi, and the eternal

Forum of Trojan (go where you will we always come to it); to the Temple of Mars Ultor, a great fragment with three gigantic Corinthian columns, whose bases have been excavated from beneath the soil; then to the Temple of Pallas Minerva, an exquisite fragment of a very rich frieze and two Corinthian columns, with a statue of the goddess above. To the Forum, and first examined the Basilica of Constantine, a gigantic ruin; then to the Temple of Venus and Rome, built by Hadrian after his own designs, just facing the Coliseum, the only part standing is a depressed apse, with a decorated roof. Then to the glorious Coliseum itself, basking in a cloudless, intolerable sun, the sky through its many openings an incredibly deep ultramarine blue; we went all over it, up to the very top, whence a magnificent view; the whole Forum, Capitol, St. Peter's, just seen over the Mount Mario, all burning under a cloudless sky; from another point Mount Gennaro, and, beyond, the snowy Apennines.

"The proportions of the Coliseum are certainly stupendous; it has a Flora of its own, on which books have been written. It is in fact the great city of the dead, where thousands have perished while millions have looked on; here Ignatius fell gloriously by the lions, and hundreds of Christian martyrs were cast to wild beasts. I thought of the thousand events crowding along the paths of history which have befallen it since.

"I felt almost giddy with the whirl of thickening recollections which centre here, as I rambled about the labyrinth of cool arcades clothed with numerous budding plants; a day never to be forgotten; would that you and the dear girls were with me. I cannot describe what I felt as I wandered away from the company to get my thoughts to myself, and sat and wrote in my memorandum book what did not express them. I hate sentiment, but I like truth, and if ever there was a spot in which the world's history centres, it is this; a memorable day it must be to any one who first sees these stupendous monuments of Roman greatness. From the Coliseum we went to the Baths of Titus, a ruin of treble interest; first, on the slope of the

Esquiline, north-east of the Coliseum, stood the house of Mecænas, Horace and Virgil's patron; then the Golden House, or Palace of Nero; and last came Titus, who enlarged this bath, and building over its garden, made the whole into public baths of gigantic dimensions; here some places were almost carpeted with maiden-hair fern; in a painted recess we saw where the Laocoon was found; on a roof some frescoes, yet visible, from which Raffaelle took his design for the Loggie in the Vatican. After this we went to the Villa Ludovisi on the Pincian, and saw some good statues, especially a Gaul killing his wife and himself, said by antiquaries to be now proved to be a portion of the group to which the so-called Gladiator belongs; but the gem of the day was the view from the top of the casino in the garden of the villa. Imagine a cloudless ultramarine sky, on one side all Rome beneath our feet, with its hundred domes and turrets and massive palaces; south the boundless level of the Campagna towards the sea; south-east the blue Alban Hills, with their graceful outlines, dotted with white villages and villas, sinking down north-east to the valley, where the road to Tivoli goes; and then the glory of the view, the splendid Apennine range rising tier over tier, clear under the cloudless sky; then round the north, seen over a foreground of pines and cypresses, Soracte unclad from snow, Fidenæ, Veii, and the Etruscan uplands in wavy, hilly unevenness, till a reach of the yellow Tiber and the Monte Mario and St. Peter's and the Janiculum bring round Rome again. It is a view only seen once in a life, because only once seen first.

"*Feb.* 16.—Yesterday we went to the Barberini Palace, where the chief feature is Beatrice Cenci by Guido; you know it by copies, but all copies utterly fail to render the loveliness and sorrow of the original. She appears to me much younger than in the copies; it is a picture of almost childish gaiety and innocence trampled out and turned into involuntary guilt by brutal usage, the eyes are brimming over with unshed tears; the face absolutely saddened with intense suffering; after a long gaze at it, I should be disposed to call it the first in point of effective expression of existing portraits. I saw here a curious picture of Christ among the Doctors, by Albert Dürer. Our Lord is a mere child, evidently less than twelve years old. He has red hair, and flowers over His shoulders, with one finger on the thumb of the other hand as if disputing; and near Him are two very queer doctors, that on the left hand with a face almost like a baboon. Holman Hunt may have seen this picture and taken a hint from it.

"To-day, Saturday (16th), we have been to the Palazzo Rospigliosi on the Quirinal, to see the famous Aurora of Guido; it is a fresco on the roof of a casino or summer-house in a very pretty garden, approached through a pergola of orange and lemon trees, full of golden fruit, as are all those which abound about Rome at this time of the year. The palace is on the site of the Baths of Constantine, and the casino is richly adorned with bas-reliefs and statues found on the spot. The fresco far surpassed my expectations. I will not attempt to describe it, but you and the dear girls must come and see it for yourselves some day. Thence we went to the Palazzo Sciarra in the Corso, where are some very lovely pictures. The famous Bella Donna of Titian, the Violin-players of Raffaelle, a very fine picture called Modesty and Vanity by Leonardo da Vinci, and a charming St. Sebastian by Pietro Perugino, Raffaelle's master.

"Thence we drove to the Protestant Burying-ground, near the Porta St. Paolo; the old pyramidal tomb of Caius Cestius points it out in the views of Rome; it is a lovely spot, very pretty and touching; the enclosed violets are from K. W. R——'s grave, of which I have made a sketch. We saw many tombs of interest here; Augustus Hare's, Shelley's, and Keats', in the old cemetery near the pyramid. Then we went to the restored Basilica of St. Paolo, which was one of the most interesting churches in the neighbourhood of Rome before it was burnt in 1823; it has been most nobly restored, has five aisles supported by rows of twenty granite pillars, and over these are medallions of all the Popes from St. Peter to Pio Nono; next we went to the Pantheon; this as you know is the only one of the great buildings of Rome which has remained at all in a perfect state; it formed most probably the great hall of the Baths of Agrippa, whose name is on the portico; it is round, and with a flat dome having a round opening into the air; its proportions are very grand and beautiful. The interest of it is that all the marble pillars and panels, which look like modern fittings of the present church, are ancient, just as they were in old Roman times; showing, which is a fact worth observing, that the present Roman way of fitting up with marbles is really nothing but a continuation of the practice which prevailed under the Empire. In the Pantheon are the tombs of Raffaelle, and Annibal Carracci and seven other painters.

"*Feb.* 17.—We have been to the Catacombs of St. Calixtus, about two miles out on the Appian Way. The sight is very curious and instructive; there are miles upon miles of subterranean passages about two feet wide and seven or eight high, with innumerable little recesses in the walls for the bodies which were buried in them without coffins; some of these recesses are six feet long, others hardly more than one; every here and there opens out some family chapel with its rude altar and fresco, with ancient Christian devices, most of these emblematic of the Resurrection. Jonah is a very favourite device, our Lord as the Good Shepherd, &c.

"*Feb.* 18.—The Vatican seems almost inexhaustible, miles of statues, many of them at every point of view; on our first day we simply took the mountain tops so to speak, the great *chef-d'œuvres* which all the world knows; very nicely arranged, and only first-rate pictures; it certainly is an event in one's life when one stands first face to face with such a picture as Raffaelle's Transfiguration [3]. I have dwelt long on this picture, perhaps the greatest of pictures,

---

[3] The full description, the result of half an hour's attentive study of this great picture, is published in "Letters from Abroad," p. 66, 2nd ed.

because I felt it very deeply, and never understood it till I saw and studied the original. That is the great benefit among many other great benefits of coming here, that for the first time great works of art reveal their meaning to one. How touching to think that this picture was the last thing which the great painter was employed on, that it was left unfinished at his death, carried before his corpse at his funeral; we may well say, may he have found that peace and consolation in Christ which his last hours felt could be found only in Him.

"*Feb.* 20.—At ten we went by appointment to Monsignore Talbot at the Vatican, to get our first work at the Codex Vaticanus. He went with us to the Library, and the celebrated MS. was produced. Then, as I expected, our difficulties began: the librarian insisted that our order from Antonelli, although it ran 'per verificare,' to verify passages, only extended to seeing the Codex, not to using it. M. Talbot pleaded our cause well and strongly, and in consequence we were allowed to use it for that morning only, amounting to one hour. We got through the passages in St. Matthew [4] about which there is any doubt. M. Talbot promises meantime to see Antonelli, and get us a special permission to work at the Codex. When turned out we went to the celebrated Loggie and Stanze of Raffaelle, also in the Vatican; the former, one gallery running round the court of the palace, opened to the air till the last few years, but now glazed to preserve the frescoes, the subjects are principally from the Old Testament History; the Stanze are a series of rooms, or rather halls, containing very large fresco pictures on the walls, nearly all by the same great painter.

"The Palace of the Cæsars on the Palatine is the ruin of

---

[4] Before leaving England the Dean made a long list of the passages which he wished to consult (see 5th edition of Vol. i. of the Greek Testament, pp. 108 and 146). The feelings of the librarian when he perceived the use which the Dean made of the Codex were only mollified by Monsignore Talbot remaining on this occasion within sight of the manuscript and its readers as long as it was in their hands.

Rome which most completely gives one the idea of devastation and overthrow. Here the great lords of the world for centuries held their court; here some of the fearfullest crimes in history were perpetrated.

"*Feb.* 21.—The Baths of Caracalla are a vast mass of ruin on the Appian Way, most striking, next, if not equal, in grandeur to the Coliseum; great halls as large as a church one after another, some still paved with the old mosaics. We climbed to the top, and sat there. Such a view over the Lateran to the ever-glorious Apennines, over the Campagna to the Alban Hills, all swimming in a mist of heat, and, over all, the clear blue sky of this delicious climate; it was one of our ever-memorable days.

"*Feb.* 22.—The Forum we have thoroughly explored, made out the uncovered foundations of the old buildings, the Basilica of Julia, Temples of Saturn, Vespasian, and Concord, the School of Xanthus, the Rostra, and the marks of the old stairs, by which in Republican times they used to climb to the Capitol; all most interesting. On our return, I deviated from the rest, and came upon a sight which I shall never forget. A procession of about one hundred monks, some with long cloaks covering their faces and holes for their eyes, and others holding large candles lighted, then a great gilded bier, and on it a young girl lying dead, white and fair as wax, her face exposed, and her hands, which were joined as in prayer and a small crucifix in them; the procession moved along singing; a most striking sight and rare, as only very old-fashioned families keep up the custom.

"*Feb.* 23.—To the Vatican. The 'Shadow veiled from head to foot who keeps the keys of all the creeds' did not appear till nearly ten; when he did we found all smoothed, and a fresh order from Antonelli, so that we used the MS. all the time, and made good progress, and advanced as far as Acts vii. I have been all through the list twice, and made *fac-simile* copies of all the principal various readings.

"At the Borghese Palace there is a vast collection of beautiful pictures; twelve rooms full, requiring a week's study. We have seen Gibson's studio. I was very anxious to see one of his painted statues. It is known that the ancients always painted their statues, and Gibson has been the first to revive it. I must own that I am quite a convert to it. Next we went to Miss Hosmer's, a very clever American sculptress; some of her works are most lovely.

"We have seen some Columbaria, one on the Appian Way very large, full of inscriptions; some were of the family of Nero, and among these I found those saluted in the Epistle to the Romans, ch. xvi., Hermas, Julia, Tryphæna, and Tryphosa[5], which was very interesting, showing that such names existed in Nero's family. The same day we saw the Circus of Romulus, and the so-called Fountain of Egeria.

"*Sunday, Feb.* 24.—I went to the early Communion at nine and the morning service at eleven, then home for biscuits and off for a walk of exploration; first for the Church of Sta. Croce in Gerusalemme, founded by Helena, the mother of Constantine, and built on earth brought from Jerusalem and mixed in the foundations. Then we went out of the Porta Maggiore, the finest of the Roman gates. It was a portion of the Claudian Aqueduct, the hollow ways for the water yet visible above it. Thence up a country lane to the Basilica of St. Lorenzo, and here we were indeed repaid for our walk. The Basilica is most striking, the most so of all the smaller ones. The ancient Basilica, now the chancel, is excavated about ten feet beneath the present level. There is a remarkable capital of a column here, with a frog and lizard, showing that it came from the Portico of Octavia.

"*March* 1.—Trench[6], Bullock, and I started off for Albano. A day among a thousand. The first nine miles along the Via Appia Nova, nearly parallel with the old Via Appia, the new road joining the old near the 'Three taverns' which St. Paul passed on his way to Rome. Soon after the eleventh milestone we began to mount over a low spur of the hills, on

---

5 He refers to this discovery in "How to Study the New Testament," Epistles, 1st section, p. 189.

6 Then Dean of Westminster, now Archbishop of Dublin.

the other side of which Albano lies. On our left, on a brow, is Castel Gandolfo, the Pope's country-house.

"At Albano we got a guide and three asses, and off we set, as queer a cavalcade as you need set eyes on. So we went up over Castel Gandolfo, through a lane darkly bowered with ilexes, and the banks bright with anemones, red, blue, and white, and reached a brow, and looked down on the Lake of Albano lying imbedded in hills on all sides. On the right Monte Cavo, the old Mons Latium, where was the temple of Jupiter Latialis, the old meeting-place of the Latin tribes, ruthlessly destroyed in the last century by Cardinal York. On a lower ridge lie the ruins of Alba Longa. We rode down to see the famous Emissary, a tunnel excavated 400 B.C. to let out the waters of the lake and keep them at a certain height; a work as perfect now as 2260 years ago. We then returned by Genzano and Nemi, celebrated by Lord Byron in his 'Childe Harold.'

"*Sunday, March* 3.—The occupation of writing to you is ever for me a daily pleasure. I am holding intercourse with her who has been my choice, and God's choice for me, to brighten my childhood, to stimulate my youth, to bless my manhood, and to cheer my advancing years; but I did not sit down to write a love-letter, so let me to my tale. I am now alone, as Bullock has returned home. To-morrow I go to Tivoli; to-day, having a few minutes to spare before church, I looked into a church very near here, called St. Andrea delle Frati, known in the history of modern Romanism as the place where the Virgin is said to have appeared to the Jew Ratisbonne in 1842; there is a picture of it in one of the side chapels. Then to church, where Trench preached a very striking sermon; subject, 'The Question of the Philippian Jailor.' After the communion (144 now, and thirty at the early communion) I took a long walk outside the Ponte Molle, leaving Rome by the Porta del Popolo, and round the back of the Monte Mario. The views were more glorious than I ever remember to have seen them; it is a Tramontane east wind, and this at Rome always makes everything clear.

"In the evening I went to dine in a quiet way with Mr. Woodward, the chaplain here, meeting the Trenches.

"*Tivoli, Monday Night, March* 4.—Here I am in the strangest little inn, the 'Osteria della Sibylla,' between the Temples of Vesta and the Sibyl, right over the falls. But let me take things in due order. At seven this morning started *tout seul,* for the first fifteen miles over the Campagna; then four or five miles are spent in winding up zigzags through an olive wood, Tivoli being situated high up on one side of a ravine. Some of the olives are very old and gnarled, and put me in mind of pictures of those in the Garden of Gethsemane. At length we passed on the right the enormous ruins of the Villa of Hadrian. Tivoli is a poor dirty place; its glory is in the cascades and grottoes, and remains of some very beautiful temples and villas. The old Roman citizens had villas very thick here, and the place is much celebrated in the poems of Horace and others. In a villa here many of the best works of art were found —the Venus de' Medici, the Dying Gladiator, the famous Mosaic of the Doves drinking out of a vase, &c. &c.

"The place is one roar of water, but the present great cascade is not that which Horace saw and celebrated. In 1826 a flood swept away the channel of the old fall, and carried away with it twenty-five houses and a church. Gregory XVI. tunnelled the rock, and made the waterfall about 200 yards farther up the ravine. I believe it is a much finer fall than before, but one would have liked to have seen it as Horace saw it, and as Quintilius Varus looked on it the morning he left his villa opposite, to take the command of the troops in Germany, where he was killed.

"*March* 5.—I have been to see all there is to be seen, ending with the grounds of the Villa d'Este, where I sketched, and, having plenty of time, coloured my sketch on the spot. The day has been cloudless; just one of those days I so much enjoy, a time of wild liberty—botanizing, sketching, and keeping my eyes for Nature to fill them. The view of Rome from here I shall never forget: half a hundred of domes, towers, and palaces glittering in the evening sun;

the Alban Hills clear and bright beyond the Campagna, which last is in the perfection of its green, pink, and blue; Hadrian's Tomb, the Coliseum, the Pantheon, the Basilica of Constantine, dappled with their sober brown the yellow of the modern buildings; while majestic in form rises the dome of St. Peter's far to the right, and intermingled with pines and cypresses. It is indeed a sight to be remembered.

"*March* 6.—To the Corsini Palace. Guido's Ecce Homo is very fine; the divine expression is caught: a most speaking picture; but it struck me the flesh was too feminine and smooth for that of one who had not where to lay His head, and must have been weather-beaten and rough-lined by suffering.

"A fine bit of rock and stream by Salvator Rosa I saw in this collection; but the sky, as is so often with him, is dashed in, in blues and whites, with apparent uselessness but admirable effect. The same is true of a picture close to this, where each horizontal white cloud is put in with one stroke of the brush.

"*March* 7.—After breakfast, having ascertained that the Frascati Railway train went at twelve, I walked off towards the Porta Maggiore, doing in my way three churches. The first was the church of the Capuchin Monks, in the Piazza Barberini, where is a very fine picture, by Guido, of St. Michael casting down Satan. The Archangel is serene in youthful beauty, triumphant but calm, and has been well called the Apollo Belvidere of the Church. The Satan is said to be a portrait of a Cardinal (afterwards Innocent XII.), who in some way annoyed the painter; but the curiosity of this church is the crypt. There are a succession of little rooms, laid out like gardens, with earth brought from Jerusalem. The little flower-beds are all graves. All round the sides of the rooms are horizontal niches; in these lie dried Capuchins; some few are upright. The arches, niches, altars, lamps, railings, cornices, are all composed of human bones. It was more like sporting with death than anything I had ever seen, and yet there was something touching in it. After this I turned aside to the Church of Sta. Pudentiana, one of the very old churches in Rome, and said to stand on the site of the house of the Senator Pudens (see 2 Tim. iv. 21), with whom St. Peter lodged, it is said. In the tribune are some very old mosaics of the ninth century, or earlier perhaps, far bolder and more expressive than any I have seen, and giving me a far higher idea of art at that time than I had before.

"Then off to Frascati, twelve miles from Rome: it lies on the steep slope of the Alban Hills. It may always be seen from Rome, glittering white against the blue hills in this clear atmosphere. There is a long ascent before reaching it, as at Albano and Tivoli, through vineyards and olive-woods. The views from Frascati beat those from Tivoli, by the very circumstance which makes Tivoli superior in its own scenery, viz. that Tivoli being in among the glorious Apennines, one loses them as a feature in the views of the Campagna from it; but from Frascati the whole lies open to view, with both ranges of hills, and all the country of old classic history. The only object of real interest near Frascati is Tusculum; it is on a high volcanic hill about three miles from Frascati, the way lying through the grounds of a villa belonging to V. E. R. D. I. (Victor Emmanuele, Re d'Italia: the pass-word here at Rome, on account of which Verdi's operas are forbidden to be performed), very beautiful, with increasingly glorious views of the Campagna and Mediterranean, the banks quite painted with violets, red anemones, squills, and periwinkles. Up, up, up, till at last we come to the ancient pavement of the Via Latina, actually worn into wheel-ruts by the ancient chariots and waggons. It was strange to think of Cicero driving up his biga (or buggy), with his head full of Tusculan Disputations. We passed what they call his Villa. 'C'était un Grand Monsieur ce Cicero' said my guide; "il était le Premier Consul de Rome.' This certainly was an historical 'find' of no small importance. We mounted again, passing a nearly perfect stone theatre and more ruins, to the arx or keep of the citadel of old Tusculum, an older town than Rome. The view from the top is truly magnificent, the crowning point certainly from which to see the Campagna and its mountains and lakes. We could see all the range of the Alban and Volscian and Sabine hills; Soracte to the north, and beyond, the mountains on the way to Siena and Florence; then, following westward, Rome; the glittering reaches of the Anio, as it flows to join the Tiber, and of the Tiber itself, till it joins the sea; then the silver shield of the sea itself, reaching right up into the sky. Beneath, the olive woods waved like a grey sea, clothing the base of the hills; and we could see, gleaming like little bits of silver in the green Campagna, the lakes of Regillus (ever memorable for the battle in which Castor and Pollux are said to have helped the Romans), Gabii (known in the history of the Tarquins), Bracciano, &c.

"On the 8th I went to the Capitol to see the pictures: they are not many, and for the most part shabby and in all conditions; but I liked them all the better, as they have not suffered at the hands of restorers and re-painters. There is a most lovely St. Sebastian by Guido, and various Guercinos, &c. I saw also the Palazzo Doria, the most magnificent of all the Roman palaces, and with hundreds of pictures, multitudes of second and third-rate things; with, however, a fair sprinkling of first-rate things. Titian's Magdalen is too much like a country-girl. . . . Claude's famous Mill very, very beautiful, let Turner and Ruskin say what they will; the water and sky seem to me almost perfect; considerably borrowed from the Roman Campagna in the ruins and places, and I am sure I discovered Monte Cavo in disguise. The gem of this collection is Leonardo da Vinci's portrait of Queen Joanna of Aragon.

"8th, 4 p.m. (from Note-book).—Coliseum; I am sitting here perhaps for the last time. Strange things have happened since Ignatius was torn by the wild beasts here: he may have breathed his soul out on the very spot where I am sitting. I own I have bad taste enough to like the presence of Christianity here, it is so speaking as to what has passed, and to itself also.

"A procession of men has just entered, in brown cloaks covering all their persons, with holes cut for their eyes, and with a Capuchin friar, who preached a sermon from the pulpit: about one hundred persons were present. The subject was the sufferings of Christ in the Garden and His capture by the Jews; it seemed to be a part of a course, and the application that it was for our sins, and therefore we must hate and forsake sin. After the sermon began the Via Crucis, the going round to all the fourteen stations, which they are now doing. It is indeed a curious and instructive sight, full of associations of the past, and speculations as to what may be in store for the future. When one looks at the monstrous state of things here, one may well exclaim, *ἕως πότε Κύριε* ['How long, O Lord?']; but when I see the apparent devotion of these poor people, I am led to hope they may be brought to a purer faith without the terrible process of all faith being broken down. The enormous iniquities of this place smoke to heaven and demand vengeance, which may not be long delayed. In her was found the blood of all the saints from Ignatius to the Waldenses.

"On Saturday, the 9th, the Villa Borghese. Beautiful grounds, carpeted with anemones and daisies, &c. Then I went to the Prætorian Camp, an interesting spot, for one of my last views of Rome. St. Paul's bonds were known *ἐν ὅλῳ τῷ πραιτωρίῳ*[7]. Here it was that he wrote his Epistle to the Philippians, his joyful, tearful, sad, happy letter, when he felt that life was Christ and death gain. Many of the vaults remain: in some of them St. Paul may have been confined when God spared him, *ἵνα μὴ λύπην ἐπὶ λύπην σχῶ*[8].

"Here, where I am looking at the remains of an ancient painting on the carved roof, he may have written:[9] *ἐπιθυμίαν ἔχων εἰς τὸ ἀναλῦσαι καὶ σὺν Χριστῷ εἶναι.* Here, where he might have seen athletes depicted running on the ceiling,

---

[7] Phil. i. 13. "In all the palace."
[8] Phil. ii. 27. "Lest I should have sorrow upon sorrow."
[9] Phil. i. 23. "Having a desire to depart and be with Christ."

he may have described himself as forgetting the things behind, and reaching forth to those before, for the prize of his high calling in Christ Jesus.

"*March* 10.—My last day in Rome. This morning I saw the relics of Becket, two pieces of linen shirt, one with a good-sized stain of blood on it: besides these, there was a small bag of blue paper tied round with a string of silk. On my asking the sacrist what these were, he answered, 'Piccoli pezzi di pietra e di cerebello e sangue di S. Tomasso.'

"This is, at all events, an interesting approximation to the question, 'What has become of the bits cut out of the stone at Canterbury?'

"I am now sitting on the steps of St. John Lateran—sky cloudless, the Apennine range as clear as it can be—a lovely purple, every depression marked in bright blue shadow; straight in front Sta. Croce in Gerusalemme, with its picturesque campanile; to the left of it an old ruin, the Temple of Venus and Cupid; then long lines of wall and aqueducts form the interesting middle distance between me and the hills. Nearer are groups of people and soldiers; outside the Porta Maggiore is just such a base of a pillar as the Roman one lately placed [1] in the garden near the Baptistery at Canterbury."

TO HIS WIFE (*continued*).

"*March* 9.—Let me wind up this voluminous letter and our Roman correspondence, by expressing a fervent sense of thankfulness to God for His many mercies to me. During this visit to the centre of the world's history, I have for the most part been thoroughly well, and have enjoyed myself exceedingly; I only hope the effects of the change may be long and effectually visible in my health. Still I must not expect too much, during the last two days my head, which I thought well, has begun its troublesome buzzing and giddiness again; but I am willing to attribute it to some passing cause."

---

[1] See p. 301.

To his Wife.

"*March* 10.

"This is my last night in Rome, and I am tired with packing, but I cannot help writing a few words to you on this day before it ends,—our twenty-sixth wedding day! We have never been separated, I think, on one of them before. May God unite us together, and if it please Him, give us many more together; and, above all, a happy eternity hereafter. I am returning home with the Trenches. We found the boat to Leghorn does not run, except the Messageria boat on Wednesday, which will be too late for us; so we have determined to exchange the perils of water for the perils of robbers, and post by land, going by Siena and Florence. In the present tempestuous weather, this is some relief, and I fancy the danger of thieves is not much."

To his Wife.

"*Bolsena, March* 11; *posted at Florence*, 13.

"Here we are more than seventy miles from Rome, having done the day's journey rapidly and safely. The road out of Porta del Popolo and over the Ponte Molle; then leaving the Flaminian just the other side of the Tiber, and taking the Via Cassia through Baccano, a town in an ancient crater of a volcano, through a beautiful ravine, over a long mountain, and down again to Viterbo.

"Siena. Here we are, having accomplished all the supposed dangerous road without an adventure, thank God, and that in two days; the Lake at Bolsena was a fine sight, foaming and roaring in the early morning; the shores of the lake are desolated by malaria. No human being can sleep a night on them in summer or autumn. Then we mounted up through bits of broken volcanic rocks clothed with gnarled oaks, very picturesque, and just like the foregrounds of Gaspar Poussin and Salvator Rosa, to a village called St. Lorenzo Nuovo, built by Pope Pius VI. for the inhabitants of the old St. Lorenzo, which was on the shores of the lake, and not healthy. We then crossed a valley to a very curious place, called Acquapendente, on the top of a ridge, with a ravine running down it; then a strange volcanic mountainous country, and, amidst this, we climbed an enormous mountain capped with wild volcanic rocks to the village at its top, called Radiofani, the frontier of Tuscany."

TO HIS WIFE.

"*Florence, March* 13, *night.*

"After a day spent in seeing Siena and getting here by rail.

"At Siena we sallied out after breakfast; first to the picture-gallery, where are a set of rooms chronologically illustrating the Sienese school of painters; most interesting, with fine expressive and noble faces and ideas. This school was celebrated for extreme care in representing feeling and devotion, and it is most instructive to see how the real genius of the earlier masters degenerated with the conventionalities of the sixteenth century, when it became extinguished altogether. In this collection is a grand fresco, by Sodoma, Our Lord tied to the Pillar; I hardly know any thing finer than this. Then we went to see the Town Hall, a grand old building with a high tower; then to the Cathedral, and what to say of it I know not; when the west front burst upon me, it almost took away my breath; imagine a front something like Milan, not nearly so large, but far more consistent in its architectural ornaments, all built of the richest and most gorgeous-coloured marble, glittering in the sun like a piece of enamel. The tower and all the pinnacles and buttresses are of black and white marble, in alternate stripes, so that the effect is rich and gorgeous beyond description; the case is the same inside, it gives one the idea of a moderately large cathedral; but it may be imagined what it would have been if finished, by the fact that the present church is only the transept of the intended cathedral; it was stopped building by the terrible plague, called the 'Black Death,' in 1356."

To his Wife.

"*Florence, March* 14; *posted at Pisa, ditto.*

"This has been a most pleasant day and a most busy day too, and I must sit down as usual to make you a sharer of it, as far as pen and ink will do so. I rose at seven, and sallied out to face a bitterly cold morning, and to make out my first acquaintance with La bella Firenze. I soon made out the principal points, the Arno spanned by its four bridges, the magnificent Piazza della Signoria with the Palazzo Vecchio, the Loggia de Lanzi, and the Uffizi, and the unrivalled Cathedral, all this I soon poked out by the light of nature. After breakfast I lost no time but went at once to the Uffizi or Offices, the building containing the greatest collection of pictures and statues; it would be quite in vain to attempt to go through all that struck me in this noble collection. I must trust to my note-book aided by photographs, and some evenings together at home, please God, to explain what I thought best to record in this my first and very cursory view. In pictures this collection is exceedingly rich; the Medici were noble patrons of art of every kind, and the authorities have kept up their character with spirit; some of Raffaelle's very finest pictures are here. The Madonna del Cardellino, so called because St. John is offering a goldfinch to our Lord, is a most lovely and affecting picture, about which I shall have much to say when we meet. In the same octagonal cabinet which contains the Venus de' Medici are about twenty pictures, enough of themselves to set up a nation with a fair nucleus of a gallery, and five or six ancient statues known all over the world, the Wrestlers, the Slave whetting a knife, the Apollo, the Dancing Faun, &c. And there are hundreds of good pictures besides two rooms of portraits of all the painters, and some most interesting sketches of drawings by the old masters; in fact, it is a gallery requiring weeks, instead of one morning to see it in.

This done, or rather not done, I went to the Cathedral: what to say of it I know not, it is quite in its own way, totally unlike any other church I ever saw, both inside and outside; it is of different coloured marbles; campanile by Giotto, and all from the south-east, where you can see the great dome, the largest in the world supported by its lesser buttress domes. The windows are especially glorious, date 1434, done by a Florentine artist at Lubeck, uniting therefore the skill of Germany with the art of Italy. The campanile in the background is a sight worth coming here for, if all the rest of Florence were nothing. I could not conceive any church on earth could be finer for grand and awing effect, the western sun streaming in through these most lovely stained glass windows. Behind the high altar is the last finished work of Michael Angelo, a Pietà. Thence to the Baptistery far-famed for its gates of Paradise[2] (as Michael Angelo called them).

"As the sun was about to set I took a fiacre and told the man to drive me to some hill near the city, where there was the best view of it, for as yet I had no idea of its situation; he took me up on one side of the Porta Romana, where the view was indeed worth the ride: there lay Florence, with its domes and towers in a basin of hills, purple with the evening light, and studded with white villas, and surrounding it like the hills about Jerusalem. Our ride issued in an engagement for him to take me out to Fiesole to breakfast to-morrow, which I will report in due time. Good night, my three beloved ones.

"*March* 15.—This morning at seven coachee appeared, and we set off to Fiesole, a Tuscan city of old times, now a mere village on a high hill overhanging Florence, three miles off. The view is very striking, of Florence and all the country round. There cannot be a greater contrast than this view and Rome with its desolate Campagna; here it is populous even to spoiling the beauty of the scene, by the innumerable white houses and villas which for miles and miles stud the

---

[2] A pair of bronze doors which contain twenty compartments, or panels, fitted with as many reliefs, consisting of scriptural subjects, besides a profusion of ornamental work in the intermediate spaces, executed by Lorenzo Ghiberti about the beginning of the fifteenth century.

broad Val d'Arno. Arrived at Fiesole, I thought of Milton's lines [3] about Galileo,—

> "Through optic glass the Tuscan artist views
> At evening from the top of Fiesole,"—

as I stood on the summit and looked on the whole broad view, a famous place for star-gazing. I went with a guide to see the old Etruscan walls of the city, and the remains of an amphitheatre, and then to a humble little inn to get some *café au lait,* which the padrona brought me in a tumbler-glass; then back to Florence in less time as you may imagine than we came, and in to see the famous Church of Santa Croce, full of illustrious tombs—Dante, Galileo, Alfieri, and others, and some frescoes by early painters; then to the famous picture-gallery in the Pitti Palace, late the residence of the Grand Duke.

It is even a finer collection than that of the Uffizi, comprising many first-rate pictures of Raffaelle, Perugino, Salvator Rosa, Fra Bartolomeo, Andrea del Sarto, &c. Here is the famous Madonna della Seggiola, the round picture of the Holy Family, with which we are all so well acquainted; here also is Raffaelle's little picture of the Vision of Ezekiel; the Three Fates, by Michael Angelo; a grand picture of St. Mark, by Fra Bartolomeo. Here too, among many other notable pictures, is a portrait of Oliver Cromwell, by Sir Peter Lely, painted by order of the Protector, and sent by him as a present to the Grand Duke of Tuscany. You may well suppose how tantalizing it was to run through such a Gallery in a couple of hours, as I was obliged to do.

"*Pisa, March* 16.—As soon as we came here last night, I just walked out to see the Cathedral and Leaning Tower, and got them finely illuminated by the sloping sun; the whole *coup d'œil,* Cathedral, Baptistery, and Campanile is one I should think unrivalled in the world. I thought I was familiar with the lean of the Campanile, the domed Baptistery, the outline of the Cathedral, and the low wall of the Campo

---

3 "Paradise Lost," Book i. line 288. Milton visited Italy in 1638.

Santo, and yet how different all and each of these now appeared; I was not prepared to see such lovely play of colour on the old walls, nor to find them thrown brightly out by such a fine background of purple blue hills, or that their former rectangular lines would be relieved by such a strange sharp outline which is traced behind them on the cloudless sky. The Tower leans very much more than I had imagined, and certainly does look very funny; it is a curious proof of men's confidence that what has been will be, that a house nestles close under the dangerous side of the Tower. I got up this morning at six, and found the ground white with frost, and the sun just rising; and went out and thoroughly examined the Cathedral, which is very curious indeed; the Baptistery and Campo Santo, or cloistered burying-ground of Pisa, where we have impressed on the walls in the coloured characters of fresco-painting, the quaint ideas of the Old Pisan school of painters with regard to Scripture history, and to the life and death and future of Man. This cloister surrounds an oblong court, the earth of which was brought from Jerusalem.

"*Spezzia, March* 16.—The road from Pisa to this place is dull for the first part of the way; we passed through Massa, in sight of the marble quarries of Carrara, and then the view became very grand indeed. The mountains rising tier above tier, the higher ones covered with snow. Some time after Massa, very picturesque old towns and castles began to appear, perched on the lovely hills, and at last the mountains fairly came across in front and blocked up the way. The road winds up a gentle rise for some miles, the banks covered with primroses, anemones, periwinkles, euphorbias, coronellas, and a white heath like the Cornish one in full bloom; the hedges here are mainly composed of myrtles. Arriving at the brow, the road winds down on the lovely Gulf of Spezzia, and I don't suppose the world can furnish a more beautiful scene than it presented when we drove down into it; for us the sun had set owing to the mountains behind, but on the opposite coast and distant mountains he was still shining. The snow-capped mountains were of the most delicious rosy pink, very faint, with the snow in white streaks; then this pink increased in depth and glow in the middle distance, till the near coast which was yellow and red, dappled with forest and town; and all this was reflected in the glassy calm gulf, which leapt and twinkled with hues almost prismatic.

"In the Gulf lay two Italian men-of-war, their hulls and rigging reflected on the water. It was a scene never to forget; if my hand can do it, I will try to give some notion of it in colour. The Gulf is a most magnificent harbour; it would hold, they say, all the fleets in the world. We mean to have an English service in our rooms to-morrow morning, and have sent round to the other hotels notice to say so.

"*Sunday evening, March* 17.—We have spent a delightful day in this most lovely place; at seven, I sallied out and climbed a little way up the Olive Terrace, and it was well I did, for the view we saw last night has not shown since. Our congregation consisted of an English father and mother and daughter, an American ditto, and a Westminster ditto; strange enough that three exactly alike should meet. Trench read prayers and I preached. Then I climbed again to an old castle on one of the Peaks with the Dean and Mrs. Trench; and after lunch I went out alone for a regular long ramble, up one of the dozen lovely glens which meet here. I never saw anything more beautiful in my life; imagine the dry bed of a torrent such as that at Invermoriston near the Caledonian Canal, but composed of all manner of coloured marbles in rocks of every fantastic shape, the chinks of the sides filled with wild flowers, primroses, pink anemones, blue periwinkles, and white and red heath in full blossom, and fringed with whole copses of myrtle and laurustinus also in full blossom, while a chorus of birds sung all around, and the bells from churches perched about on the heights were swinging with their lively sound. I took out my tin box, and filled it with many beautiful flowers and roots; ceterach and trichomanes clothed every wall; on the grass I found the spider orchis, and a curious pitcher-plant, a sort of arum, and the blue bachelors' button; there I stayed botanizing and meditating till approaching *table d'hôte*, and an approaching shower also sent me back faster than I came, which was natural, the climb being tremendous, the shower came fast and furious as I stood into Spezzia, laden with heath and myrtle, &c.

"As to our plans. We reach Genoa (D.V.) to-morrow evening, and stay till Tuesday five p.m., for which I am glad, as I never saw it; and then start by express through Turin and Susa to the foot of Mount Cenis. Then cross next day, which takes twelve hours, to St. Jean de Maurienne, where the rail begins, and there sleep. Then on Thursday to Macon, where the Trenches stay; but if I am in good order I shall probably post on to Paris all night, as I want a day there. To make safe, in case this letter should not reach, I will telegraph from Paris about my return.

"Send all my letters and a waste-paper basket in the carriage to Dover, then I shall gain time and know what is doing; and let me have a note to say how all is going on.

"If either of the dear girls like to come down, *tant mieux;* but if it will be awkward waiting about, don't suppose I expect it, or consider it a thing of necessity. We have only just missed an earthquake here.

"P.S.—*Genoa, March* 19.—Got here in safety about eight last night, after eighteen hours posting through, for the most part, most lovely scenery. We got a mountain storm of east wind and hail, which nearly took the carriage off its wheels, but when we came down to the shore the roads were dusty. The road baffles all description in beauty: it keeps the coast, now on the level, now winding up the promontories. The hedges are of aloes and orange, trees thick with fruit hanging over, and the grand waves tumbling in evermore on the left, in phosphoric sparkles along the shore. Genoa is a city of palaces spread along the shore, and up the mountain streets, narrow but grand."

JOURNAL.

"After sleeping at Susa, where we arrived from Genoa at

midnight, we started at nine a.m. to cross. There had been during the night a tremendous hurricane, accompanied at Susa by rain in torrents, and on the mountains by a deep fall of snow. We had five miles in our carriage, winding up by steep ascents, with splendid views of the valley and Susa to the first relay; then we were told that further progress was impossible. The diligence due at three a.m. had not yet arrived, and in fact nothing had come from the top; all was stopped. So there was nothing for it but for us to stop too. This we did for nearly three hours, during which time we lunched and I took a coloured sketch and finished it. At last the diligence arrived; the *conducteur* reporting that passing was impossible, for the *quantité de niège* was *énorme*, and the wind *horriblement fort*. On this we started, and a mile or two higher exchanged our carriage for a sledge, as we were now on the edge of the snow. We very soon came to large drifts quite obstructing the road, and in some cases rising twenty or thirty feet above it. The passing over these was certainly formidable enough, the road itself being only a ledge in the precipice cut in zigzags, a great drift had spread itself down over the brow covering all the zigzags. Along the steep surface of this snow a track had been extemporized, generally sloping considerably outwards, and sometimes covering itself by new drifts.

"To keep our sledge from falling over, we had two wild but most efficient fellows from among the Cantoniers of the road to hold us up; and, but for them, we should certainly have been over more than once. At one place, just past the barrier at the summit, we hung partly over the edge, and the men showed some anxiety, calling out 'Faites attention' to the postillion, and it was not till they had fastened both traces to one side and pulled us round sideways that we got right again. At last we began to descend over great plains of snow and through forests of zigzags, which, with our horses reduced to one, we trotted very rapidly down, and arrived mercifully preserved at Lans le Bourg, where we slept at a nasty inn. Glad enough, and thankful, especially when we heard that last night's diligence, which preceded us, had got into the worst of the storm, and had been turned over down one of the slopes by the force of the wind. It fell sixty or seventy feet, and then rested on the snow, no one being badly hurt.

"The scenery was very grand, but we could not enjoy it much from the constant risk of impending danger.

"Happily the wind had fallen before we passed, so we were spared that element of peril. Mrs. and Miss Trench behaved admirably, though of course thoroughly frightened."

He reached England on Saturday, March 23. In his way through Paris he paid a visit to the great ecclesiastical warehouse of the Abbé Migne, which then stood in the Rue D'Amboise, outside the Barrière d'Enfer. There he bought all that was published of the Abbé's "Patrologia," a series of Greek and Latin Fathers, amounting, with some subsequent additions, to upwards of 380 volumes, and extending over 1200 years. This valuable acquisition was not likely to lie idle in his library. On April 1, writing to his friend, the Rev. W. H. Gurney, he says, "I am just setting to work at an English critical edition of the New Testament with a popular Commentary;" and on April 5 he heard from his publisher that a new edition was already wanted of the Second Part of Vol. iv. of the Greek Testament, which had been only published two months previously.

He took his family to town at the end of May for a fortnight. "Heard Mendelssohn's 'Antigone' on June 1;" and on the following day, after preaching in Quebec Chapel in the morning, he "heard Mr. Liddon preach at Westminster Abbey in the evening a most striking sermon." On the 5th "we went to the opening of the Horticultural Gardens; Prince Consort there, with the Prince of Wales and Prince Louis of Hesse. The Prince Consort planted a tree."

On the 9th he was invited for the first time to preach before the Queen. "The Prince Consort, the King of the Belgians, the Princess Alice, and the Prince Louis of Hesse, were present with Her Majesty." His text was 1 John iii. 18[4].

---

[4] Not long afterwards this sermon gave occasion to a clever quotation.

In the course of the fortnight he visited the Royal Academy and National Gallery, and received some instruction in water-colours from Mr. Burrell Smith, with whom he went to spend a day in Richmond Park in sketching.

He returned to his Canterbury ordinary work; but his health was not in a perfectly satisfactory state. He records July 4, "awkward giddiness in the head; I must be careful in diet and prepare to be ready for death." A few days afterwards he went with his younger daughter to Winchester on a visit to Dr. (now Bishop) Moberly, and there he was introduced to Mr. and Mrs. Keble. At the end of July, Canterbury was the appointed place for a meeting of members of the medical profession, and the Deanery was not backward in contributing to their hospitable reception.

About this time a plan was under consideration for extensive repairs of the Cathedral which cost him some anxiety and perhaps contributed to his uneasiness about his health. It fell to his lot to hear a sermon which he describes as wandering from its proposed object, and "really levelled at the cathedral and all connected with it, assuming that none had any religion who cared anything for the beauty of nature or art, or for the regularity or decency of Church ordinances. O when will better days dawn on our poor Church?"

On the 1st of August he made an effort to go to the house of his friend Sir Culling Eardley, at the dedication of a church built under peculiar circumstances, where he says, "did not preach the written sermon I had prepared, but an extempore one." At a Bible Meeting here he met the Archbishop of Canterbury (Dr Sumner), Lord Chancellor Cranworth, and some eminent Nonconformist ministers.

A clerical friend under the pressure of sudden illness asked the Dean to preach for him. This sermon was delivered accordingly to a less select congregation than that for which it was written. The clergyman thanked my husband for having "tuned to please a peasant's ear, the harp a king had loved to hear."

He soon returned to his ordinary work, the composition of sermons, and the preparation of new editions of portions of his Greek Testament, but it is now described in his journal as "harassing."

At the end of August we all went for a holiday to the Lake country, spending a day at Doncaster (Dr. Vaughan's) by the way. A little cottage, Loughrigg, was engaged for six weeks through the kind help of Mrs. Arnold. It was on the bank of the Rothay, and about half a mile from Rydal Chapel. Next to sketching, my husband's chief amusement was the completion of his translation of the first half of the Odyssey, which was published after our return to Canterbury. A few extracts from his journal will show how the time passed, and they may be suitably prefaced by a letter which I received a few months ago from Miss R. Quillinan, with whom and with Mrs. Arnold, we enjoyed much friendly intercourse in this holiday.

"Well indeed do we both remember your sojourn in our sweet valley, when we were such near neighbours, and so thoroughly enjoyed the friendly little meetings we occasionally had with your gifted husband, his wife and daughters. One evening comes back vividly before me, which we spent at Fox How, when we all joined in a poetical game, and Dean Alford was so kind and entertaining, and read out our productions so delightfully, that they sounded much better than we had ventured to expect; and again when Miss Arnold and I were walking together to Rydal Chapel, he ran out from Loughrigg Cottage and gave me the poem so kindly composed for my album [5].

"I recollect his saying that it partly came into his mind whilst listening to a peculiarly depressing sermon, and certainly the latter part of Dean Alford's verses is a complete antidote. . . . .

"The last time we met was upon the occasion of your eldest daughter's wedding in Canterbury's glorious cathe-

---

[5] "Life's Question," Poems, p. 334.

dral, when we were kindly invited to a charming oratorio, held in the Chapter House. We adjourned to the Deanery afterwards to supper."

JOURNAL.

"*Sept.* 7.—Expedition to Langdale, the same we took in 1838; sketched under difficulties, the weather is so wet; first my umbrella, then my sketching folio fell into Dungeon Ghyll.

"*Sept.* 20.—Fishing and sketching, and very busy with my Odyssey. Dined at the Arnolds', Fox How, and met many of their nice neighbours.

"*Sept.* 26.—To Coniston, driving by Tarn Hawes, where we had a most splendid view of the mountains; Langdale Pikes, Coniston Old Man; by train to Furness Abbey.

"*Sept.* 28.—Drove to Easedale and lunched at Lancrigg, Sir John [6] and Lady Richardson's pretty place; on our return looked at Wordsworth's grave in Grasmere churchyard.

"*Oct.* 2.—Walked on the terrace towards Grasmere. In the evening to Doves-nest [where once Mrs. Hemans lived for a time], now the abode of Miss Napier and Mr. and Mrs. Graves; met many people there.

"*Oct.* 4.—Though wet, to Buttermere, where we slept; the next day to see Scale Force, Honister Crag, and Borrowdale; splendid scenery, saw Lodore, Skiddaw, &c., which looked most beautiful at sunset.

"*Oct.* 9.—Went to the Arnolds' to play croquet; before, called at Rydal Mount, and Mrs. Hill most kindly took us all over the grounds. Twenty-three years ago Fanny and I saw these grounds; then Wordsworth was living there.

"*Oct.* 14.—Sketched above Fox Ghyll, in the evening drank tea at the Arnolds'; met several of our neighbours, and had an amusing round of the American game.

"*Oct.* 17.—Sketched three hours at Yewdale and on to Coniston; for a wonder, glorious day, thank God for it.

"*Oct.* 18.—Drove to Grasmere up Dunmail Raise, and turned up St. John's Vale, lunched in drizzling rain under some rocks."

---

6 He was associated with Sir John Franklin in the Polar Expedition, and in old age went in search of him. He died in 1865 at Lancrigg.

Soon after our return from the Lakes the Deanery received a guest, in intercourse with whom my husband always found great pleasure.

"*Nov.* 7.—At three Dr. Tregelles came, a most wonderful man for information on all subjects. I took him to see the library and the lions. He kept us amused during his visit.

"*Nov.* 8.—There was a meeting in St. Augustine's Hall to hear Dr. Camilleri's statement about religion in Italy. He and the Warden of St. Augustine's, Mr. Butler of St. Thomas' Hill, and Hake, dined at the Deanery. Dr. Tregelles most amusing."

Through these months the journal supplies frequent evidence of overwork. At the end of the year the following entry occurs:—

"How many mercies have followed me through this year. I have visited the wondrous Rome, one great wish of my life, and have had a very pleasant autumn at the Lakes with my dear ones in good health; my situation here is one of comfort and honour, and I am surrounded by mercies. May I be found ready, so that when He calls, I may joyfully answer. Every year after fifty is a new blessing, which I have no right to expect."

But a fortnight before this was written, an event occurred which agitated all England, and long fixed the attention of loyal hearts on that house of mourning, in which the chief sorrow was borne by the Queen.

My husband writes in his journal:—

"*Sunday, Dec.* 15.—As I was going up to the communion rails, to take my part in the Communion Service in the cathedral, I was told by a verger of the death of the Prince Consort. My voice faltered so much whilst I was reading, Fanny was frightened. I changed the music to a solemn tune, and made an allusion to the subject in my afternoon sermon [7]. Poor Queen!

---

[7] [Printed in "Sermons on Christian Doctrine."] "But though my time is run out, and I have said what I had to say on my subject, none of you I am sure will to-day grudge me a few minutes more. I little knew when I wrote of times of national dejection what deep occasion we should have for it before that sentence was uttered here. A prince and a great man has

"Toll from out thy towers, toll on, thou old cathedral,
Filling the ambient air with softest pulses of sorrow;
Toll out a nation's grief dole for the wail of the people.
Bursting hearts have play'd with words in the wildness of anguish,
Gather'd the bitter herbs that grew in the valley of mourning,
Turn'd the darksome flowers in wreaths for the wept, the lost one.
Toll for the tale that is told, but more for the tale left untold;
Toll for the unreturning, but toll tenfold for the mourning;
Toll for the Prince that is gone, but more for the house that is widow'd."

In the above unfinished lines he expressed his first feelings. Some hexameters which are included in his Letter to America ("Poems," pp. 340), refer to the same event:—

"Full in the midst of all our calm when we thought us securest,
Came the angel of death and smote our sovereign's household,
Smote the stay of the throne—the wise and faithful adviser:
Left our Princes fatherless—left our Queen a widow.
Never in history's day have a people mourn'd as we did.
All to this hour is black in Church and home and assembly;
All speak sad and soft, and pray each day for the mourners."

The following extracts from the sermon which he preached in Canterbury Cathedral, on Dec. 23, shows his estimate of the results of the Prince Consort's public life (pp. 13—17):—

"He came to us in 1840, fresh from a liberal education; and in becoming one of us, and that in an undefined and exceedingly difficult position, he determined to bend the great powers of his mind, and to use the influence of his exalted station to do us good. The early days of his residence among us were cast upon troubled times; the gloomy years between 1840—1848. First, before we speak directly of his great national work, deserves mention the high

---

this day fallen in Israel. At the very time when the vessel of the state requires most careful guidance, and none can tell what dangers are before her, one of those nearest the helm has been mysteriously snatched away, when none thought it, when it seemed as if unbroken prosperity were almost the heritage of our royal family. In one night our princely house is fatherless, our queen a widow. I pause not to day to draw out the solemn lessons which such an event suggests. The blow is too fresh, the effect too numbing just now. All I say is this: first, pray loyally, fervently, constantly, for her whose grief is now uppermost in all our thoughts; and, secondly, waken more than ever at this solemn moment to the claim of our national Christian duties. Let not the astonishment of your present grief supersede your zeal for God's work to which you are called; rather let the softened heart, the stricken spirit, acknowledge God as nearer, His voice as more plainly heard: and may this and all other duties to which He summons you, make you more ready to say, 'Lord, what wouldst Thou have me to do?'"

example of that royal household, whose unstained purity, and ever cautious and punctual propriety in all civil and Christian duties, has been to this people a greater source of blessing than we can appreciate. At last the hour of trial came, and the eventful year 1848, which overturned so many thrones, passed powerless over our favoured land. Our royal house was beyond danger, for its foundations rested in the hearts and prayers of the people. And now a period of calm succeeded, during which our Prince's designs for the good of our people found scope and time to unfold themselves.

"The Great Exhibition of 1851, the effects of which for good have been so many and so universally acknowledged, is believed to have been his own conception; and the plan of it, though filled in by many able hands, was sketched out by himself and constantly presided over and brought to maturity by his unwearied care. The event of that year opened to us views with regard to the intercourse and inter-dependence of foreign nations and ourselves, unknown to English minds before, and suggested to us improvements which have shown new paths of industry and advancement to thousands of families among us. To him we owe, as a direct consequence of this his plan, our Schools of Design, which have called out so many a dormant mind, and brought blessing and competence to so many a household in the lower ranks of life. Of one great society, the 'Society for the Encouragement of Arts, Manufactures, and Commerce,' he was, to the last, the active and indefatigable President.

"Only a week before his death, he determined an important point connected with the building designed for the Exhibition of this year. Besides these efforts you will all remember the interest which he took in our agricultural progress, and in a matter of more vital import to our national well-being—the better construction for decency and comfort, of the cottages of the labouring classes. He has left us his views to be carried out, his schemes to be completed, his example to be followed. Each citizen, each head of a family, ought long to remember, and will long remember, the lessons of his life: we shall not go back again from the higher level to which he has raised us, but shall, I am persuaded, go on in the same course, with more earnest endeavour, with more scrupulous anxiety, because to all other motives is added that of not doing dishonour to his memory, nor violence to what were his known wishes."

A few years afterwards when he had to lay out a plan for filling with images the numerous niches at the west end of Canterbury Cathedral, he assigned a position in one of them for a statue of the Prince, where it was placed by the liberality of her Majesty, opposite to one of herself.

This sad event was not forgotten even in the midst of his hours of relaxation, as will appear from the following letters which he wrote to his brother, Mr. B. H. Alford, who was then sojourning with some pupils at Nice; and whose glowing descriptions gave the first suggestion to those later tours, of which my husband's book on "The Riviera" (published in 1870) is a memorial.

To Mr. B. H. Alford.

"*Dec.* 29, 1861.

"Thanks for your journals and letters. I'll tell you what it is: your descriptions of Nice are so *nice* that they make my mouth water. Why, if nobody else won't come with me, why I shall take two Sundays out of Lent, and run away from Monday till it's Saturday fortnight, and get ten days' roaming and sketching about your parts.

"Well, we have been in sad trouble here about our poor Prince: it is a terrible blow, and the loss will be spread over years to come. The Queen bears up very tolerably, I hear, and the family are admirable. You never saw anything like the sorrow here in England. I remember nothing like it since the Princess Charlotte's death, 1817, which I do remember well. On Monday, 23rd, the day of the funeral, we had our morning prayer here at eleven. I preached a sermon, which I will send you in due time by book-post, with another preached this afternoon. The cathedral was crowded: the Mayor and Corporation and all Canterbury attended. We are all hung with black, every bit of red in the choir covered.

We know nothing as yet about war with America, but all is unfavourable that leaks out. We give our Christmas treat to the choristers, but our theatricals, as also those of the King's School, are given up on account of the Prince's death.

"Three days' frost last week brought about visions of skating again; but it all gave way, strange to say, before a north-east wind, and to-day it is as raw as a cab-horse's hips. All well; the Dean better than usual, and painting at leisure hours a large sunny picture of Thirlmere and St. John's Vale. I certainly will come, please God, and beat up your quarters ere long."

TO MR. B. H. ALFORD.

"*Jan.* 12, 1862.

"It is really and truly my intention to give you a look in March. Here we have had no winter; in Paris they are and have been skating, and the same has been the case in Somersetshire, but not in Kent, I think. I shall sleep at Sens the first night, and not in Paris. In Sens is a cathedral I wish to see: it is said to be very like Canterbury.

"You inquire about our poor Prince. The man's real worth now comes out. He certainly was an immense benefit to our national tastes and habits: the greatest, I have ventured to say in my printed sermon, since the great Alfred; and it is strictly true, no royal personage has ever given himself up as he did to exalt the standard of taste and comfort, and to promote intercourse with other nations. The Exhibition of 1851 was his idea, and has been, for the effect it has produced, the greatest of our times. This coming one, too, which will be even greater, was promoted by him, though he was not exactly on the Commission. The Queen is behaving admirably. You see we are out of our great Yankee fix; and, what is even more wonderful, it was taken sensibly by them from the first, as the correspondence showeth. Since you left I have finished and framed a big picture, and I have now in hand another of the Campagna, from the back of Monte Mario: a bright afternoon mist. Won't I get some sketches of your glorious country! Your description makes my mouth water. The world is at issue about my Odyssey: high praise and high blame."

His own state of health was far from satisfactory, and he made up his mind to pay a short visit to the attractive country where his brother was staying. Two sorrowful occurrences in his own circle of friends are recorded in the following letter:—

"*March* 7.

". . . All is well at home except that Paterfamilias is out of sorts, not up to work, and sadly wants change. Out of doors very bad things are going on. Mrs. Stanley died on Wednesday, after only a week's illness. The Queen was most kind, and offered to telegraph for her son, but it would have been no good, he was gone so far up the Nile. Poor Gurney is very ill, and in great danger: there have been prayers for him in the Marylebone churches. He came here to lecture on Monday week on 'The Letters of the Poets,' but was so poorly I was obliged to read the lecture for him. Next morning he returned to his doctor, and ever since has been in the same low way; no rest, no food; typhoid fever has set in, and I much fear the worst. How he will be missed by his family and parish and friends! So it really seems as if gloom was gathering round; but God rules, and we are all in His hands."

This apprehension was too soon justified by the event. Mr. Gurney died a few days afterwards. In a letter written, on March 16, to the Rev. J. H. Hamilton, my husband says:—

"What a loss we have had in poor dear Gurney! Who would have thought that his strong, heroic, useful course would come so suddenly to an end? Where shall we find such another man, who, with all his faults, was almost the only bold, fearless assertor of what he held to be truth, in the present miserable days, when men pick their ways among safe professions of opinion, and conceal their real views of things? You probably heard of his coming down to Canterbury; how he was too ill to give the lecture him, self, and I gavo it for him. His two girls were with him, and they were to have stayed with us some days; but on the Tuesday morning he thought, and I thought, that he had much better get back without delay, to see doctors, and get to the bottom of his illness. He had had no sleep and no appetite for a week, and his tongue was as white as snow; so he went on Tuesday at noon. We had much talk before he went, and he left in good spirits. I was never to see him again. There is hardly any man who could be worse spared, in spite of many eccentricities and prejudices, than our poor friend. It is indeed a mysterious and most afflicting dispensation of Him whose ways are not our ways, and whose judgments are past finding out."

The same letter refers to another event, our daughter Alice's engagement to the Rev. W. T. Bullock :—

"I have not seen you since our dear Alice's engagement. We have every reason to be thankful for it . . .; and I do believe she, and we all, will have reason to bless God to all eternity that the engagement has been made. All details have probably been told you by your girls."

When he wrote the following letter to his daughter she was on a visit to the family of her future husband :—

"I half regret going to Nice, and thus losing a month of my dear girl's last spring at home; but then another thought came, that I should enjoy more the four months coming. Your empty room makes me quite sad. The day brings its work and its church, and its saunter to Mrs. Baker's wood. With the 'Lady of Garaye' *en poche*, and another slim little lady in my thoughts, and my heart seething like a kettle, I thought of the day when the little feeble cry first sounded in my ears, and I thought on and on, all the way through all our daily joys and loves and our two great sweeps of sorrow, and then all these undeserved mercies here, our talks before the Communion, &c."

And a little later, in a letter written to her from Nice, he speaks in the same strain :—

TO HIS DAUGHTER ALICE.

"This place is not picturesque, but has a sort of dreary

uniformity and propriety about it. In front of the high row of houses in which the Hôtel des Princes forms one, is a row of low houses, with a public walk on the top of them as at Genoa, below them a public road, below that the beach. The boys here are good and nice, what is called retiring, which means that they wear their social sides inwards. I must comply with poor ——'s request; I cannot find in my heart to refuse him, and will write by this post to arrange it. I hope all is right about his prospects, but that is his concern not mine. Mine is to help my friend, and leave the issue with Him who knows the hearts. . . . . Many, many thanks for your nice note, which breathed gentle balm into the paternal heart, the one fortress in the vaunted quadrilateral which has fallen before the foe. Ah, dear child, it will be void indeed. For who is it that has ever been my playful companion in all my little lovings and pursuits, to whom else did I ever take flower or leaf or insect, sure of a kindling eye, and of a present interest, and where shall I take them now? . . . . With all love, thy sorrowing ancestor."

He set off on March 10 for his journey to Nice, the course of which is thus recorded in his journal:—

"*March* 11.—The cathedral of Sens is a sad degeneracy from ours: like it in some particulars, e. g. the apse in the choir, but evidently later, the Geometrical Early English as we call it prevails over our chaster Late Norman, and the height is not much more than half ours, which is low enough. The most interesting resemblance was in the four windows of the nave of the choir, which I believe must have come from the same manufactory as ours in the same situation, in the treasury; they have some of Thomas à Becket's ornaments, his chasuble and various other treasures in the relic line. . . . . The fine old Christian city of Vienne looked very striking in its basin in the broad gleaming Rhone.

"*March* 26.—Nice is surrounded by the queerest country, a land of yellow ridges of earth and pebbles, sometimes hardened into a kind of conglomerate stone, and channelled deep by water-courses into hollow gullies; the walks are up steep paths, strong and earthy, and all kinds of wild aromatic shrubs and flowers grow by the side of them; here geraniums are in full flower in the gardens, almond and peach-trees covered with bloom, and the whole place smells of violets. St. Remo is a most curious place, said to be the warmest in the Riviera, only here do the dates ripen upon the palms; the old town is built upon a very steep hill, with the cathedral at the top. The streets are like those at Clovelly, but dark, going under arches continually; every now and then you look through an opening into a torrent with quaint old bridges and houses hanging over it. Along the coast to St. Remo is very beautiful, some of it literally answering to its name the Corniche, being a shelf in the mountain right over the sea. We pass Ventimiglia and Bordighera: the former was the ancient Intermelium, and was where Agricola was born, and where his mother was murdered by some marauding troops of Otho's. Bordighera is the place where the inhabitants have the privilege of furnishing the palms at Rome.

"*April* 1.—Set off at seven with Mrs. Bryant and her friend from Cannes, but delayed three hours for want of horses; took a walk and found out Lord Brougham's villa, and took a sketch[8]. The Estrell is clothed with cork trees and white heath.

"*April* 2.—Left Mrs. Bryant at Toulon and started alone for Paris at eight p.m.; beautiful night, Marseilles, Arles, Avignon, Orange, all by star-light. At Valence the day broke, the loveliest of morning lights over the Rhone, and its hills glowing in the risen sun; Vienne picturesque as always, Lyons a rushing whirl of gathering smoke, and here am I at 8.40 flying past Villefranche writing this in the rolling train with difficulty."

---

[8] This drawing has a subsequent history. It was sent many months afterwards to the Amateur Exhibition for the Benefit of the Distressed Operatives of Lancashire, where it was sold for ten pounds. In a review of the exhibition in "The Reader," it was thus noticed:—"The Dean of Canterbury wins our approval by his grappling, and not unsuccessfully, with a most difficult subject, 'Waiting for Horses at Cannes. A fine day after all.' While occupied with his serious work, he has ever welcomed the artist faculty, which would have made him a great landscape painter, had he not, either from preference or necessity, become a great Greek scholar and a Dean."

TO HIS WIFE.

"*Nice.*

"It will not do for me to remain long at Canterbury at a time. If I could get some place with good air to run away to now and then, I think I could hold out, but without that I am sure I cannot. A few weeks more as I was when I left home I should get past the point of rallying.

"What a loss we have had in poor Gurney! where can such another honest man be found, where such another antagonist of bumptious bishops and dilettanti deans? it is indeed a grievous blow to us all, and a warning to us who are left behind. I should have exceedingly liked to preach his funeral sermon, but now of course it is impossible. You cannot think what a change even these three days have made in me in a country 'ever charming, ever new.' May the effect of the present journey be to strengthen and restore me for God's work as long as He will have me to do it here on earth."

TO THE REV. E. T. VAUGHAN.

"*Nice, March* 18.

"I am out here for a fortnight to see my brother and to recruit my health after a winter's work at Canterbury, the climate of which always tries me if I remain as long as five months at a time. What a loss London and Christendom have had in poor Gurney! He was with us at Canterbury ten days before he died; who can tell what meeting in this world may become a solemn one by being the last? He was full of sympathy, full of burning zeal for justness and fairness, and it is indeed a loss to sit down and weep over, did we not know that there is no chance in the event, but that One has taken him from us, who knows what is good for him and for us. . . . . As to Alice, God has been very merciful to us in this matter of our dear child's engagement; our hearts are brimming over with gratitude. . . . . There are not six men living to whom I could with comfort leave my Greek Testament in charge. Bullock is one of them —need I say who is another?"

Soon after his return from Nice, on the 5th of April, he published his eighth volume of Sermons, "On Christian Doctrine," which had been preached chiefly on Sunday afternoons in Canterbury Cathedral. Describing them in a letter to the Rev. J. H. Hamilton, he says, "They were indirectly provoked by 'Essays and Reviews.'" He prefixed to them a touching dedication to the Christian memory of his friend, the Rev. J. H. Gurney (see page 343).

In April he visited Oxford, to take part in a course of Lenten sermons at St. Mary's Church; and in the following month he went with our daughter Alice to spend a week in the friendly rectory of Loughborough, and in the neighbourhood which was endeared to us by the recollections of eighteen years.

Our home at Canterbury received a welcome visitor in Mr. Lowes Dickinson, who was engaged in a painting of our two daughters, and who gave my husband useful suggestions for his improvement in what was now his favourite relaxation, drawing in water-colours.

On the 1st of July the important domestic incident, for which we had long been preparing, took place—the first marriage in our family. My husband thus records it in his journal:—

"*July* 1.—Dearest Alice married; she came down to prayers and breakfast as usual. At eleven we went to the Cathedral, general company first, then groomsmen with the twelve bridesmaids, and Alice and I bringing up the rear. All went off most nicely. In church Dr. Russell read the greater part. I joined their hands and blessed them. Psalms chanted; I took the choral part. Then the breakfast, most successful."

The following letter, written two days afterwards, carries on the story of the wedding-day:—

TO HIS DAUGHTER, MRS. BULLOCK.

"*July* 3, 1862.

"After our eminently successful day on Tuesday, and when you were no more amongst us, we adjourned to a *levée* of

King Croquet. Then came the concert, which was a great success; the music well performed, and the Chapter House full, but not overflowing; then the 'Middle Passage' to the Deanery, and to supper, also very successful.

"And so what was to be has been, and now you are a married woman, entered into the higher and more perfect state of human existence, and responsibility, and blessing. Yours has been a singularly happy lot through your life, chequered, it is true, by personal struggles and family sorrows, but still full of bright sunshine. One, it is true, is gone from us who might, in the pride of recent manhood, have brought you into church, and given you away for me. Let us not wish him back, but wish ourselves one day sure of joining him at a more blessed bridal. Our other might have been with us by this time at Oxford or Cambridge; but if we are without the joys of their presence, we are also free from the fears of their falling away: they are safe. But I was speaking of your youthful days. You have been differently brought up from other girls: yours has been a home of truth and fairness, and your character has nobly reflected both. Go on, dear child, and lead the rest of your life according to this beginning; go on in the strength which this beginning gives you; belong to no party, adopt no man's saying for your rule, be all your life as you were on your wedding-day, the thoughtful adviser, the warm-hearted friend, the upholder and consoler of others, and, above all, of him to whom it is your life's work to minister."

We remained at Canterbury a few days afterwards. The Dean had to make many arrangements previous to the first meeting, in the cathedral, of the Diocesan Choral Union. Their first service in the cathedral, on July 9, was very effective, as might be expected, from the union of 550 trained voices.

On the 10th of July we set out for a Continental tour, in the course of which we hoped to overtake the newly-married pair.

My husband's journal records our progress. This was the first time he indulged himself with the luxury of a courier:—

"*July* 10.—From Dover to Calais and Amiens, but much more comfortable with a courier. Found the cathedral more magnificent than ever, the height and ancient stained glass. The west front has been well restored, and all the trumpery La Gloire, &c., is to be taken away from the inside, and the church put back as it was in the thirteenth century. Next day to Creil and St. Quentin; a stiff old town. The church is a very fine one of the Transition, with some mixture of Latin styles.

"*July* 12.—Left St. Quentin for Laon, a strange place, on a hill, like Lincoln; cathedral fine, and peculiar; five towers, of very beautiful style; interior chaste and most interesting; double triforium.

"At eight got to Rheims, and to an hotel close to the glorious cathedral, and under its shadow we proposed spending our Sunday.

"*July* 13.—At nine into the cathedral, one of the grandest I know; the west *façade* is one mass of sculptured figures, defying all representation, except by photographs: the inside is most magnificent, the effect grand in the extreme; the west end, with two rose-windows, as seen from the choir, is the noblest possible—likest, perhaps, to Westminster Abbey, but higher and larger; painted glass very fine. After lunch, our own service in our own room; then to the cathedral, expecting a sermon, which, however, was not.

"*July* 14.—Before breakfast sketched a buttress and pinnacle, with a view to the Corona of Canterbury. At ten left for Strasburg, and next day, after seeing the cathedral and waiting for the clock to strike and seeing the figures go round, off to Basle.

"*Berne, Sunday, July* 20.—Corrected proof of my sermons just come from Canterbury. Morning, English service. . . . Afternoon to the cathedral; German service. Evening a drive round the town, ending with the Enghe."

TO HIS DAUGHTER, MRS. BULLOCK.

"*Berne, July* 20.

"We have seen the Münster Thal, and we went in a

char-à-banc up the Weissenstein; such a climb! Burkhard (our courier) and I on foot. At the hotel; at the top such a view! All Switzerland stretched out; a glorious range of snowy tops—the Wetterhorn, Schreckhorn, Jungfrau, Eiger, &c., and the town of Soleure under our feet; the Aar winding in endless courses through the plain; the lakes of Bienne, Neufchatel, and Morat; Mont Blanc westward: all the Oberland. On the 18th we went to Soleure and Berne, and next morning off to see Freyburg, a most curious place in a deep ravine, with a church tower, which might be a Somersetshire one, and two wonderful suspension bridges over the gorges on which the town is built. The second bridge is 312 feet above the river; we heard the organ and a storm imitated. On the 21st we go to Thun, on Tuesday to Interlaken, &c. On Saturday week I hope we shall meet at the Schweizerhof at Lucerne."

JOURNAL.

"*Interlaken, July* 22.—Came here yesterday by steamer from Thun. Up at 6.30 to sketch the Jungfrau, which was glittering in the blue sky in all its graceful majesty. At eleven started for the Giessbach.

"The peculiarity of this fall is the succession of waterfalls down the steep of the mountain; there are four considerable ones, besides several lesser ones. The path is carried behind the second fall, and the effect of seeing the landscape through the falling water is very curious. The whole scenery of the Lake of Brienz is very fine; no snowy mountains, but more of the picturesque than usual in Switzerland; rocks and trees such as N. Poussin loved to paint.

"*July* 24.—From Interlaken to Lauterbrunnen, and, having a day to spare, devoted it to the Lauterbrunnen Valley, composed of limestone rocks of various colours; the flowers most abundant and beautiful.

July 25.—Up at 3.30 a.m. to look at Mont Titlis; most glorious before and after sunrise. At ten left for the Wengern Alp; glorious day, without a cloud in the sky. View from the inn on the Wengern Alp truly magnificent. Heard several avalanches, and saw one immense one. At sunset came to Grindelwald.

"*July* 26.—Started for the Faulhorn (where we propose spending Sunday), a most steep but beautiful ride; the views back, over the Wetterhorn and its glaciers, glorious; as we approached the top, the clouds gathered; then we were enveloped in mist, but a glorious sunset lifted up the mist, the colours changing from pale gold to deep gold, then to copper; then fading away to that queer corpse-like hue which succeeds the loss of the sun.

"*Sunday, July* 27.—Called at four to see the sun rise; but everything was shaded by a line of clouds. Service in our room with two Englishmen, members of the Alpine Club.

"Afternoon walked out in the zigzags and gathered flowers; then a mist came on, which 'eventuated' in a magnificent thunderstorm, the lightning which was worst at the receding of the storm, surpassed anything I had ever seen, it struck the earth almost close to us; and as I stood talking to Burkhard, I distinctly saw the light of a flash between him and me; after the storm, such a rainbow; as near as it could be, a complete circle; a remarkable and most happy day; thank God for it; 'to-morrow to fresh fields and pastures new.'

"*July* 28.—Sunrise next morning magnificent; left for the Scheideck and Rosenlaui; latter part not so grand, but very beautiful; through forests almost like park scenery. Went to see the glacier at Rosenlaui.

"*July* 29.—Down the valley of Reichenbach on to Guttanen, and up the splendid valley of Oberhasli.

"*July* 30.—Rode to Handek, and saw the great Fall of the Aar which looked finer than ever, lighted up by a magnificent rainbow.

"*July* 31.—Through Meyringen, over the Brunig, past Lungern, Sarnen to Lucerne [here we met Mr. and Mrs. Bullock, with whom we were to travel as far as Trèves].

"*Aug.* 4—To Weggis by steamer; and then up the Rigi on horses.

"*Aug.* 5.—Called at four to see the sun rise, which he did

splendidly; every Alpine point was as clear as possible, and one after another was lit up. We made out with a glass the inn at the Faulhorn, and indeed, every one of our old points; it was a great success, and one which I never expected. Twenty-one years ago, Fanny, Burnett, and I, saw nothing from this spot, scarcely the whole of the then small hotel! That evening got to Zürich.

"*Aug.* 6.—Saw the town library, and in it letters of Henry IV. of France, Lady Jane Grey (beautiful writing), Frederick the Great, Lavater, Zwingle, Cranmer, and the First English Bible ever printed; examined a file of the 'Moniteur' for the French account of the Battle of Waterloo; at six left for Romanshorn, on the Lake of Constance.

"*Aug.* 7.—Having crossed the great Lake almost like a sea, got to Constance in time for the *table-d'hôte;* then saw the Cathedral, the Council-chamber and Huss's Prison, and various antiquities.

"*Aug.* 9.—Got to Comburg, about one mile and a half from Hall; an ancient fort on a hill, where the Wurtemberg Invalides are commanded by General Von Stadlinger. Here we stayed till the 12th with our kind friends. On Sunday, 10th, went to the Protestant Domkirche at Hall, to see a new clergyman inducted; the ceremony of investing and laying on of hands very interesting. He preached a very good sermon, and told us the story of his life, which I suppose must be usual on such occasions.

"*Aug.* 13.—From Heidelberg to Bingen on the Rhine, and from there we went up the Nahe-Thal to Kreuznach and Aberstein; the latter a very curious place, built on the river under very precipitous volcanic rocks.

"*Aug.* 15.—From Coblentz in the steamer on the Moselle to Trèves, sleeping at a little mean inn at Trarbach; getting to Trèves on Saturday night and spending Sunday there.

"*Aug.* 17.—Morning; went to the service at the Basilica, and a very fine church it makes; service well done, and a good expository sermon on the Gospel; the Litany was from Bunsen's book, and the responses were well given by the choir. After this we had service in our own room in the Hotel.

"*Aug.* 18.—After breakfast went to see the town library, where is the Codex Aureus, and many MSS.; saw a letter of Luther's and other curiosities; then saw the cathedral; at twelve left for Luxemburg, where we dined all together. At the station left them [Mr. and Mrs. Bullock] to return home to town, we going on to Metz.

"*Aug.* 19.—Went to see the beautiful cathedral at Metz, Geometrical or Early Decorated; very high within, splendid stained glass, mostly of the King's Chapel character, date 1500; an old round church incorporated into the nave, and an old episcopal chair of cippolino. At twelve off for Paris, and went to the new large Hôtel de la Paix.

"*Aug.* 20.—In a carriage to the Russian Church, to St. Ferdinand's Chapel, Bois de Boulogne; and saw the Parc de Monceaux, a new little garden, very near the Arc de Triomphe.

"*Aug.* 21.—Out all day to the Place de la Bastille and Hôtel de Sens, the Hôtel de Ville, very much enlarged and splendidly fitted up inside; then to Petit Montrouge, and to show them the Abbé Migne's shop.

"*Aug.* 22—Not at all well; the sun yesterday too much for my head; obliged to have a doctor. [His verses entitled, "Life's Answer" ("Poems," p. 336) appear from a note-book to have been written at this time. He evidently felt uneasy about his health.]

"*Aug.* 23.—Better, thank God; out seeing lots of churches, Jardin des Plantes, &c.

"*Aug.* 26.—Drove to Sèvres, along the banks of the river, by the side of the Champs Elysées Avenue; the latter part of the drive pretty; Prince Jerome's Château to the left and St. Cloud to the right. Saw the china but not the manufactory, it being now forbidden.

"*Aug.* 27.—Started at nine for Versailles; had to walk through miles of galleries; what most interested me were some pictures of Horace Vernet's, and two rooms full of small portraits of the old historical characters of France; the garden is curious, and in its way pretty. Saw the Grand Trianon, &c.

"*Aug.* 28.—Devoted this our last day in Paris to the Louvre and Luxembourg. Went through the galleries in the Louvre rapidly; the pictures certainly are glorious. The Luxembourg now contains chiefly the pictures of living artists."

To Mr. B. H. Alford.

"*Paris, Aug.* 25.

"I have not been well since I have been here, but it is only the old story, the action of years of overwork on the nerves and brain, which is increasing as age comes on. I have called in a doctor who has prescribed, and I am a trifle mended, or rather patched up; for the evil I fancy is passed mending."

To his Daughter, Mrs. Bullock.

"*Grand Hôtel de la Paix, Paris, Aug.* 24.

"On Thursday we had a very fatiguing day in a broiling sun, and I was entirely prostrated by it, so that the next morning I could hardly stand or see. The doctor said it was nervous debility. I am better, and yesterday did a good day of sight-seeing. Metz is a very fine city, with a really glorious cathedral almost equal to Amiens, the painted glass is superb. Paris utterly surprises me, everything here is being pulled down or altered. There is not a church, nor a street, nor a theatre, nor a palace, where there is not some demolition, and reconstruction going on. The fact is, it is necessary for him [Louis Napoleon]; the moment it comes to an end he comes to an end.

"How dreadful about the poor B.'s. You remember our seeing them the Sunday we were at Quebec Chapel, with their children. I have written to M—— to inquire about the poor widow. God bless you in your new home!"

The first volume of Bishop Colenso's book on the "Pentateuch," was published in the following October. A portion of it was circulated privately by the author before it was made public, and in the beginning of September it was sent to my husband. He writes the following letter to the Bishop on the subject:—

"*Sept.* 15, 1862.

"I have looked through a considerable portion of your book, and coming engagements will prevent my going on with it. So I return it by this post. I must say, that all your arguments do not seem to me to affect our position with regard to the Pentateuch. It seems to me that there are two ways of approaching and considering this subject. First, from the *unbelieving* point of view, proceeding thus to argue from the improbability or discrepancy of details to the unhistorical character of the whole; this method assumes that we understand all the details, and deal with them as ascertained and undoubted elements in the inquiry. Secondly, from the *believing* point of view, proceeding thus to argue from the acknowledged historical character of the whole to the existence of a key to difficulties of detail, provided we could thoroughly understand all circumstances regarding them; this view assumes Jesus Christ to have been the Son of God. If He *was*, the Pentateuch is historical; for He treats it as such. The former of these methods, it seems to me, is yours. The latter I am content shall be mine. I send you a volume of 'Sermons' which I have just published [Vol. viii. 'Sermons on Christian Doctrine']."

Soon after our return to England, Archbishop Sumner died on September 6th. On the 12th my husband mentions in his journal, that he "attended Archbishop Sumner's funeral at Addington, not strictly private, though comparatively so. Most of those present were relations or friends. So ends the career of one of the best and holiest men of the age. May the next be like him."

To a friend who suggested to him that one consequence of the Archbishop's death might be his own appointment to a bishopric, he wrote:—"I do not apprehend any such consequences as you picture, so I look round on all my own comforts, and thank God. I am too outspoken, and too little leaning to any party for them to take me. If I am passed over by the fatal bolt this time, I am safe for the future. . . . If I am called I shall go, but we are hoping to be let alone in our happy, pleasant home,—I to finish my English Testament, now going on well.

"We have had a most successful tour, and are now embarking on our round of home duties. At Lucerne our neogams met us. I am, perhaps, not so well as could be desired (as, indeed, I have never been since the Apocalyptic pull in February, 1860), but not ill. An English physician whom I consulted in Paris, called it nervous debility, and pronounced it not a question of bodily health so much as of rest and bracing of the nerves. Who is to succeed the Archbishop is a most anxious question. I should like Longley above all things; so mild and kind and fatherly, with a background of firmness withal—his manner is certainly most sunny."

Both these anticipations were fulfilled. His journal soon afterwards records:—

"The Archbishop of York has accepted the Archbishopric of Canterbury. Thank God for this."

And the new Bishop was our friend Dr. Ellicott, then Dean of Exeter, of whose appointment he says in a letter:—

"I am delighted. Besides higher qualifications, he is an excellent man of business, and will be a great acquisition to the bench of Bishops."

The enthronement of the new Primate in Canterbury Cathedral involved my husband in a vast amount of business of a kind which was certainly not congenial to him, though he won universal approval by the manner of performing it. He writes in his journal:—

"*Nov.* 7.—Alone with my dearest ones for the first time since this day three weeks; head giddy from overwork; lots and lots of letters to write, and arrangements to make for the enthronement, now fixed for the 12th.

And again:—

"*Dec.* 12.—The enthronement. A bright sunny day, and all went off as well as possible, and every one was very kind and reasonable; not an unkind word with a soul all day. Crowds at lunch, and a large dinner-party last night. Our house is quite full of the Archbishop's party, Bishop of Oxford, &c."

His reflections at the end of this year are in a somewhat different tone from those of former years:—

"*Dec.* 31.—Sat up till the end of the year; heard the clock strike amidst the ringing of bells. So ends 1862, a year of great mercies and some important events to me; during it, my darling Alice has been happily married; a blessing, indeed, of no common kind. I have had two pleasant journeys: one to Nice in the spring, and one with Fanny and Mary to Switzerland in July and August. My own health has, I fear, been somewhat impaired; my head is often weak, and I cannot stand the work, either physical or mental, which I could some years ago; but this has improved of late. My sight has become much impaired, which shows that old age is coming on. O may I be ready whenever the Master calls; very much longer it can hardly be. I have worked harder than most men, and must in the course of nature go sooner. Lord, make me fit to meet Thee, not by my own righteousness, but by growth in Thy grace, and in knowledge of Christ my Lord. Keep me in spiritual health, if bodily be denied me. If I live, may it be to work for God and for Him—if I die, may my end be a Christian one, and my waking after His likeness be my soul's eternal satisfaction. May He bless, also, my dear ones, with whom He has made me very happy!

"Far from the Light! O why, O why?
Is not my Light within?
* * * *
But ah, I fear no chink of sky,
To look through canst thou find.
My bank of clouds is all too high,
And Thou art still behind.
O for the breath divine to blow
This inward mist to clear.
In tempest, if it must be so,
So Thou my light appear."

CHAPTER X.

1863—1867.

New Testament for English Readers—Queen's English—King's School Rebuilding—Consecration in Canterbury Cathedral—Winter in Rome—Canterbury Harmonic Union formed—Sojourn at Callander—Attends Norwich Congress—Year of Prayer and Year of Praise—Autumn Home at Vine's Gate—First Canterbury Mission—Lectures at Glasgow—Netherton-on-Sea.

ALTHOUGH the reflections with which the last year were closed were of a less bright character than usual, they certainly did not indicate a decline of intellectual activity. His journal affords evidence of his employment in the beginning of 1863 in improving his Commentary on St. John (Greek Testament); in preparing his New Testament for English Readers; in the composition of a sermon on Holy Scripture, which he preached in St. Paul's Cathedral on the 11th January to 5000 persons, and which was afterwards published by the Society for Promoting Christian Knowledge; in the completion of a short course of sermons on Creation, preached at Canterbury (published 1865); in the enlargement of certain lectures into the book published in 1864 under the title of the "Queen's English," and in the composition of several new poems, viz.:—"Evening Hexameters," p. 327. "A Greeting to Spring," p. 331. "Be Just and fear not," p. 332. "Filiolæ Dulcissimæ," an Easter Offering, p. 334.

Whilst employed in these more serious works, he found leisure to make the arrangements for an Amateur Concert, in which Sir Sterndale Bennett's "May Queen" was performed, at the Deanery on 5th January; and to complete a series of water-colour drawings, the outlines of which he brought home from the last summer's tour in Switzerland. And another subject to which he gave much attention was the rebuilding of the King's School, Canterbury, the plans for which were settled principally on the responsibility of the Dean and Chapter.

On March 7 he went to town to be present at the arrival of the Princess Alexandra.

He enters in his journal:—

"At ten a.m. to St. Paul's, south side. Crowd immense.

"At 3.30 the procession came. The Princess Alexandra, our future Queen (D.V.) is fair, and prettier than I had imagined from her photos. When she had passed, I went off and joined the rest of my party. Home by eight. Memorable day."

Through the kindness of friends, our daughter Mary was one of those who were admitted to St. George's Chapel to witness the marriage on March 10.

The day is thus described in his journal:—

"*March* 10.—Marriage of the Prince of Wales. The Mayor and Corporation came to the Cathedral; we met them at the south door and preceded them up the nave, chanting the two wedding Psalms. I preached[1]. Then to the Dane John. Then to lunch with the Mayor, and with him to the Exchange to say grace for the old men and women who had dinner given them.

"Then off to town to see the illuminations and seek after Mary, who is gone with the Archbishop's party to Windsor to see the royal marriage.

"The squeeze at Ludgate Hill was fearful, much more than I liked; so I made for the Farringdon Street Railway, and in a few minutes was in Baker Street. Mary did not return till after midnight, when she came in one of the Archbishop's

[1] Sermon called "Rejoice with them that rejoice." Printed.

carriages; they had been three hours getting from Westminster to the Horse Guards."

Canterbury Cathedral was now to be again, after an interval of fourteen years, the chosen place for a Consecration of Bishops, and one of those who were consecrated on March 25th, Dr. Ellicott, the new Bishop of Gloucester and Bristol, was, in consequence of their fellowship in critical works, one of the most intimate friends of my husband, who was selected to preach the sermon. The text was St. John x. 11.

And he thus speaks of the office of a Bishop:—"None can mistake the engrossing nature of a bishop's employments; none can suppose that there remains anything for him, except to give himself up henceforward simply and entirely to the work he has undertaken. A bishop has almost to bid farewell to leisure, that ever more and more valuable luxury of the advancing years of busy men; the great tide of overwhelming responsibility has flowed in and filled up all the chinks and intervals of disposable time. He has only become greatest that he may be the servant of all. You are passing out from among us into the heat of public gaze, and under incessant question and criticisms. Where the least trip will be exaggerated and the most trivial error magnified, how easy it will be for you to bring dishonour upon Christ, how difficult so to walk that He may always be glorified in you." Dr. Mesac Thomas, the first Bishop of Goulburn, was consecrated at the same time, and he is referred to in the following words:—"It is a joyful and proud day for our ancient Cathedral when she thus again vindicates her position as the centre of England's Christianity, when she can send forth to the ends of the earth founders of churches descended from her, and remembering her with affection, and can be made again the place of consecration of a bishop of her own province."

At the end of the month he went again to Oxford to take part in the annual Lent Lectures in the University City; and in May he spent some days in London attending Convocation. A characteristic entry occurs in his diary:—

"*May* 22.—Heard of two deaths, very sad, Sir Culling

Eardley's and Henry Streeten's[2]. Arranged my money-matters for Fanny in case of my death."

It was in this month that the first volume [Part I.] of his "New Testament for English Readers" came from the press. The object of this book was to give to persons who do not know Greek as much as possible of the information contained in his work on the Greek Testament. The first part of the first volume (452 pages) included the first three Gospels in the Authorized Version; with his own amended translation of certain phrases in notes beneath, marginal references, and a large body of explanatory notes, mainly, though not entirely, adapted from the notes to his Greek Testament; there are also copious Introductions prefixed to each book. He regarded this work as an important step in carrying out his purpose, which was always on his mind, of contributing to extend a deeper knowledge of the Bible in all ranks of society.

In June he spent a day on an object in which he always took much pleasure, and for which he was peculiarly qualified, a holiday with the young. He writes:—

"*June* 26.—Started with a party of King's Scholars, Clergy Orphan boys, and others, nineteen in all, for Calais; showed them, accompanied by a commissionaire, the town, ramparts, and cathedral. Dinner at an hotel there, and supper at the Deanery."

The following letter, written in July, from Lord Camden's House, "The Wilderness," near Sevenoaks, to his younger daughter at Taunton, records another day of relaxation:—

TO HIS DAUGHTER MARY.

"*July* 16.

"We have had such a nice day at Old Penshurst, 800 people; Lord De Lisle gave luncheon to all, and Mr. Parker of Oxford lectured us on the grand old house, begun in King John's time, and finished in Elizabeth's. I missed one little face there, but it was very jolly none the less.

---

[2] A young Lieutenant in the Navy crushed to death by a boat which was torn from its fastenings during a fearful gale, just as the ship had entered the Channel on its return from China.

Lots of other Kentish people were of course with us to-day, Lord Sydney, the Archbishop and Miss Longley, and Bishop Trower, &c.

"To-morrow we are going to Knowle. On Saturday I am off to the old place. Only think, what will my filiola say when she hears that Stanley was down at Canterbury yesterday with Prince Arthur. He went to church and sat in my stall; lunched at the Harrisons; saw St. Augustine's and returned in the evening. Was it not a pity we were not there? He of course would have lunched with us; love to darling mamma and all in mountain and marsh.

"P.S. I hope I shall find the three gables in front of the Deanery nearly finished, what an improvement it will be!"

A few days afterwards he paid a brief visit in the West of England, and spent part of a day at Dunster, so well-known to him in early days. He writes July 23:—

"Up early and out early to sketch the castle and church. I am here in the same large room in the 'Luttrell Arms,' where my father and I were in 1824, Paget and I in 1831, Bickersteth and I in 1832, dearest Fanny and I in 1838, my dear ones, Eliza Mott, and I in 1848, and now M. and I in 1863. How great God's mercies have been to me."

Another pleasant visit was paid to our friends, General and Mrs. Hutchinson, then at Government House, Devonport.

It was this autumn that he preached in Wells Cathedral a sermon for the "Five Church Societies," which was published separately.

Two new plans were now first presented to him which eventually occupied much of his time. Mr. Strahan, the publisher, proposed to him to edit a new periodical to be called the "Contemporary Review;" and Mr. Pfyffers, a Belgian sculptor, submitted to the Dean designs for the statues to be placed outside the south porch of Canterbury Cathedral.

Although the restoration of the cathedral was carried on on a liberal scale from funds connected with the edifice, the Ecclesiastical Commissioners thought it best to leave to voluntary contributions the work of completing the west front by filling the numerous vacant niches with appropriate statues. The Dean accordingly put forward in the winter of 1862 a proposal for a public subscription for erecting fifty-six statues, one of our Lord as the Good Shepherd, and the others commemorative of personages whose fame was connected in some way with the ancient cathedral. A complete list of them is given in the Appendix. The first list was put forth in 1862. In six years thirty-one statues had been erected; another effort was made, and before the winter of 1870 nearly all the niches were filled, and this portion of the outside of the cathedral was probably in a more complete state than it had ever been previously.

I have written *nearly all;* for amongst the vacant places on the west front, was one which is now filled by a representation of him by whose mind the whole plan was formed. As early as 1864, some ladies of Canterbury privately raised a sufficient fund for the erection of a statue of the Dean among the others; but as soon as the intention was made known to him, he prevailed on the friendly contributors to change their purpose and to present to the cathedral one of the statues previously proposed; that of Edward the Black Prince was chosen, and it took the place thus intended for the Dean. But eventually the original intention was fulfilled. On October 15, 1871, a statue of Dean Alford, executed by Mr. Pfyffers at the cost of members of the Canterbury Harmonic Union and other friends, was placed in a niche on the west front, and publicly unveiled and presented by Mr. Precentor Hake, the representative of the donors, to the Dean [3] and Chapter.

---

[3] Dr. Payne Smith, the Dean of Canterbury, in accepting the statue for the Cathedral body, said, "It must be a great pleasure to them to see such a memorial of one who had done so much towards establishing their Society. The late Dean was a man of many accomplishments, and, besides being a scholar, was a musician and a poet. He was also a great hymn writer, one of his compositions was that Harvest Hymn, 'Come, ye faithful people, come,' which was being sung in church throughout England at that season of the year. It was very appropriate that Dean Alford should occupy a place in that series of statues which he had himself originated, and also that he should be placed next to Erasmus, being, like him, a notable com-

In the autumn of 1863 he determined to spend all the ensuing winter on the Continent. His annual relaxation from work was usually for a much shorter time. Some of his reasons for prolonging it on this occasion are stated in the following letter to the Rev. J. H. Hamilton; and, as the reader is aware, he had cherished the wish to revisit Rome with his family. It was on this second visit that he wrote "Letters from Abroad," which after first appearing in successive numbers of Strahan's monthly magazine, "Good Words," were published in a separate volume.

A beautiful memorial of this tour was preserved in a large manuscript volume containing more than 600 photographs of pictures, places, and statues, &c., some prints and a few original sketches arranged in the order in which the places were visited, and connected by a manuscript diary. This was in later years one of the favourite ornaments of the drawing-room at Canterbury. So far as the details of this tour are of general interest, they will be found in the following letters.

We left Canterbury on 30th November, a party of four (our niece, Miss H. E. Alford of Taunton, supplying the place left vacant by the marriage of our eldest daughter), with a courier, Burkhard.

To the Rev. J. H. Hamilton.

"*Toulon, Dec.* 2.

"Many thanks for your affectionate farewell letter, received just before we left. As you say, our contemplated absence is for a long time, and no one knows what may happen before we return; but we are kept in His hands who has preserved me and mine for His work hitherto, and will do with us what is best for His service and glory. We have prospered very well hitherto. We left home on Monday, the 30th, and here we are on Wednesday, 800 miles from home, without inconvenience or unusual fatigue. . . .

---

mentator on the Bible." He concluded by calling upon those present to sing the 229th Hymn in the Dean's own collection [The Year of Praise]. "Ten thousand times ten thousand."

"I would not have run away from my duties and from England for so long had I not felt that I have been for many years expected to do more than I ought to do, and had I not been anxious both to get a good winding-up for what may be to come, and to put an interval between what has been my former life of incessant toil and what, if God spares me, I hope to enjoy as an eventide of useful, but less persistent, work."

TO THE REV. J. H. HAMILTON.

"*Genoa, Dec.* 8.

"We left Nice on Saturday morning, spending Sunday at Mentone; from Nice here we have, literally, not had a cloud in the sky; the mountains and the glorious sea in all their splendour. The whole Riviera is perfumed with orange blossom; in some places the trees for miles are one sheet of white bloom. If you have ever travelled the Corniche road, you will not need telling that no words can describe its beauty. First of all, you have as your companion throughout, the lovely sea full of gorgeous colours, from the emerald green of the curling waves to the turquoise and purple of the near distance, the steady sapphire blue of the middle distance, and the deep ultramarine of the far-off sea-line. This on the right; then you have also on the left the ever-varying mountains. Sometimes you are skirting and tunnelling their promontories, gaining new views as each is turned; sometimes you are threading the olive-clad hills which form their buttresses over the sea; sometimes, again, crossing the wide pebbly beds of the torrents which descend from them, and up their course, catching glimpses of the snow-clad giants of the main ridge of Alps, over banks of silvery green and shining villages perched on the heights. And then the towns glittering many-coloured, quaint with their narrow smooth-paved streets, shady and lofty, looped together with frequent arches from side to side, to steady the houses in earthquakes; hundred-towered as Alberga, lying all of them hot and glaring on the smooth beach of their little bays. The views, as Genoa la Superba is approached, of the maritime cities increase continually in splendour, till at last, after a cut over a pine-clad promontory, the fair vision of the Queen of the Riviera spreads before you.

"To-morrow we hope to make a long run for Spezzia, next day Pisa, then to Siena, where we spend Sunday; on Monday (D.V.) to Orvieto, Tuesday Viterbo, Wednesday or Thursday Rome. I have given you our tour as it has been, and we hope it will be."

To his Daughter, Mrs. Bullock.

"*Hôtel de l'Europe, Rome, Dec.* 16.

"Here we are all safe, without having gone over any precipice, or had a single *contretemps* of any kind. We have every reason to be most thankful for our prosperous journey. From Toulon here we have not had a drop of rain, hardly a cloud in the sky. We examined thoroughly the Cathedral, Baptistery, and Leaning Tower of Pisa, and the interesting frescoes of Benozzo, &c., in the Campo Santo; the Sienese School of Siena, from Guido da Siena to Beccafumi. The front of the Cathedral of Orvieto is a very miracle of art in graven work and colour: the upper portions are entirely occupied between the buttresses with the most gorgeous mosaics of scriptural and traditional subjects. At Ficulle we hired a *vetturino* for Rome. Saw St. Peter's fourteen miles off, and entered Rome as it was bathed in the glorious hue of a golden sunset.

"*Dec.* 17.—We have seen more than twenty sets of rooms, and gone up some hundred pairs of stairs; at last we fixed on a very nice set in the Piazza Nicosia, near the Borghese Palace."

To Canon Robertson.

"*Rome, Dec.* 16.

"Here we find ourselves, after a journey without a hindrance or drawback. I was not prepared to find so much beauty in Central Italy. I had gone through it by another route with Trench in 1861, by Radiofani to Siena, and could hardly have believed that the deviation by Orvieto, now made necessary by the temporary terminus of the rail being at

Ficulle, could have made so much difference. The scenery is quite gorgeous: oak forests clothed in the brightest autumnal tints, melting into the tenderest purples in mid-distance, and a perfectly ultramarine blue in the distance. We got to Rome at five this evening. Certainly the way to approach Rome is by the Via Cassia.

"At the fourteenth mile-stone you see St. Peter's alone, with a wide horizon of Campagna; then mile by mile more and more bursts on you till the descent to the Ponte Molle, when all becomes full of interest. Besides, St. Peter's never looks so well as from a height, and it is by this approach only that you can get it from a height.

"But let me say a word of the cathedral of Orvieto. I had no idea of anything so beautiful being there. It, rather its west end, is a mass of the brightest mosaics, framed in exquisite carving in marble. The mosaics (thirteenth century) are as fresh as the day they were done, and the delicate carving, by Nicolo da Pisa, almost uninjured."

TO CANON ROBERTSON.

"*Christmas Eve*, 1863.

"We are leading a very cosy life, as snug as may be, working at Italian, drawing, and letter-writing in the morning, going out to see sights in the afternoon, or—as we have hired a carriage here—we take drives in the Campagna, taking our lunch and sketching till it is time to return; in the evening reading up for to-morrow's sights. The weather has been magnificent. This afternoon we spent among Louis Napoleon's excavations on the Palatine under a cloudless sky. The view of Rome and of the distant mountains beautiful beyond description, and the heat quite as great as was comfortable. We are going to shirk the late idolatries to-night, and quietly hear the Pastorale at the St. Maria sopra Minerva, said to be the best in Rome, and from ten to twelve."

TO THE REV. B. H. ALFORD.

"*Rome, Dec.* 26.

"Here we are in the midst of the gorgeous old city

looking more lovely than ever. Such noons and moons, and sunrises and sunsets, and the old ruins blushing with deeper colour than when I saw them before in February, 1861. Well, Christmas is over, and we saw our share of its ceremonies. On Christmas Eve we had no mind for the fight to get into and out of the Sistine; so, having been told that the sight was good at the Minerva, we went there at ten p.m., and after waiting an unconscionable time, during which the Dominicans chanted a tedious service behind a screen at the farther end, the chief man went up to the high altar, uncovered what I had supposed to be the sacred elements, but it proved to be a wretched little wax doll, about eighteen inches long, on a cushion; this he solemnly carried under a baldachino with heaps of lights round it. All the Dominican body followed him with lights round the church; this done, he placed himself and the baldachino and lights at the end of the south aisle, and every one of these Dominican fathers—constituting, mind you, the Holy Office of the Inquisitors, judges of books to be prohibited—came up and kissed the toes of the miserable little idol, and reverentially pressed his forehead against it. This done, an inferior priest took the bambino and carried it to a side chapel, where a rail was run out at which the people knelt, and the idol was carried round to railfull after railfull, who kissed its toes and pressed their foreheads against it. This done, the priest mounted on the altar of some chapel, and deposited the doll in a cradle, over which leant figures of Joseph and Mary. The whole thing was sickening and disgusting to the last degree. And this, thought I, as I returned, is the Rome in which St. Paul preached!

Well, at nine a.m. we went to St. Peter's. As a whole, I should say the procession was a failure: it was gorgeous enough in colour, certainly, but there was no study given to arranging the colour effectively, and the poor old Pope looked the image of ill-repressed nausea. We stayed but to see him flinging his censer behind the altar, and then off to our own church, which was a treat.

"In the afternoon I preached from Luke ii. 34, 35

extempore, for my heart was full. Service being ended, we drove to Sta. Maria Maggiore, which was certainly superb, lighted with thousands of candles, the whole church full of people and spectators; for there is but one congregation in Rome, and that is outside the Porta del Popolo. To-day after lunch we went to St. Stefano Rotondo, thence to the Ara Cœli to hear the little children preach, which was very funny. Quaint little souls of five and six, put up on the side of a pillar, hold forth with abundant action about the Nativity, as if they had seen it. Never was a day so glorious, the unclouded sun bathing all the old ruins in rich orange light, and the everlasting hills in their tender purple beyond."

TO THE REV. J. H. HAMILTON.

"38, *Piazza Nicosia, Dec.* 28.

"We arrived here on the 16th, having been favoured with most lovely weather throughout. Since we have been here most of the days have been cloudless, wind north and north-east, but the sun very powerful. The mountains and the old ruins have looked most lovely in colour. It has been very tempting to sit out sketching, and to enjoy sunsets on the Pincian and Janiculum; and the consequence is we have had colds. Bradley will have told you how we fared on Christmas Eve and Day. We saw quite enough to make us all doubly thankful to Him who hath called us out of darkness into His marvellous light. The idolatry is unspeakably degrading, worse than I could have believed. A person here who knows Rome well, told me last week that the lower orders are heathens; their whole creed and practice are Pagan. The procession in St. Peter's disappointed me; considering how important they regard it as being, and what their facilities are for getting it up, it ought to be far grander than it is. The transition to our own service, 290 communicants, was indeed enough to make one most thankful. The outward changes in Rome are very striking. All now is order and outward good government, and I hear now the city is as well ruled as any in Italy. They have determined not to yield so they have taken to reforming. The letters are punctually delivered. But the Neri hold themselves as high as ever, and the Papal regulations are as strict. Permission has been refused to our Consul to hold a supplementary service in his house for the hundreds who are turned away from the English Church! . . .

"*Jan.* 6.—Since I wrote the above (which I thought I had sent), we have patched up the difficulty about the English service by having an additional morning service in the present church at 9.45, full morning service with a sermon[4]. The same with the communion and sermon at 11.30, and evening service at 3.30, besides two evening weekday services and the communion on the festivals. I take it we are by far the best appointed church in Rome, and the only congregation.

The Emperor's excavations on the Palatine are most interesting, wonderful remains of the kingly, republican, and imperial periods have come to light; among other things, the ancient Porta Mugonia, one of the gates of Roma Quadrata, when it was confined to the Palatine Hill. Signor Rossi, who has found it all, was a man persecuted by the Neri, but the Emperor found out his value, and gave him asylum on his newly purchased Orti Farnesiani, and made him superintendent of the works, and gave him a guard of French soldiers, so that the Pope cannot touch him. He has given us private permission to go there and sketch when we like."

To his Daughter, Mrs. Bullock.

"38, *Piazza Nicosia, Feb.* 17.

"Many thanks for your letter which I found this evening on our return from Ostia; the day was not unfavourable, but it suited well that strange country between this and the ancient port of Rome; the visit was most interesting, some portions of the old city having been excavated like Pompeii, and there are streets and houses just as they were, with their splendid mosaic pavements of marble. Ostia once had

---

[4] The Dean does not state that this service was undertaken by himself during our stay in Rome.

80,000 inhabitants, and now has not one hundred. We spent two hours in seeing the excavations, and in picking up bits of marble; then we went to Castel Fusano[5], in a magnificent pine forest which extends sixty miles along the coast, and here we had our lunch. We have seen such glorious works of art at the Vatican. The splendid golden colours of the groups in the Transfiguration, and the beauty of the little angel in the Madonna del Foligno much struck me. I have not been idle professionally, I preach at the 9.45 service.

"About the middle of January it was very severe weather here; they say there has not been such a winter since 1806. The Triton in the Piazza Barberini was frozen. We have given several days to the Vatican and we give more before we leave, and we are getting on with our sights famously.

"On January the 11th we went to Cervaro, where mamma sprained her leg in stepping over a little ditch in the Campagna, and for ten days she was obliged to keep in, but now she is well again, and this afternoon she has been with us picking up marbles on the sunny side of the Palatine, with sun gloriously hot, but a bitter tramontane coming round the corners. Afterwards we saw the two churches in the Cœlian, and ended with the preaching in the Coliseum. We are going to see Gibson's and Story's studios."

TO THE REV. J. H. HAMILTON.

"*March* 23.

"Our time here is drawing fast to an end, and we have been so comfortable and happy that we are quite sorry to leave Rome. We wait for the girandola on Monday night, and then on Tuesday start for Tivoli, returning here on Thursday, and next day we leave for Albano, whence after having made some excursions, we go on towards Naples on Tuesday, stopping at San Germano to see the famous Monte Cassino. After seeing Naples, Sorrento, Salerno, Pæstum, and Capri, we hope to return through Rome about May 2, and by the Perugia road to Florence, Bologna, Ravenna,

---

[5] See Mr. A. J. C. Hare's "Memorials of a Quiet Life," vol. ii. pp. 421, 422.

Venice, Verona, Milan, Lago d'Orta[6], perhaps, and Geneva, reaching home, please God, about June 20."

To Canon Robertson.

"*Capua, April* 5.

"I should have written to you before I left Rome, but really there is so much to do, *tanta roba*, that I could not find time; we got away on Tuesday to Tivoli, exploring the waterfalls that afternoon; and on Wednesday attempted to get to Licenza, to Horace's farm, but the weather rendered it altogether out of the question,—rain, hail, thunder, snow, wind. So we pulled up at Vicovaro, where I made acquaintance with a miraculous winking Madonna, and the testimonials to the same, to the future edification, I hope, of the readers of 'Good Words.' Thursday morning, happily, was glorious, and we got unaccompanied into the ravine, and sketched and enjoyed it vastly; in the afternoon we returned to our rooms in Rome for the last night; we had become quite attached to them and to the people, who have been most obliging. On Friday we left for Albano, where we stayed till Monday, seeing the Emissario on Friday, afterwards the Caput Aquæ, Ferentina, Rocca di Papa, and Monte Cavo. On Saturday I walked home by a way of my own to satisfy myself as to the site of Alba Longa, and Genzano, and the Lake of Nemi. On Sunday we saw the illumination of St. Peter's from the Porta Romana at night (it having been put off by reason of bad weather on Easter Day). On Monday we took the train at Albano Station, and came to San Germano and Monte Cassino; there we slept last night in a veritable Italian locanda; and this morning mounted Monte Cassino[7], fortified with a letter to the Abbot from

---

6 We crossed this lake and over the Colma to Varallo. His journal says, "In the most fearful thunder-storm I was ever out in, we took refuge under the roof of a châlet, and literally had to walk in water nearly two miles to reach Varallo, where next morning we went up the Monte Sacro and saw forty-six most curious chapels, full of life-size figures representing the events in our Lord's life." Between Foligno and Perugia we went to Assisi, a description of which, and a sketch of the monastery there, will be found in "Good Words."

7 "A Monastery founded by St. Benedict, who, flying from the corruptions

Dr. Smith, but we were in high luck, it being St. Benedict's day. The church is incomparably the richest in adornment I have ever seen. St. Peter's is mean compared to it. The whole floor, walls and altars, are Florentine mosaics, flowers, and arabesque patterns in the most gorgeous marbles and alabasters. The monastery is of course full of interest, the library far smaller than I expected. The good monk who showed me over, when I ventured to doubt whether Hildebrand himself wrote in a Charter the whole of 'Ego Aldobrandinus Archidiaconus R. E. subscripsi,' and pointed to the similarity of handwriting of all the column, said this was only because the handwritings of the time all looked alike to one unaccustomed to them, as he added, do the English handwritings of the present day. By-the-bye in the stranger's book he pointed, by way of illustrating this his position, to the signatures of Stanley and Hugh Pearson!

"We have stopped at an indifferent locanda here, partly to see the great amphitheatre in the morning, and partly because I did not like to face the crush at the Naples Station. We shall make our entrance quietly by a local train at noon to-morrow."

TO HIS DAUGHTER, MRS. BULLOCK.

"*En route from Naples to Rome, May* 2.

"You are the best in the primissima class of good girls for writing so long and so often. Now for a jog, as the train has started. As Mary has told you all about everything in the journal line, I will confine myself to general impressions, especially as I am already writing descriptions in my own journal and in 'Good Words.'

---

of Rome, had taken refuge in the caves of Subiaco. Then he removed from holes in a precipice to the summit of a mountain, and on the sunny ridge of Monte Cassino, which rises above the valley of the Liris, and commands a splendid panorama among the hills and over the valley of Campagna; he founded in 494 that retreat which for more than 1300 years has been one of the most famous monasteries in the world." (Duke of Argyll's "Iona.") In 1869 when other monasteries were suppressed, it was allowed to remain.

"Our journey to the south has been a great success; we began with cold, unfavourable weather, but since then the sky and sea have been glorious. . . . The inhabitants of South Italy are a fine race, but they are miserably degraded by centuries of despotism, and spend their wonderful energies in spasmodic excitement, instead of honest, sober exertion. The Italian Government has a most serious and difficult task before it, to bring about the sense of order and responsibility in this wild demoralized population. At present the effect of being citizens of a free country is one for the worse rather than for the better, but this is only what might have been expected. It will take a quarter of a century to make the Neapolitan shriek into a musical tune. We have this minute crossed a large river, whose name is given by the following riddle, which, if you have to give up, William will doubtless be able to explain:—

'Entire I flow; headless, I shine in war;
Curtailed, I fly; embowelled, have a scar.'

"I am in a state about my third paper in 'Good Words.' There is no paper of mine in the May number. I shall write to Strahan forthwith. . . .

"On April 9th we went to Pompeii; it is wholly unlike any other place. It is, and it is not a ruin; it fell asleep, and ages passed, and it has awakened to a new world.

"On the 14th.—From the top of Vesuvius the eye surveys the broad lands round its base, glittering with the sunny towns of this our century; and among them we saw one city, dark in the sombre brown. This was Pompeii.

"On the 16th, as we went to Sorrento, we passed on that beautiful coast-road a spot where last year some carriages were stopped by brigands. From Amalfi, on the 18th, we went to see the old Moorish town Ravello, which once had 30,000 inhabitants and thirty noble families; now it can only be approached by a mule track.

"On the 25th.—From Salerno we went to Pæstum, a long drive of twenty-four miles. Where the temples stand is now a cultivated district, and no longer the haunt of buffaloes and wild horses. Poor, miserable, naked children beset the ruins, which are most magnificent. There is no inn there. We lunched and took sketches from one of the temples. On the 10th preached at Naples, for the new English church, from Acts xxiv. 12—14. After church Mr. Maitland, the Chaplain, took us over the church, and walked with us up the hill behind, below Castle St. Elmo."

TO THE REV. W. T. BULLOCK.

"*Palazzo Barbano, Venice, May* 30.

"We are now enjoying cloudless skies in this most lovely, but, under present circumstances, most miserable cities; two-thirds of the inhabitants have migrated, and more than half the houses near the Grand Canal are shut up. But the natural beauties of the place are indestructible; and we have been, as it were, in paradise, for the last four days living chiefly in our gondola, and in the evening making excursions on the lagoons.

"On the 11th of May we passed the lake of Thrasymene. I made out satisfactorily the Sanguinetto and the field of battle, and the pass which Hannibal blocked up in the second Punic War about 217 B.C.

"In the Uffizi Gallery, Florence, I was more than ever delighted with the Madonna del Cardellino; and with the beautiful picture, "The Salutation," by Albertinelli. At Ravenna, where we spent last Sunday, we saw Dante's grave, and had a drive in the great pine forest there.

"We saw the mosaics in the choir of San Vitale; they are most gorgeous, and very interesting historically, representing the Court of Justinian and Theodora, about A.D. 565, each holding vases, and surrounded by their courtiers. We saw a grand procession on the Angels' Day, the next Sunday after Corpus Domini, wherein, in addition to usual pomps and idolatries, some half-naked children, with sheepskins and wings, personated angels.

"On the 20th of June we hope to reach Canterbury. A consecration in our cathedral comes off on St. Peter's Day. Please remember we want servants."

We returned to Canterbury in time to prepare for the guests who were present on June 29, at the consecration of Bishops Jeune (Peterborough), Bromby (Tasmania), and Crowther (Niger Territory).

Soon afterwards, in addition to his regular daily work at the New Testament, he began to write the series of papers published first in the "Sunday Magazine," and afterwards in three volumes, under the title of "How to Study the New Testament." He also prepared a new and revised edition of the "Queen's English;" and a paper on "The Special Education of the Clergy" (published in 1869 in "Essays and Addresses") was written for the Church Congress at Bristol.

A day's absence was the cause of his missing two royal visitors, the Princesses Helena and Louise, who unexpectedly came, on July 2nd, to visit the Cathedral and other antiquities of Canterbury, including the Deanery.

The following letter was written, on her birthday,—

To his Daughter, Mrs. Bullock.

"*Deanery, Canterbury, Oct.* 22.

"Many, many happy returns of this day. I have nothing but a blessing this time for you, for you are in the situation of one in the Psalms, 'whose right hand is full of gifts.' . . . Well, my child, you have been much in our thoughts of late, and are so day by day. We evermore pray for you, and look for every letter from you with increasing interest, and thankfulness to Him that you are so well. I suppose Mary tells you all the news in a far more interesting manner than I could if I were to try. Mr. Moore's house is half down, Mr. Blakesley's looks as if it were coming down too, and the old school-house is all to pieces. I have built an additional little green-house for the black Hamburg vine, warmed by an extension of the pipes of the other house."

On December the 4th he was summoned to preach for the second time before her Majesty at Windsor, where he was the guest of the Dean of Windsor. He says in his journal:—

"Preached at the Chapel from 1 Cor. xiii. 12. After

service the librarian showed me the library. Whilst we were there, the two young princes came in to look at some portfolios of drawings and photographs of Raffaelle's Stanze. They are nice intelligent lads. Prince Arthur is handsome.

"On my return to the Deanery I heard the Queen had sent to say she wished to see me with the Dean at three. We were shown into a small room, the Prince Consort's private sitting-room, full of furniture, with many little comforts about. The Queen entered by a door opposite. We all stood; the interview lasted about half an hour. . . . Her manner was very kind and gentle, quite such as to lead one on, and make one at home."

He writes on January 1, 1865:—

"O praise the Lord, my soul, for all His mercies! Here I am alive and well, whilst many of my youth's friends are cold in their graves."

Another mercy was soon added. Early on Sunday, February 5, he received a telegram announcing the birth of our first grandchild, Margaret Alice Bullock. I had gone to London a few days previously, and I received in Blandford Square the following letter, dated February 5, from my husband:—

"Thank God for the news which the telegram brought. It arrived just as I was in the middle of pondering my sermon. It was rather a trying dose for an extempore preacher just going to church. It is tantalizing that we cannot hear particulars till post time to-morrow. Give my best love to my darling girl, and tell her we have just been drinking the health of 'La Marguerite des Marguerites.' When we got this message,—must it be told?—we both began to cry. . . . I shall long to realize my new treasure in a few days.

"The 'Creation' went off very well, on the whole, on the 2nd. On the 20th I had a great meeting of amateur singers, Longhurst, and others; and we are forming a 'Canterbury Harmonic Union,' for performing oratorios, &c.

"Mary and I have had a musical party, I sung 'Herz,

mein Herz' with her, also a new duet of mine, accompanied by Longhurst."

He was present at the baptism on 24th February, in Christ Church, Marylebone, and wrote thus from Canterbury to the Rev. E. T. Vaughan:—

"*Feb.* 26.

"Many thanks for your kind letter of congratulation. It is, indeed, a serious thing to be grandpapa; it seems to show the lengthening of the shadows, and to whisper a prayer, 'Abide with us; for it is now evening, and the day is far spent.' O my dear friend, what a blessing of blessings it is to be able to look back on a life, in which though very very full of unworthiness, I may thankfully say, that childhood's faith has never been beaten, and my dear Lord's presence never removed. As the shades fall, of course there is a solemn feeling; but it is not dread, only the natural result of uncertainty as to details, not as to the final state, but as to the interval between the change and the resurrection.

"Dear Alice and her little Margaret are right well. The christening was on Friday, Ernest Hawkins, Miss Bullock, and Mary being sponsors. In the evening we left for Canterbury, I not being sorry to have my solitude relieved by the return of mamma and Mary.

"To-morrow week I go with my Precentor, Hake, who is also my Biblical Secretary, for a parson's three weeks among the French cathedrals. We have been working very hard all the winter, and both of us want a change. Really the work is getting gigantic."

The following letter was written to our daughter, Mrs. Bullock:—

"*Deanery, Feb.* 26.

"I write a line to-night, my darling child, because I think you may feel solitary to-morrow when Miss Von Stadlinger is gone, and would like a little cheerfulness. What a month of mercies you have to look back upon, all has been so nicely ordered for you, that it seems more like a pleasant tale, than one of the stiff realities of this contrarious world. And you have your dear little one, not exactly, indeed, in the nearest and dearest of all points entirely your own (and this privation is, doubtless, ordered for your good), but still a matter of infinite thankfulness, and to pray and hope over, and watch and order continually, and see growing up from week to week.

"Not being able to nurse it, is a physical relief to you; but on one account I rather regret it, that you lose the discipline in patience and long-suffering which makes the bloom of the maternal character. A mother who has borne with her infant's thousand wearing and worrying ways, who has given up her employ by day and her rest by night for it for months together, will be likely to bear with its moral faults and exercise patience in disciplining it for Christ, better, perhaps, than one who has been spared all this.

"Bear this in mind, dear child, and pray that your loss may not be for the worse, either for yourself or dear little Margaret. I wish I could get a sight of you on Thursday, but it is simply impossible, as I have a Ladies' Committee at 2.15, at the Adelphi, and I want to get away at three."

In March he went in company with his friend, the Rev. R. Hake, a minor canon and Precentor of Canterbury Cathedral, to visit some of the French cathedrals. An account of this tour was published in "Good Words," under the title of "Three Weeks among the Churches in France." His impression of the cathedrals of Chartres and St. Ouen are described in his journal:—

"I examined thoroughly St. Ouen, Rouen, the most beautiful church, perhaps, in the world. As to Chartres, nothing can be more graceful and beautiful than the west end of this exquisite cathedral: the spires are not twins, as they have been called, but rather brother and sister of different ages, one full of elaborate ornament and all kinds of varieties of lines, the other plain and severe, but not ungraceful, as I now sit on a stone step on the Place d'Armes, looking on them in the bright March sun with a black cloud behind."

And in a letter of condolence to a former pupil (the Rev. W. H. Gurney), he refers to his tour:—

To the Rev. W. H. Gurney.

"*Easter Eve.*

"I am ashamed not to have sent you before this some words of sympathy. Your letter arrived during a short run in France which I made in Mid-Lent, and got into the accumulation which awaited me on my return. You know how we feel for you, far better than pen-and-ink can tell. You were with us in our first great sorrow (1844, Easter): we shall ever be with you in all yours. After all, what are they, being translated into Christian language? what but, as each comes, one treasure *less* on earth, and one *more* in heaven. I wish you and your wife could come and see us some time before the summer, it would be a real pleasure to get a little friendly intercourse again, and especially now that, as you say, there is this new tie between us. I had a very cold but very enjoyable run in France with my Precentor, steeple chasing. We saw about a dozen glorious cathedrals, a report of which you may perhaps see in 'Good Words' in the September number. My present work consists of Vol. ii. of the English Testament, which, I hope, will appear (at least, Part I. of it) in a few weeks; several volumes of the Greek Testament are going through the press for new editions, a business which keeps me and my secretary, Hake, always employed, as I make a point of keeping the book always up to the present mark of information."

The summer passed without any very remarkable occurrence. His journal records a garden party (which afterwards became an annual institution) in the Deanery on June 20, to the Canterbury Harmonic Union: "160 singing, tea and ice in the garden, supper in the dining-room, music, &c., &c., up-stairs;" and his attendance at a meeting of the Palestine Exploration Fund, in which he took much interest.

On July 20 he writes, "Ecclesiastical Commission in the morning; afterwards to the Bishop of London's at Fulham, to meet the Queen of the Netherlands. Then with Fanny and Mary to the Royal Academy. In the evening at Lady Franklin's to meet Queen Emma of Hawaii; one does not often meet two queens in one day. I asked Queen Emma to come to Canterbury in the autumn, which she has consented to do. On Sunday I am to preach at the Westminster Abbey Evening Service."

Our autumn holiday was spent this year in Scotland; he undertook the service of the church at Callander in Perthshire. Leaving London on July 25th, we visited the Rev. Lord Arthur Hervey (afterwards Bishop of Bath and Wells) at Ickworth, and the Rev. H. Fearon at Loughborough, whence we went once more to see Wymeswold.

His journal will supply a record of our abode in Scotland, and of his visit to the Norwich Congress in October:—

"*Aug.* 2.—Edinburgh, after breakfast took a drive round the Queen's Drive, glorious day, views exquisite; then up Salisbury Crags, and returning by Canongate and High Street and Grass Market. Off at four for Callander, and on from thence to our small farm in Bocastle plain, just under Benledi.

"*Aug.* 4.—After arranging and unpacking, drove over to Callander to fetch Vaughan, who is to spend a fortnight with us.

"*Aug.* 8.—Busy with my September article on the Acts of the Apostles for the 'Sunday Magazine;' also preparing for the coming 'Contemporary,' and the new Hymn Book for Canterbury Cathedral. Our mornings are spent in study, our afternoons in drives and sketches, generally having our afternoon tea in some pretty spot; and in the evening I read to them, and we practise the 12th Mass, which is to be sung at our Harmonic Union at Canterbury.

"*Aug.* 14.—We all four went to spend a few days with the Macnaughtens at Invertrosachs; the house is most prettily situated, looking down Loch Venachar.

"*Aug.* 15.—Started over the hills with Mr. Macnaughten, Vaughan, &c., to the Clachan of Aberfoyle, and on to Loch Ard; next day sketched and fished at Landrick Mead.

"*Aug.* 19.—We went to Stromvar, Mr. Carnegie's, on Loch Voil; most beautiful place. We were rowed on the lake by four men in red shirts to the end of Loch Voil, where we landed and crossed over to the little Loch Doyne. We did not get to our home under Benledi till eleven o'clock. A most enjoyable day.

"*Aug.* 24.—The Hakes and Harry Thornton came by coach and alighted at the hill above our house. It is pleasant to have our Canterbury friends in our highland home.

"*Aug.* 26.—Working at the Hymn Book with Hake; this morning set off in a carriage for Loch Menteith and Loch Ard. We had our lunch on the heather at the top of Loch Ard, which is very beautiful. In returning crossed to Inch Mahone.

"*Sept.* 10.—Very hoarse and throat bad; happily Mr. Maclagan turned up and read prayers for me. A. K. H. B. at church twice. We drank tea at Mrs. Scott's in the evening to meet him.

"*Sept.* 11.—Fanny, Mary, and I by train to Duncrub; a magnificent house, the whole party were photographed outside the front porch. After dinner we played croquet in the hall by gaslight.

"*Sept.* 12.—Had much talk with Lord Rollo on men and things. He is an excellent specimen of a young Christian nobleman. Chapel attached to his house, and a parsonage for the chaplain, and everything done in a hearty genuine manner which delights me.

"*Sept.* 13.—Left Duncrub and got to the Macnaughtens for dinner, and met a nice party there.

"*Sept.* 14.—For a wonder a fine day; went with a party rowing across Loch Venachar to the Trosachs and Loch Katrine, and then by the steamer to Stronachlachan, lunching by the lake, and on our return having tea by a waterfall in the Trosachs, then crossed Loch Venachar against a head-wind.

"*Sept.* 16.—Left for our cottage, having spent a dissipated week as to work, but a very pleasant one as to society.

"*Sept.* 25.—Met Mr. Buchanan Hamilton at the bridge, and walked up Benledi with him; yesterday I forgot to bring my sermon with me to church, so I preached on the ten virgins from the second lesson. Received an article from B. Shaw on Ritualism, being the first article sent for the 'Contemporary Review.'"

We give some extracts from two letters written to Canon Robertson from Scotland:—

"*Bowcastle, Sept.* 8.

"The weather is simply execrable; water-colours are lying on the shelf, the sun making a point of retiring as soon as I appear with a sketch-book. The fish I suppose are washed away, at least, I can get none. Such is the state of things, yet we manage to enjoy ourselves between whiles, and I sally out rain-proof over the country, climbing all sorts of out of the way crags. Sometimes the ladies in our trap set me down and go on to Callander for letters, groceries, and flesheries. We have the Buchanan Hamiltons close to us, at Leny House, and two families near we know: the Troughtons of Cambusmore (where Walter Scott wrote his 'Lady of the Lake') and the Ainslies at the Gart. I am to foregather with A. K. H. B. (Dr. Boyd) at tea on Sunday evening.

"*Invertrosachs, Sept.* 14.

"Our Rollo visit was most successful. He is a very choice fellow, a specimen of a Christian nobleman of the very best kind, unpretending, liberal-minded. He has a princely place at Duncrub, and is still enlarging it. We are making out a dissipated week at the Macnaughtens; we had a glorious day at Loch Katrine yesterday, and my shaking hand is due to a hard pull against a head-wind across Loch Venachar on our return, which used up and blistered my hands. The weather as you may surmise by my last sentence has taken a turn (owing I suppose to the Queen's arrival). By all means persuade Blakesley [8] to dispense with his wall."

---

[8] Now Dean of Lincoln.

JOURNAL.

"*Oct.* 3.—Slept at York on my way to the Norwich Congress. Went to the Minster; service well done, but more than ever disappointed with the building; no genius, bald, and unharmonized; width too great for height. Met Howson, and secured him for the 'Contemporary Review.'

"At Norwich met Willie Gurney, who took me off to Earlham. In the evening appeared some men from the Congress. Off in a break on the 4th to the Congress; Goodwin read a paper on Cathedrals. Seymour also one, which I answered.

"*Oct.* 5.—Pusey read a remarkable and beautiful paper on the 'Application of Science to the Bible;' I read my paper on 'Preaching: its Adaptation to the Present Times' [in Essays and Addresses]; and then off all night through York, Berwick, and Edinburgh, and home by 11.30; thus hurried, as in a few days we are leaving Scotland."

After our return to Canterbury, we met with a disappointment in the failure of Queen Emma (in consequence of a sudden attack of cold) to pay her promised visit. A large party, including Sir Brook [now Lord Fitzwalter] and Lady Bridges, Mr. Beresford Hope and Lady Mildred Hope, and other friends assembled at the Deanery to meet her.

At this time two schemes occupied much of my husband's thoughts; the first of a personal character, the second of more general interest. He had long wished to possess a private house in addition to his official residence; partly with a view to provide a home for myself and our daughter in the event of his own death, and partly for the reason thus stated in a letter to a friend: "I wish to provide myself with a home in case I am unfit for my duties as Dean, for I have ever disliked the conduct of men retaining office in the Church after they were past their duties: and I long ago resolved, that if such should ever be my case, I would resign and retire." He fulfilled this intention by purchasing a lease of a small house commanding a remarkably fine view, named Vines Gate, about a mile from Brasted, near Sevenoaks. It became afterwards a pleasant occupation to add year by year something to the furniture of the house, or to the grounds.

The other scheme which now engaged him was the establishment of the "Contemporary Review" (see page 363). A great deal of time and trouble were given to engaging the assistance of a sufficient staff of contributors for a monthly magazine of about 150 pages, and to defining the ground which it was intended to occupy, and the subjects of which it was to treat. In a letter to a friend he says, "I trust we are doing good service against Ritualism and extravagancies of every kind, and are serving literature and art too."

The following letter glances at his various employments in the last months of 1865.

TO THE REV. J. H. HAMILTON.

"*Dec.* 18.

"I really am ashamed ('and so you ought,' echo) of the time since I have written to you; but if I were to mention the very busiest period of my busy life I should name the last two months. Since our return from Scotland, I have had many irons in the fire; my ever-pressing Greek and English Testaments; the preparation, in union with the Precentor, of a Canterbury Hymn Book, complete with tunes for the Sundays in the year. The editorship of the now nascent 'Contemporary Review,' which has gathered round it a staff of nearly fifty of the best men in the country, and is really a thing worth doing well. The multifarious cares of our Cathedral and this, in a time of growing reform, both in buildings and institutions; and added to all, a pleasant supplement, yet requiring time and travel, the arrangement about our new second home, now almost matured. I have heard of a farmhouse converted into a 'cottage ornée,' belonging to Mr. Tipping, of Brasted Park; it is in a most lovely spot, on a hill half way up Toy's Hill from Brasted, commanding a view down a wooded glen over Lord Amherst's and Lord Stanhope's parks, and away as far as Sevenoaks. This place I hope to take for a long lease."

The following reflections entered in his journal on December 31, 1865, may conclude the account of that year.

"It has pleased my gracious God wonderfully to preserve me and mine during another year. It has been one of peace and domestic happiness for us all, and full of blessings. The chief event in it has been the birth of our dear little grandchild.

"I have become Editor of the 'Contemporary Review,' the first number of which came this morning. I have got through much of the last part of my English Testament, and have written much in the 'Sunday Magazine' on the Use of the New Testament Books. After our return from Scotland dawned the project of a cottage in West Kent, and I am now in treaty for Vines Gate near Brasted.

"In health I have been very much better than for some years past, having nearly lost palpitations, and feeling clear in my head; able for any amount of work. Praise God for all His mercies to me and mine."

In the beginning of 1866 two events gave pleasure in our family circle: a second granddaughter, Edith Mary Bullock, was born on January 29th, and he went to London for the christening on February 24th. Almost contemporaneous with this event was the engagement of our younger daughter Mary to our neighbour, the Rev. H. E. T. Cruso, at that time a Master in the King's School, Canterbury. My husband refers to it in the following letter:—

To the Rev. J. H. Hamilton.

"*Feb.* 27.

"Many thanks for your congratulations and wishes; all has indeed been most mercifully ordered for us and our dear child; she has had sound sense and discretion enough to choose one in every way worthy of her. Thank you too for your kind sympathy on our coming loss of Mary. I shall feel it very deeply; but I should feel far more deeply the having, in any the least degree, interfered with her prospects in life, and I have always found by experience that in proportion as in any of our acts self is forgotten, just in that proportion is a rich reward reaped.

"You see what a terrible accident has befallen our poor Master[9], I fear likely to be fatal; a sad end for so great a man. I am just putting the finishing stroke to the Apocalypse for the English Testament; it will be quite another life when it is done."

He took part in a Mission held at Reading in February, and in a course of Lenten Sermons at Oxford. The good effects which he traced to such efforts, suggested to him the plan of a similar attempt to revive spiritual life in his Cathedral city; and he arranged a course of popular addresses in school-rooms attached to the different parishes (as will be seen) in the following December.

In July we went with our daughter and Mr. Cruso to visit our relations in Somersetshire; and my husband, leaving us there, made a short excursion by himself into Cornwall, the fruits of which were a considerable addition to the increasing number of his water-colour sketches.

The following letter was written from thence to our daughter Mary:—

"*Lizard Town, July* 17.

"Who would have thought that my first occupation should be writing to you? well, so it is, I remember the little figure, the affectionate chiselled face, as it stood at the door of the Mount, and a certain cord pulled and I gave way. The journey was long enough. The calm decorum of Exeter spread over its hill with its two-towered cathedral, like a hen brooding over it; then the well known line of red coast and the accustomed pang and tear in the eye as a certain bay of sorrow came in sight. Sixteen years ago—oh darling, what would he have been now? Yes, but what is he now? Then the town of Dartmoor, to the right far looming in grey mist; then the varied majesty of Plymouth, its well known haunts of great cork-trees, and the massive towers of docks. The roaring rush over Saltash bridge into Cornwall; then

[9] Dr. Whewell, Master of Trinity College, Cambridge, who died a few days after a fall from his horse.

the succession of wooded glens and tall viaducts, and town after town until we came to the end of the terminus at Falmouth, with the spruce, well be-vesselled basin on the left, and the roaring ocean to the right; then half an hour in a smoky coffee-room, and a two-horse fly and a tedious drive of twenty-two miles, till it grew dark, darker, and darkest. I at length with head out, looking for the flare of the Lizard lights, twice mistook a glowworm on the heath for them; at length a hazy luminosity ahead, lo it is done. I am going after breakfast to put in the outline of a picture of the Bumbles; then to the Cove, to which I remember going with you between the Lizard and Penolver Head, and make as good a picture as I can without any sun."

The fruits of his literary activity this year will be seen in the Appendix. One of them requires particular mention. "The Year of Prayer" is a book which contains original family prayers, and a calendar of short lessons for every day in the year; and, after its publication, it was constantly used in our own household. Its daily plan is simple, and may be thus generally described: first, a passage of Scripture of about ten verses: secondly, an original prayer appropriate to the day of the week—there are fourteen of these, one for each morning and evening; thirdly, another original prayer appropriate to the Church season, and generally founded on the Epistle or Gospel of the week; this prayer is designed to be used throughout the week, and sometimes to be followed by another special prayer; fourthly, the Lord's Prayer. The twenty-four prayers for special occasions of family or local interest, many of which are peculiarly original, are collected together in an appendix. The introduction of a hymn is suggested on Sunday evenings. In the preface he points out three distinct features of the book: its constant reference to the course of the Church's Year, its attempt at great plainness of language, and the frequency with which the prayers are addressed to the second Person in the blessed Trinity.

He notes with thankfulness in his journal, in March, 1866, the completion of his New Testament for English Readers, by the publication of the Second Part of the Second Volume. He regarded this and his Commentary on the Greek Testament as constituting one whole labour, his principal occupation for twenty-four years.

It may not be amiss to give a few unconnected extracts from his journal, by way of showing the diversity of his occupations in this year:—

"*April* 6.—The King's School athletic sports. Vocal rehearsal of music of 'Judas Maccabæus.' Off to-morrow for Cambridge, where I preach for four Sundays.

"*April* 7.—Cambridge. Rooms in my old staircase. Chapel in the morning, with M——. After breakfast to see St. John's new Chapel and the cricket-ground and rifle-butts behind the Colleges. At two at St. Mary's, and preached on the Resurrection. After dining in Hall left at 5.20 for town, caught the train at Ludgate, and got to Canterbury at ten, where I found the Archbishop, who confirms to-morrow.

"*April* 18.—Returned yesterday in time for the Diocesan Meeting. Lord Sydney, Lord Camden, Lord Romney, Lord Amherst, Lord Sondes, and others, came to the Meeting, and all the world to lunch at the Deanery. In an old wall in the Mint-yard were found some boys' names cut, dated 1553.

"*May* 2.—Convocation: then Literary Fund Dinner in Willis's Rooms.

"Some of our old Deans[1] are sent up to the Portrait Gallery Exhibition this year."

In the autumn we removed for two months to our new and quiet house, Vines Gate, near Brasted; and from thence he

---

[1] Twenty-eight portraits of successive Deans, beginning with Nicholas Wotton, 1541, adorn the walls of the hall and the principal rooms in the Deanery. They are heirlooms, and it seems to be the recognized custom for each Dean to leave his portrait. One or two of them, particularly Dean Bargrave, and perhaps Dean Rogers (see "Letters from Abroad," p. 99, 2nd edit.), are valuable, not only from their antiquity and local association, but as works of art. Dean Alford's portrait was the work of our friend, Lowes Dickinson, and was painted in the year 1860. Dean Bargrave's portrait is the work of Cornelius Jansen, who lived several years in England during James I.'s time.

paid a visit (to which he often referred with peculiar pleasure) to the Rev. Sir F. G. Ouseley, at Tenbury, Gloucestershire. They had been brought into communication by Sir F. G. Ouseley most kindly writing some tunes for my husband's projected Hymn Book; and my husband went to preach at a Choral Union at Tenbury. He says in a letter:—"I had a most awful headache on the day of preaching, but, happily, it held up just in time for service. All at Sir F. G. Ouseley's most charming, all his own work. A college for training gentlemen's sons chorally, no Ritualism, but all thorough Church, like a splendid great concert."

"The Year of Praise," which was published in 1867, had been in careful preparation for many months. Among its contents are several original hymns, which my husband composed in his solitary daily walks in the neighbourhood of Canterbury. His journal shows that five of these (148, 158, 174, 213, 229) were thus produced in five consecutive days. The tunes were mostly chosen, and some, indeed, were composed, at a weekly meeting between himself and his friend and coadjutor, the Rev. R. Hake, on Sunday evenings. The primary intention of the book was to serve as the means of introducing congregational hymnody into the service in Canterbury Cathedral. It contains 326 hymns, each printed with its music, four hymns being assigned to each Sunday or principal holiday, and about fifty being appropriate to special occasions. Previous to the publication of this book, and while his mind was full of the subject, he wrote in the "Contemporary Review," March, 1866, an article on "Church Hymn Books," in which he criticizes at considerable length the contents of nine of the most popular collections.

To the Rev. J. H. Hamilton.

"Vines Gate, Sept. 6.

"'The Family Prayers' have been ready for publication for three weeks; Strahan is only keeping them back for the publishing season. 'The Year of Praise' is rapidly getting on, and will be ready before the end of the year. The Dean of York sent me an invitation to come and make a speech at the Congress on 'the use of Cathedrals, Ecclesiastical, Musical, and Spiritual,' to last ten minutes! I respectfully declined; the thing will become a farce unless they diminish the number of speeches, and have but one essay on each subject, I am employed at this moment on lighter literature. 'Felix Holt' was mine in the September 'Contemporary,' and I am now writing an article on 'Recent Poetry,' besides various notices. In one of these I have rather a fierce slap at our friends the Church Milliners; for as to Ritualism, I am, and ever shall be, its uncompromising foe."

JOURNAL.

"*Nov.* 13.—After dining at Mitchinson's, went into the Green Court to see the meteors. They began about twelve, a most magnificent display; many at a time in the sky gliding from north-east to south-west, and leaving a trail which lasted many seconds. At its height at 1.15, then declining.

"*Nov.* 27.—To town at Hamilton's. Lectured at Exeter Hall on 'True and False Guides.'

"*Dec.* 13.—The rest dined at Mr. Bell's. I stayed to address the people in St. Mildred's School-room.

"*Dec.* 14.—Went to the early Communion at St. Mildred's.

"*Dec.* 20.—To town: Ecclesiastical Commission; dark as night. Telegraphed to say I could not return, but did in time for Mr. Woodward's address in St. Paul's School Room."

TO THE REV. J. H. HAMILTON.

"*Nov.* 22.

"I send you two books, 'The Family Prayers,' (or 'The Year of Prayer,') of which you know; and another, of which the only remarkable thing is, that the whole edition sold on the day of publication ('How to Study the New Testament'); so that I had great difficulty in getting six copies for my friends. I lecture at Exeter Hall on the 27th.

"We had a Consecration at Brasted on Saturday. The Archbishop preached.

"I return this afternoon to a school examination to-morrow at Canterbury. On Saturday Audit begins. On Monday I have arranged an Advent Mission in the slums of Canterbury this year, Dr. Miller begins by an Address on December 4th."

The marriage of our daughter Mary was an important family event in the early part of 1867. The following characteristic letter was written with reference to it to our intimate and valued friend, Fräulein Caroline von Stadlinger, then living with her father, General von Stadlinger, at the castle of Comburg, near Hall, in Swabia. Her presence at the wedding was especially desired by her former pupil, and my husband thus made the wish known:—

"*Deanery, Canterbury, Dec.* 18.

"Will you, can you, 'come over and help us'? Our darling child is to be married in the middle of February, and she says, 'O that I could have Caroline here! no one could be so useful, or give me so much help.' I too urge the same request. Much devolves on me at such times, and the legs are more liable to get worn than they were ten years ago. Mary is, thank God, much better, but obliged to be careful and to avoid fatigue. Your presence would just ease her from many little exertions which she would have otherwise to make; and so do come, there is a dear girl! and make us all happy. It would do if you were here on the 1st of February, and if you could stay a little after the event it would be a great pleasure; but this must be, of course, according to your own engagements. Alice and her children are well, and are to spend Christmas with us. There will, of course, be a family gathering at the wedding. Excuse me for adding that your journey shall be no expense to you. Please say all that is kind to your father and *die liebe* Emma."

Whilst he was busy in preparation for the wedding, and was anticipating with natural depression the vacancy which was about to be made in our house, his attention was diverted to the necessary accompaniments of an event of a different kind. On February 2nd Bishops R. Milman, of Calcutta;

W. C. Sawyer, of Grafton and Armidale; and C. R. Alford (our distant cousin), of Victoria, were consecrated in Canterbury Cathedral.

The wedding took place on February 12th. His record of this and the preceding days is as follows :—

"*Feb.* 7.—To town; Ecclesiastical Commission. Brought Etty [Alford] down with me. Caroline came a week ago, all the way alone and from Germany, during the severe frost and snow, to be present.

"*Feb.* 9.—Alice and her babes and Granny[2], who is much aged, came. Very pleasant altogether in the evening. Last days of happiness, i. e. of one sort. Happiness alone and with God we may have again, but with our children never.

"*Feb.* 10.—A large party at church. God grant that her approaching marriage may be for His glory and her own good!

"*Feb.* 11.—Very busy all day preparing. People come arriving all day. Very sad thoughts, but it is for the best for her and for me.

"*Feb.* 12.—My darling child married. She went through all, and we also, most cheerily and happily; our guests, too, were most kind, and all pathos was avoided. It was a day to thank God for. A large party in the evening. Songs, &c., from the choir. Everything went off well: δόξα τῷ Θεῷ."

Canon Selwyn sent two epigrams to be read at the breakfast. These may be interesting to some readers :—

EXEMPLARIA QUÆDAM, NULLIUS PRETII, HOC ARGUMENTUM EXHIBUIT.

Μηδὲν τοῦδε γάμου μετάνοιαν, χρυσὲ, παράσχοι,
μηδ' ὑπὸ τῆς πολλῆς (1) τειρομένῳ λαλίας·
μηδέ ποθ', οἷα πάλαι πρόγονος σέθεν ἔκλυε φωνῆς
πολλάκι (2) φασκούσης, "Χρύσ' ἐλεεινὲ" κλύοις
χαίροις, ὦ φίλε χρυσὲ, περιπλομένων ἐνιαυτῶν
ἀεὶ τῇ πολλῇ (1) τερπόμενος φιλίᾳ.

Hæc serioris esse notæ nemo sanus non videt; verborum lusus puerilis indicasse sufficiat.

(1) Videtur ἡ πολλὴ inepte alludere ad novæ nuptæ prænomen "Mary" quod Anglice = "Polly."

(2) Idem jocus insulsus in voce πολλάκι narrationem Robinsoni Crusoe

---

[2] The widow of his father, the Rev. H. Alford, see p. 72.

tangit, qui solus in insula deserta vitam degens Psittacum suum (Anglice *Poll*) clamitantem audiit "Poor Crusoe!" "POOR CRUSOE!"

Χρυσὲ φίλ', εὐκαίρως ἄλοχον πάγχρυσον ἔγημας
πλήθουσαν χαρίτων ἄμμιγα παντοπόρων (1),
ἣ φιλέουσ' ἀρετὴν, σοφίην τ', ἐπιηράτε πάντα,
ἓν μόνον ὑστερέουσ',—οὐ φιλόχρυσος ἔην.
κυκλοτερεῖ χρυσῷ ζευχθέντε, φιλήσετον ἄμφω
χρυσὲ σὺ τὴν χρυσέαν· ἡ δὲ σὲ χρυσὲ, πάλιν.

(1) Videtur familiam Alfordianam innuere.

A few days after the wedding he went to London, to take part in an important debate in Convocation, and he records:—

"*Feb.* 16.—A most pleasant evening at the Deanery, Westminster. Met the Duke of Argyll, Mr. and Mrs. Gladstone, Mr. and Mrs. W. Cowper, Plumptre, Mr. Rogers of Charter House, and Dr. Norman Macleod."

But the excitement, mixed up with depressing feelings of which this month was full, brought on a slight illness, and he sought relief in a short visit to the Riviera. Two notes which he wrote about this time to his grandchildren will show the warmth of his attachment even to the youngest of his family. The first is tinged with the sadness which oppressed him at that time:—

"DEAREST LITTLE MARGARET,—This is your third birthday, and Grandpapa wishes to give you his blessing and all good wishes. Perhaps Mamma will put by this letter for you, and you may read it on some birthday years hence, when the hand that is writing it is lying still in its coffin under the ground. If this is so, remember, dear child, that there is but one way to be happy, and that is the fear of God and the love of your parents. God bless you, dear girl, prays

"Your affectionate Grandfather."

By way of acknowledgment of this birthday greeting, he received on the thirty-second anniversary of our wedding a locket containing photographs of the two children, which drew from him the following letter to Margaret and Edith (written very large, and in jagged letters):—

"*Deanery, Canterbury, March* 10.

"DEAR LITTLE WOMEN,—Grandpapa feels so very old; he has been married thirty-two years, and his hands shake from age. But he must have some strength left, for he has two young Bullocks hanging at his watch-chain, and they don't tire him. Thank you, little darlings, for your kind present, and God bless you both. By, by, Margaret! ta, ta, Edith! From your venerable ancestor."

In obedience to an invitation from Archbishop Longley, he went to Lambeth in Ember Week to preach the Ordination Sermon. He records the visit in his journal:—

"*Feb.* 16.—Found my sermon to the candidates for Ordination was to be in the Parish Church instead of the Chapel. Had to sit up and rewrite it at night.

"*Feb.* 17.—Ordination at eleven. The candidates asked me to publish my sermon. Dinner with them all at two. Spent a pleasant day. The Archbishop very nice in his own house.

"*Feb.* 18.—After breakfast Mr. Longley took us over the Lollards' Tower, and Mr. Stubbs, the Librarian, showed us the Library."

He left England on March 27th, and returned on April 20th. This tour added to the materials, both literary and pictorial, out of which his book on the Riviera was subsequently composed. Two or three extracts from his letters will supply a sufficient record for these pages:—

TO THE REV. J. H. HAMILTON.

"*Cannes, March* 31.

"I am out for three weeks after our great event, which left me, when the excitement had passed away, in low spirits, and, according to everybody's opinion, needing change; but I dreaded leaving home, and I don't find as yet that my dread was unfounded. I came straight without stop, leaving at nine on Wednesday morning, and arriving here at 5.30 on Thursday afternoon; seeing the English Channel and the Mediterranean on consecutive days. At Orange lilacs were in bloom. At Marseilles we had green peas; the spring flowers are over, and the gardens are in full bloom. I propose exploring some of the lateral vallies at right angles to the Riviera road from here to Bordighera; they are reported very fine, with villages perched on rocks, and grand mountain views. Here there are great tracts of forest, rocks full of scrubby firs, with an undergrowth of ferns and myrtle; but the sea is glorious, and the view of the Estrelle Mountains also is always fine."

To his Wife (*on first leaving home*).

"Now one has got away from home, the events of this eventful spring look like a dream.

"I flitting away from home, a boy of fifty-seven, to enjoy a holiday a boy of twenty-five would despise. It all looks so strange and *bizarre*, but far above it all is an atmosphere of calm, sunny thankfulness to think and feel, 'Not more than others I deserve, but God hath given me more.'

"Life has entered on a new phase for us both, and I suppose we must make the best of it for God's work while it lasts. I am taking this tour in hopes of being set up physically for the work which God may yet have for me to do. I am sure I must be the dullest of companions, for I am sensible of not speaking one word where I used to speak ten.

"Thou who art weeping
When all are sleeping,
Sad vigil keeping
Far into night,
Nurse not thy sorrow
Into to-morrow;
From Jesus borrow
Comfort and strength.
Long though He try thee,
Still He stands by thee;
He shall supply thee
Richly at length."

To his Wife (*a few days after*).

"I had a bright, almost a cloudless passage, the sea retaining some traces of the storm the day before. I ran on through Paris, dining at the Gare de Lyon; the morning broke with splendid sunshine, and the Valley of the Rhone was burning and sparkling all the way to Vienne. On the mountain tops was snow, and dense vapours soon rolled up and shut out the sunshine. I am at the Beau Site at Cannes by A. Hare's advice; their society here is a great pleasure to me. I have been sketching a good deal; a view on the high road to Toulon, on a picturesque knoll, with pines and cypresses, and a little hermitage chapel called St. Cassian. I went to a village the other side of the bay under the Estrelle Mountains called Napouli; here I had only an hour for my sketch; it was a glorious view of the coast down to Bordighera, with such a background of snowy Alps behind in all their glory. From the Parc, a lighthouse at the top of the promontory, there is one of the most glorious views in Europe. It is now like June in England, orange trees all in blossom. I am trying a sketch from my bedroom window looking over Lord Brougham's grounds; above is a hill, with his pine wood, and the usual undergrowth here of a thousand flowers; to the right Cannes and the deep blue sea; the Isle of St. Marguerite, where dwelt the Man in the Iron Mask [1686—1698]. I have been to lunch at the Riddells. He looks ill. His daughters look more blooming every time I see them. I have been to Turbia, where Charles Albert abdicated, in 1849, after the battle of Novara; there I sketched, and made my fifth luncheon off the potted meat and biscuits.

"*April* 12.—I am off to Ventimiglia and Dolce Acqua, the village of Dr. Antonio, and sleep among the palms of Bordighera. I have had a sharp feverish attack, and could neither sleep nor eat. I exposed myself too much to the sun in my anxiety about finishing my sketches. Thank God, I am now convalescent. It was very funny to see Miss Leycester to-day scolding me, 'What is the use of our having wise Deans if they do such foolish things?' She came here last night, had a most stormy passage, saw the Exhibition in Paris, and was the only English person there.

"*Paris, Good Friday, April* 19.—I have been to Notre Dame, to hear the Père Felix. I got there at five to get a good place, but the service did not begin till 7.30. He preached nobly to a vast congregation."

At Canterbury he returned at once to his usual occupations: his afternoon services in the cathedral; the improvement of the volumes of the Greek Testament in new editions; and contributions to the "Sunday Magazine," in a series of articles on "How to Study the New Testament."

His attention to the affairs of the Ecclesiastical Commission drew him to London nearly every Thursday. One day he brought home from a committee of that body a *jeu d'esprit,* which he wrote apparently while waiting for some episcopal members to make up a quorum. A few lines from it may be acceptable to the reader:—

"I'm glad I'm not a Bishop,
To have to walk in gaiters,
And get my conduct pull'd about
By democrat dictators.

"While I by my Cathedral
Sit writing at my ease,
And fanning my grey temples
With the wanton summer breeze;—

"From Longley down to Sodor,
From Exeter to Lincoln,
They've knots to cut, or to untie
Would make me mad to think on."

In July he was honoured with a command for the third time to preach before the Queen at Windsor. His text was 1 Kings xix. 12, "After the fire a still small voice."

At the Choral Meeting this summer at Canterbury Bishop Hamilton of Salisbury, was the preacher, and was our guest at the Deanery. This led to a most pleasant visit to the palace at Salisbury in the autumn. The following letters mention this visit and his summer rambles; and in a letter to me he describes his Cornish trip, which furnished him with materials for some sketches and an article in "Good Words," called "A Week on the North Coast of Cornwall."

To the Rev. J. H. Hamilton.

"*Deanery, July* 13.

"We have had your uncle's bishop (Hamilton) here

preaching, the most kind and agreeable of men, and he preached a really good sermon. Mrs. Alford and I are going to stay with him at the end of September.

"What an extraordinary political phenomenon we have witnessed in the last few weeks!—a Tory Government taking office because their Liberal opponents proposed a Reform Bill which went too far for them, at last carrying through one themselves ten times as democratic as the wildest dream of the demagogue whom their opponents were supposed to be following. I doubt whether anything in our times has been so damaging to the theory of party Government as this. What will 1967 see? What sort of a future does Mr. Disraeli contemplate for us! If the next century is to witness twenty Governments, each outbidding the other for popular favour, who will govern us after the end of it?

"I have had two days' tour in France with a Marlborough sixth-form nephew[3], and it was very pleasant. We went to Ricquiers, a very fine old church, six miles from Abbeville; we were only one night out, returning in the middle of the next night. ——— is much improved, being more like other people, without ceasing to be like himself."

In August we spent a fortnight in the West of England. Mr. Bullock had taken charge of the parish of Pitminster for a summer holiday, and lived with his family in the vicarage. We resided with them for a part of the time.

TO THE REV. J. H. HAMILTON.

"*Pitminster Vicarage, Taunton, Aug.* 21.

"Bullock and Alice are here taking duty for August, and we have come to share in his labours and their housekeeping till September 8; then I leave my wife with her sister and go for a ramble with my sketch-book into some unexplored part of Devonshire or Cornwall, joining her in time for our Salisbury visit, and then eastward to Vines Gate for October, and so home into winter-quarters. The country here is very

[3] Mr. Robert Alford, son of the Rev. Walter Alford, of Drayton.

beautiful, rich, and somewhat over-timbered; elms, 300 feet, rather choke up the valley, and really injure the view.

"Alice's eldest child is developed into a rosy blue-eyed little chatterbox as amusing as a kitten; the younger a shrewd sensible little soul, just passing the boundary of infancy into childhood, and talking a *patois* somewhat puzzling to comprehend. I am working in the mornings at the 'Contemporary Review,' and proofs of the Testament, and spending the afternoons in croquet, or walks forwards and backwards over the four miles which divide us from our local metropolis."

To his Wife.

"*Columb Port, Sept.* 10.

"I started on a glorious morning for this place; all day sketching, but the tide is rather awkward, the scenery here is all low water. I took three sketches, and a long walk on the sands besides. The finest part of the coast is not here but at Bedruthan, a sort of Kynance Cove of this part of Cornwall. There is one rock exactly like Queen Elizabeth, crown, features, ruff, hoop, and all. The day has been the very best for sketching that could be imagined; blue clear sky, with clouds in the horizon. One sketch was taken under difficulties; an immense flock of pigs kept surrounding me, and as I was washing in my sky in haste, for fear of edges drying, some ladies came up with, 'May we see your sketch?'"

To the Rev. W. H. Gurney.

"*Weston-super-Mare, Sept.* 24, 1867.

"I was truly sorry to see your sister's death; how sad it must have made you all; and the poor husband so helpless. May you and may he find all the comfort which we declare is to be found in our holy faith at times when we only look at sorrow. I have ever found that more comfort comes than I could possibly have looked for, and in more merciful ways than I previously could imagine.

"We have been about these parts now for nearly two months. We joined the Bullocks in a vicarage where they took duty near Taunton, and now we are lingering about and visiting our friends one and another till next Saturday, when I am due to visit Salisbury, and to preach in the cathedral there. We shall be at the Palace for a few days, and then we go to Vines Gate."

JOURNAL.

"The Palace at Salisbury is a great rambling house like two of my deaneries.

"*Michaelmas Day.*—Preached in the morning, extemporary, at St. Edmund's for the organ; in the afternoon I preached in the nave of the Cathedral from 'A little lower than the angels.' The Bishop of Arkansas and Mrs. Lay are here, having come to England to attend the Pan-Anglican Meeting; they have promised to come to Canterbury in November.

"*Oct.* 1.—Sketched from the garden; lovely day. Drove to Bemerton and Wilton. Only such a sky could justify the Italian Church and Campanile at Wilton. Home by Old Sarum, meeting the Bishop, and walked home with him.

"*Oct.* 2.—Finished my sketch. A dull drizzling day, but went with Mrs. Hamilton to Stonehenge."

On November 1st he was present and was placed in the chair at a complimentary dinner which was given in London to Dr. Norman Macleod[4], previous to his departure for India, whither he was sent by the Established Church of Scotland to visit and report on the state and prospects of Missions to the heathen. Among the speakers, in addition to the chairman and the guest of the evening, were the Rev. E. H. Plumptre, Mr. George Macdonald, the Rev. Dr. Mullins, Mr. De Liefde, and the Rev. A. Saphir.

The "Contemporary Review" was at this time a cause of some anxiety to its editor; and the following letter relates chiefly to it:—

TO THE REV. E. T. VAUGHAN.

"*Deanery, Nov.* 15.

"A real effort will be wanted to carry on the 'Contem-

---

[4] Who died in the summer of 1872.

porary Review;' effort to catch the popular interest worthily. My own earnest wish is to carry it on with a view to a nucleus being formed of a better yearning for Christian union than now shows itself among us. A rallying ground for a party (if party it must be called) which should recognize with heart and hand, not after the unctuous platform fashion, but honestly and consistently good and loyal men, to whatever denomination belonging, recognizing them (not with any idea of proselytizing from them) as *religiones licitæ* within the limits of our common Christianity, sticking to one's own, and prepared to defend it, but preparing also to maintain the thesis, that our Reformers did not, and we will not, regard our own form of Church as *de rigueur* or force it upon others. This is the only consistent following out it seems to me of our principles, and the only way of being loyal to that state of life (using familiar words in a wide public sense) to which it hath pleased God to call us. I am preparing a lecture for the young men at Glasgow, to be given on December 4th on 'The Christian Conscience[5],' founded on the Trichotomy, but going into its functions as regards present matters, in which I hope to utter some sentiments of this kind. Somebody ought to be up, and speak; good and true and loving men are too reticent it seems to me, but perhaps we think differently on this."

To an old friend who consulted him as to the interpretation of Colossians ii. 2, he wrote as follows :—

"*Deanery, Canterbury, Nov.* 26.

"DEAR MISS LEYCESTER.—The τοῦ Χριστοῦ can hardly be anything but 'personal.' Your idea is an ingenious one; but can hardly stand when one puts beside it the fact that St. Paul uses the same τοῦ Χριστοῦ a few verses down, chap. ii. 11, of the circumcision of Christ, which, of course, can only mean the strictest personal reference, seeing that on this personal reference the very sense depends. Nor do

---

[5] Afterwards printed in "Good Words," and in "Essays and Addresses," p. 45.

I see that your sense would make much difference. The mystical Christ is only so by being summed up in His Person: the personal Christ can only be said to be completed by being expanded out into His mystical Body. We seem to come to much the same either way. And either way, what a universe of glory and grace the words open before us! How true it is, dear Miss L., that the longer life becomes, and the more it groups around the sayings of the Word, the more its whole voice becomes, 'Thanks be to God!'

"How I envy you old Rome again! Could you not give us a day in your way out? Mrs. A.'s best love.

"Ever yours,

"H. A."

On December 2, his new Hymn Book, 'The Year of Praise,' was used for the first time in Canterbury Cathedral, and he refers to it in a letter to his daughter, Mrs. Cruso:—

"To-day was the first Sunday of the new Hymn Book in the Old Cathedral, and it sounded very nice. I preached on the subject in the afternoon from Ps. lxvii. 3—5[6], but not to an overflowing congregation; for the spouts were overflowing instead, and a storm was raging, and blowing the windows.

"The new Library makes progress."

In the same week he went to Glasgow, to deliver the lecture which has already been mentioned (p. 403). Perhaps it is not saying too much to describe this lecture as one of the most thoughtful and characteristic of his writings, and most important in its bearing on practical life. His theme is the Christian Conscience—its origin, its description, its operation, its present extent of influence on public and private opinion and action. No one without the training of his peculiar studies could have written the former part of it: and few men would have arraigned so boldly the violations (as he regards them) of Christian conscience exhibited

---

[6] This sermon was printed with the title of "Cathedral Hymnody," and copies were also distributed by the author to the members of the Cathedral Choir.

in the practice of our commercial men and of our legislators, in the attitude of a large section of the Church of England towards other communities, and in the inexact handling of the Word of God by "all the Churches of the realm." The long-cherished opinions which he here expressed concerning our "depreciation of the Nonconformists," and the defects of our Authorized Version of the Bible were avowedly carried out, as we shall see in the course of the following year.

To his Wife.

"*Glasgow, Dec.* 5.

"The long journey passed prosperously, though so cold. I am in a most beautiful and luxurious house. My host is the Mr. C—— who twenty-three years ago was to have been my pupil, but his father changed his plan, and to compensate me gave me £10 towards our Wymeswold west window; only think!

"I have been to see the new University building in the Park this morning, close to Dr. Caird's church, where we went in 1859. I lunched with the Blackburns[7]. L. came in, whom I had not seen for thirty years, when we saw him and D. at Bonn. The latter is very ill. You remember he and his daughters went up Vesuvius with us April 14, 1864."

On his return he writes to his younger daughter of what he saw whilst passing through London:—

To his Daughter, Mrs. Cruso.

"I must write and describe one of the great sights of my life. I arrived from Glasgow at ten, and went to the Athenæum for some tea, having ordered a bed at the Grosvenor for the 7.25 a.m. train on Saturday. I had drank my tea, and had been looking over some man's travels in Abyssinia, and seeing it was eleven o'clock got up to go off to bed. I had been conscious for some minutes of a woody burning smell, and fancied one of the fires had gone out and had been fresh lighted; but just as I rose to go, Mr.

---

[7] Hugh Blackburn, Esq., Professor of Mathematics in Glasgow University was once a pupil at Wymeswold.

Bunbury came by, and said, 'This smell is increasing, there must be a fire somewhere;' we both went to the window and drew aside the curtain, and lo! the flame was just bursting through the roof of the Queen's Opera House.

"In a few minutes all in the drawing-room were in utter dismay; the general cry was 'They must be just coming out, hundreds will be burnt!' then some one said it was not an opera night, and one breathed freely. I rushed down to get my hat and coat, and all went to the balcony; the sight was grand; as the flames increased at last (that last was not more than ten minutes), they shot up full three times the height of the roof, 400 feet high, and as the keen north-east wind rose and fell they swooped over Pall Mall, sometimes almost touching the United Service Club, and covering its roof with burning pieces of wood and paper: it was at one time in some danger. The heat in our balcony was very great; I got both blackened and scorched. All the houses round the Arcade and Waterloo Place had caught more or less. The engines had by this time arrived, whistling furiously as they tore up the street in full gallop; they instantly began working on the blazing roofs, smoking and snorting as loud as a train, and the effects were soon visible. The enormous mass of water from the steam fire-engines soon got the mastery, and every roof one after another sputtered, and smouldered and steamed; among them Rivington's, to my great delight, though still my Greek Testament may be spoilt by water. By this time the Queen's Opera House was a mere shell, and the flame had sunk down within. The two gables stood grinning at each other, capped by its high water tanks in solemn irony; the gas-lamps ceased to look green sparks, and returned to their wonted splendour; the moon and stars resumed their government of the night; the Queen's Opera House took itself off into the realms of history, and myself to bed at the Grosvenor."

In his journal he writes, "Took notes of this fire for future use." Use was made of them a few months afterwards. A niece, Miss E. M. Alford, was engaged in the composition of a work of fiction, and consulted her uncle as to the arrangement of the plot. Beginning as adviser he became a joint author, and when "Netherton on Sea" was published in 1869, many incidents in his own life, many early recollections and scenes with which he was familiar were described in this novel. Thus the account of the conflagration of the factory ("Netherton on Sea," 2nd edition, 1870, page 69) is founded on what he observed of the destruction of the Opera House. His recollections of Ilminster Grammar School supplied the description of that of Netherton (pp. 34—36). The Church of Ars and its Curé (pp. 201—204) are sketched from his own observations in 1868, so is the scenery of the Riviera (ch. xxvi. and xxvii.). The local descriptions of Rome (ch. xxix.), and many of the remarks in that chapter were familiar to those who shared his visit to Rome.

CHAPTER XI.

1868–1870.

Archbishop Longley's Ordination at Canterbury—Visits Cornwall and the Isles of Scilly—Death of Archbishop Longley and Enthronement of Archbishop Tait—Visits to the Riviera—Revised Version of the New Testament—Lectures at Liverpool, Leeds, and Bradford—Illustrated Books in Contemplation—Commentary on the Old Testament—Scheme to visit the Holy Land—Company for Revising the New Testament—Last Tour on the Continent—Autumn at Vines Gate—Visit to the East Coast of Scotland.

THE Mission or course of addresses which was held at Canterbury in the latter part of 1866 (p. 393), had appeared to some persons to be capable of repetition with still better effect at another season of the year. Accordingly the Dean suggested to Archbishop Longley that Canterbury should be chosen as the place for the ordination in Lent, 1868, and that his Grace should deliver an address in a course of Mission Services to be held at the same season. This was done; and on March 8th Canterbury witnessed for the first time in fifty years, the striking and instructive ceremonial of an ordination. The Archbishop resided for a week at the Deanery, and the candidates for the ministry, while under examination, were hospitably accommodated in houses in the Cathedral precincts and at St. Augustine's College; a room for the examination was supplied by the Deanery.

The Archbishop at the cost of much personal exertion contributed to the good results of the Mission by giving on

March 3rd "a most kind and fatherly address" to an assembly of working men, &c., at the Broad Street National School-room.

Soon after Easter my husband, accompanied by his brother the Rev. B. H. Alford, went to the Riviera. The results of this tour appeared afterwards in the illustrated book on the Riviera (published in 1870) and in some accounts of the famous Curé d'Ars in the "Contemporary Review" (1867, pp. 209. 297), and in "Netherton on Sea."

He wrote to me from Cannes, on April 20 :—

"All has prospered; weather most beautiful; the sun arose as we were leaving Lyons, lighting up first Our Lady of the Fouvières, then all the windows on terrace after terrace, with ruby light.

"As we passed on, old legends were ever in my thoughts: the Roman Arch of Triumph and vast Theatre at Orange; the massive palace of the Popes at Avignon, &c., &c. On the stony plain of the Cran between Arles and Marseilles, the mirage was very remarkable, the distant trees and hills looked as if a sea were between us and them, and one could even see them reflected in the water—all a delusion. All the valley of the Rhone was brilliant in sunshine, and the salt lakes and the sea as we approached Marseilles most heavenly in colour. I think I told you of the palms at Hyères. I have seen nothing like them before; they quite beat those of Bordighera in size, but the difference is, in Bordighera they are wild and by hundreds, at Hyères only in gardens. We went in a little carriage from Hyères to St. Tropez, partly through plains full of peach orchards, with china roses all in blossom; and partly through cork-tree forests. St. Tropez is situated on a peninsula which makes a land-locked bay; it is said to be the very best place for consumptive patients. Next day, the 18th, we walked out to a grand pine on the Hyères road, where we lunched, and I sketched the pine, and late that evening I got to my old quarters at Beau Site, Cannes; on the 19th I took a long fatiguing walk to the Chapelle de St. Antonio and to St. Valerien."

"*Oneglia, April* 29.

"On the 20th we went to Nice, Bradley and I, to make calls; and I alone to Villa Franca harbour, which I sketched with you in 1863 on our way to Rome. Here I wrote a description for future use.

"The next day we set off for Grasse, and on to the famous Pont à Dieu. At St. Vallier we left our carriage, and with a guide went a glorious tiring walk of five miles over a stony waste, then an ilex grove. The bridge is made of tufa in a deep gorge over the Siagne. I took a sketch amidst the ilexes and periwinkles and maiden-hair fern, to the southward face of the bridge. We have been to some glorious views near Antibes (I have three views of these parts in my Rome and Nice Sketch-book). We went from Vence in a shandrydan to see the beautiful Var villages, perched on rocks in the gorge of the Var: at one spot one sees eight of them, with the snowy mountains at the head. There I drew from the olive terraces, in the midst of nightingales, till sunset. On the 27th I was very poorly and fit for nothing, but next day we set out at ten, up the course of the Nervia to Dolce Acqua, and there sketched and lunched; and on to Bordighera. I was much better, but not quite well. To-day I have been colouring my last year's sketch of the palms; also taking a sketch of the scene of the upset in Dr. Antonio. My incident book will tell you more particulars.

"The heat is very great here."

TO HIS DAUGHTER, MRS. BULLOCK.

"*Latour, the Capital of the Vaudois Valleys, May 3rd.*

"We followed our plan till the heat made it impossible, so we broke off our Riviera part at Oneglia, and thence we crossed the Alps to Turin, and came here to look up our friends the Vaudois. They are a nice, hearty, merry people, bright-eyed, lots of pretty children and girls; and they live in valleys with rushing waters, and vines trimmed over pergolas, and quaint houses, with galleries all round; their service, which we attended, is dreary enough.

"To-morrow we leap on asses at 6.30, and go to see other valleys. Did I tell you, from the promontory of St. Jean, near a place called Petite Afrique in the Riviera,—such a hot place,—I saw the Island of Corsica very plainly?—white cliffs bright in the sun, 120 miles off: on that spot there are splendid aloes and carouba trees (a glorious evergreen)."

To his Wife.

"*Turin, May* 4.

"On approaching Turin from Garessio, the hills were clothed with chestnut forests, an undergrowth of box, ruined castles placed on the heights above; five miles from Garessio we passed the Tanaro, on a bridge all of white marble (flecked with grey); soon after the road rises up a small hill and passes along the ridge of a gorge, the river and rocks below, and at the end the distant snowy mountains. The Alps here were perfectly wonderful. Monte Viso, the chief of them, looking from his proud domain like the god of this nether world; this became more and more so as we got farther on, for the country got hidden by mists, and the top of Monte Viso shot faint and mysterious gleams up into the sky, like an approaching strange planet. Mondovi is a small city on the banks of a torrent; it has several churches picturesquely situated. I took an outline from the train as we passed. We have just taken our last excursion to the Val d'Argogna up a path taking the east side of a fine gorge, snowy mountains at its head; vegetation most luxuriant; we got many roots of lilies, ferns, and gentians, &c.

"Here we found such a budget of news. The Duke of Edinburgh shot at. The Emperor Theodore in trouble, &c.

"You remember Turin in 1837, an uninteresting, straight-built modern city, but surrounded with the glorious chain of the Alps on three sides. We mounted up on a height on the other side of the Po, and the whole lay before us basking in the still bright heat of a summer's day; on the left Monte Viso, the giant of the Dauphiné mountains, the Mont Cenis, and farther round Mont Blanc, Monte Rosa; full 200 miles of Alps! What do you think we have seen? a great Romish procession, the only one I have seen at all.

"We mean to return by Ars, Paris, and home."

TO HIS WIFE.

"*Paris, May* 8.

"On the 6th we went from Lyons to Ars. Most interesting: the old church just as it was in Vianney's time. A truly village church, with the plainest seats and simple country people; pilgrims kneeling about. The vicarage, pulpit, confessional, the chapels of St. Philomen and St. John the Baptist, preserved exactly in the same state as in his time. A grand new church is being built containing the old one. We were shown the Presbytère and his own room by M. Tassi, and were taken to a Mademoiselle Ricotti, a well-to-do woman, who has bought up everything belonging to him for his poor people, even his teeth at five francs each. She has a room full of all sorts of furniture of his, his coat, hat, &c. I sketched the village and church, and we called on M. Toccania, his successor, who showed us his house and gave us some photographs. To-morrow, please God, you will see me. So ends my spring tour in joy and thankfulness."

One result from his lecture at Glasgow on "The Christian Conscience" now appeared. Early in this year he had written to his friend, the Rev. R. P. Graves:—

"I send you a lecture I gave at Glasgow on December 4th, which you may not have seen in 'Good Words.' It has led to much correspondence and two practical results: first, a movement of recognition of Nonconformists; secondly, a pressure on me to undertake a revision of the English New Testament, which I have done, more to incense men's minds and bring on the movement than with any idea of doing much service. The work ought to be done by many, not one."

His lecture at Glasgow led to correspondence with many Nonconformists; and a proposal was made to him that he should take a prominent part in a centenary celebration at

Cheshunt College[1], Herts. Before consenting, he made careful inquiries into the object and condition of the College, and then wrote as follows, on March 30th, to the Rev. Dr. Allon:—

"I have carefully read the papers which you have sent me, and am more convinced than ever that Cheshunt College is exactly the institution where ground can be broken in our movement most appropriately, and with the strongest case in favour of such an act; I shall therefore put myself at the disposal of the College for the purpose for which they invite me."

On June 14th he was staying at the Deanery at Westminster, and preached in the Abbey on "Charity the End of the Commandment." The sermon is printed in "Essays and Addresses" (p. 113).

Ten days afterwards he writes in his journal:—

"In town again. Next morning (25th) drove to Cheshunt College. Service, Church of England. Newman Hall read; Dr. Binney preached. I presided and gave a written address, and spoke. Returned at eight p.m., and went to a clerical meeting at the Rev. J. Oakley's, Hoxton."

The address which he delivered is printed in "Essays and Addresses" (p. 137). The subject is "The Requisites of an Education for the Ministry in the Present Day."

In the course of another week (on July 1st) an annual garden party was given at the Deanery in connexion with the Canterbury Harmonic Union, and to this party he invited three of his entertainers, viz. Drs. Binney, Stoughton, and Allon, and showed them over the Cathedral. In the following

---

[1] "This College, it is said, was founded by Lady Huntingdon for the purpose of training up lay-preachers for meeting-houses. Lady Huntingdon, though a pious woman, was unquestionably not a member of the Church of England, but what is strictly and properly called a Methodist, professing the doctrines of George Whitfield, and educating young men to preach those doctrines without episcopal ordination." ("Bishop Porteus's Life," by Hodgson, p. 268.) In the last century the Rev. Dr. Draper, a clergyman of the Church of England, went so far as to become President of the College and preacher in the chapel, and consequently fell under the censure of Bishop Porteus, who himself was subject in his generation to "the common sweeping imputation of methodism."

December he renewed his intercourse with some of the party in a visit which he paid to the New College at St. John's Wood.

A few days afterwards a sorrowful event occurred, which is mentioned for the sake of the letter to which it gave occasion. Mrs. Cruso, the mother-in-law of our second daughter, died suddenly at Vines Gate, where she was staying on a visit to her son, then Curate of Brasted. My husband wrote thus on July 8th to our daughter:—

"So it is over. Well, dear child, you have been brought face to face with your own and your husband's trouble. One's own first sorrow is a very real thing, very different from even one's dearest friend's sorrows. The grief is closer; the comfort is closer; more actually in the heart, and less about its borders. When we lost Clement I felt as if I had never sorrowed before; as if the fire which had been trying others was now indeed brought near, and tearing my own nerves. Even this and its greater repetition you, darling, hardly felt with ripened feelings. The child and the maiden have the pangs of grief, but not its dignity, not its enduring impression. Now you have all. God bless them to you, and you in them, both in smiting and in healing. Pray say to Henry all that you know I wish to say. Words are poor things in the face of sorrow. . . ."

On July 30th the new Chapter Library (see Appendix) at Canterbury became a rendezvous for the County Archæological Society. Professor Willis read a paper, and conducted a party round the precincts. In the evening there was a *soirée* at the Deanery, and a visit to the Cathedral by moonlight. Next day St. Augustine's College and various places in the city were visited by the antiquaries.

In August he went with Mr. Burrell Smith for a sketching tour in Cornwall.

He wrote to his niece, Miss E. M. Alford, Taunton, on August 1st:—

"So the month for rambling and unbending the bow is begun, and by the same token you are about to be besieged by two flies, which will perch down on your Mount on the 6th, reaching their pasturing ground at Tintagel—far from all railways, the enchanting abode of King Arthur and Sir Galahad and the rest—that night; for are they not twenty miles from the Bodmin station? Now as to Scilly. . . . It not the King[2], but the priest I go to visit, . . . the faithful Dan."

To his Daughter, Mrs. Bullock.

"*St. Mary's Vicarage, Isles of Scilly, Aug.* 29.

"Our time is spent here in boating and sketching. The weather is superb, sunny, and breezy; the sea, ultramarine and emerald, even surpasses the Lizard and Mediterranean. It is a tiny, jolly place, 145 granite islands, glowing like gems in the heaving heart of the deep. This place is quite a town, streets and shops, and a harbour and a pier. Opposite is Tresco, the Imperial residence; I was there from Monday to Wednesday this week, and I am going again next week. The Emperor [Mr. A. Smith] is full of reading and anecdote, and the pattern of hospitality."

To his Wife.

"*Tresco Abbey, Isles of Scilly, Sept.* 1.

"We got to Tintagel at seven on Friday, such a long cold drive from the station. Next day we went down to the Cove and began sketching. I found a lady there who came here owing to my article in 'Good Words' (1868), 'A Week on the North Coast of Cornwall.' On Sunday I preached for Mr. Kinsman at the quaint old church. On Monday, after lunch, Mr. Kinsman drove us with his three ponies to Bowcastle, where Burrell Smith and I drew; and then on to a high cliff, where we also drew a splendid view from the latter. We had very bad weather for the Lizard and Land's End, but Burrell Smith and I drew a good deal, and we met Mr. Hart, the Lizard artist. I have ordered

---

[2] Augustus Smith, Esq., who died in 1872, was for forty years proprietor of the islands under lease from the crown. The Rev. D. P. Alford, the Dean's nephew and brother of his correspondent, was at this time Vicar of St. Mary's in the Isles of Scilly.

of him the sketch we saw him taking, and also one of Kynance Cove; and Burrell Smith took one for me of Tintagel and the coast below. I came here on the 20th. The islands seemed low at first sight.

"I sailed across in the Imperial boat to lunch on the 31st, and stayed till the 3rd. This place is just like Nice or Cannes in the garden growth. Huge aloes, with their blossom stalks, palms, forests of mesembryanthemum cactuses, and all manner of geraniums, great bushes covered with bloom; the weather is perfectly elysian. To-day I saw from my room the sun rise out of the sea behind the Land's End; and this evening, I saw the most glorious sun set clear into the sea.

"We have been a large sketching party to St. Helen's Island, more beautiful than I can possibly describe; fern, heather, and rocks, all of gorgeous colours, the sea perfectly calm inside the Archipelago, but outside thundering on the rocks with clouds of spray. My host goes with his guests in his boat in all directions. I hope to draw a great deal whilst I am in these parts, to illustrate my article in 'Good Words' ('Cornwall Again,' No. II. 1868). The rocks are so bright, and the sea most lovely in colour, the views are very curious; the sea bristling with dozens of rocky islets, whichever way you turn. On Sunday, 30th, I preached at Tresco for the Truro Infirmary; the second lesson for the morning gave me a text, Acts xxviii. 9. I came back in Mr. Smith's boat, and in the evening I preached for Dan at St. Mary's; and, after church, we had a moonlight walk to see the little grave of their dear babe, whom I buried on the 26th. What a fearful railway accident there has been!"

The death of Archbishop Longley occurred in October [3]. Shortly before, he wrote as follows to my husband:—

"Though I have returned from my Continental tour much improved in general health and strength, I have, unfortunately, brought back with me an asthmatic cough, which

---

[3] In the Dean's second "Fireside Homily" ("Sunday Magazine," Dec., 1868) are some remarks on Archbishop Longley's death.

my medical adviser says would render it very imprudent to undertake such an exertion as the fortnight of Visitation necessarily entails. . . . I intend, however, to print my Charge and send it to every clergyman in the diocese.

"Believe me, my dear Dean,

"Very sincerely yours,

"C. T. Cantuar."

On 28th October his journal records :—

"Heard of the Archbishop's death in the evening, Bell Harry[4] tolled from eight till ten. Whom shall we have?"

At this time he was preaching in the Cathedral a course of Sermons on "The State of the Blessed Dead," which were afterwards published in a small volume.

It was in the month of October that we had a visit from the Rev. Dr. Tristram, which gave great pleasure to my husband. A project was then revived of a journey to the Holy Land, on which he had set his mind. Arrangements were made for a tour, in which he was to be accompanied by Dean Howson, Dr. Tristram, the Rev. E. Venables, and the Rev. E. H. Bickersteth, of Hampstead. More than once a time was appointed for the departure; but unforeseen occurrences intervened, and the project was never fulfilled.

I record here a visit which we received a few months later from the Rev. Dr. Stoughton, the respected Minister of the Congregational Chapel, Kensington. More than two years afterwards Dr. Stoughton writes with reference to this visit:—

"Of Dean Alford's eminently companionable habits I have a pleasant remembrance, as I call to mind a long walk which I took with him in January, 1869, when we passed near the churchyard of St. Martin's, where, in so short a time, he was to sleep his last sleep. He spoke freely upon Church questions, manfully maintaining his own views; he explained and defended his opinions on fixed theological questions, that of baptismal regeneration in particular; and he dwelt much upon his ministerial experience and his London life, his ministry at Quebec Chapel, and his intimacy with Hampden

[4] The large bell in the cathedral, so called after King Henry VIII.

Gurney—for whom he had a great affection, as I know Hampden Gurney had for him. I shall never forget the feeling with which, ever and anon, he pointed out natural objects, or some striking feature in the wide historic landscape opened before us; and how with poetic sensibility, he called my attention to the fact that the soil of the ploughed field seemed so brown and bare as we crossed it, assumed a delicate shade of green, as we looked back and saw in perspective the delicate spires of corn peeping above the furrows that glorious winter afternoon: and when the walk was over, and we had passed under the shadow of the grand Cathedral by moonlight, calling up speculations upon the Church's future, there followed in the evening a train of travelling reminiscences, full of description and anecdote; hints as to a tour I was intending to take over the same ground; and notices of school-boy and after-life, all bright, genial, heart winning. I make no apology for thus alluding to private intercourse; for it illustrates traits of character which do not appear in an author's books or a preacher's sermon, or in any of the generally known proceedings of a public man. As in his writings on great subjects, so in his conversation respecting them there was a wholeness of heart—a unity of spirit, resembling 'the cloud which moveth altogether if it move at all."

He attended the crowded meeting of the Society for Promoting Christian Knowledge, at Freemasons' Hall, on December 8, where that Society rejected by a majority of 765 against 674 a proposal to grant a large sum of money for the purposes of Bishop Macrorie in Natal. The meeting made a deep impression on the Dean, and he wrote an article on it, entitled, "The Next Step," in the "Contemporary Review," January, 1869.

On the 16th December he wrote the following characteristic letter to his old friend, Archdeacon Bickersteth, on the occasion of the Archdeacon's election to the chair of Prolocutor in the Convocation of Canterbury:—

"It is, indeed, a pleasure to find that in the midst of widely diverging Church opinions Christians' hearts can ring true to one another, and to their great Lord. It was a cause of real delight to me that I was called on to propose you on Friday. I doubt we have a stormy sea of sessions before us, but you in your august chair may sing 'Suave mari magno' over us, whose frail barks are tossed thereon."

A list of his literary works published this year will be found in its place in the Appendix. It might appear to some readers of these pages that the seasons of relaxation, which are so fully described in his numerous and interesting letters, occupied too large a portion of his time. But that impression will be removed when it is considered how many hours of mental labour were given to the production of his various writings—hours of which the only record must be the abundant fruit which they bore. His articles in the "Contemporary Review" and editorial correspondence occupied much time. Amongst the articles in the "Sunday Magazine" I must single out the series of Fireside Homilies, in which he took great delight, and poured out his reflections on passing events, as well as agreeable reminiscences of the past. It was his intention to republish these Homilies in a separate volume. A list of them will be found in the Appendix. The fifth edition of his Poems was published this year, including his most recent pieces. "A surprising proof," as a friendly reviewer observed, "of the springiness and lightness of his mind after the *improbus labor*, which has been his lot for so many years past."

The following reflections are entered in his journal at the end of 1868:—

"Another year! the shades are beginning to close in, and the windows want cleaning, but won't clean. However, blessings have not been and are not few. The past year I have done much literary work, and have been led to come forward more boldly for what I believe to be the best for the Church and her members.

"Health and strength are now more than ever cause of thankfulness. After fifty, whatever happens to the body, we have no right to complain. God grant me energy for work, or, if not that, patience to endure; and this and every year (if there be any more) may He, by work or by endurance, ripen me for the great final state now dawning in the horizon."

On February 3rd, 1869, the new Archbishop (Dr. Tait) came to Canterbury for his enthronement, and remained till the 8th. The preparations for the ceremonial occupied much of my husband's time for many previous days; and I find in his journal notices of frequent pains and weariness, which indicated a lower condition of health and strength than he was then supposed to possess. He was rewarded, however, by the universal satisfaction with the regularity and order with which all the complicated arrangements were carried out.

At eleven a.m. on the 4th the enthronement took place at the morning service in the Cathedral. Not the least effective part of the ceremony was the procession of more than 200 clergymen, two and two, in surplices, who, after forming in the Chapter House, preceded the Cathedral body, the Archbishop, with his chaplains, train-bearers, and seven accompanying bishops, through the cloisters, and the great western door of the Cathedral, up the nave, until they took their places on the steps leading up to the altar. Whilst this striking spectacle was passing before the eyes of more than 2000 persons assembled in the nave and choir, first the choristers striking up as they entered the western door the clear ringing chant to which they sang the processional Psalms [cxxi., cxxii.], and then the organ, filling the Cathedral with the sound of the "Hallelujah Chorus," rivetted the attention of every hearer; next the Dean's single voice was heard intoning the opening sentences of the Morning Prayers. In the course of the service the Archbishop is seated (each time with a suitable declaration), first in the throne on the south side of the choir by which it is supposed his possession of the spiritualities of the see is indicated; next in the ancient marble chair, now placed in the south transept, which marks his possession of the temporalities; and lastly in the Dean's stall at the west end of the choir, which exhibits him as the head of the Cathedral body. Afterwards the members make promise of canonical obedience to their new chief. Archdeacon Harrison (as proxy for the aged Archdeacon of Canterbury) and the Bishop of London, as Provincial Dean, took the most prominent part in the Ecclesiastical portion of the ceremony, and the Queen's mandate was presented by the Vicar-General and read by the Auditor. Both the choir and nave were full of people. After the enthronement there was a large luncheon party in the newly-built Library. Two speeches[5], and only two, were made on the occasion, which, on account of their peculiar felicity, will not be forgotten by those who heard them.

In the evening a large number of guests came to the Deanery to pay their respects to the Archbishop.

On the 5th my husband records a visit with the Archbishop to the Clergy Orphan School at St. Thomas's Hill, where his Grace gave an address to the scholars.

The Deanery was the scene on the 6th of a levée where nearly one hundred clergymen and laymen waited on the Archbishop in the course of the morning. After the afternoon service in the Cathedral, a visit was paid to St. Augustine's College and to the old church of St. Martin.

On Sunday, the 7th, the Archbishop was in the Cathedral in the morning, and assisted in the administration of the Holy Communion, and in the afternoon preached to an enormous congregation.

He and his party left the Deanery the next day.

Two days afterwards the Dean was in town, preaching the Whitehall sermon on Ash-Wednesday (February 10).

About a month before he wrote thus to a niece :—

"I have drifted into a plan with the booksellers of making a book about the Riviera for a Christmas book for next year, and doing the drawing and the description; in fact, the whole. They have made me a generous offer, and the thing seems in every way delightful. After the enthronement is

---

5 One by the new Archbishop, one by the Dean.

my time, for I am sure I shall be knocked up by it; for there is scarcely a soul to help me, so on these eyes and hands the whole burden must lie, to say nothing of the anxiety on such occasions. How stand you about the possibilities of a visit here during my absence?"

With a view to increase his materials for his book, he visited the Riviera twice in 1869. Leaving home alone on the 15th, he wrote thus on the 27th from Monaco:—

TO HIS WIFE.

"*Monaco, Feb.* 27,

"I had a very favourable passage, and arrived to the moment at Paris, and had time for dinner, but at half-past four on Tuesday morning when we were pulled up near Villefranche by Lyons, we were detained there two hours and a half by a luggage-train off the line; seven trains were all waiting together. After spending Sunday the 21st at a curious little old hotel at Antibes, I went on to Nice, where I found the Bishop of Gibraltar, who is on his visitation tour. I meant to have gone to Corsica with him, but owing to the gloomy sky and continued rain I have given it up. Lord Thomas Hay is here, also the Dean of Windsor and Mrs. Wellesley, and Lord Rokeby. On the 25th I strolled out with my sketching materials, and was drawing a carouba[6] tree with a little bay and rocks beneath, when down came the most pouring shower; happily I had my tweed with me, but I was several miles off, and had to do as we did at Orta[7] in June, 1864, thereby preserving the trowsers dry. In the evening I set off for the Casino, which is a new one a mile off towards Mentone. There I saw hell in all its vice, and listened to some splendid music.

"Yesterday I walked to Eza with a gentleman I met here, Mr. Lucas. It is about nine miles off, all mountain paths, and some very stiff climbing, having lunched and sketched at that quaintest of places, we made our way up into the Corniche road not far from Nice, and returned by Turbia, whence you and the girls walked down to Monaco [on our

---

6 See "Riviera," p 121.

7 See *ante*, p. 373.

way out to Rome]. Our day's walk could not have been less than nineteen miles; as we descended on Monaco the sunset on the Mediterranean over Mentone and Bordighera was glorious. After *table d'hôte,* seeing it was moonlight, I sallied out to the gardens facing the sea, and there was the brightest full moon, with such a path of light on the waves. I sat watching it, and jotting down its phenomena for an hour or two. I have not done much in the sketching line, and what I have done has been very unsatisfactory, as I am confined to nine inches by five, a size I am not accustomed to.

TO HIS WIFE.

"*Mentone, Feb.* 28.

"I started at ten this morning from Monaco in a burning sun, and left my traps to come on by a 'bus, and had my lunch and a little service under a rock near Roccabruna. I could not abide staying any longer at Monaco, for although I was at the old hotel where we dined in 1863, and not at the grand new one at the Casino, the people who were about and at the *table d'hôte* were almost entirely gamblers, and talked of nothing else."

"*Hôtel d'Angleterre, Bordighera, March* 5.

"Here I am detained in a very pleasant place and civil people and comfortable quarters, but grievously against my will waiting for my luggage. Most fortunately I have some sketching materials with me. I have made an expedition to St. Agnese on a donkey, a wonderful village on the top of the cliffs. Here I sketched; Gobio too I sketched. Yesterday I spent entirely in drawing the splendid palms, and finishing three sketches on the spot."

"*March* 12.—Fine day for a wonder; cloudless sky, and sea bluer than I can make it with such a cold wind from the north numbing ones fingers as one draws. I have put in a sketch first of Monaco, then Mentone in the western sun. I have been sketching a good deal, but under difficulties, at Albenga; it was terribly windy and cold, at night a regular tempest. I ordered a fire, but six French ladies took possession of it; we were, however, very good friends.

"On the 13th I went by rail from Genoa to Rapello, and

walked from there to Chiavari; it was very glorious. I got two sketches and some splendid views of land and sea, but the weather is most provoking for a water-colour drawer, sometimes scudding showers, then snow and wind cold enough to skin one; I fear my projected book will suffer fearfully. I am a victim to the bad weather which has now fairly (or foully) upset my tour; what makes it strange some days are most lovely, blue sky with light clouds round the horizon, just the day that raises one's spirits about the week that is left; but now it is worse than ever, and my aneroid is gone down immensely; strange to say I am feeling quite dull, having no books with me, and not seeing the fun of making sunshine out of my own head for sketching. I slept at a most primitive inn at Chiavari, at five in the morning began the usual timtam of bells from the Campanile. I sketched it, and the chimes seemed to be in all variety of clashing, the note really is F. On leaving Margarita I encountered two Englishmen, one of whom has a castle at Porto Fino, a little land-locked harbour of the loveliest deep torquoise water, and a village built round it. The two Englishmen turned out to be the English Consul at Genoa, Mr. Montague Brown, and his brother. He offered me to go to his castle to lunch, which I did; nothing can be more lovely than the view from the windows of the castle, the whole coast is seen from St. Margarita to the end of the Gulf of Spezzia. After lunch my host and his brother walked with me over the mountains towards St. Remo, a stiff walk. On my way I sat down, and left my water-proof tweed where we sat; Mr. E. Brown kindly went back for it, but was obliged to return to catch the train; 'Never mind,' said the Consul, 'the people here are all honest; it will be sure to be brought to the authorities, and I will send it for you to England[8].' I came in for a procession in a glen behind Savona. Some hundreds of people, including a bishop.

---

[8] In about two months it made its appearance at Canterbury, and on inquiring after its fortunes, we were informed a peasant had found it, and had taken it to the priest, by whom it had been asked in church, and had thus been tracked by the Consul.

"At Oneglia I fell in with some of our Canterbury neighbours. When at St. Remo I called on Mr. Isaacs, and found him much better. My Southern sojourn is now over for this time; it can hardly be said to have been successful in attaining its end of faithful sketching, as I have not in more than two or three cases been able to sit before a scene till it was finished. Fillings up at home are eminently unsatisfactory; they are contributions, not out of the endless stores of nature, but out of one's own wits with inadequate gatherings from those stores: still sometimes they produce more successful drawings as drawings. The memory does the office of the artist-eye in minute details, and in gathering the general effect."

Soon after his return, his son-in-law, the Rev. H. E. T. Cruso was presented to a Chapter living, the Vicarage of Bramford, Suffolk, in consideration of his claim as having been a Master in the King's School and a Curate for three years in the diocese.

My husband's Revised Version of the New Testament, which it will be remembered he undertook on the suggestion of friends and rather against his own judgment (p. 412), was completed before he went to the Continent: on April 12th he received from the publisher the first copy, and he refers in his journal to the gratifying letters which it brought him, two of which (from Dean Goulburn of Norwich, and from the Rev. Dr. Angus) were preserved. In this month he speaks regretfully of the distraction of his work:—

"London has now so many calls for me, I scarcely get four days a week at home, and those are crowded with arrears never overtaken; as to a clear day, it is as rare with me as with the English climate."

On the 1st of May he was a guest at the Royal Academy Dinner, and it was the subject of the following letter:—

To his Daughter, Mrs. Bullock.

"Deanery, May 2.

"I thought you would like to hear about the great dinner: first of all the pictures are very good,—out-and-out the best exhibition one has ever seen. The building inside (it seems to me it has no outside) is all that could be desired; grand spacious rooms, and all the pictures well hung for seeing. The big hall where we dined is devoted to the principal pictures; the finest—the President said it was Sir E. Landseer's *chef-d'œuvre*—is a lot of eagles attacking a swannery. The dinner was, of course, a fine sight; all the grand folks of all departments, in and out, Ministers, Prince of Teck, Duke of Cambridge, many Dukes, and inferior Lords past number. After dinner there was some amusing talk at the tea-counter between the Archbishop and John Bright. I left Prince Teck and Bright going round the statues in the room together."

He went to London by the early express on May 10 to attend a meeting of Deans, whom the Archbishop had invited to Lambeth to consider the subject of "Cathedral Reform." He records:—

"To town by early express to Lambeth to a meeting of Deans; nothing decided on, except that all adopted the Archbishop's proposition of thorough reform being wanted.

"*May* 11.—All the morning seeing pictures with Fanny, then with her to dine at Lambeth; large party of forty. Dr. Schaff from America there, who wants me to come to America next spring and read a paper at the Christian Union."

Some months afterwards he published in the "Contemporary Review" for September and November, two articles on this subject, called "Cathedral Reform," which exposed him to much criticism. Without entering into details, I may say here that he maintained the absolute necessity of a change in our Cathedrals:—"Set the position and wants of the Church on one hand, and the actual life and work of any Cathedral body on the other, and it must be plain to fair-judging men that the same age cannot hold both." He wished an end to be put to the present capitular system, and with it to the extra-diocesan position of Cathedrals:—"They never can be made available for the purposes of the Church till they become part of the ordinary machinery of the diocese, under the direct superintendence of the Bishop." (See below, p. 431.)

On the 30th May, his step-mother, Mrs. Alford, died at the house of her son, the Rev. B. H. Alford, at Hoxton. She survived her husband seventeen years. The Dean always felt towards her, and treated her, as a mother. She was a person of strong feelings in matters of religion, though never wanting in consideration for the feelings of others. The fulness of her information on historical subjects, and her lively and endearing conversation, made her a general favourite.

In May his volume of collected "Essays and Addresses" was unfavourably noticed in the "Pall Mall Gazette." He records the fact with the observation, "I must try more and more to be utterly above all such things, and simply to live to do good."

His literary work was diversified this summer, by such incidents as his assisting (May 24) "to adjudge Sidney Cooper's Prize at his Gallery;" by a performance of Mendelssohn's "Elijah" at Canterbury; by the annual Choral Union (May 25); by attending (June 24) a meeting of the "Palestine Exploration Fund;" by a visit to his son-in-law, the Rev. H. E. T. Cruso, at Bramford, where he officiated at the christening of another granddaughter, Mabel Louisa Cruso, who was born on June 10; by going to the "Literary Fund" dinner (July); by a meeting of the "Canterbury Choir Benevolent Fund" (August 17), followed by an evening concert.

On August 27, having for his chief object to improve and increase his materials for his book on "the Riviera," he set out with Mr. and Mrs. B. H. Alford, for a visit to the North of Italy.

In the course of this tour he wrote the following letters:—

TO HIS WIFE.

"*Quatre Nations, Genoa, Sept. 2.*

"After three days' outing in the Riviera, I return here

almost eaten up with mosquitos, and my feet disabled with dust which was four inches deep. I slept at Loano on Sunday, and got up early next morning to draw under the bridge. After breakfast, I walked to Finale and had a glorious bathe near the Finale tunnel.

"On Tuesday, I set off after a seven o'clock breakfast to paint Finale from about a mile off, and another sketch I took under the rocks approaching the Noli tunnel.

"Though we were half an hour late at Paris on the 23rd, we just caught the Lyons train, and went on through the night, changing at Lyons, and going on through a country getting more beautiful; a district gradually rising till we got between great banks of precipitous rocks, two or three thousand feet high, with snowy mountains at the end. Grenoble is most splendidly situated; several Alpine valleys meet and form the citadel; you look up the valley of the Isère and see Mont Blanc at the head of it.

"Chambery is a more interesting town, older and more quaint than Grenoble. When we were there, it was being all decorated with flags, for the visit of the Empress of the French and the Prince Imperial on their way to Corsica. The character of the Dauphiné valleys seems to be richness, you can't see the mountains for the trees. Large avenues of walnut-trees are common. The ash, oak and beech, seem to vie with one another which shall grow highest and largest; at St. Laurent we turned up the gorge to the convent; it is exceedingly fine, and very narrow, and almost choke-full of large trees, with enormous walls of bright limestone rock; there are several fine points of view. The Grande Chartreuse is an immense pile of seventeenth century building, looking as one approaches, a wilderness of dark slate roofs and bell-turrets. When we arrived we were separated, C. being consigned to the care of some sisters; we were taken to see the whole building by one of the fathers. There are a series of very long cloisters, one of them ancient and gothic, the rest modern; then we rejoined C. outside, and went up with a party and a guide to the chapel and fountain of St. Bruno, a steep climb of about 1000 feet above the convent; then we returned to dinner; there were that day sixty or seventy guests. The dinner was funny; first some soup, simply sago and water, just coloured with milk like a "forgotten pudding" of the worst kind; then an omelette, then a very rich muddy carp, and a petit verre of the celebrated Grande Chartreuse liqueur as strong as brandy; strange that men who never eat nor allow meat should manufacture this potent spirit. Then a star-light ramble with B. and C. My bedroom is a small square white-washed room, ill plastered, loose red-brick floor, bed, table, crucifix, altar (which was also a cupboard), and a small saucer to wash in. I got up to the midnight office, anxious to see the fathers come in with their lanterns; the howling was awful. There is a fine thirteenth century cloister here, and a library which looked to me in too good order for much use. I got a sketch in the morning.

"The Mont Cenis railway is most wonderful: up and down the most rapid steeps, and round the most rapid curves and corners, the little engine pants its way most vigorously, and soon comes to numbers of tunnels and arches, giving one no idea of danger but all of admiration of the genius that could accomplish such a thing."

"*Venice, Sept.* 4.

"On my way here from Milan, I came by Pavia, from whence I went to see Certosa, another Grande Chartreuse of a very different kind. I took a little vehicle from Pavia, and saw the churches and battle-field of 1525, and by another train on to Certosa, which is the next road-side station. The great charterhouse there is the most gorgeous specimen in the world of the early Renaissance style, the over-florid gothic covered with arabesque, &c. The ornamentation is very much in white marble and terra-cotta, and the whole interior is painted in arabesque, with buds and flowers by Bourgognone, one of Raphael's contemporaries. It is the very marvel of decoration of all kinds; a splendid metal screen, altar all blazing with precious stones, every side-altar worked in front in mosaics by the inmates themselves: it would take a week to see it thoroughly in detail. There was only a very homely osteria near the station, where I got half a poulet whose flesh had somehow been extracted, or it was sitting in its bones owing to the heat. . . . .

"We have been to Torcello, which I have seen thoroughly three times. You remember its old, old cathedral, which we saw on our return from Rome in May, 1864, and the little octagon chapel of Sta. Fosca. On the 9th we leave for Innspruck and Saltzburg, spending Sunday at Königsee, the most beautiful of all lakes; then I leave them and go straight home by the 15th, so as to get over the change to Vines Gate during that week, as the next week I must go to Bristol."

TO HIS DAUGHTER, MRS. BULLOCK.

"*Botzen, Tyrol, Sept.* 11.

"We left Venice on Thursday, and came to the foot of the Lago di Garda, and then by steamer to sleep at Riva, the head of the lake, which is one of the most beautiful situations I ever saw; thence in a carriage, on a magnificent new road through a mountain gorge, to Trent, where we stopped two hours to dine and see the place of the Council, where half the world's Creed for 300 years was settled.

"I have enjoyed my three weeks exceedingly. Venice was perfect. We had a long boat excursion on Wednesday to the mouth of the lagoons south-east of the city, and returned with a glassy sea and moon and stars reflected; and I saw a big meteor as big as a cricket-ball, which burst into the sea and left a white track across the sky for some minutes. I sent the account of it to the 'Times.'"

He wrote the following letter on his return:—

TO HIS DAUGHTER, MRS. CRUSO.

"*Sept.* 19.

"You will be wanting to know something about me and my fortunes. Well, all you supposed about Venice is correct; it is a very different place. The Piazza, the evening of this day fortnight, was a sight. Full as it could hold, an Italian band and a touching ring of piccolini, and we seated inside the circle of the band. In the evening we had a glorious row to Malamocca, the mouth of the Lagoon, a grand breakwater of miles long, and the roaring Adriatic outside.

"On Thursday we left at six for Desenzano, thence up the Lago di Garda to Riva, next day down to Trent. Such a church! almost as bad as Quebec Chapel. Then we took train for Botzen, where we slept; and then crossed the Brenna on a railway, wonderful! and slept at Innspruck; next to Saltzburg. On Monday to Berchtesgarten and Königsee. Glorious. You remember them in 1857: the renewed acquaintance convinces me Königsee is the grandest lake and Berchtesgarten one of the loveliest spots on earth. Back to Saltzburg and home.

"Kiss the Mabelline's soft cheeks for me."

Before the end of September he paid a short visit to the West of England, which he thus records:—

"Off to Bristol, and preached at the Cathedral there for the Church Fund, then on to the Palace, Gloucester. Much pleasant talk on many and deep subjects with Bishop Ellicott. Much speculation about the new bishops."

At this time he wrote the following letter:—

To the Rev. R. P. Graves.

"*Oct.* 6.

"I have been for three weeks with my brother and his wife to Italy, Venice, and the Tyrol; and returned on Sept. 16, the very day when the 'Times' travestie of my Cathedral Reform scheme come out. I am writing a second article supplementary, in which I make it clear (not that it needed clearing) that to leave the present office of Dean alone was the farthest possible from my intention; the best solution of my view would be to make the Bishop Dean of his own Cathedral."

To the Rev. Dr. Allon.

"*Vines Gate, Oct.* 14.

"Have you ever seen 'Catholic Thoughts,' by the late

Mr. Myers of Keswick? two privately printed volumes, one on the Church of Christ and the Church of England, one on the Bible and Theology; very remarkable, especially as written 1834—1848, containing the largest views now urged by any of us, put out by a devout Christian Churchman. Mrs. Myers would not consent to publish it, so some of us contributed to the private printing, and I got a number of copies as my *quid pro quo*."

On his birthday he writes in his journal: "My sixtieth year, praise be to the Author of all my mercies," and he thus replied to a congratulatory note from his eldest daughter:—

To his Daughter, Mrs. Bullock.

"Many thanks, dearest Alice, for your affectionate wishes. Many returns there cannot be. Whether they are to be happy ones, very much depends, I daily feel, on whether the remainder of my life is to be spent in the Master's direct and active work or not."

A few weeks afterwards he refers to the state of his health in the following letter:—

To Mrs. John Cunliffe.

"I am far from well, and in the doctor's hands. Old enemy, palpitations and irregularity of heart, more obstinate than ever before, but with sixty in sight one must not be surprised. I have long regarded every day as a new mercy straight from the spring up there."

In this month he went, after a visit to Maidstone, to deliver lectures in Liverpool, Leeds, and Bradford, where he met with hospitable friends, as the following letter will show:—

To his Wife.

"All has prospered. Mr. and Mrs. Stuart at Maidstone are nice hearty people. I preached in the morning, then a walk in Lord Romney's park to think over my evening sermon to the young men, a vast congregation. At Liverpool.

I was received at Fulward Park, about three miles from Liverpool: nice religious people, with three jolly little boys. My host took me to see the Lions of Liverpool, the New Exchange, and Free Library. Our old servant, A. K. turned up, and inquired for you and the young ladies. The next day I went to Leeds, through Manchester. Flags half-mast everywhere for Lord Derby's death. Mr. B. took me out to Burley. I lectured in the vast new Town Hall. Next day off to Saltaire, where I was shown everything most interesting. To-morrow I go to Chipping Norton, and home next day."

The following entry in his journal is the first reference to a new work undertaken at this time:—

"*Oct.* 11.—Mr. Pickersgill has proposed to me to write something for some beautiful designs of his, to bind the whole together by descriptive letter-press. I shall make it a poetic whole of different metres called 'Children of the Lord's Prayer.'"

This book, published at Christmas, was his last attempt at poetry of any considerable length. The first part of it, as far as the Fourth Chorus, had been written thirty-two years previously (see page 110), and he now finished it. In a letter to a niece he thus refers to it:—

To Miss H. E. Alford.

"You will find at home some signs of my autumn employment. It was very pleasant to find myself building up verses again after more than thirty years' disuse, at least as far as a long poem is concerned. In the late gale we lost a venerable member of the Cathedral body,—the old mulberry-tree in the Deanery garden, which you saw Stanley explain to the Princesses Helena and Louisa, July 2, 1864 (see p. 377). The Church of Rome[9]—is it not ominous?—was snapped off about seven feet from the ground, and lies a hideous wreck."

---

[9] There was an old mulberry-tree in the garden, from which early in the present century a branch was broken off in a violent storm, and was driven into the ground at no great distance from the parent stem. Where it was

A letter of later date to the Rev. Dr. Allon, 14 Feb. 1870, will tell the fortune of this book :—

"Let me thank you most heartily for your kindly notice of the 'Lord's Prayer.' It has had fondling lavished on it all around, but it is only a puling infant after all. I believe it came out too late. The drawings were not shown me till Oct. 11 (a time when most Christmas books are out), therefore the booksellers had made up their sets, and we had no chance."

Another illustrated book (" Our Lord and His Disciples ; a Series of Photographs after the Crayon Drawings of Leonardo da Vinci ; edited, with a History of each Disciple, by Henry Alford, Dean of Canterbury ;") was undertaken at the request of his publishers. During its progress it was kept a secret from me, and the first copy was given to me as a surprise, at Christmas, 1869. This volume, being published at a high price, has not attained the popularity which in the opinion of many persons was due to its literary and artistic merits. The illustrations are photographs of drawings from Leonardo da Vinci's great picture of the Last Supper, painted in 1497 on the east wall of the Refectory of the Dominican monastery of the Madonna delle Grazie, at Milan. It occupies a space of twenty-eight French feet, and the figures are colossal. The fresco is now nearly obliterated, as the materials used by the painter were not good. In 1500, a flood much damaged the building, and at the time of the French occupation the Refectory was used as a stable. An etching of this picture by Rubens was found by my husband in an old curiosity-shop at Bury St. Edmund's, in 1834. He had the missing parts restored, and the old dilapidated roll covered with dust became one of his favourite pictures.

---

thus rudely planted, it struck root and grew ; and in our time it used to bear more abundant fruit, in proportion to its size, than the older tree. I do not remember whether our friend Dean Stanley, or some one else, was the inventor of the parable ; but it was customary to point to these two trees as representatives of the Churches of Rome and England. The accident to the old tree in 1869, happened just whilst the world was expecting the assembly of the Œcumenical Council at Rome.

The publication of his book on the Riviera was postponed, as is explained in the following letter :—

TO HIS WIFE.

"I have had a letter from Bell, saying that the Riviera book was so serious a speculation, that it had better be postponed to another year. This of course has but one meaning, it will be just as serious a speculation next year as this, and I cannot consent to spoil another year's work. I have been two journeys to the Riviera expressly for it, and I have been toiling at it a good deal; so I have lost nearly a year's work, and moreover the money which I had intended for Palestine. This of course is provoking, but I am surviving it pretty cheerily. Yes, the Riviera catastrophe will be submitted to, and the year's work sacrificed. Never mind, worse things might have happened. Just now the Fates are adverse in many quarters, but I suppose things will right themselves again, or, if they don't, worldly success is a trifle after all. There is another crown which may brighten as the lower garland fades, so I give up Riviera and set to work thoroughly arranging my library."

The following entries in his journal will show the variety of his occupations in the last fortnight of the year 1869 :—

"*Dec.* 15.—To town by 12.43 train, called at Ludgate Hill ; Strahan had gone home ill. "Metaphysical[1]" in the evening, paper on Memory as an intuitive faculty; walked back to the Athenæum with Dr. Carpenter; at Bradley's at night.

"*Dec.* 16.—To Ecclesiastical Commission; to the British Museum to examine a reading in Acts iii. 25; walked back to the Athenæum, and read articles in 'Temple Bar' on Tennyson, &c. Mrs. Cunliffe came for me in a tremendous storm of rain, dined and slept at her house, great gale at night.

"*Dec.* 17.—Home by 10.30 express, found that our great mulberry-tree had been snapped off in the gale, utterly spoil-

---

[1] The name of "The Metaphysical" was given to a sort of private society of persons known to one another, who about this time agreed to meet periodically for the discussion of certain subjects in which they felt a common interest.

ing the grass. In the evening had all the King's Scholars (twenty-five) and others. Charades. Successful evening.

"*Dec.* 18.—Working at sermon and lecture amidst numerous interruptions. In the evening a meeting of the Canterbury Harmonic Union; all at sea what to do, referred to public meeting January 4.

"*Dec.* 19, *a.m.*—Very good sermon from the Archdeacon. I preached on the Parable of the Ten Virgins. In the evening, reading 'Rob Roy on the Jordan,' which Macgregor has sent me.

"*Dec.* 20.—No end of interruptions to getting on with my lecture for this evening. The Le Marchants came from Ramsgate to lunch, very pleasant. Attending to the old mulberry-tree, and making fac-similes of New Testament MSS. Lecture in the evening well attended. Mr. Burgon sent me some photographs of the old manuscripts K. L. M., and some modern MS.[2]

"*Dec.* 21.—Church, and installed Mr. Jenkins as Honorary Canon; in the morning writing an article on Tennyson's new poem; dined at the Hiltons' at Nackington.

"*Dec.* 22.—Writing my article on Tennyson, lots of interruptions. Attending to the poor wreck of the mulberry-tree; patched up a new tree out of various large branches, and sent branches to plant, to the Harrisons, Robertsons, and Truemans.

"*Dec.* 23.—All the morning writing my notice of Roma Sotteranea, and various volumes of sermons. After church walked with Robertson; dined at the Foleys.

"*Dec.* 24.—Finished my notices.

"*Dec.* 25, *a.m.*—I preached on Acts iii. 25. 'Ye are the children of the prophets,' &c. The Jewish mayor, Mr. Hart, at church. Only Archdeacon Harrison and the Parrys here. The Archbishop slowly improving. Miss Hole came to dinner.

"*Dec.* 26.—Archdeacon in the morning; good again. Afternoon, I on Acts xiv. 22, 'Much tribulation.' Happy evening together.

---

[2] This was his last lecture.

"*Dec.* 27.—Morning, arranging library. At 4.40, William, Alice, and the two little ones came, all well. Dinner, and the evening chat. News of the Bishop (Lee) of Manchester's death.

"*Dec.* 28.—Working at Mrs. Whitney's novels for an article. Walk with Bullock. Our dinner party.

"*Dec.* 29.—Writing a review of 'Hitherto.' Walked with Bullock in the afternoon beyond the turnpike on the Dover road. Mr. Geary installed Six Preacher by Harrison. I had an engagement to go over the old Church House to see pictures for Scharf.

"*Dec.* 30.—A very nice notice of the 'Lord's Prayer' in the 'Guardian.' Out with Alice to buy toys, &c., for to-morrow, and spent the evening in arranging them.

"*Dec.* 31.—All day more or less preparing for the Choristers' party which came off in the evening. Had the usual gathering of little ones besides Choristers. Alice's two, Foster's three, Longhurst's three, one Parry. I showed the Jackdaw of Rheims, John Gilpin, Robinson Crusoe, in Matthew's magic lantern; all seemed very happy. So ends 1869, full of mercies to me and mine."

In the beginning of 1870 he undertook the last great work of his life, a Commentary on the Old Testament.

Soon after he took his degree at Cambridge, he gave some time to the systematic study of Hebrew (see page 84). But for the last thirty-five years he had made no attempt to increase his knowledge of that language, using it only occasionally to investigate the meaning of any text to which his attention was specially called. He undertook, therefore, only to prepare for ordinary English readers the best explanation of the sacred text which he could gather from a perusal of the principal modern commentaries, leaving to more advanced Hebrew scholars the discussion of many grammatical questions for which he did not think himself qualified. He intended to produce a work which should range with his New Testament for English Readers, and not to address himself (as in his Commentary on the Greek Testament) to Theological students and ministers. The work was to be published by the firms Bell and Deighton, of Cambridge, and Strahan, and Co., of London; and he entered into an agreement with them to complete the commentary, if life should be spared, in the course of seven years, and in five volumes of about a thousand pages each.

The actual commencement of his work appears from his journal to have been on the 21st Feb., and he left off on Nov. 15, at the verse, Exod. xxv. 40, "Look that thou make them after their pattern, which was showed thee in the mount." The unfinished fragment was published in 1872.

A letter written to one of his nieces in January, enters on his reasons for addressing himself to this task:—

TO MISS E. M. ALFORD.

"*January.*

"I have been busy preparing a new edition of the "Queen's English" (third), in great part re-written and considerably augmented by subsequent correspondence. And now comes rash act number two. It behoves me to look out for some worthy employment for the evening hours of life, sixty. . . Editing Reviews, writing in 'Good Words,' &c., &c., does not quite seem heavy material enough for luggage for the long journey, whenever it shall be due. So not without advice, attention has been turned to the Old Testament; and it has appeared to the present writer that 'The Old Testament for English Readers,' might, if life be spared, be accomplished by him; and that worthy service might be done by him if he could throw himself into the gap, and, if necessary, victimize himself, in trying to make out some honest account of the acknowledged difficulties consistently with holding all that Christians hold. So I am now in the throes of a treaty with booksellers, and probably shall soon be engaged in the great work; and with a view to it shall relinquish the 'Contemporary Review,' and shall buckle to in earnest. Happily, it is a work which admits of instalments; Pentateuch, Historical Books, Lyrical Books, Prophets major, Prophets minor."

A few notes from his journal refer to his other occupations about this time.

"*Jan.* 12.—The Canterbury Harmonic Union constructed on a different footing. Writing a course of sermons on the Self-witness of Jesus.

"*Feb.* 7.—To town to attend a Conference at the Society of Arts, on Education. Archdeacon Denison's motion to discuss Bishop Temple's consecration lost by forty to sixty. The withdrawal of the essay was announced, and Denison gave up his opposition. 'All's well that ends well.'"

"*Feb.* 28.—Much perplexed about sermons; five this week. Genesis every day when I am at home. The work is very interesting to me.

"*March* 1.—Dean Howson came to Canterbury on his way out to the Continent. Our Palestine expedition was settled for next year, D.V.

"*Ash-Wednesday, March* 2.—Up to town to preach for Dean Jeremie at Whitehall, but in the service he appeared, and I was not wanted. He preached a grand sermon, twenty times as good as mine; then I preached for Dr. Barry at King's College Chapel; very full congregation.

"*March* 3.—Preached at Quebec Chapel; very nice to be again in the old place. Off to Bramford with H. Cruso, and all next morning (4th) busy about site of his new vicarage; home at ten, and found lots of letters.

"*March* 9.—Began writing my St. Paul's sermon for the 13th; finishing article on Biblical Revision, and preparing another [third] edition of 'Queen's English.'"

On March 10, the anniversary of his wedding-day, he wrote to his son-in-law in London:—

To the Rev. W. T. Bullock.

"Thirty-five years I have been racked out of my life by London engagements. Last week I did not touch Genesis from Monday morning till Saturday night. I am going to read a paper from the pulpit of St. Paul's, on Biblical Revision, on Sunday evening."

This sermon, on "Biblical Revision, its Duties and Condition," was published in due course. Going to London to preach it, he stayed for two nights at the Rev. B. H. Alford's vicarage, Hoxton, where he met with an accident which entailed painful and inconvenient consequences. He thus describes it in a letter to his niece:—

TO MISS E. M. ALFORD.

"*March* 22.

"I was indeed grievously damaged, and have but just recovered my power of writing. I was staying at Bradley's, having preached the night before at St. Paul's. I was getting up to go to Canterbury, by the 7.40 train from Ludgate Hill. I saw a cab in the street, and threw up the window to hail it; it was a sash without a weight to hold it, as they make them in Scotland; it fell down on my right thumb, and squashed the top of it quite flat, the pain for about two days was certainly greater than I ever felt before in my life. I have been obliged, till a few days ago (when the nail came off), to write with my left hand, and to take twice the time dressing, and so forth; even now it is very stiff and tender, and will be for some weeks, if not longer."

He went again to London to preach (on March 25) at the Consecration of Dr. E. Parry as Bishop Suffragan of Dover. His sermon ("The Compacted Body") was published at the request of the Archbishop. On the same evening he had the pleasure of renewing, after an interval of thirty-seven years, his acquaintance with Tennyson, whom he met at dinner at Clapham.

The Lower House of Convocation was engaged at this time in discussing the question of Revising the Authorized Version of the Bible; and he made a speech which I have been told was one of the most effective in the debate. On the same day he wrote to me:—"All right; we got over our Committee work at one sitting, resolving unanimously that the Revision should be undertaken, and reporting for the appointment of a body by Convocation, to invite the co-operation of men eminent for scholarship, to whatever nation and religious body belonging; so that I am now at liberty to be at home (D.V.) by 9.45 to-morrow."

I may here insert a letter to myself from Archdeacon Bickersteth:—

"When the subject of revising the Authorized Version was brought before Convocation, and a Committee was appointed to undertake the work, it fell to my lot as Prolocutor to suggest the names of members of the Lower House who should discharge the responsible duty. I need hardly say that the name of Dean Alford was the first that occurred to me, and it added greatly to the interest which I felt in the matter, that I now found myself associated in such a work with the companion of my boyhood, and my earliest friend. I looked forward to some years of happy intercourse in promoting this holy work, with all the advantages of his Biblical scholarship."

On Easter Day, April 17, John Campbell Colquhoun, Esq., died. He was the author of several works, and was well known to us during our residence in London, and afterwards our neighbour in Kent. This is referred to in a letter to the Rev. J. H. Hamilton:—

To the Rev. J. H. Hamilton.

"*Easter Tuesday.*

"I cannot tell you how shocked I was when Harrison told me, as we were coming out of church, of our dear friend's death. From your letter I had not expected such an ending; I suppose he had a relapse. Well, who could not die on such a day, the day of all the year when death hides its head ashamed?"

Mr. Hamilton himself was an invalid at this time: in answer to his request, conveyed by Miss Hamilton, my husband promised in the following letter to supply his place at St. Michael's church in the morning of April 24.

"Of course I'll come; 'Whoso seeth his brother have need,' &c. Tell papa, with my best love, I am good for more than the morning; if he wants it, I could take the afternoon as well. The thumb still lives a retired life, being not presentable; a nail seems long coming. I wish I could buy a temporary one, but if I did, I fear I should not hit the right nail on the head. On the 22nd we did the 12th

Mass and the Dettingen Te Deum; very successful. Miss Henderson was our soprano; she stayed with us."

Of the debate in Convocation, which he attended at this time, he gave the following account in a letter :—

TO THE REV. J. H. HAMILTON.

"*Jerusalem Chamber, May* 6.

"I have not had a moment to answer your letter till now. And now in my place here we have been sitting all yesterday and the day before, and, thank God, with victory in every case. The Lectionary is now safe, and the Revision started. Even the 'Times' gives us an article of commendation; it has been hard work, and I am feeling somewhat fagged by it. To-day we go to the Education Bill. I cannot fix a day to preach for you on account of the Queen's wish that I should preach again before her soon."

The following entries in his journal touch on his occupations and his projected visit to the north coast of France.

"*April* 29.—Very busy all day to finish next week's Genesis, for to-morrow we go to Kensington Palace for a week.

"*May* 1.—Took Hamilton's duty morning and evening at St. Michael's; called on Miss Leycester in the evening.

"*May* 7.—We breakfasted early, and went to the Royal Academy and spent five hours and a half there, and thoroughly examined the pictures; from thence we went to the Houses of Parliament, and saw every thing, and the Chapel in the Crypt; dinner at six at Kensington, and home to Canterbury by 8.35 mail train.

"*May* 9.—Letters, and Genesis; Longhurst's Concert in the evening.

"*May* 14.—Got to Genesis xxi., the work interests me more and more; proofs of wood-cuts and chromos for my book ['Riviera']. I shall preach to-morrow, the 15th, about Abimelech and Abraham, as my mind is full of this subject.

"*May* 21.—Morning, Genesis, I am getting on very well with it; afternoon gardened; evening framing pictures.

"*May* 25.—In town. Our Revision Committee met to arrange plans, and agreed on action; the meeting lasted through the day; home by express 8.35. I am off to-morrow for a change to the north coast of France, as I could not have my usual outing this spring; for I am again down on the axle-springs, and I must be braced up. Cornwall is too far to reach, although a most tempting invitation has come to explore between Bude and Bedruthan, for I have but the inside of a week, and that a scanty interior, only five days to call really my own, so the thoughts turn nearer home, and strange to say their alighting point is a foreign shore. From Canterbury to St. Valery-sur-Somme only from 8.20. a.m. to 4.30. p.m., and then I can work along the coast of Normandy to Dieppe: so then let it be; but I must be back on June 2, as then Fanny and I go for a few days to Stonehouse, to see the Archbishop."

Before setting out he had the gratification of receiving the following letter from the Archbishop of Canterbury, just then recovering from illness.

"*Stonehouse, St. Peter's, Thanet, May* 25, 1870.

"MY DEAR DEAN,—As I am now allowed again to write with my own hand, I will not fail to address my fourth letter so written to you. I wish to thank you with my own hand for all your kindnesses in the matter of the Suffragan; for all the kind interest you have taken in my illness. Mrs. Tait and I hope to be here for a month. It will be a great pleasure to us, if next week, please God, you could come over with Mrs. Alford and spend a night or two here. We shall of course be quite alone, except Mr. Sandford is with us. Ever yours,

"A. C. CANTUAR."

An account of the five days which he spent in France is given in three letters to myself. I find in a note-book the following reflections jotted down in the steamboat on May 27:—

"Whilst we are steaming along mid-channel, one cannot help thinking what a queer world one has left behind, and at the same time what an earnest world just now. At the base of society absolutely no stir; throne and law rivetted down in every English breast. But short of the base, all in stir, all in change. Never so universal, never so rapid as now. Wonderful it is how all the old barriers of prejudice seem to be giving way together. Imagine our Committee of Revision last week voting in one dissenter after another to sit and work with us. Imagine the Universities Test Bill passing with only sixty-nine voices against it. Imagine again the Education Conscience Clause universally accepted throughout the kingdom, and Forster's Bill, which five years ago would have awakened a howl from hundreds of obstructives, now winning universal approval!"

TO HIS WIFE.

"*St. Valery-sur-Somme, May* 27.

"All prospered; such a passage, 1 hour, 25 minutes. I hardly thought we were more than half way, and I looked out, and we were close to Calais Pier. I found I must leave the train at Boulogne and take a slow train which stopped at Noyelles, the junction for this place; the branch-line crosses the estuary on an immense long wooden viaduct, like the bridge at Teignmouth, and the place is very like some of the places in the Devonshire estuaries; a Grande Rue parallel to the river, then a steep low hill behind, covered with back streets and gardens and surrounded by a wood full of nightingales. I suppose this is a specimen of Normandy; the people are most civil, touch their hats as one passes. The country full of orchards in blossom, and such green leaves; the women are short and good-looking, but very modest. No improvement in the auricular appendages [3] as yet, but the air is delicious, and I have enjoyed the day immensely; it has been worth coming, even to a deserted watering-place, for the air and change."

"*Dieppe, May* 28.

"Here I am safe and sound, but not without adventures.

[3] Referring to a discharge behind the ear: see p. 446.

I left St Valery at eight in a *petite voiture*, to spend the mid-day and lunch. I stopped at Treport, and came on here in the evening. All went as intended. The road is about the very dullest I ever travelled on; on high land over the sea which is hardly ever visible. At length we descended on Treport, which is striking, with an immense chalk cliff on each side, something like Dover. When about four miles and a half from here the horse began to show symptoms of fatigue, and by-and-by down he came, smashing the off-shaft in so doing [4]. It was a curious scene; the road was full of Saturday market-folk, in carts and gigs returning from Dieppe, and in a few minutes we were the centre of a crowd of vehicles and farmers' wives. At length the beast was got up and proved unhurt, the carriage was attached to a waggon returning to Treport, and the horse to a cart to go back to the last village to recruit. The young man who drove was in terrible distress and was sobbing like a child, so I consoled him by doubling his *pour-boire*, and shook hands with him, he smiling through his tears; *pour moi*, I got hold of a peasant to carry my bags, and trudged on to Dieppe. This is an interesting old town with chalk cliffs, but low, and a splendid old Gothic church."

"*Lisieux, May* 31.

"This is a curious place with heaps of old houses and a glorious church; every house is a study here. I have been to St. Valery-en-Eaux, Fécamp, Honfleur, &c.; have taken several water-colour sketches, and bought some photographs. To-morrow, I go to Paris, not being afraid of small-pox. I shall sleep there one night, and then home."

After his return we went (June 2nd) on "a very pleasant visit to Stonehouse," where he saw Mrs. Tait's Orphanage.

---

[4] This incident is referred to at the end of his last article in "Good Words," "The Bullers of Buchan," written Aug., 1870; published in "Good Words," April, 1871.

At Whitsuntide the Deanery was "brightened" by the arrival of Mr. and Mrs. Cruso and their "good-natured and cheery" infant daughter.

On Whitsun Tuesday, June 14th, the Tenth Festival of the Parochial Choirs of the Canterbury Diocesan Choral Union was celebrated by services in the Cathedral, performed by 900 voices. The Dean had been a very active encourager of the Society from its commencement, and it was his custom "at each recurring Festival in a wonderful five minutes' address to gather up and drive home to the hearts of his hearers the distinctive lessons of the day." This year he took even more than ordinary interest in it, and it was said that all previous difficulties were smoothed over by his kindness. After it was over he made arrangements with the Society for the performance at their next Festival (Whitsun Tuesday, 1871), of a Processional Hymn, for which he furnished the words and music. It was his last composition of this kind, and will be found in the Appendix.

On June the 16th his journal records a symptom of the state of his health:—

"Went to see a physician about my exema: he found fault with my general appearance, and told me to take quinine and steel."

The meetings of the Company to whom was committed the Revision of the Authorized Version of the New Testament, now claimed his presence in London at regular intervals. On June the 22nd, the Company met to receive the Holy Communion in Wesminster Abbey, an act for which some of those who met were severely censured. It is thus recorded in his journal, and in a letter which he wrote to a brother-in-law at Bristol.

"*June* 22.—Long day at Revision. Communion in Westminster Abbey. All denominations knelt round the tomb of Edward VI.; a most striking sight, and one to be thankful for. Began our revision, went on right well. All dined at Bishop Ellicott's."

To W. F. Morgan, Esq.[5]

"*Canterbury, June* 24.

"I have just returned from our first Revision meeting. Nothing more interesting has been done since the Reformation. We received the Communion round Edward VIth's tomb, three bishops, two deans, two archdeacons, several clergymen, an Independent Professor, a Wesleyan ditto, a Scotch Presbyterian ditto, a Scotch Establishment ditto, a Baptist ditto and a Unitarian: such a body meeting around Edward VIth's tomb was a sight England has never seen before. I am determined to give up for this important work a long cherished journey to Palestine with Dr. Tristram. If I went, it would be equivalent to resigning my place on the Revision Committee, which I should be sorry to do merely for personal enjoyment, as this revision has been one of the earnest wishes and prayers of my life."

On June the 23rd, he solved the conflicting claims of the Revision Company in London and the commencement of the Audit, by giving the day to the former, and coming to Canterbury by the night-mail. The next Sunday (June 26), after preaching in his own cathedral on "Brotherly love," he went in the evening to preach for the Society for the Propagation of the Gospel in Rochester Cathedral; "nice service and striking sight in the nave; text, Ezek. xlvii. 8. Supped with Dr. Griffith, and returned to Canterbury by the night-mail." On Wednesday, July 6, he went again to London to attend the meeting of the Lower House of Convocation, which was deprived this time of one of its most conspicuous members by the alarming illness of Archdeacon Denison. This is referred to in the following letter, in which my husband writes to thank the Prolocutor, Archdeacon Bickersteth, for his Sonnet on the Communion of June the 22nd in the Abbey.

---

[5] Whilst this sheet is passing through the press, my brother-in-law has been taken to his rest: his life prolonged through more than seventy years, full of faith and good works, came to an end on December 9, 1872. No member of our family had a larger portion of the respect and love of the younger generation; none had learned more thoroughly amidst early adversity that entire self-denial and trustfulness in God which enable the elder to influence the younger most effectually.

TO ARCHDEACON BICKERSTETH.

"*July* 4.

"Many thanks, dear friend, for the Sonnet. It was, indeed, a day much to be remembered; how very sad about poor dear Denison, and how we shall miss him. I don't know a man who can worse be spared. The kindest and most generous of opponents; a man of unerring refinement, of boundless self-sacrifice and of iron courage, often gloriously wrong, in victory never despising those he had beaten, even in defeat never laying himself open to contempt. I have spoken and written against him as much as any one, but there never passed between us any word but of brightness and kindness; certainly we shall never look upon his like again. I fear there is no hope, nay, even now he may have passed from us. Hodie illi cras nobis.

"I forgot the object of my letter—to say, that owing to our King's School Speeches, at which my presence is *de rigueur*, I cannot be present till Wednesday."

The following letter to a niece refers to nearly the same subjects.

TO MISS E. M. ALFORD.

"*July* 5.

"So you cannot conceive how one who denies the atonement in our sense can receive the Holy Communion with earnestness: but I can. Unitarians, I think, often beat us in their intense 'thankful remembrance of Christ's death,' regarding it as the great central act of love, though not in the sense that we do. It was for that one I was most especially thankful, and how any Christians can have said about it what they have said, passes me to comprehend. We have worked together all this past week; it is quite delightful to see the harmony and Christian forbearance of all. The good Archbishop did us the honour to pay us a visit on Wednesday, his first public appearance, to mark his sense of what has passed; it made me thank God and take courage.

"You will see an article about it of mine in the next 'Contemporary;' also some remarks in my tenth Fireside Homily, in the 'Sunday Magazine' [November, 1870].

"You will be glad to hear that 22,000 of my small revised Testament have been sold already in less than three months.

"How sad about poor dear Denison, the noblest and best fellow, full of heart and courtesy! whom no foe ever made afraid, no victory ever rendered insolent, and no defeat ever irritated. We shall be dreary indeed without his merry voice and red-hot energy."

The first of his three days in Convocation was agreeably relieved by an evening "at the Queen's Concert at Buckingham Palace; very interesting; Nilsson, Patti, and old Mario, &c."

After a few days' work at Canterbury on his Commentary on Genesis, there was another call to London; and his entry on July 15th is "Third day of Revision, Matthew iii. iv. On Wednesday at the 'Metaphysical.' Harrison read an essay on 'Limits of Human Thought.' War declared between France and Prussia. Papers full of the war, lots to read."

On the 1st of August appeared the last article which he wrote in the "Contemporary Review." Its subject was a volume of essays entitled "Ecclesia," written by Nonconformists. Towards the end of the article some remarks were made on the present aspect of Church and Dissent. After describing and commenting on the celebration of the Holy Communion in Westminster Abbey on June the 22nd in connexion with the Revision of the English Bible, he concludes the article with the following solemn words of advice and encouragement to those who share his views and aspirations:—

"That which has passed has taught us a double lesson: of which however both the branches tend one way, and ultimately unite. The one is, rather to leave the onward steps of our work to the unfolding of God's Providence, than to be restlessly and anxiously devising them for ourselves. Like those who have had to deal with another well-known 'religious difficulty,' we encounter our greatest trouble not in the matter of deeds but of words. Let a proposition be once put forth, and it thereby becomes impracticable. Words, like weapons, are soon whetted to keenness when war is in the air. The most important steps towards our great end will be drawn on, one after another, by the deep working of Christian public opinion; in other words, by the wisdom of God's Spirit. They will come in the train of other and unsuspected designs; they will not be recognized as of great import till they have passed by. Many a deed is done, many a word is spoken, which not a soul on earth contemplated an hour before, but which, when done or spoken, shifts the level of human thought, and opens a new era for mankind.

"And the second of our lessons is that great fact to which our last sentences have pointed: that the Spirit of truth is opening the way before us, both rapidly and surely. In every direction the barriers of intolerance and exclusiveness are falling. We watch the progress from year to year, and we wonder as we gaze. It is not that men are becoming less faithful, less watchful, less anxious to prevent change. At no time has obstruction been so obstructive as now. Never has exclusiveness been asserted in stronger words, or by more indefatigable champions. But the adverse host, as each conflict arises, crumbles away and is not found. Public measures have already passed in our day, are now passing, or are contemplated as sure to come, which a few years since were but the dreams of the over-sanguine. Truths are now cited in all companies as axioms of the common sense of mankind, which would in our younger days have been voices in the desert. And the results are coming thick upon us: not in the unwelcome outbreaks of revolutionary violence, but in the irresistible bearing onward of national conviction: results, compared to which all that we have seen and rejoice over, shall seem to those that shall witness them but as the dawn that ushered in the day. Never was there a time in the course of history, never in the lifetime of the Church, when the intelligent Christian, when the faithful and loyal citizen, had more reason to thank God, and to take courage."

It was his intention to visit the Tyrol this year, and afterwards to witness the Passion Play at Ammergau; but the outbreak of the war between France and Germany caused a change of plan, as will appear from the following entries:—

"*Aug.* 2.—Genesis xlix., very difficult. News of a great defeat of the French on Sunday at Wörth. I have decided not to go on the Continent this summer, though I have written to the parish priest, Herr J. N. Müller, to engage lodgings for me, and a stall at the great performance. My plan was to go to the Passion Play at Ober Ammergau, and then to the Dolomite mountains in Carinthia, and perhaps to Trieste and the coast of Istria, and, if I could, back to Vines Gate by September 1st; and I have, I think, earned the run, for I have had hard work since November last. But the cruel necessities of the war have quite changed my plans. I should not like now to go abroad and make Fanny anxious about me; and I hear 'Christus,' 'Judas,' and 'Petrus,' are called to the front, and the Passion Play will be given up for this year.

"*Aug.* 3.—Finished Genesis, thank God. Packing: off for Hoxton on the 6th, then Bramford for a week, and then to Vines Gate for the autumn, unless my scheme about the Bullers of Buchan comes to anything.

"*Aug.* 15.—Left Bramford with Fanny; decided to go to the Bullers of Buchan with Burrell Smith, who is to meet me at Berwick on the 22nd."

Before his departure for Scotland, he wrote from Vines Gate to our friend Caroline von Stadlinger, whose father, a general in the Wurtemburg army, remained at his post in Suabia, being disqualified by reason of old age from joining the German troops. I print this letter at length, as representing his views at this time, although they were afterwards much modified. The letters to myself which follow, were written during the Scottish tour. On this, as on many other occasions, my preference for home-life, especially after the temporary failure of my health in our Pyrenean tour in 1855, led me to forego the pleasure of being his companion in travel; a circumstance from which I now reap an advantage not then foreseen, in being able to communicate to others the graphic descriptions of his progress, which he never failed to send me.

TO MISS VON STADLINGER.

"*Vines Gate, Aug.* 21, 1872.

"In the midst of all these terrible events, our thoughts turn to you and yours, and we long to hear something about you. First, I need not tell you how all England, except one or two of our journals, rejoices in the success of Germany, and looks with silent awe upon the signal vengeance which seems to be overtaking the French Government. Who could have thought that in one short fortnight the (angebliche) first military power in the world would so utterly collapse? Miserable generalship, and the distrust of the people, seem to have done all the mischief. Yet how nobly their soldiers have fought! and how admirably yours. What a story that was this day week, of the Prussian Cuirassiers. All the officers killed, the regiment reduced from 800 to 147, and yet taking six guns and two eagles, and coming out victorious; but what mourning and privation there will be in all Germany! God grant a speedy and lasting peace! But how? This is one of the most difficult questions. You have no right to Alsace without consent of the people, and France would never forgive it, so the peace would not be lasting. But God will find a way, we trust.

"I suppose your father is past being called out into service. I fancy you employed in receiving poor wounded men in your fortress. We are doing all we can for the International Society, and have sent them large supplies of money and nurses. Many English ladies have gone out to the battle-field. Some mischievous people tried to make out that we were favouring the French by trading in coal. But it was not so, we could not help ourselves. The law of nations had determined that coal was not contraband, but must be carried at the risk of the carrier. If we had forbidden it, we should have at once violated neutrality. It was unfortunate that, France being strong by sea, we were thus doing harm to our friends; but we could not help that.

"We are now here for the autumn. We have been visiting Mary; her little Mabel is the loveliest child, always laughing and happy. They are building a new Vicarage at Bramford. Alice and hers are at Eastbourne, in Sussex, by the sea. I am just going for a fortnight to Scotland, having been disappointed of seeing the Passion's Spiel at Ammergau. Mrs. Alford is quite well, and enjoying this beautiful place. Do write soon. Our best regards to the General and to *die liebe* Emma."

To his Wife.

"*Aug.* 23.

"We left Edinburgh at 6.48 for Perth; Stonehaven to Dunnottar Castle, very grand cliff scenery. The castle something like Tintagel, but larger. At Berwick, we had to sleep on two sofas in two sitting-rooms. My bed was made up with chairs which would not keep together, but parted in the middle, so I introduced my Scottish tour by sleeping in a glen. On Wednesday we were off after breakfast on foot to Dunnottar Castle, and in the bay beyond the castle I did a large picture. After lunch another view, then by rail to Aberdeen, where there is a grand, new Town Hall. . . . Peterhead is an important place, the capital of the herring fishery; the barrels, which are thousands at Stonehaven, are ten thousand here. The Bullers of Buchan is six miles from Peterhead. It is a grand, rocky coast, very like the Lizard, lots of coves, one much like another, and all wanting days and days to paint thoroughly. The Bullers (Boilers) is a great hole or chasm in the granite, opening to the sea by a natural arch. When the sea is rough, it is said to boil like a caldron."

"*Banff, Aug.* 28.

"Yesterday a long drive of forty-two miles along, for the most part, a magnificent rocky coast from Peterhead here. We stopped to bait at Aberdour, and went down to the shore. At that point begins high cliffs of slate and granite, and red sandstone, and they increase in height and grandeur for several miles. We walked along the cliffs, taking an occasional sketch, and met our trap again at a house vertically above the village of Pennan, which, inaccessible by wheels, nestles under the cliff on the beach. My ears are very fiery;

let us hope the benefit of this tour will come afterwards. Horrid news of the war; people starving, crops being burnt."

"*Fisher's Hotel, Pitlochrie, Aug.* 30.

"This place is so much enlarged since we were here in 1856. We went to sketch at the bridge, and then on to our old quarters at Dunfallandy. All the old people at the cottages are dead; but they remembered hearing of my preaching in the barn [6]. I feel this glorious air is doing me good."

"*Edinburgh, Sept.* 1.

"After I wrote you last from Pitlochrie, we went in a trap to Killiecrankie, and had a sketch of the Queen's View over Loch Tummel and the Falls. As I was sketching, two little highland lasses with bare legs were sporting round us. I found they were sisters of the page at Fisher's Hotel. I drew the falls of Tummel on my way back. An eyelash or something got into my eye. After much pain I went to a doctor, but he did me no good; so you must expect to receive a Cyclops. Burrell Smith is to draw for me a large picture of the valley of the Tummel, just over Dunfallandy."

"*Whitby, Sept.* 4.

"As Bradley and I were descending into the town yesterday, we met a boy with a big placard rushing like mad. 'Peace! peace! Surrender of Napoleon.' The news is indeed enormous; such a fall has not been, I think, in history. But I fear much it will not bring peace. My eye is still painful. I fear Exodus must not be undertaken just yet, which is a plague. I am longing again for our pleasant home, and the shady wood, and the one quiet voice. On the 6th I hope to get to Vines Gate, but I must get some dinner at the Club, and copy the 'Pall Mall' article about the Bullers of Buchan, and a description by Johnson for my article in 'Good Words.'"

On September 6 he returned to Vines Gate. It became necessary to protect his eye with a shade, but, notwithstand-

---

[6] See page 260.

ing the irritating effect of the pain of it, he continued to spend the entire forenoon as usual in his study, working at the Commentary on Exodus, arranging the account of his tour for publication, and completing the sketches which he brought home, which were engraved and published with the article in "Good Words" in the following April.

Mr. and Mrs. Bullock and their children came on the 15th September to spend a few days at Vines Gate. The condition of his eye was evidently working a change for the worse in his health and spirits, which gave us some anxiety. Medical skill had hitherto failed to arrive at the origin of this trouble. Nevertheless he continued his daily literary work notwithstanding our remonstrances, and took as much pleasure as ever in a game of croquet on the lawn, or in a long afternoon walk among the heathery woods of Toy's Hill. The following riddle on the word "Chassepôt," which was his contribution to an evening's amusement, showed that his facility in versification was still undiminished :—

"Loud clangs the horn as early morn
Hangs on the Lombard hills,
My *first* is up, away, away,
The cry each spirit fills.

"Across the plain they rush amain,
Each cheek with ardour glows,
Till broad across their onward path
In pride my *second* flows.

Foremost their chief in bright relief
Against the sky gleam'd red;
Whom Milan and whom Naples proved
Worthy to be their head.

"Ah, different far the shout of war
Along Mentana's height,
With other red that west is dyed,
And dim those glances bright.

"Dig deep the grave for legions brave
Where in their ranks they fell:
Relentless blazed my dreaded *whole*
And rung their glory's knell."

On September 19, he wrote to his niece, Miss E. M. Alford :—

"We are listening every day for the guns at Paris; is it not awful? poor Paris will have to eat dust and ashes, and it is (though excusable) very foolish for not giving in. I was talking to an M.P. yesterday, who has lived much in France, and he says the Red Republic and reign of terror must come before the air is cleared. If you want to see my Scottish trip, is it not written in the 'Good Words' of Alexander Strahan for November[7]?

"I am now touching up my drawings for him. But I got a stray eyelash into my right eye in Scotland, and it has been sadly irritable ever since. Meanwhile, the work goes on. I have to-day done Exodus vii. Genesis is ready for press.

"*Sept.* 25.—Preached at Brasted for the sick and wounded in the war.

"*Sept.* 29.—Finished Exodus xii. and part of xiii. Augustus Hare[8] is spending a day or two with us; he showed us his drawings, and gave us a wonderful account of the terrible flood at Pisa. He and his mother, Mrs. A. Hare, happened to be there at the time. News of the surrender of Strasburg.

"*Oct.* 3.—Exodus xiv., but in pain and weariness with my afflicted eye; unless some change comes, I must abandon my life's work. At 12.30 in a fly to Sevenoaks, and to Canterbury, staying at Parry's.

"*Oct.* 4.—At 12.30 Meeting at Canterbury for an educational movement to work the Government Bill. Archbishop spoke well . . . . got to Vines Gate to a 7½ dinner.

"*Oct.* 6.—Exodus xv.; eye better. Samuel Alford, who has been spending a few days with us, left this afternoon. In the evening I was able to read the papers once more to Fanny.

"*Oct.* 7.—Eye not so well. My sixtieth birthday. All thanks to my good God."

Wearied with the increasing pain in his eye, he went up to London for the day, and called on his old acquaintance, Mr. James Dixon, the oculist. The result is told in the following letter :—

TO MISS H. E. ALFORD.

"*Vines Gate, Oct.* 9.

"Many thanks for your birthday good wishes. It is a

---

7 It appeared in April, 1871.

8 Augustus J. C. Hare, author of "Memorials of a Quiet Life," 2 vols. "Walks in Rome," &c.

serious thing, this being sixty,—looks as if it were time to say good night. But it is an endless comfort that with the good night will come a good morning on the other side. The day (7th) was curiously celebrated. My damaged eye had become unbearable any longer, so I went up to Dixon to have it examined. His practised eye instantly detected, and his skilful hand extracted—what do you think, of all things in creation?—a fish-scale! The pain had begun while I was sketching the falls of the Tummel at Pitlochrie, a well-known salmon-leap. There was a brisk breeze blowing from the fall, and it must have carried into my eye a scale which was tossed in the spray. It has proved to me Apostolic Succession; for I doubt whether I am not the next link to St. Paul, it cannot have happened to any one since. See Acts ix. 18. I should so like to get to Rome and see it next spring. But this must depend on a great many things, of course. It is so pleasant to write without pain.

"This is our Revision week, so I shall be in town all the week."

To her sister, Miss E. M. Alford, he wrote:—

"Many thanks for your good wishes. I only hope the Master's work may be got done by bedtime—the falling asleep and the awaking. I have told Etty the way in which I have kept my birthday, and the curious result. Tell papa it had got worn down during the five weeks it had been in, till it was quite thin, and just like a little watch-glass: it was springy, and, when touched with an iron point, as we were examining it, hopped away. This terrible war is going on sadly too long. I am not French in my sympathies; more than from my heart I pity them now. They have paid the penalty of a people without reality, and the nation as it has been since 1789 has simply collapsed. It is vain trying to dislocate the empire and the people; it was their child, and for it they must be held responsible. Their ingratitude to Louis Napoleon, who did more for them commercially than any man in his time, is abominable. But I begin to fear the Germans are set upon building up even a greater and falser state of things than the French ever did. The French fallacy was supremacy by means of an army. The Germans' is the greater crime of universal military life, and by means of it the unchristianizing of Europe; at least I fear so. I should like to see an answer to the question, 'Why is Paris besieged?' I have never been able yet to answer it.

"My Riviera book is just out."

On October 11, he went to town for four days' work on the Revision of the English New Testament. On the 14th he wrote to me from the Athenæum:—

"After my revision work on the 12th, I preached Bradley's Harvest Sermon from Ps. lxv. 1. Many clergymen, and to supper afterwards. Next day sad headache, the inevitable concomitant of supper; but better after breakfast, and we had a hard day's work at the revision over Matt. v. 22—37. Then I dined with the Hamiltons; and then a gathering at the Deanery, Westminster, of all the small world of London there. The news of course you have heard. 'The Royal maiden all for Lorne,'—is it not remarkable? What will she be called?

"How funny that I should spin by you in the express this afternoon, on my way to Bettshanger, where I am asked to meet Count Bernstoff. On Tuesday, as I passed on the railway, I saw distinctly the house, and the mirror glittering. *Conservez-vous, ma chère.*"

In the following week we received visits at Vines Gate from the Rev. R. Hake and Mrs. Hake, and afterwards from Mr. Burrell Smith, his companion in the recent Scotch tour, to whom he was indebted for much of his progress in water-colour drawing, and who on this occasion came to sketch some of the pretty Kentish scenery in the neighbourhood of our house.

He mentions in his journal:—

"*Oct.* 24.—Magnificent Aurora; finest seen in this country. All the sky except south crimson, in great pillars and radii. Burrell Smith sketched it from the window, and I put in the foreground."

A visit which we paid on Oct. 22 to Lord Stanhope, at

Chevening, and the sight of the splendid collection of all sorts of MS. letters, old books, relics, &c., &c., are mentioned with delight in his journal.

The following letter was written to the Rev. Dr. Allon, who had just sailed on a voyage to America :—

"*Oct.* 20.

"You will indeed find things here not altered but thoroughly swept away. France is for our time gone, vanished from the nations. I paid a four days' visit in June, running in traps along the north coast from Boulogne to Havre, and I look upon it now as the last interview with an old friend. I shall never see France again. The plains and hills and rivers I may, but France never. The merry laugh of bustling industry is changed for the execration of revenge, *exit* monkey, *enter* tiger. The feeling is growing here, that the Germans are pushing too far. But to-day I have a note from a friend with whom Count Bernstoff has been staying, and he says that there is a little hope of peace. The lull before the bombardment of Paris, I fancy, is due, not only to the getting up of the siege-train, but to negotiations also.

"The New Testament Company met again last week, and we have got to the middle of Matthew vi.; slow work, but steady. I am working on with Exodus; Genesis was finished before coming here. At its conclusion, I went off to the north-east of Scotland, with an artist friend. . . . You will also find a new era in postage begun. The halfpenny cards (begun October 1st) have become a great institution. Some of us make large use of them to write short Latin epistles on, and are brushing up our Cicero and Pliny for that purpose. I hope you may be able to come down to Canterbury this winter, and tell us about your trans-Atlantic adventures.

"I wish you a safe and pleasant voyage."

The next week, business took him twice to Canterbury. Both journeys were hurried, and exhausted his strength; on one occasion he went to officiate at the wedding of a young friend [9], on the other, to preside at a public dinner.

We received as visitors at Vines Gate our friends Mr. and Mrs. J. Cunliffe, and Mr. B. H. Alford.

The following letters were written to his nieces :—

To Miss H. E. Alford.

"*Vines Gate, Oct.* 30.

"Tell Bessie I was deep in her story, at Ashford, when a guard looked in with 'Like a paper, sir? Metz has fallen,' so exit Bessie for the 'Times.' Poor France, she must succumb now, I suppose. To resist any longer would be to make all France a horde of brigands, for there is no army left; but their lying rulers will keep them a month in ignorance. The war is a dreadful tragedy; Carlyle says, more like Michael and Satan than anything in history."

To Miss E. M. Alford.

"*Oct.* 31.

"There is a most interesting telegram of two columns in to-day's 'Daily News,' from their Metz Correspondent, giving the whole detail of the surrender. There are signs of Aurora again to night; how grand they were on Monday and Tuesday last! We are just going to dine at Lord Stanhope's, three miles off; so we shall have a good view."

The first few days of November were spent quietly at Vines Gate. One of the daily entries in his journal is a specimen :—

"*Nov.* 3.—Exodus in the morning; took dearest F. in the afternoon over Westerham Common to the old sham ruin, and a very beautiful spot in the Squerries Woods, where the beech leaves looked bright burnt sienna against the strange metallic green of the grass. Evening as usual; read the papers to her."

On the 7th of November he went to London for four days' work on the Revision. On the 9th of November (Lord

---

[9] Leaving Vines Gate at 6.45, and returning late the same evening.

Mayor's day) there was a remarkably dense fog in London. In the evening he wrote to me:—

To his Wife.

"*Athenæum, Nov.* 9.

"As dark as night the greater part of the day. I hear from Merivale that he saw the Lord Mayor, and how during half an hour it cleared, and it was very pretty on the Embankment. We have done a good day's work; all chap. vii., and part of chap. viii.

"Yesterday, what with Revision in the morning, and Metaphysical at night we had a hard day. It was a capital meeting."

In this week his journal begins to record frequent complaints of troublesome feelings, of oppression in the head, buzzing in the ears, and sleeplessness at night. He returned to Vines Gate on Saturday, Nov. 12. On Sunday, after preaching in the morning in Brasted Church, he wrote in the evening a Fireside Homily on "The Gospel of the Children."

On Tuesday, Nov. 15, he records, "Finished Exodus xxv., and left off work for the present[1]." Our friend, the Rev. T. S. Huxley of Canterbury, was our visitor this week.

On Sunday, Nov. 20, he preached again at Brasted, and in the afternoon a change in the weather enabled us to walk to Toy's Hill, and enjoy the view from thence.

The next day we left Vines Gate to spend four days with Mr. and Mrs. Bullock at Kensington; there we met at dinner a family whom my husband knew previously only by a correspondence. Mr. Govin Chunder Dutt, a Christian Hindoo, had come to England for the purpose of giving his daughters some educational advantages which cannot be procured in Calcutta. The father, at and after the time of his conversion, was a reader of "Alford's Greek Testament." From reading the notes[2], he conceived so deep a regard for the author, that he wrote from Calcutta a letter full of gratitude and affection,

---

[1] This Commentary on "Genesis and part of Exodus," was printed in 1872 in one volume (338 pages), and was published by Strahan and Co.

[2] And from a perusal of "Alford's Poems."

and expressed the same feelings in a poem and sonnet [3]. The pleasure on both sides was very great when they met at Kensington. And in the evening of the 24th we returned to Canterbury, where he was required for the business of the Audit.

---

[3] The "Dutt Family Album," published by Messrs. Longman, in which these poems are printed, is a small collection written by two or three authors. Its versification would be highly creditable to a literary Englishman; but considered as the production of persons who had never seen England, it is a most remarkable work.

CHAPTER XII.

1870–1871.

DECLINING HEALTH—REVISION WORK RELINQUISHED—OLD TESTAMENT COMMENTARY SUSPENDED—LAST DAYS—FUNERAL—OPINIONS OF HIS CHARACTER AND WORKS.

WHEN we came to Canterbury he made no attempt to resume the composition of the Commentary which he had laid aside a fortnight previously. And now the usual record of a morning spent in literary work disappears from his journal; but in its place there are such entries as "arranged room and correspondence by way of being idle, as I am told to be," &c., "as yesterday, arranging," &c. Was this an unconscious preparation for the approaching event?

On his first two days at Canterbury, he records his "gladness to get once more into the old place" and "pleasure after our long hill solitude to see old faces once "more.

"*Sunday, Nov.* 27.—Morning, Bishop Parry, capital sermon. I, first of four sermons on the war[1], "Cease ye from man, whose breath is in his nostrils: for wherein is he to be accounted of?" Isaiah ii. 22.

"*Nov.* 28.—Audit; numberless applications for aid to schools in consequence of the new Education Act. Rhode's Concert.

[1] These four sermons were published. "Truth and Trust: Lessons of the War;" and the book was passing through the press at the time of his death. In page 20 will be found some remarks on the breaking up of a household; perhaps he had in his mind the decay of his own health.

"*Nov.* 29.—Meeting about education plans.

"*Nov.* 30.—Audit; King's School dinner; Mayor on my right; I proposed his health.

"*Dec.* 1.—To town, to Ecclesiastical Commission; afterwards to Bramford; all well, and new house getting on famously.

"*Dec.* 2.—To Ipswich, to buy grates for the new house.

"*Dec.* 3.—Snow; writing letters, and polishing to-morrow's sermon for Windsor; at one to town; about an hour at the Athenæum; then to the Deanery, Windsor.

"*Sunday, Dec.* 4.—At twelve to the Castle service; Queen there; preached on "Except ye see signs and wonders, ye will not believe," John iv. 48 [2].

"In the afternoon to Eton College with Mr. Marriott; most striking sight; 800 boys, choral service. Hugh Pearson and Lord A. Hervey dined at the Deanery.

"*Tuesday, Dec.* 6.—'Literary' dinner last night; returned to Canterbury by the early train. Arranging, &c., in the library; evening, Harmonic Union practice.

"*Dec.* 7.—Audit again; snow most unpleasant; our dinner party twenty-one."

On Thursday, Dec. 8, and again on the 10th, he went through the snow by special request to pay a ministerial visit to the Rev. J. B. Reade, then lying on his death-bed in the Rectory-house, Bishopsbourne [3].

On Sunday, Dec. 11, he preached his third sermon on the war, and four days of the following week were the last which he devoted to the work of revising the English New Testament.

After spending the morning and afternoon of Tuesday, the 13th, in that work [4], and the evening "at a Metaphy-

---

[2] This sermon is printed in "Truth and Trust," page 31.

[3] It is not easy to avoid recalling the visit, in the winter of 1600, of a Prebendary of Canterbury (Dr. Saravia) to the Rectory of Bishopsbourne, "about one day before the death" of Richard Hooker, then Rector. See Walton's "Life of Hooker."

[4] A post-card written that evening was the last communication I received from him. "Ma très chère,—Tout va bien; hier et aujourd'hui nous avons finis chapp. x. et xi. de l'Evangile de S. Matthieu. Tout à vous, H. A."

sical" meeting, he woke the next morning "at four, with buzzing in the head and throbbing, as during last Revision week."

The same work was repeated on Wednesday and Thursday[5], followed each time by the same evil symptoms. At the suggestion of the Rev. J. H. Hamilton, in whose house he was staying, he consulted on Friday Dr. Battye, who "pronounced the brain overworked, and ordered total rest even to-day from Revision. I am to take phosphates, Hungarian wine, cauliflour, and do nothing. I went to bid farewell to the Revision Company, and telegraphed to Fanny to say, 'I shall be home to dinner; I have not been well.'"

The following letters connected with the events of this day were received two or three days afterwards.

From the Rev. J. H. Hamilton[6].

"How are you? is the head quiet and comfortable again, &c. . . . We have had many an anxious thought about you since you left us; while grieving over the forced abstinence from hard work, and the loss of its fruits to the world, we admire more than I can express, the way in which you submit to the self-denying ordinance; the fear, perhaps, may be lest in feeling well again after a certain rest you should be tempted to resume your old toil."

From Archdeacon Bickersteth.

"I fear I but imperfectly expressed yesterday my sympathy with you in your breakdown; but I trust it is only temporary, and that you may be spared for some years of usefulness; we missed you sadly, and shall be glad to have you back to Jerusalem Chamber, January 31st, please God."

---

5 Ending his work with the Company of Revisers at the twelfth chapter of St. Matthew. "For whosoever shall do the will of My Father which is in heaven, the same is My brother, and sister, and mother."

6 Now Canon of Rochester.

I insert in this place the two next letters, because they relate to this time: they were written some weeks afterwards.

To MYSELF, FROM THE REV. J. H. HAMILTON.

"On his last visit to us, we were more struck than ever before by his sunny, holy, loving state of mind; even Dr. Battye's opinion, giving a death-blow to his most fondly-cherished work, never disturbed his equanimity for a moment. Not a murmur escaped him, but cheerfully he expressed his submission and determination to obey the doctor's desire. My wife and I were lost in admiration of his conduct, and indeed his whole spirit and conversation, all the time he was here, were sweet and bright beyond measure. This was the more remarkable, as he had little sleep, and felt the pressure of the Revision work daily more and more.

"On looking back, we feel that he was ripe for glory. . . . He has left his mark on the mind of this generation as few others have done. Those he has left behind will now learn more fully what a noble work he achieved, and what a benefactor he was to the whole Christian Church."

To MYSELF, FROM ARCHDEACON BICKERSTETH.

"The Dean of Canterbury was one of my earliest and dearest friends, and our Revision labours had brought us into such delightful intercourse again, that I was quite cheered and refreshed by it. I little thought when he left our Company on the 16th of December, in consequence of what we all thought was but a passing indisposition, that I should not see him again on earth. I need not say that his loss is, humanly speaking, irreparable to us. He was looking pale and worn, and told me his medical adviser told him to strike work immediately; that there was congestion of the brain looming in the distance, which could only be averted, under God, by immediate cessation from labour and entire rest for several weeks. So he swept off his books and papers never to return to us; though, happily for us, leaving behind him the printed records of his toil and thought, to which I need not say a frequent reference is made in the course of our labours."

Next day my husband wrote from Canterbury to his niece, Miss E. M. Alford:—

"And now I have some tidings for you about myself, grave but happily not (or not yet) sad. This week was one of our Revision sessions; in our last, in November, I had not felt well or up to the mark. But this time it became much worse, and robbed me of an increasing portion of each night. So I went to a big doctor. The brain was pronounced overworked, and system poorly provided with blood. I was ordered to do as little as possible at present; relinquish editing the Old Testament; and take to lighter and more varied work, mischief having arisen from too continued tension on one anxious subject. So after all you were right, and it was a rash act to undertake the Old Testament; the doctor told me it was too late in life to enter on a new and laborious department of study. So now it becomes my employment to amuse and benefit others. I am heartily glad of the change, for I am beginning to feel the work telling on strength and spirits. As to being low about it, I cannot see it so. If God's good hand has brought me to sixty in vigour, surely all after is pure gain, in whatever form it may please Him to shape it. One result will be more visits, a speedier sight of friends. It is a pity the Continent is shut out, or one might get a nice run to the South."

On Sunday, Dec. 18, he preached on "Trust as a Lesson of the War," and his condition of health is recorded as "tolerably well all day, but the noise in the attic unremoved."

On Wednesday Dr. Battye requested him to abstain from music (he was then practising for a performance at Canterbury of "Acis and Galatea").

He wrote to his daughters as follows:—

To Mrs. Bullock.

"The old trouble of seething and throbbing head kept

me awake three hours on Tuesday night, and four on Wednesday. And on Thursday, it was very much worse than I had ever had it before. So on Friday morning, I went to Dr. Battye, and got regularly overhauled, and he said it was brain overworked, and with too intense straining on one subject; this he said at once, and that it would come to mischief in a few months if work were not given up. He begged me not to go to the Revision on Friday, ordered me peremptorily to give up the Old Testament, as too much for the mind at my time of life. All, he thinks, will be well again, now it is taken in time. So a change has come o'er the spirit of my dream, one which I am not on the whole sorry for, as I was getting sure I could not go on with full work. I am better, and have slept better since Friday. My own view is, a man who has lived to sixty has so much occasion for thankfulness, it ought to overpower every other feeling; so it has not occurred to me to be in low spirits. I shall now look up the colour-box and the garden tools, and the fishing-rods of old days, and take up light literature once more."

TO MRS. CRUSO.

"*Dec.* 18.

"Dr. Battye pronounces what I always expected, the brain to be overworked with being fixed on one subject. Forbade me going on with the Revision on Friday, and, on my confessing the Old Testament plan, said I must give it up, as too great a strain at this time of life for the brain. I am to do as little work as possible just now—to draw, garden, travel, everything but mental puzzle; all will come right with rest and great care. I was becoming painfully conscious that I could not carry out the Old Testament work. It is too late to begin an arduous new pursuit, involving a new language; the effect on the whole will be, if all goes well, to make me better company and more useful to the generality of men. Sermons, articles, a tour or two, &c.; and as to lowness of spirits, it is not my way of taking such things. God's goodness has brought me past sixty. I owe

Him too much ever to murmur at what He does with me now. I am painting a large picture for the Huxleys. On the 27th is our Choristers' treat. How I do wish you and yours could be here. All love to the venerable pastor, and the one solitary lamb of the flock. The most blessed of Christmases, and happiest of New Years to you all, prays your loving ancestor."

On Thursday, the 22nd, he writes:—"Saw the eclipse of the sun very well, the last certainly I shall ever see. Dined at the Parrys."

The following letter to his niece was written on this day:—

To Miss H. E. Alford.

"*Dec.* 22.

"I thought you would like to have a report of progress. I am getting on, I think, just a wee bit; more and more sleep certainly, but the swarm of bees not yet hived. The doctor commands rest from mental work of every kind for at least a month, and even then no resumption unless natural sleep and silence in the attics. Alice and her chicks come to us on Monday for a fortnight, and will be, of course, a diversion from the occupation of sitting and listening to the hubbub within. After that could you come to us for a few weeks? I feel as if you would be a great comfort in the way of reading to me and sitting with me.

"My visit to Somersetshire must be put off till the 18th of January, as on the 12th I am engaged to dine at Tyler Hill, to meet the bride; and on the 17th our Choristers give their annual Concert, at which my absence will sadly disappoint the poor boys; so we will say the 18th provisionally, but I will write again. On the 27th is our Choristers' party. A Christmas tree and Charades, in which I act with them."

On Christmas-day he preached on Romans i. 1—4, and in the afternoon he complained of feeling unusually tired and sleepy in the service. Our neighbour Miss Hole dined at the Deanery, and he adds, "we thought of the poor people in the war."

His journal goes on, on December 26th:—

"Preparing dining-room for the usual Choristers' party to-morrow. At 12.30 William, Alice, and their children came from London, and afterwards Alice B. from Ramsgate; evening with them. Felt pretty well, thank God. Rehearsal in the morning of the Charade with the Choristers and Hake.

"*Dec.* 27.—Poorly all day, but much to do in preparing for the party. Rehearsal at eleven; party went off well. We acted 'Horse-spy-table,' with incidents of the war, ending with the King of Prussia and Bismarck being taken prisoners by Trochu, and let off on condition of yielding the Rhine frontier."

In the next three days he completed a painting of "The Land's End in Stormy Weather" for his friend the Rev. T. S. Huxley. He records agreeable walks with Canon Robertson:—"Frost continues unabated; much skating, but I have not been this year. Health gradually improving, I hope."

On the 31st December he writes:—"Afternoon, looked in at Canon Stone's children's costume party; very pretty. Rehearsal at the Music Hall.

"Sat up to the New Year. God be praised for all His mercies during this year of great events. He only knows when this my course will end. May its evening be bright, and its morning eternal day."

New Year's day, 1871, was a Sunday. He enters in his journal, "Good sermon from Bishop Parry on Isaiah xxx. 21. I preached on Ps. iii. 5 and iv. 9. Evening and morning thanksgivings. 'I laid me down and slept, and rose up again; for the Lord sustained me. I will lay me down in peace and take my rest; for it is Thou, Lord, only that makest me dwell in safety.'

"God only knows whether I shall survive this year. I sometimes think my health is giving way, but His will be done."

Happily a young friend has preserved a few notes taken down at the time of this his last and most striking New Year's extempore sermon:—

"The secret of the peacefulness with which the Psalmist

went each night to rest, undisturbed by the cares of the past day or fears for the morrow, is answered in the second verse I have quoted, 'For the Lord sustained me.' . . . Let us heartily thank God for His goodness to us in times past, and pray to Him still to guide our steps during the year which has just begun, without longing too anxiously for the gratification of our own particular wishes, which must be shortsighted and may be wrong. Let us humbly leave all in God's hands; for which of us can even imagine what one year or day may bring forth? If we look for a warning near home[7], we shall find it in the death of one who has been among us for many years; one whose removal we feel the more strongly, from the regularity of his attendance at the Cathedral services. Any of us may be summoned to follow him before this year is over; then let us lose not a day in preparing to meet our God. If we turn to the affairs of Europe, how fearfully do they show man's utter inability to look even a few months into the future. Well may we tremble at the unthought-of ruin which has so suddenly fallen on France. How many of those now present will meet together here next New Year's day, or what public events may then have taken place, it is not for us to consider. Our duty is to trust wholly in God's love, 'Casting all your care upon Him, for He careth for you;' and to strive earnestly to become less and less unworthy of His love and care."

On the 3rd of January he attended a meeting to establish a Relief and Mendicity Society, and on every day this week he was engaged in some meeting or conference on this subject; for whilst no doubt was expressed as to the desirableness of such a society in Canterbury, there was a great difference of opinion as to its constitution. The Dean and the Mayor were named chairmen of two separate committees, and it was my husband's chief care throughout the week to bring the two into union. He had interviews with various persons, and thus he was many times exposed both to the outside air while snow was falling or thawing on the ground, and to the

7 Referring to a member of the congregation who had died suddenly.

trial, even more severe to a person in his state of health, of protracted discussions in cold rooms.

On Thursday, the 5th, we dined at Bishop Parry's, and the following letters were written :—

TO HIS NIECE, MISS E. M. ALFORD.

"*Jan.* 5.

"There is just a loose point or two about my plan of coming to you. My doctor does not like my travelling this severe weather. He does not absolutely forbid it, but says getting chilled in the way up to see him would do more harm than he could do good. And we have just arranged a permanent Poor Relief and Mendicity Society, of which I am chairman, and this occupies the mornings, as long as the severe weather lasts. But, still, I am in hopes all these will get out of the way by the 18th. Only I tell you in order to provide for contingencies. I am better; sleep has returned nicely, the noise is not gone, but not so loud. I can do everything but literary work."

TO THE REV. D. P. ALFORD [8].

"*Jan.* 5.

"Many thanks for your kind invitation, which it would give me great pleasure to accept if it were possible, but I have not yet got my doctor's leave to go even to Somersetshire. I am, I hope, getting on : I can do pretty well everything but the one thing which is my natural occupation—literary work. Next week my Harmonic Union will perform 'Acis and Galatea,' and the 'May Queen,' and the rehearsal employs many evenings; so that, although knocked off work, I am by no means idle. I fill up my time by painting. If you would like a view at 'Scilly' for your walls, I shall be happy to execute your order. Mention any particular one you fancy; I have in pencil a view of St. Mary's from the way to the Telegraph, which has never been coloured; would you like that? the colouring would not be, perhaps, quite correct."

The drawing above mentioned was never begun. But he

---

[8] Incumbent of St. Paul's, Tavistock; formerly Vicar of St. Mary's, Isles of Scilly.

had found similar occupation in the two previous days in painting a picture of St. Michael's Mount, Cornwall, from a sketch taken in July, 1860, which he intended for his daughter's drawing-room at Kensington. When her husband arrived at the Deanery, on Friday, the 6th, it was agreed that one feature was wanting to complete the picture, and a cart was sketched in on the following Monday. The picture now remains with this unfinished addition.

On the 6th he entertained a dinner party of twenty persons, and no change was observed in his health or spirits. The next morning, though the snow was thawing in the streets, he walked with Mr. Bullock towards the railway, and parted from him in Castle Street; his intention being to call on a friend and concert farther measures for putting an end to the differences respecting the Relief Society. The last entry which he made in his journal relates to this subject:—

"*Saturday, Jan. 7th.*—Mr. Elgar called to try to make peace, and I went to the Mayor with the same purpose."

Mr. Elgar is a member of the Society of Friends, and in a letter to the Dean on the next day, he says:—

"The result of thy visit to the Mayor has been much before me, and more particulars I had from him in an interview last night; my heart was warmed when in the course of the evening I heard of thy liberal donation of £5 to the Mayor's Fund; my heart does indeed rejoice. And it is with me to tell thee that I do feel, that not only in thy individual capacity, but as Chairman to your Association thou hast done what thou couldest; and the prayer of my heart is, that the blessing of Him who so emphatically said, 'Blessed are the peacemakers, for they shall be called the children of God,' may rest upon thee. Accept my sincere thanks for thy kind donation of £2 2*s.* to the 'War Victims' Fund.' It is liberal, for I am sure thou hast many claims."

On Sunday, the 8th, he helped in the Communion in the morning, and preached an extempore sermon, as well and as energetically as usual, from "Verily Thou art a God that hidest Thyself, O God of Israel, the Saviour." Isaiah xlv. 15.

After church he walked to the Dane John. That morning he first mentioned an uncomfortable feeling behind the right ear, and he had a restless night; but he dined with us as usual, talked to his grandchildren, who came in to dessert, and heard the eldest read. But his spirits failed very soon after this, and instead of writing or reading to himself as he generally did in the intervals of our conversation, he allowed us to read to him.

On Monday (9th) he got up at his usual time, and read prayers himself with our household at eight o'clock. The portion of Scripture, according to the calendar prefixed to his "Year of Prayer," was Rev. xxii. 1—7, ending with "Behold, I come quickly: blessed is he that keepeth the sayings of the prophecy of this Book;" and in the prayer appointed for the day in the same Book of Prayers were the words: "In all time of temptation this day; in all times of flattery or success; in case we are sick, in case we have to die, Good Lord, deliver us." Soon after breakfast, though he was aware that he had caught a cold, he went out to a meeting, which unfortunately happened to be held in a cold room. When he returned home, his friend and secretary, Mr. Hake, was announced, who had come for a conference on some of the literary work in which his assistance had been found so valuable in recent years. My husband, who usually was ready to see him at any time, now asked me to go with a message to the effect that he was not well, but would nevertheless see Mr. Hake, if it were necessary. After lunch he went into his library, saying that, as he felt unfit for severe work, he would finish his picture of St. Michael's Mount for Mrs. Bullock. But he soon got tired of this, left his work unfinished, and sent for Mr. Hallowes, his usual medical attendant. Mr. H. treated him for a cold in the chest and neuralgia, but did not restrict him from going out; and, accordingly, he walked for a short time in his garden, and then went into the town. On his return he complained of restlessness, chill, and failure of appetite; instead of going down to dinner, he lay on a sofa in the small drawing-room, and took only some tea.

Next morning (10th) he was not disposed to rise, and his breathing was short and laboured, but he spoke cheerfully, and we thought the remedies were taking effect. His letters which came that morning were read to him, and he gave directions concerning them, and dictated and signed an answer to one. The newspapers also were read to him. He was able to see his grandchildren, and appeared to be amused by their talk. That evening he would not allow his daughter to be absent from the concert given by the Harmonic Union, though he was unable to accompany her as had been arranged, or to receive visitors from thence that evening. During her absence he slumbered a little, and scarcely spoke. On her return he showed a desire to hear the details of the concert, for he had spent much time in the practisings and rehearsals which preceded it; and he asked her many questions as to the performance of various parts.

On Wednesday (11th) morning he woke after a longer sleep, the effect of medicine. But his drowsiness and difficulty of breathing continued; he showed little appetite; he did not care to have his letters read to him, and he took no interest in passing events, making no remark when he was told of any occurrence.

This day had been previously fixed for the return of his daughter and her children to their home in London. She felt some hesitation; but after consulting the doctor and myself, and finding that there was no apprehension of danger, but an expectation, that with rest and nursing all would soon be well, she left us in the afternoon. When she took her children to bid good-bye to their grandpapa, he spoke to them in a way which seemed to show that it cost him an effort to fix his attention on what he was saying.

After their departure I did not leave his room. He seemed too much exhausted to speak more than a few words. I offered to read to him, but he said he would rather try to sleep.

About nine in the evening the doctor came to see him; and when his bed had been made, he seemed composed and refreshed by the change, and he put out his arm to turn off the gas-light by the side of the bed, and after I had prayed with him, he tried to sleep. But as the night advanced he became increasingly restless, though he spoke no word of complaint.

I caught some incoherent sentences, "I must give up the School Board." "The Revision is now beyond me; I fear I cannot go on with it." When I spoke to him, he said, "Attending the Relief Society every morning has been too much for me." And once I heard, "I don't think I shall ever get over this illness. I shall not leave my bed again."

In the morning (12th) he lay quite prostrate, never speaking except to say "Thank you, darling," for any little act of attention. After prayer together, I sent to his doctor, and gave him his breakfast, for which he apparently felt some appetite.

The doctor on arriving about nine, saw at once that a change had taken place, and that wandering was coming on. He said to the Dean, "I am sorry to hear you have had a bad night," to which the answer was, "No; I have not had a bad night." He inquired, "Have you any pain?" "No, no pain!" He then told me that the Dean was in considerable danger, and that I had better send by telegraph for his daughters.

On my suggestion, Dr. Lochée, the physician, was called in. Meanwhile Mr. Hallowes sat down by the fire to watch. Presently the Dean beckoned to him to come close, and said "Will you tell the Arch—?" "Do you mean the Archbishop?" "No, not the Archbishop." "The Archdeacon, the Bishop of Dover?" "Yes; *will you move a vote of thanks for his kindness in performing the ceremony?*"

When Dr. Lochée arrived he was able to learn something of the symptoms from the patient himself; and by his order strong external applications were used, and stimulants were given. But they produced no visible effect. He was fast sinking. His eye was fixed on me, and followed me when I moved. I felt a slight pressure on my arm, but the power of speech and consciousness gradually forsook him. He was, in the doctor's opinion, quite free from suffering of mind or body.

Soon after twelve o'clock his brother, Mr. B. H. Alford, in accordance with an appointment made a few days before, arrived at the Deanery with the purpose of paying us a short visit. My husband sent him on Tuesday evening a message to the effect, that he had a bad influenza, but should probably be well again in two or three days.

The shock was great when he was aware of the change which had come over all our expectations that morning. When he entered the chamber of sickness, his brother did not recognize him by word or sign. He went out to make a last effort to ascertain from the physician whether any further advice could avail, and to bespeak the prayers of the congregation in the cathedral. Meanwhile the doctor and I remained.

A haze was observed coming over his eye; there was a very slight muscular movement of the chin and lips. The doctor said, "It will be very soon." I was able in a few earnest words to commend my beloved husband to the care of our Heavenly Father, and to ask for strength. And then with a gasp but no struggle, his spirit returned to God who gave it.

In the next few days whilst addresses and numerous letters of condolence showed how wide was the circle of friends whose respect and affection he had won, the scattered members of his family assembled at the Deanery. In accordance to his well-known wishes, the funeral was to be as simple [9] as possible in its arrangements.

The Library was chosen as the fittest temporary resting-place which the house afforded for his beloved remains. Every part of the room seemed to be a distinct memorial of some of the works in which the energy of that active spirit was spent. There was the recessed window which enclosed what we were used to call "the New Testament desk," between shelves filled with the most recent works of German and English critics on the Greek Testament;

---

[9] He always adhered to the sentiments which he had expressed many years ago in his sermon on Funeral Pomp.

the place of many a morning's work alone or with his Secretary. There was his reading-chair beside the fireplace, in which he sat to receive visitors in the Library, and in which most of his recent original compositions, sermons and essays, had been written: and over the fireplace, an antique Italian clock which he brought from Rome; an aneroid barometer, his companion in all his tours; a paper always displayed conspicuously on the chimney-piece, reminding visitors in that room to "call on a business man in business hours, only on business, transact your business, and go about your business, in order to give him time to finish his business." In the centre of the panel above the chimney-piece, was an engraving of a Virgin and Child after Andrea del Sarto, on which he had often gazed when a child in his father's study[10]; and round it were two favourite engravings, of the Virgin Mary and St. John the Baptist, and two photographs from statues in the Vatican, Demosthenes and Pudicitia. There was the little table which he kept for letter-writing. There was the desk at which he was wont to work chiefly on his Commentary on the Old Testament; beside it, on a stand, the first volume of the Chapter Library copy of Walton's Polyglot lying open at the Book of Exodus; and at the foot of it was the travelling bag, still unopened, containing a work of Tischendorf, and various papers, which he had laid down there after his return from the last meeting of the Revision Company. Behind him, when he sat there, were the shelves which held the Abbé Migne's collection of Greek and Latin Fathers, his last large addition to his Library. Next stood the table with his box of colours and other drawing apparatus, and propped on its little easel the picture of St. Michael's Mount, on which he had spent his last minutes in that room. His harmonium stood open, with music-books beside it, in the window beyond, from which, when he sat there, he looked out on the Cathedral, and on the Green Court, the playground of the school over whose interest he watched constantly.

---

10 See "Fireside Homily," iv.

DEAN ALFORD'S LIBRARY

Between the windows was a collection of Greek and Roman Classics, many of them prize volumes. The other shelves were laden chiefly with theological works, the gatherings of his lifetime—literature of other kinds having found ample place in other parts of the house.

Amidst these memorials of his life-long toils he was laid, until the earth claimed its own.

On Tuesday, the 17th of January, the day of the funeral, no sign was wanting by which the whole city could show its sympathy with the sorrowing family.

The Harmonic Union, which regarded him as its founder, had a place assigned to its members in the Cathedral. The Corporation of the City, the Volunteers (whose Chaplain he was), and the Clergy of the diocese, united with the Cathedral body and his family in the procession; and it was followed by friends from various parts, among whom were several Nonconformist ministers, and by fellow-citizens in unusual numbers, from the Cathedral to St. Martin's Churchyard.

The pall was borne by the Deans of Ely and Westminster, Captain Brinckman, M.P., and Mr. Tipping, M.P., the Rev. W. G. Humphry, and the Rev. Dr. Stoughton, who met in the Chapter House and proceeded thence by the cloisters.

The former part of the service took place in the nave of the Cathedral; and there, when the Bishop of Dover (the Canon in residence) had finished the lesson, the Dean's hymn was sung:—

"Jesus, when I fainting lie,
And the world is flitting by,
Hold up my head:
When the cry is, 'Thou must die,'
And the dread hour draweth nigh,
Stand by my bed!

"Jesus, when the worst is o'er,
And they bear me from the door,
Meet the sorrowing throng:
'Weep not!' let the mourner hear,
Widow's woe and orphans' tear
Turn into song.

"Jesus! in the last great day,
Come Thou down and touch my clay,
Speak the word, 'Arise!'
Friend to gladsome friend restore,
Living, praising evermore,
Above the skies!"

The concluding portion of the service was read in the churchyard by Archdeacon Harrison; and lastly the Dean's hymn was sung:—

"Ten thousand times ten thousand,
In sparkling raiment bright,
The armies of the ransom'd saints
Throng up the steeps of light:
'Tis finish'd—all is finish'd,
Their fight with death and sin;
Fling open wide the golden gates
And let the victors in.

"What rush of Hallelujahs
Fills all the earth and sky!
What ringing of a thousand harps
Bespeaks the triumph nigh!
O day, for which Creation
And all its tribes were made!
O joy, for all its former woes
A thousandfold repaid!

"O then what raptured greetings
On Canaan's happy shore,
What knitting sever'd friendships up,
Where partings are no more!
Then eyes with joy shall sparkle
That brimm'd with tears of late;
Orphans no longer fatherless,
Nor widows desolate.

"Bring near Thy great salvation
Thou Lamb for sinners slain,
Fill up the roll of Thine elect,
Then take Thy power and reign:
Appear, Desire of nations,—
Thine exiles long for home:
Show in the heaven Thy promised sign,
Thou Prince and Saviour, come!"

He had himself expressed a wish to be buried in St. Martin's Churchyard. The spot chosen for his grave is beneath a yew-tree on the brow of the hill on the south side of the path which leads up from the lich-gate to the western door of the ancient church. At the distance of about half a mile to the west the towers of the Cathedral look down upon his tomb.

Among his papers was found the following memorandum, which, of course, was carefully obeyed:—

"When I am gone, and a tomb is to be put up, let there

be, besides any indication of who is lying below, these words, and these only:—

DEVERSORIUM VIATORIS HIEROSOLYMAM PROFICISCENTIS

i. e. the inn of a traveller on his way to Jerusalem."

A day or two before the funeral[1], the following letter arrived at Canterbury, having been written on the day of his decease for whose eyes it was intended.

FROM THE ARCHBISHOP OF CANTERBURY.

"*Mentone, France, Jan.* 12, 1871.

"MY DEAR DEAN,—Mrs. Tait and I have heard with much distress that you have not been well. I write to beg you to give yourself immediate and lengthened rest. Let my example be a warning to you. But I suspect your literary work has been a greater strain than my necessary occupations of business in London, and in my first nine months of Lambeth and Kent. I earnestly hope that we shall soon hear that you are quite well. If you have never read, read at once Sir B. Brodie's 'Psychological Researches,' and see what amount of literary work he thinks the human frame can stand. Your most interesting 'Riviera' reached London the day we started, but it was brought out to us, and it is a great help to us along the coast. I think you are severe on St. Remo, which, if we could only have found beach walks, we should have greatly enjoyed. We stayed there a month, and had many most lovely drives. Will you not come here and refresh yourself at once? What can we look forward to before it is time to turn our faces towards England? The fear of passing through France oppresses us. The French who are here seem resolved not to believe that any real evil can happen to Paris, and bear as good a heart as possible on the sad state of things. Would that the love of Christ had so taken possession of men's hearts that wars were impossible. Mrs. Tait sends kindest regards to you and Mrs. Alford.

"Ever most truly yours,

"A. C. CANTUAR."

---

[1] A handsome memorial window has been subscribed for, and is about to be placed in Canterbury Cathedral.

It was followed by another letter to myself :—

FROM THE ARCHBISHOP OF CANTERBURY.

"*Mentone, France, Jan.* 18, 1871.

"MY DEAR MRS. ALFORD.—Last week I wrote to your dear husband, begging him to take care of his valuable health, and to give himself some rest, and now I hear his Heavenly Father has taken him to his eternal rest. I need not say that our hearts bleed for you, deprived so suddenly of one so justly loved and honoured by all, and who was to you every thing the world can give. Deeply do we grieve also for the Church, at this time so requiring such spirits as his to be her aid. I feel for myself I have lost a kind friend and helper. How mysterious that I should be living, and he who seemed so full of health and vigour when you came to visit us at Stonehouse, should be gone. But his Lord had need of him, and has called him elsewhere, and whilst we mourn we feel the confidence and quiet resignation which attends the departure of one of Christ's own people. May the great Comforter pour abundantly into your heart those consolations which have sustained so many Christian widows when their loved ones have fallen asleep in Jesus. I will not write more, and would not have ventured to intrude on your grief but for the real affection I bore for your husband, and my deep sense of the greatness of our loss. Mrs. Tait knows how to feel for you.

"Affectionately yours,

"A. C. CANTUAR."

Her Majesty was graciously pleased to send through the Dean of Windsor, a message expressive of her "very sincere sorrow for the sudden death of so able a man, and one whom she had seen and heard so recently, and of her sympathy with the family."

I cannot but record with a feeling of gratitude that friends at a distance, to the number of nearly two hundred, were good enough in that season of sorrow to send us letters of condolence.

A complete review of Dean Alford's works and character will not be expected from the editor of this volume. Some of his contemporaries, who are most competent to speak of him as a commentator, a preacher, and a poet, have recorded their sentiments, and I am allowed to give them a place here. I venture to preface them with a few observations on some points which might escape the notice of his less intimate friends.

No one who lived with him could fail to be struck by his extreme quickness in observation, thought, and action. He was the first to notice any alteration, for instance, in the furniture of a room, or in the appearance of any person whom he met frequently, the first to read any inscription by the roadside. The gradual developments in the growth of plants in the garden, the changes of the sky seemed to chronicle themselves in his mind as soon as they occurred. Although on public occasions, as when he was in the pulpit, his utterance was measured and deliberate; yet, when he was quite at ease in his family circle, there was something unusual in the rapidity as well as vivacity with which he would follow up a train of thought to its conclusion, or would recall one after another recollections of his early days or travels. At dinner parties, even in his own house, he rarely appeared to lead the conversation. A certain shyness kept back the expression of his ready thoughts, or confined it to his next neighbour: but his mind knew no rest[2]; and when he chose to speak he never hesitated for a word, and always by a peculiar felicity seemed at once to hit on the word or

[2] This will be illustrated by the following remark in a funeral sermon preached at St. Mary's Bredin, in Canterbury, on 15th Jan., 1871, by the Rev. G. B. Lee Warner:—

"If I might be permitted to point out a fault in the well-nigh perfect character of our departed friend, a fault, indeed, which was but a virtue carried to excess, I would say it consisted in his habitual forgetfulness of a precept contained in those very New Testament Scriptures which were so familiar to his mind—a precept, too, which fell from the lips of Christ Himself, whom he so endearingly loved and served, when He said to His disciples of old, and says to His disciples still, 'Come ye yourselves apart, and rest awhile.' So averse was the departed Dean from all idleness, either in spiritual or temporal things, that in very truth he seemed to be, and I believe really was, incapable of resting."

phrase which expressed most exactly his idea. It must not be concealed that his sensitiveness and quickness in decision sometimes led to hasty action; but this was checked by the natural comprehensiveness of his mind, and by that genuine humility which kept him always ready on reflection to see, to avow, and retrace any error. If in his early days specially he was, as he has himself stated, apt to be intolerant of those who differed widely in opinion from him, or to be impatient of dulness or inaccuracy, yet that failing disappeared as he advanced in life, insomuch that he was once publicly pointed out by a determined but generous opponent in Convocation, as a man whom it was impossible to provoke; and, in private, instances have been known of his apologizing for the use of what he regarded as hasty words to persons who themselves had seen nothing unsuitable in them.

The versatility of his powers has been abundantly illustrated in this Memoir. In his home it showed itself by the ready and sympathizing interest which he took in every occupation of every member of his family: sometimes he would anticipate, even to an inconvenient extent, the decision of those about him, in what they regarded as their own concerns; but the gentleness of his character always disarmed opposition.

The same versatility and ready sympathy constituted, perhaps, one cause of the general exclusion of personal and trifling conversation from his fireside. I should not venture on this remark, had I not heard it from visitors. His interest in a multitude of pursuits, almost always supplied topics of talk, without wandering into detraction, or into over warm discussion, and never allowed stagnation.

One of the lesser traits of character manifested in his daily life was his punctuality, a quality which is not often found in combination with versatility, poetical temperament, and extreme readiness to enter into the pursuits of other persons. He had his regular hours for everything. He did not allow himself to be taken off his literary work in the morning; the business of the study was very rarely indeed suffered to encroach on the afternoon out-of-doors exercise; and the evening was systematically assigned to conversation, fireside amusements, or some book "well chosen, and not sullenly perused in selfish silence." No meal ever waited for his presence. He was usually the first to appear in the morning at our eight o'clock family prayers; and the first to retire to his study, after those at ten in the evening. This habit, of course, had the effect of leading all around him into similar regularity. Few persons, I believe, were so punctual in keeping an appointment. And he always seemed to do this, not because he piqued himself on the small virtue of punctuality, but because he knew by experience, that this was the only way of getting through his numerous occupations every day.

In these remarks I have purposely confined myself almost to his domestic life. Even in it there are many other points too sacred to be dwelt upon. I will now give place to the observations of others, who saw him in different spheres of action. Among them, the first place is due to a letter written at my request, by his early and intimate friend Dean Merivale:—

"It is not every one who would wish the annals of his youthful career to be too closely scrutinized, even by those in whose affectionate sympathy he might have the greatest confidence. But no man, as far as I have known, lived a more consistent life from the first than your husband. His strength and his weaknesses were ever the same, and the deep regard and respect he inspired in his latter years, showed how much the strength overbalanced the weakness, in the estimation of all who knew him then, just as it did in the estimation of his earlier associates.

"It was with great regret, and some little shame, that I found myself obliged to answer your natural application for some of the letters I have received from him, with the confession that I had very needlessly allowed myself to destroy almost all of them. Some two years ago, I had occasion to make a removal from an old home, and on such occasions one's impatience sometimes gets the upper hand, and impels one to clear away old books and papers with reckless precipitation. I am distressed now to think that among the boxes full of old letters, accumulations undisturbed for years, which I then sacrificed, were, I should think, some hundreds of my old familiar friend. The idea of being called upon, as I now am, to pay a tribute to the memory of one younger, and as I always thought stronger, than myself, had never once in my life occurred to me: and I seemed to be so thoroughly imbued with his views and sentiments upon all the subjects which ever came into discussion between us, that those fugitive records of them seemed but the shadow of the man himself, while I still possessed, and never thought of the time when I should no longer possess, the substance of them in himself.

"One packet, indeed, I find that I have still retained, and this I have had a melancholy satisfaction in communicating to you, containing as it does a history, month by month, or almost week by week. of the first year or two after I parted from him at Cambridge; when he was first entering upon the duties of the profession to which he devoted himself; when he was laying out the scheme of life which he had long before contemplated, and crowning it with the wedded union which had been, as you know, one of his earliest aspirations. You have found little or nothing, I imagine, in these hasty jottings of his pen, which would seem fit for general perusal, but I am glad to know that there is much in them which has an interest for yourself, and that you do not grudge me the share I had in his confidence and sympathy, even in that spring-tide of a young poet's affection.

"The re-perusal indeed of those letters, and the recollections they bring back to me of my familiar converse with your husband, during those early years, suggest to me what was perhaps throughout his career the most characteristic of his moral features. I really think he was morally the bravest man I ever knew. His perfect purity of mind and singleness of purpose, seemed to give him a confidence and unobtrusive self-respect which never failed him.

"A young provincial, fresh from the very quiet domestic training of his father's vicarage, or from an obscure country school, he was flung, as it were, into the amphitheatre of the society of Trinity at Cambridge, among hosts of young men distinguished for self-assertion no less than for ability, backed by every advantage of social recommendation. He came to Cambridge with the acquaintance of some two or three fellow-pupils; after a couple of years of contented obscurity, he had won his way to acceptance and respect among the most popular and most gifted of his contemporaries. Then, as throughout his career, he was singularly remarkable for the versatility of his talents. If one of the friends among whom he was then held in estimation, was more eminently gifted in verse, another plunged more deeply into the dark profound of juvenile metaphysics, a third promised to take higher rank in classics, a fourth in mathematics, Alford at least could hold his own with all of them, could appreciate all, could sympathize with all, and could gain in return the sympathy of all. As soon as he had taken his degree, not without considerable Academic honours, he was desirous, like many young men, of marrying. But, unlike most young men, he had already for years fixed upon the object of his affections, and kept it steadily before him. When he intimated his wishes to his father, he was met, like other young men, with hesitation if not remonstrance. How will you keep a wife? I will take a curacy and pupils. The arguments pro and con that followed need not be repeated. At least, said the anxious parent, stand for your fellowship: achieve me that honour: *nullam patiere repulsam.* Alford continued to work for the fellowship, which, in the second or the third year he obtained, having already taken orders, and entered upon the duties of his father's curacy. He then sought for pupils and obtained them, occupying the vicarage from which his father from ill-health was absent, and prepared to carry his long cherished object into immediate effect. Just then, fell vacant the small college living of Wymeswold, so small, so obscure, so much, for a long period, neglected, that no senior fellow cared to take it; and thereupon he married his wife, and buried himself for a period of eighteen years.

"Many a young man has done the like, and has not shown himself brave therein, but foolish, rash, and selfish. But it was not so with Alford. He justified, I would say he glorified, his act by the unwavering courage and confidence, and the unflagging exertion with which he faced and battled with the consequences. The population to whom he ministered numbered more than a thousand, and there were few or none among them from whom he could derive much help in his ministrations. The habits of the people did not demand, nor perhaps did the usage of the clerical school in which he had been trained suggest, the constant house-to-house visitation which might be looked for in rural parishes in these days; but he carried on his three full services single-handed every Sunday, he built and superintended his schools, he almost rebuilt his church, and his earnestness and evident self-sacrifice won him the unbounded love of his parishioners. All this time he maintained himself and an increasing family by constant tuition, and still finding time—for I never saw him throw himself back in his chair and lounge for one minute—for writing some books and editing others, for skirmishing in reviews and lecturing in local centres. For some years he was a periodical Examiner for the University of London, and in his trips there found opportunities of preaching not unfrequently in London pulpits. His great gift of preaching, which one friend at least had marked from the beginning, at last attracted the attention it deserved, and he received the 'call' to the pulpit of Quebec Chapel, from which his rapid rise in his profession, and the wide extension of his reputation as a preacher, are dated. From that time, relieved entirely from the work of tuition, and in a great degree from parochial cares, he was enabled to centre his still untired energies upon his edition of the Greek Testament, and to work another, and perhaps the richest of the many and various mines of talent, which he developed successively or together.

"But this, too, is an old chapter in human life. Many

others before him, having deliberately thrown themselves upon their own resources, have worked to the end steadfastly and indefatigably, and made the best of the difficulties in which they had involved themselves. But this was not all with my friend. His bravery was manifested in the unfailing serenity and confidence with which he encountered his work, and the cheerful undoubting satisfaction with which he looked both forward and backward. I never heard one murmur from him, I never saw him despond, I never knew him look about anxiously for the means of bettering and advancing himself. His mind seemed at perfect peace, as one well assured that his work was appointed him, and that he was doing it. I knew many of his troubles. You knew them all, and I appeal to you with confidence for the confirmation of what I say regarding him, that this brave spirit of his, anchored in domestic love and religious faith, never quailed before any of them. It would be little, perhaps, to add that this moral fortitude was not unaccompanied in him with physical courage also, of which I could give examples, if it were sufficiently to the purpose. But the side of his character which I have thus illustrated is that which is brought most forcibly before me, on reviewing the years of our long-cherished intimacy; and the little tribute I am enabled to pay him will, I trust, be not ungrateful to the friends who survive him."

The following passages have been selected from an article in the "Contemporary Review," by his early friend, the Rev. E. T. Vaughan :—

"Throughout his course at Cambridge many of the same qualities which marked his after-life were conspicuous—simplicity and purity of character; affection both warm and lasting, quick sensibility, unusual powers of acquiring and reproducing knowledge; much freshness of thought, combined with singular felicity of expression, whether in speech or in writing; not a little of that undefinable something which distinguishes the man of genius from the merely clever or able man. His versatility was wonderful. Outdone by many of his competitors in each department, he could do more things very well than any of them, and succeeded accordingly. His father's early care and prayers had not been in vain. His inner life was always that of a truly religious man, and his outer life morally blameless.

"His family life is a subject almost too sacred for the pen even of an intimate friend. I can only say that, from first to last, at Wymeswold or at Canterbury, it was the simplest, the fullest of affection abundantly returned, of thought and care for all who came within its circle, the purest from all alloy of selfishness or worldliness, that I have ever known or could have imagined.

"A shrewd and rather severe judge of sermons who heard him in 1855, on being asked what he thought, said drily, that 'he thought it spoke well for London that such sermons should be so popular.' This critic from the north had expected, doubtless, to hear either a great orator, or a very powerful and original thinker, and had been disappointed. But he had felt truly that the sermons had a peculiar charm for people who went to church, not for an intellectual feast, but to gain help in living the Christian life; and that it was a token for good that the people who went for this purpose were so many. Such was, indeed, the real attraction of his preaching. To put forth clearly and fully the great truths on which the Christian life depends for its existence and development; to unfold to view the nature and practical fruits of the life itself; to appeal earnestly to the conscience of every man on the question whether he himself was in it in reality; to help and encourage those who were struggling to begin it, and to carry it on to its completion; this, and this only, was the preacher's aim; but truth was always presented, not as a formula, but as a living reality, freshly apprehended. Prevailing errors of practice, the fashionable sins and selfishness of private and public life, were fearlessly exposed, with manly warmth and earnestness of expostulation. Eloquence was never sought, but the unconscious eloquence which clothes high and holy thoughts in language worthy of its object and its aim was seldom wanting. Those who came for Christian instruction and guidance never went away disappointed.

There were sermons of which very far more might have been justly said. But so much as this was true of his sermons, always and everywhere, in country churches, in London, at Canterbury.

"The work which he did in making those critical and exegetical helps, which had hitherto been the property in England only of a few readers of German, to become the common heritage of all educated Englishmen, was a work which no other man of his own generation could have achieved equally well, or was likely to have attempted. His industry was wonderful, his power of getting through work such as I have never known equalled. No man could sum up more clearly and concisely the conflicting opinions of others; none could, on the whole, exercise a fairer or more reasonable judgment between them. No man could be more honestly anxious to arrive at truth; he shirked no difficulty which he felt; he kept back nothing which he believed. On all critical and exegetical questions he was always open to conviction, and never ashamed to confess a change of opinion.

"Above all he knew but one aim—to approximate as nearly as his knowledge would allow to that exposition of every passage which should truly express the mind of the Divine Author. He dreaded theories of inspiration; but no man ever lived and studied under a deeper conviction that every part of Scripture was given by Inspiration of God, and expressed a wisdom which no human mind could exhaust. To trace out the truth revealed everywhere, and apply it for the building up of mind and heart in the knowledge and love of God, was the one object with which he worked as expositor; even as his one aim in criticism was to approach, as nearly as the available evidence would allow, to the original verity of God's word written.

"We read now with a solemn feeling of its entire truth the language in which, nine years ago, he expressed his own desire with regard to the success of the great work of his life, then just completed.

"'I have now only to commend to my gracious God and Father this feeble attempt to explain the most mysterious and glorious portion of His revealed Scriptures; and with it this, my labour of now eighteen years, herewith completed. I do it with humble thankfulness, but with a sense of utter weakness before the power of His word, and inability to sound the depths even of its simplest sentence. May He spare the hand which has been put forward to touch the Ark! May He, for Christ's sake, forgive all rashness, all perverseness, all uncharitableness, which may be found in this book, and sanctify it to the use of His Church; its truths, if any, for teaching; its manifold defects, for warning. My prayer is and shall be, that in the stir and labour of men over His word, to which these volumes have been one humble contribution, others may arise and teach, whose labours shall be so far better than mine, that this book and its writer may ere long be utterly forgotten.

ΑΜΗΝ ΕΡΧΟΥ ΚΥΡΙΕ ΙΗΣΟΥ.'

"Those who knew the Dean will feel that this was with him the language of simple truth. In the spirit of those words, those who knew him best are sure that his whole life had been spent. He had not sought wealth, or fame, or influence. If any of them were given, he accepted them thankfully, and enjoyed them fearlessly as a gift from God. But they were not his object, whether in the pulpit or in the study. He aimed to know God's truth for himself, to speak it to others, and to live it faithfully. And as he lived, so in the appointed time he has died—in the simplicity of a child-like faith. His appointed work was done, and he lay down to rest like the child at evening."

The pages of this Memoir contain too little reference to one of my husband's most intimate friends, Dean Stanley. But I am glad to insert here the following extracts from his article in the "Contemporary Review" for February, 1871:—

"Of all the more intellectual ecclesiastics of our time, he was the most active and indefatigable workman. His study was literally an *officina librorum*. The handicraft which he possessed in so many other branches—mechanical, artistic, musical—reached its culminating point in his literary achievements. Others, no doubt, have written, in our time, more profoundly, more eloquently, more philosophically, but we doubt whether any of his ecclesiastical contemporaries rivalled Henry Alford in the amount of genuine labour undertaken. Many objections, both general and in detail, may be brought against his edition of the Greek Testament. But its great merit is, that it was done at all; and, being done, although far from reaching the idea of such a work, and inferior in execution and conception to that which is displayed in particular portions of the sacred writings as edited by others, it remains confessedly the best that exists in English of the whole volume of the New Testament. To have done this, at once elevated its author to a high rank amongst the religious teachers of his country. It is premature to speak of his work on the Old Testament. It was when it became apparent to him that, in all probability, his ecclesiastical life was likely to run on in the same quiet channel as it had run heretofore, that he undertook to devote his remaining years to do for the Hebrew Scriptures what he had done for the Greek. It was a gigantic undertaking for a man already past the middle term of his existence; but he threw himself into it as heartily and as energetically as if he had been a young man of five and twenty. And we cannot but believe, from the spirit in which he entered upon it, that his execution of the task would, far more than any other exegetical attempt of a like kind in England, have faced the difficulties of the sacred text, 'divided rightly' the word of truth, illuminated the dark places of the venerable records of the chosen people.

"He was a 'scholar' in the sense of constantly learning. Few ecclesiastical writers of our time have gone more steadily forward in a wider appreciation of Christian truth; and few high dignitaries have obtained a clearer view of the duty of placing the Church on a truly national basis. His relations to the Nonconformists were such as would have led as much as any other single cause to the mitigation of the 'watchful jealousy' with which so many even of the best members of the Nonconformist Churches have of late years regarded the Church of which Dean Alford was unquestionably a faithful representative, at once by his tolerance and his culture.

"The gathering of distinguished Nonconformist ministers round his grave, and the genuine expressions of sympathy that his death has called forth, are cheering pledges that his kindly relations to them were fully appreciated, and will bear a lasting fruit.

"One of the latest projects of his life was one which singularly united his ecclesiastical predilections and his Biblical studies. It may truly be said that to him, more than to any one man, may be traced the scheme for the Revision of the Authorized Version of the Scriptures. He advocated it whilst it was still deemed rash and premature. He pressed it forward the moment that others had taken it up. He gave himself to it with all his energy when its necessity was recognized. He was, perhaps, of all the members of the Company for the Revision of the New Testament translation, the one who could least be spared.

"It would be taking an inadequate view of Dean Alford's literary career, were we to omit that sphere with which it began—his poetry. It may be that there will not be many of his poems, graceful as they are, which will live beyond the present age, yet it is no light service to have contributed at least one hymn which has almost become the Baptismal Canticle of the English Church.

"And it was but a just tribute to his poetic fire that when he was buried amidst the mourning of the whole population of Canterbury, two hymns were selected from his volume, not unworthy of the stately pile in which his obsequies were celebrated, or of the sacred hill of St. Martin's Churchyard, whence, from beneath the venerable yew-tree, his grave looks out on that historic prospect which he knew so well."

The Bishop of Gloucester and Bristol (Dr. Ellicott) has obliged me greatly by writing (December, 1872) the following letter for this Memoir:—

"You have done me the kindness and honour of expressing a wish that I should add to your life of my dear and valued friend some few remarks on the nature and influence of his theological labours, and especially of his great work, the 'Commentary on the Greek Testament.'

"I do so very gladly. I must, however, ask you to receive these pages rather as a friend's criticism on a completed work than as a contribution to the history of its progress. The reason for my asking you thus to regard this letter may be soon stated. Our dear friend and I were both very hard-working and busy men, and had but little time for correspondence. The notes that passed between us were for the most part brief and hurried, and do not in any way tend to illustrate the literary history of his Greek Testament. We conversed much on our common subject when we met, but wrote on it hardly anything.

"Thus, from very want of materials, my comments must, for the most part, take the form of estimate and criticism. Yet I can make a humble contribution to the history of the first volume from the relation in which I stood to it soon after its appearance. It is now with very mingled feelings that I notice what has, I have no doubt, been mentioned in the body of your volume[3], that my first connexion with your dear husband's great work was as a hostile reviewer in the 'Christian Remembrancer' some twenty or more years ago. I write this with strangely mingled feelings, as, on the one hand, I dare not deny that my stand-point (as the phrase is) remains now what it was then; and yet, on the other, it is a very pain to remember the crudities and ungentle comments that disfigured that article. My stand-point was reverence for what is called Catholic interpretation, combined with a readiness to subject that sort of received interpretation to the established rules and principles of grammatical criticism. The Dean's—so far as I then understood it, and as, perhaps, it substantially remained to the very end—was different. He entered fearlessly into the critical field, perhaps, even with a slight bias against what was merely received and patristic; he warmly denounced every attempt to gloss over difficulties in harmony; he paid no greater heed to any inter-

[3] Page 205.

pretation, however time-honoured, than its simple merits required; he considered himself free to use all the material that foreign criticism had collected, and, in his earlier volumes, was sometimes led, by his sympathy with the results arrived at, to adopt the arrangement and exegetical details of the distinguished modern writers whom he principally consulted. Everything, however, like his own gentle and noble nature, was patent and undisguised. He knew none of those mean and despicable arts by which the use of another's labours can be disguised, and a show and semblance of research put forward, which really goes no farther than the volumes that are supplying the collected material. No, not a trace of such ignoble manipulation of results and references can be found in any part of his great work. He used others freely, but it was ever so plainly and clearly, that no doubt could have been left on any mind of the liberty which he claimed for himself and acted on. He did, however, thus leave himself open to criticism, and the more so as in his early days as an interpreter he was to some extent under the influence of two or three leading interpreters, such as De Wette and Meyer, whose views at the time certainly were not always in harmony with the general current of English theological opinion. As time went on, he soon felt his own great powers, and discussed on equal terms with these guides of early days each passage as it came before him, and showed his real mastery over the materials or opinions which he had collected. But it seemed to be otherwise at the time of which I am now speaking. My friend replied to my article in a temperate and well-written pamphlet, which, I well remember, made me desire to know personally a man who could write with such ability, as well as kindness of tone, in answer to an unfriendly criticism. A year or two after this time I had the happiness of becoming acquainted[4] with my generous antagonist. He was then in Hamilton Terrace, St. John's Wood, with a genial library of books round him, working steadily at his Commentary, and

---

[4] See page 245.

adding weekly to his reputation as an interpreter by his lectures in Quebec Chapel,—all which you will, I am sure, have fully mentioned elsewhere. I will, however, venture to add my remembrance of one of those lectures, as illustrating his power as an interpreter. There was a large and interested audience, many with Greek Testaments, and all evidently gathered together to be instructed. The lecture was a model of pulpit exegesis. It was extempore, but so clear in diction and so happy in expression, that if the whole had been taken down *verbatim* hardly a word would have had to be altered. What struck me particularly was the easy and connected flow of the address. Special points were noticed, difficulties fairly met, differing interpretations lightly but sufficiently noticed; but all flowed onward easily and limpidly. The mastery over the materials was complete, and the power of placing the mind of the sacred writer before the audience such, as I believe, has never since been equalled. Most expositors in their oral addresses make you feel that you are but hearing, instead of reading, notes. While the verse lasts the interest is maintained, but it closes with the verse, and has to be called out anew when another verse or period is commenced. In fact, the usual expository discourse flows on by jets, instead of forming a regular and continuous stream, and attention becomes proportionately fatigued. My friend's lecture was in every respect the reverse. Whether it was by his quick perception of the general scope as indicated by the language of the original, or by some delicate and subtle sympathy with the mind of the passage, or whether, again, it was the simple tact of the practised interpreter, it is, perhaps, not easy to say; but the fact and results were clear enough: all were sorry when the lecture was over. The student portion of the audience closed their Greek Testaments, I can well believe, with the inward resolution of returning; the general hearers were conscious of an interest in Scripture different to what they had felt before; the few critics or strangers that the reputation of the lecturer had attracted left the church with the difficult question uppermost,—What, after all, was it that made the lecture so thoroughly interesting, so popular in the best sense of the word? The answer, perhaps, may not always have been rightly given, but it was this—that the lecturer had the rare gift of the 'exegêtical sense,' as our German friends would say, that gift which, it may be, was found in an eminent degree in those whom the writers of the New Testament speak of as 'prophets,'—men with the gift of setting forth the full mind of Scripture, and of revealing its hidden and deeper meanings. The two travellers to Emmaus were permitted to realize this in its highest and holiest form.

"Not long after this I had the happiness of being associated with my friend in a work that, if I remember right, extended over some three years—a revision of the 'Authorized Version of St. John's Gospel, and six or seven of St. Paul's Epistles.'[5] The work has still some little circulation under the title of the 'Revision of the Five Clergymen.' It was the first fruits of that which is now being done more completely, and was the one work which predisposed the conservative mind of Bible-reading Englishmen to tolerate the idea of a new revision. In this work all the high qualities of the Dean's mind (he was called to the office he so worthily filled while the work was in progress) were very conspicuous. If any of us imparted any thing to him it was, perhaps, more punctilious accuracy in grammar; what he imparted to us was something much more subtle. It was again that happy exegetical instinct, to which I have already alluded, that sympathy with the continuous mind of the passage, so hard to define in words, but so readily accepted and welcomed whenever manifested. He was thus a contributor to the work of an importance which, I think, fully justifies my saying that without him the revision would not have been what it is, nor would the work have met with the reception that was given to it by students both at home and abroad. It is pleasant to linger in memory over those days, —our early efforts, our difficulties, our experiences, and

---

[5] See page 262.

especially our good-humoured but vigorous conflicts when it was thought that much turned on the proper rendering of a particle, or when the subject matter was the retention or extrusion of some poor innocent 'has' or 'have' in the ever-recurring question of the best mode of rendering the Greek aorist; and then, at last, the subsidence of the *motus animorum* by the sprinkling of a little common sense, and by an appeal from very exhaustion to that safe arbiter, English idiom, and English usage. All these things it is pleasant to recall, and in any criticism on the Dean's great work, it is, at any rate, necessary to allude to them, as it can hardly be doubted that our critical and grammatical discussions exercised considerable influence on our friend's own work. It may be clearly seen in the latter half of his Commentary. The first and second volumes had been written before we commenced our revision; and in them the grammatical element will be found more sparingly introduced. The Dean was from the first a thoroughly good scholar; but, if I may so express myself, he was so, rather by instinct than by direct study of details. His early interpretations are probably not less trustworthy than those in his later volumes, but in the first and second volumes there is not the same force and certitude of statement on the grammatical bearings of a passage that we find in the volumes that followed. Our frequent discussions did us all good, and especially our quick and clever colleague. He entered, I remember well, with the keenest interest into the delicacies of grammatical criticism. His fine perception made him appreciate distinctions, and his clearness of thought enabled him to express them with ease and precision. He became soon more than a match for most of us in our gentle encounters, and he acquired, with characteristic rapidity, that technical knowledge which up to the time he had not fully acquired, but for which he evidently had always a natural aptitude.

"I am now brought to the consideration of his Commentary as a whole; and, in obedience to your wishes, will endeavour to form some estimate of the characteristics of those honourable and honoured labours. My comments must be threefold,—on the Introductions, the Textual Criticism, and the Notes.

"The great value of the Introductions, or Prolegomena, is in the digested information they abundantly supply to the student. Every view taken by any interpreter of eminence is noticed clearly and succinctly, and in several cases—as for instance in the Introductions to the Ephesians and to the Pastoral Epistles—criticized with great power and ability. In both cases the doubts that have been entertained as to the authorship of the Epistles in question are disposed of in the most clear and convincing way. If I could wish anything otherwise in these Introductions, it would be that they had been written in a more continuous style. The division of each chapter into several sections, rather breaks the continuity of thought, which, in critical estimates such as these Introductions really are, proves always so welcome to the general reader. Still this may be certainly said, that no student will ever refer to this part of the work without finding every point that has been raised, whether as to the scope, characteristics, age, or style, of the writing, discussed with that clearness and perfect candour and impartiality which mark everything that the Dean wrote. He was sometimes, I have ventured to think, a little hard on some systems of Scripture criticism, such, for instance, as the system of the Gospel harmonists, but the seeming hardness was but the expression of his own honest aversion to anything that seemed to him to be uncandid or evasive. His thoroughly honest mind could not tolerate anything that in the faintest degree bore even the appearance of pious fraud or conscious subterfuge.

"On the Text it is somewhat difficult to speak. The work was commenced at a time when our critical aids were much fewer than they now are, and when the important modern principle of laying great weight on the convergence of representative testimonies was very imperfectly recognized. Though the Dean ever kept his work, in its successive editions, fully up to the latest standard, still, in a matter where subjective considerations necessarily enter so largely, as they certainly do in the construction of Text, it is always difficult to modify the leading principles which were originally followed. These principles, as the Dean's excellent chapter on the subject in his first volume very clearly shows, were the best and most approved at the time he wrote; but since that time wider and more accurate information has tended to modify some of those principles, and to suggest altered groupings of authorities. The result is, that the Text is thoroughly good, but yet not likely to become a standard text. The service, however, that the Dean has rendered to the general cause of textual criticism can hardly be overestimated. At a time when but little interest was felt in the subject, he helped greatly to popularize the study of critical authorities. He supplied the student, especially in his later editions and later volumes, with short clear statements of the principle on which one reading had been preferred to others. He never fails to exhibit tact in the subtle question of the exact worth, in any given case, of internal evidence, and always shows a freedom from critical bias that has, perhaps, never been exceeded by any critic of recent times. His indirect effect on textual criticism in this country has thus been very great; and has, perhaps, never yet been sufficiently acknowledged.

"Still his present and future fame both is and will be connected with his Notes and Exegesis. Here the fine qualities of his mind, his quickness, keenness of perception, interpretative instinct, lucidity, and singular fairness, exhibit themselves to the greatest possible advantage. Rarely, if ever, does he fail to place before the reader the exact difficulties of the case, and the true worth of the different principles of interpretation. He never leaves any doubt as to the view he himself takes, and he takes it on grounds and evidence which it will always be found very difficult to shake. If he does not convince, he yet never fails to make the reader pause, and often pause long, before he rejects the view ultimately placed before him. There is no special pleading, no latent principle at work, no theological bias (some, perhaps, may wish sometimes that this had been otherwise), no reserve of any kind; the reader feels that he is taken into fullest confidence, and is under a thoroughly impartial guidance. He may in the sequel sometimes fail to be satisfied, nay, from the very fairness with which the case is stated, may adopt some opposed view to that of his instructive guide, but, if he does so, it will always be with a sense of gratitude to a writer who so well supplies the very materials for the divergence in judgment.

"Of the many merits of these Notes perhaps one of the greatest is the clear view they give the student of the connexion of the inspired thought, especially in the epistolary portion of the New Testament. This it will be observed is done in two ways,—first, by giving (after the manner of De Wette), before each group of connected verses, a summary of their substance; secondly, by drawing out with careful precision the meaning of the connecting particles. The student is thus enabled to follow as it were the mind of the sacred writer, and is inured to the first duty of every earnest interpreter, viz. that of weighing each passage *in reference to its context*, and allowing that context to give its proper hue of meaning to the inspired words. Amid the many great services the Dean has rendered to the cause to which he devoted so many years of his valued life, I rate none higher than the assistance he has afforded to the student in the matter of contextual interpretation. His Commentary on the Hebrews, the fullest and, perhaps, in some respects, the best portion of his great work, is a lasting monument of his success in unfolding the mind and reasoning of his author. I have alluded to one portion of the fourth volume, but I cannot close these remarks without specially calling attention to one other portion of that volume which has not, I think, been sufficiently noticed by critics—I refer to the Commentary on the Apocalypse. This is a noble close to eighteen years of continuous labour. It reflects all the high qualities of the mind of the interpreter, perhaps even more clearly than any other portion of the whole work. The clearness, candour, and wise simplicity of the Notes; the fulness and completeness of the Introduction; and the judicial calmness with which the various systems of interpretation are discussed, show clearly enough that this was a true labour of love. I do sincerely trust now that the Revelation forms a part of our Lectionary, that this closing portion of the work will receive more attention than it has yet received. There are portions in the Introduction of truest Christian eloquence, and the tender and pathetic words with which the eighth chapter of that Introduction closes, can never be read by any gentle and sensitive reader without the feeling that they represent what should ever be the aspirations of the true Christian scholar, and form a simple yet befitting epilogue to a really great and genuinely noble work.

"My last remembrances of my dear friend are those connected with his share in the Revision of the Authorized Version of the New Testament that is now going on. Long[6] and eagerly had he looked forward to that work; greatly had he prepared the way for it; steadily had he advocated it. At last he was permitted to see it in progress, and himself to take a leading part in it. From the first day the New Testament Company met to the *last*[7] sad morning, when he gently and resignedly gathered his books together, and told us that 'the doctors had forbidden his continuance of the work,' he never was absent from one of our meetings. Always ready in suggestion, and yet always as ready to point out any objection that could be urged even against what he himself might have put forward; quick in perception, felicitous in expression, subtle in discrimination, with all the wisdom acquired from long practice, and that knowledge which only experience can give, he was felt by us all to be a colleague and helper of the highest order, and he was honoured and valued, and—let me not fail to add—loved as he deserved to be. Never was man more tenderly regretted by those with whom he worked; and when, at our first meeting after he had been called to rest from his labours, the Collect for All Saints' Day was added to our simple

---

[6] See pages 121, 412, 425, 439, 440, 447.
[7] See pages 465, 466,

prayers, never were its touching words more deeply felt by those that heard them than by us in the Jerusalem Chamber that sorrowful day.

"I have now, dear Mrs. Alford, completed, as well as I have been able, the estimate and criticism that you, in your kindness, have wished me to attempt. I wish from my heart more time had been at my disposal, but these lines have been written in the midst of incessant work, and must be accepted rather as what they desire to be than as what they are. They are designed to be a friend's sympathizing sketch of a friend's labours; but now that the sketch is finished I feel how imperfectly it sets forth the original. Such, however, as it is I send it."

My husband had some valued friends, who were not members of the Church of England. I am indebted to an article by one of them, the Rev. Dr. Stoughton, for the following remarks:—

"The merits of his 'Magnum Opus' have been largely discussed—it has been severely as well as favourably criticized; but the upshot of all is, the high place assigned to it for usefulness by scholars of different creeds, and different countries. In the library of most English ministers, Conformists and Nonconformists, you are sure to find conspicuous on the shelves, 'Alford's Greek Testament.' In conversation on disputed passages, the question is often put—'What does Alford say?' And in America, I know, from the testimony of my friend, Dr. Schaff, himself a superior judge of Biblical attainments, that no other English critic is, on the whole, valued so highly. The book has, no doubt, imperfections, as everything human must have. It may, and doubtless will, be surpassed in value by some other edition some future day, when the inquisitiveness of scholars, now working in different departments of the great field, shall have provided richer and ampler materials than the present age places at any one's command. But, in comparison with the actual past, not in comparison with the possible future, must the Dean's critical labours be estimated; and, tried by this standard, there is no doubt as to the verdict pronounced by those who are competent to form an opinion on the subject.

"There was a strong poetic element in his mind from boyhood. It gushes out with irrepressible fervour in his 'School of the Heart,' and it found what quickened its impulses in the English club at Cambridge, where he wrought together with Tennyson, and witnessed 'the gradual modulating into harmony of some of those sweetest strains which are now known and felt throughout the world.' Some of Alford's lyrical pieces and hymns, though they lack the exquisite word-music, the perfect finish, and the condensed power of the 'Poet Laureate,' abound in what is natural, true, picturesque, touching, and holy; the whole poured forth in mellifluous strains, only sometimes too little restrained.

"His career as a literary critic was much more important than his career as a poet. He might be said to have inaugurated, as Editor of the 'Contemporary,' a new line in the history of criticism. There is no want of keenness in the critiques he wrote or admitted, ignorant assumption and incompetent ventures received their due; but all honest, industrious, well-informed authorship he treated with respect, and by him, perhaps for the first time, all sectarian and class prejudices were banished from the pages of a leading Review. Many persons were filled with surprise at articles representative of different schools of thought being admitted into a periodical conducted by a Dean, and at notices, just and genial, of works ignored in other quarters, or dismissed with a contemptuous sneer. 'The Contemporary Review' has been valuable for its own sake; but, as a pioneer in a new path, as an example of independent, unprejudiced, and disinterested criticism, it claims honour which will be more appreciated hereafter than it is at present.

"Many of his lighter pieces, such as appear in 'Good Words' and the 'Sunday Magazine,' manifest considerable literary skill, and some of them, as regards descriptive power, particularly those describing a tour on the Cornish coast, attain to pre-eminent excellence in that department of composition. He had an eye ever open to what in nature is beautiful and sublime; and, combining the painter with the poet, he admirably sketched in water-colours what he admirably described in words. I remember hearing high testimony borne to his drawings, by one of our most celebrated Academicians; and it was very affecting to see in his library on the day of the funeral, a beautiful picture of St. Michael's Mount, which he had nearly completed on the Monday before his death.

"These various pursuits indicate his industrious habits; but, in addition to his being a critic, a poet, and a painter, he was a musician and a mechanic. Triumphs of his handicraft adorned the Deanery; his talent for music found appropriate scope in the Cathedral Services; his study, with different tables for different kinds of work, showed a love of methodical arrangement; and other contrivances, interesting and amusing to his friends, indicated the value which he set on hours and minutes.

"Great industry and methodical habits unfit some men for social intercourse. When you are in company with them, you see that they are ill at ease: their hearts are away with their business or their books. Not so in the present instance. Dr. Alford's nature was formed for kindly and loving companionship, and he had the gentlemanly instinct which enables a man to show himself at home in whatever society he appears, because he feels a moral kinship with his fellow-creatures, however different their training and habits from his own.

"Dr. Alford throughout his whole ministerial life, judging from his writings, and from the testimony of those who knew him best, kept a fast hold upon those great truths commonly termed Evangelical, without ever identifying himself with the party in the Church of England which bears the distinctive name. Some love to reveal the secrets of their spiritual history; with others it is indeed 'hid with Christ in God,' save as it comes forth in deeds, not professions. I did not enjoy the intimate acquaintance which would enable me to bear personal witness to Dr. Alford's character in this respect, but I should infer that he belonged to the second and nobler type I have mentioned, not to the first. 'By their fruits,' says the all-seeing Judge of character, 'by the doings of the life, not by the utterance of the lips, shall ye know them.' The appreciation of virtue is a Divine gift: reverence, prompting an utterance of blessings over the holy dead, is a Divine impulse. I recognize a sign of the Master's approval, a reverberation of His voice, who says, 'Blessed is that servant whom his Lord when He cometh shall find so doing,' in the consentaneous expression of regard and love to Henry Alford's memory, by different organs of religious opinion—by ministers and people of all Churches—by many representatives of them gathering round his grave—by the touching references made to him at Canterbury, as '*The Good Dean*,' and by demonstrations of public feeling when the whole city was moved, and went forth to see the last Christian rites celebrated at his grave."

A friend from Canterbury had especial opportunities of forming from his own point of view an opinion of my husband, and he has obligingly stated it in the following remarks:—

"I would speak of him as Dean of Canterbury, as the leading citizen of that ancient city, as the eloquent preacher in the Cathedral pulpit, and as the kindly loving friend; for however much we might and did differ on some great points both of doctrine and politics, it was impossible to resist the attraction of the warm loving heart which drew to him all who were admitted into the circle of his friends. One great change which as Dean he introduced into the Cathedral service was the establishment of a sermon on Sunday afternoons, for which for many years he was alone responsible. This, which at first was considered a great, and by some an undesirable, innovation, proved a complete success. Very large congregations, drawn from all parts of the city, filled the choir of the cathedral. The Dean's voice, well modulated, distinct, and clear, could be heard in every part of the choir, whilst the language, 'drawn from the well of English undefiled,' in which he clothed the original and striking ideas which he introduced in his sermons, was such as went home to the minds and hearts of his audience, and sent many a one away deeply impressed with the truths which had been so eloquently brought before him. To the very end of his life his sermons continued to make a strong impression upon his hearers, and were listened to with what in many cases had become an affectionate interest in the preacher. Nor was this the only way in which he was qualified to be the Dean of a large cathedral. The present Bishop of Carlisle, speaking from his recollections as Dean of Ely says, 'It is a considerable advantage to a Dean to have some knowledge of and taste for music; this enables him to take his own proper part in the choral service, and also to speak with some kind of authority when the music of the service is bad.'—Cathedral Essays, p. 15. When Dean Alford entered upon his office it was a very rare thing for a Dean or Canon to be able to take his part in the musical service. On what are technically called 'Precum Days,' the great Choral Festivals, when the choicest treasures in the musical repertory of the Cathedral are selected to celebrate with glad praise and thanksgiving the great truths of our salvation, it falls to the Dean and canons to say the service for the day; and when they are unable to intone the prayers and sing the versicles, the perfectness of the rendering is sadly marred. On such occasions Dean Alford's sweet and musical barytone voice sounded throughout the choir, and could be distinguished even at the lower end of the nave.

"I can well remember that upon one of the choral festivals of parochial choirs, when a portion of the congregation were seated in the nave, he tried the experiment of saying the service at the choir door standing facing the north; and that the prayers were easily heard and joined in by the large numbers assembled both within and without the choir. It was at such gatherings, too, which tend to reunite what have been too much separated, the cathedral body and the clergy and laity of the diocese, that his great powers of organization and arrangement were conspicuous. So far as he could manage it, places were found for all who came, whether as singers or as members of the congregation. The available space within and beyond the choir was used to the utmost, and the whole of those who were present were conducted to their appointed places in an orderly manner. It is not my intention to say anything of his intercourse with the members of the Cathedral body, even were I competent to do so; but I can speak from my own knowledge and experience of the beneficial influence which his residence in Canterbury exercised upon the citizens generally. No scheme of public utility or of charity was proposed which he was not ready to further with kindly countenance and with very liberal gifts from his purse. All the established institutions, such as the hospital and the dispensary, were very largely indebted to his help; whilst two of our largest national schools received very liberal contributions, and in one of our poorest and most populous parishes a considerable portion of the curate's salary was for a long time paid by him.

"It was, however, in our social life that we felt so greatly the benefit of his being amongst us. In most Cathedral cities, and in Canterbury not less than in others, there is too great a tendency to keep up a wall of exclusiveness to protect the dwellers in the Precincts from the intrusion of those living in the City. To break down this barrier as much as possible, and to promote the kindly intercourse of different classes of society was one great object at which the late Dean aimed and in the attainment of which he was, to a great degree, successful. Amongst other means adopted for this purpose was the foundation of a musical society for the practice and performance of the Oratorios and other standard works of our great musical composers. In this society persons of all classes were enrolled, and during its continuance it has been the means not only of rendering some of the Oratorios of Handel and Mendelssohn in a way which gave pleasure to the audience, but also of bringing together people who would otherwise have had little or no intercourse with each other.

"That by this and other kindly deeds the late Dean had

gained for himself the love and goodwill of the citizens of the cathedral city was shown most plainly on the sad day of his funeral. So suddenly, indeed, was he removed from our midst, and so short was the illness which preceded his death, that few had realized the idea of his life being in any danger when the great bell of the cathedral proclaimed the sad tidings of his death. On the day of his burial the cathedral was filled; and, notwithstanding the uncertainty of a January day, a large number both of clergy and laity joined in the funeral procession from Christ Church gate to the quiet resting-place which had been chosen on the green hill of St. Martin. Long, indeed, will it be before the memory of the good Dean Alford is forgotten in Canterbury by those who knew and loved him for his own and for his works' sake. Long will it be before the impression grows faint which was made by the holiness of his life and the consistent earnestness of his Christian character. To myself personally, having known him so intimately not only in the cathedral city, where he was so incessantly occupied with literary and other labours, but in his country home, where he allowed himself more relaxation, it will ever be a painful pleasure to bring to mind all the little incidents of our warm friendship. Whenever I recall the well-loved features, the genial smile, the hearty welcome, the warm grasp of the hand, I feel how great has been my loss, and can only hope that, should my own course be guided aright, I may meet him again in that happier world where sorrow and partings shall be known no more for ever."

APPENDIX A.

WORKS OF DEAN ALFORD IN THE ORDER OF THEIR PUBLICATION.

1830.

SOME Hymns, sent to the "Christian Observer" and "Christian Guardian."

1833.

An article on Ancient Music sent to the "Philological Museum," No. II.

"Poems and Poetical Fragments." J. J. Deighton, Cambridge; and Rivington, London. Pp. 97.

1834.

"Address to the Inhabitants of Bury St. Edmund's and neighbourhood in regard to the Lord's Day." Gedge and Barker, Bury St. Edmund's. Pp. 9.

"Faith Explained and Enforced: a Sermon preached at Ampton Church." T. C. Newby, Bury St. Edmund's. Pp. 21.

1835.

"The School of the Heart, and other Poems;" in two volumes. Pitt Press, Cambridge; Longman and Co., London; Deighton, Cambridge. Pp. 169. 129.

1836.

"Hymns for the Sundays and Festivals throughout the Year, with some occasional Hymns; adapted for use in Churches where the Psalms of David are Sung." Longman and Co., London; Cartwright, Loughborough. Pp. 58.

"The Practice of Infant Baptism asserted on Scriptural Grounds, in a Letter from a Clergyman to one of his Parishioners." Cartwright, Loughborough. Pp. 8.

1839.

[Memoir prefixed to] "The Works of John Donne, D.D., Dean of St. Paul's;" in six vols. Edited by H. Alford. J. W. Parker, West Strand.

[Various articles in] "Dearden's Miscellany."

1840.

"The Clergy Watchmen unto the People: a Sermon preached at Melton Mowbray at the Primary Visitation of the Lord Bishop of Peterborough." Rivington, London; Dearden, Nottingham. Pp. 28.

1841.

"Go, and Sin no More: a Sermon preached before the Wymeswold Friendly Society." Rivington, London; Dearden, Nottingham. Pp. 11.

"The Abbot of Muchelnay. Sonnets, &c." W. Pickering, London. Pp. 120.

"Chapters on the Poets of Ancient Greece." Dearden, Nottingham; Rivington, London. Pp. 263. [Reprinted from "Dearden's Miscellany."]

1842.

"Hulsean Lectures for the Year 1841. The Consistency of the Divine Conduct in revealing the Doctrines of Redemption. To which are added two Sermons preached before the University of Cambridge." Deighton, Cambridge; Rivington, London. Pp. 194.

1843.

"Hulsean Lectures for the Year 1842. The Consistency of the Divine Conduct in revealing the Doctrines of Redemption." Deighton, Cambridge; Rivington, London. Pp. 160.

1844.

"Psalms and Hymns adapted for the Sundays and Holidays throughout the Year; to which are added some occasional Hymns and Prose Hymns, chiefly from Scripture, Pointed for Chanting, and adapted to the Sundays and Holidays throughout the Year." Rivington, London. Pp. 275.

"The Restoration of Churches the Bounden Duty of a Christian People: a Sermon preached at the Restoration of the

Parish Church, Beeston, Nottinghamshire." Dearden, Nottingham; Rivington, London. Pp. 31.

1845.

"Address to the Inhabitants of Wymeswold on the approaching Completion of the Restoration of their Church." Dearden, Nottingham. Pp. 8.

"ΠΡΟΓΥΜΝΑΣΜΑΤΑ: Passages in Prose and Verse from English Authors for Translation into English and Latin; together with selected Passages from Greek and Latin Authors for Translation into English: forming a regular Course of Exercises in Classical Composition." Deighton, Cambridge. Pp. 204.

"Poetical Works." Two Vols. Third Edition. Rivington, London. Pp. 135 and 165.

"An earnest Dissuasive from joining the Communion of the Church of Rome." [Tract.]

1846.

"A History and Description of the restored Parish Church of St. Mary's, Wymeswold." 4to. Printed in aid of the Restoration Fund. Vizetelly Brothers. Pp. 23.

"Plain Village Sermons on the Lord's Prayer and the Beatitudes." Rivington, London; Dearden, Nottingham. Pp. 125.

1848.

"An Address presented by the Inhabitants of Wymeswold to Rev. H. Alford and his Reply." Pp. 12.

1849.

"The Inspiration of Holy Scripture. Preached before the University of Cambridge as an Exercise for the Degree of Bachelor of Divinity." Deighton, Cambridge. Pp. 18.

"The Greek Testament. Vol. I. With a Critically revised Text; a Digest of Various Readings; Marginal References to Verbal and Idiomatic Usage; Prolegomena; and a Critical and Exegetical Commentary. For the use of Theological Students and Ministers." Rivington, London. Pp. 664.

"Four Lectures on the Influence of the Fifth Commandment as the great Moral Principle of Love of Country and Obedience to constituted Authorities; delivered in the Theatre of the City of London School; having gained the Prize offered by a Benefactor to that Institution." Rivington, London. Pp. 73.

1850.

Prælection [read at Cambridge, 14th Feb. 1850]; "ad Ephesios revera dabatur Epistola illa canonica, Paulo non Pseudopaulo auctore."

"Sermons." Rivington, London. Pp. 335.

1851.

"Select Poetical Works." Rivington. Pp. 76.

Article in the "Christian Observer" (October), on Paget's "Unity and Order of St. Paul's Epistles."

Article in the "Christian Observer" in the form of a letter, referring to a letter headed "Alford's Prolegomena."

1852.

"Sermon preached at the Re-opening of St. Martin's Church, Leicester." Crossley, Leicester. Pp. 19.

Article in the "Edinburgh Review" on Conybeare and Howson's "Life and Epistles of St. Paul."

"Greek Testament. Vol. II." First Edition.

[ADVERTISEMENT[1].—The principal points of difference between this volume and Vol. I., which I have explained more at length in the Prolegomena, are the following; in this volume:—

1. The text is arranged on critical principles, regard being had to the internal evidence for and against every reading, as well as to the external evidence of manuscripts.

2. The reasons for adopting or rejecting every reading are given in the digest.

3. The digest embraces a complete account of the various readings; those of the later cursive manuscripts, and those of minor import, which were excluded in Vol. I. being here inserted.

4. The various marks of variation from the received text, of divided manuscript authority, and probable spuriousness, are omitted in the text of the present volume.

I have to express my thanks of especial obligation to—

1. The 2nd Leipzig Edit. of Tischendorf, on the digest in

---

[1] It seems desirable to print here those "Advertisements" to certain editions of the volumes of the Greek Testament which record any change of plan or any important addition to the contents of previous editions.

which my own is mainly founded, and from whose account of MSS. versions, and Fathers, I have borrowed largely.

2. The Commentary and Critical Notices of Meyer. Though often differing widely from him, I cannot help regarding his Commentary on the Epp. to Corinthians as the most masterly and complete that I have hitherto seen on any portion of Scripture.

3. The archæological and illustrative labours of Messrs. Conybeare and Howson.

4. The able and satisfactory treatise of Mr. Smith on the Voyage and Shipwreck of St. Paul.

I must leave my many other obligations to speak for themselves. None can tell how much and how kindly I have been helped, but those who find in the exercise of that kindness its most acceptable return.]

1853.

An American edition of "Poems." Dedicated to Longfellow. Ticknor, Reed, and Field, Boston. Pp. 398.

Article in the "Edinburgh Review," "Saul of Tarsus."

1854.

"Memoir of the Rev. H. Alford." Rivington. Pp. 259.

"English Descriptive Poetry: a Lecture." Pp. 27.

"Greek Testament. Vol. I. Second Edition. By Rev. H. Alford, B.D., Minister of Quebec Chapel, London, and late Fellow of Trinity College, Cambridge."

[Advertisement. 1854, May.—This second edition will be found to differ from the first in being conformed to my second volume, as regards the revision of the text and digest of various readings. This latter has been entirely re-written, and the text being now revised on the critical principles announced in the Prolegomena, Vol. II., differs considerably from that in the first edition. I would request the reader, before entering on the work itself, to consult the following portions of the Prolegomena:—

Chapter VI. § 1. Of the arrangement of the text in this edition.
2. Of the various readings.
3. Of the marginal references.

Chapter VII. § 1. MSS. referred to.
2. Versions referred to.
3. Fathers, and other ancient writings referred to.

I would also take this occasion of stating that the matter of the Prolegomena, digest of various readings, and notes throughout my work, must be understood to be gathered from all sources to which time and opportunity have afforded me access. Of these I would especially mention, in this first volume, Meyer's and Olshausen's "Commentaries on the Gospels," Stier's "Reden Jesu," Tischendorf's second Leipzig edition of the "Greek Testament," De Wette's "Handbuch," and Luthardt's recent admirable work on St. John's Gospel; I only regret that this came into my hands so late that I have been only able to make cursory references to it in revising the Notes on St. John.]

"Quebec Chapel Sermons. Vol. I." Rivington, London. Pp. 408.

"Intelligent Study of the Scriptures." Lecture in Exeter Hall.

1855.

"Quebec Chapel Sermons. Vol. II." Rivington, London. Pp. 311.

"Heal the Sick, the Duty of the Christian Church in all Ages: a Sermon preached in Quebec Chapel on behalf of the Samaritan Free Hospital for Women and Children." Rivington, London. Pp. 15.

"Quebec Chapel Sermons. Vol. IV. Divine Love in Creation and Redemption." Rivington. Pp. 307.

"Greek Testament. Vol. II. Second Edition."

[Advertisement. 1855, February.—This second edition is little more than a reprint of the first. Errors have been corrected where discovered, and a few important changes made; but in almost all respects the volumes are identical. That this is so is owing, not to want of will to consider and revise, but to want of time at present, with the preparation of the remaining volumes pressing on me, to work over the ground again. The first volume of this work being now in the editions since the first assimilated to the present volume, I need only refer the reader to the Prolegomena.]

"Greek Testament. Vol. I. Third Edition."

[Advertisement. 1855, London, Dec. 22.—Little more than a reprint of the second. In the text I am not aware of having introduced any alteration, except, indeed, Ἰωάννου for Ἰωνᾶ in John i. 43, which latter was already marked as an erratum in the second edition.

In some places in St. John I have added a few explanatory and other remarks to the notes; and throughout that Gospel, for my former analytical titles of the various sections, I have substituted in the main those of Luthardt, which regard not so much its outer historical surface as its inner theological coherence. That such corrections and additions occur in St. John only is owing, not to my supposing the other part of my book complete without them, but to my being just now engaged in my pastoral work on a regular exposition of that Gospel.]

1856.

"Quebec Chapel Sermons. Vol. III." Rivington. Pp. 471.

"Quebec Chapel Sermons on Christian Practice. Vol. V." Rivington. Pp. 333.

"Sermon preached at All Saints' Church, Belvedere." Daniel and Oakley, London. Pp. 24.

"Two Letters to J. Sperling, Esq., on the Lord's Day Question." Rivington. Pp. 24.

"Greek Testament. Vol. III." First Edition.

[ADVERTISEMENT. 1856.—It has been thought better to extend the number of volumes of the work to *four*, partly on account of the great size to which the third volume, according to the former plan, would have extended, and partly because the publication of this portion would thereby have been so long delayed.]

"Greek Testament. Vol. II. Third Edition."

[ADVERTISEMENT. 1856, December.—In this third edition of my second volume I have cursorily compared some exegetical works which have appeared since the publication of the second edition, and have inserted in many places remarks on and extracts from them. These authors will be found mentioned in the "Catalogue of Books referred to" at the end of the Prolegomena. I only regret that time will not yet allow me to give this portion of my work a more thorough revision. It is a trial incident to the preparation of such volumes as these—to be obliged to reissue from time to time many things which I could wish to see more thoroughly and laboriously done, and to be content still, in some instances, to put forth views which subsequent experience has chastened and deepened. But so it ever will be with those who labour at God's Word. The mine is unfathomable: and the deeper research of the work, as it advances, seems also to show how much deeper it might have been carried before.]

1857.

"Quebec Chapel Sermons. Vol. VI." Rivington. Pp. 291.

"Why will ye Die? a Sermon preached at the Special Services at Exeter Hall." Seeley and Co. Pp. 15.

"Quebec Chapel Sermons. Vol. VII." Rivington. Pp. 348.

"Homilies on the first ten Chapters of the Acts of the Apostles." Rivington. Pp. 208.

"Poverty and Riches: a Sermon preached at the Temple Church." Pp. 19.

"Separation for the Spirit's Work: a Sermon preached at St. Paul's Cathedral at the Ordination by the Lord Bishop of London." Rivington. Pp. 19.

"Greek Testament. Vol. III. Second Edition."

[Advertisement. 1857, June, London.—A few necessary corrections. In the "Pastoral Epistles" notices have been inserted of Mr. Ellicott's work, published about the same time as the first edition.]

1858.

"Pulpit Eloquence of the Seventeenth Century." Lecture delivered in Exeter Hall. Pp. 50.

"Four Sermons on the Parable of the Sower." Deighton and Bell. Pp. 115.

Various Articles in the "Dictionary of the Bible" edited by Dr. W. Smith. Published by Murray.

1859.

"Our Lord and the Gadarenes: a Sermon preached at Westminster Abbey," taken down in shorthand. Pp. 13.

"Greek Testament. Vol. IV. Part I." First Edition.

[Advertisement. 1859, June, Carlisle.—The division of this fourth volume into two parts has been occasioned by the amount of time necessary for the preparation of the Apocalypse.]

"Greek Testament. Vol. I. Fourth Edition."

[Advertisement. 1859, August, Oban.—The whole digest of various readings has been re-written, and the body of marginal references much revised and enlarged; corrections and additional comments have been occasionally inserted in the notes.

Particulars of these changes will be found in the Prolegomena, Chap. VI. § 1, 22 ff.; § 2, 1 ff., iii.]

1860.

"Greek Testament. Vol. IV. Part II." First Edition.

1861.

"Odyssey of Homer: in English Hendecasyllable Verse." Longman. Pp. 208.

"Greek Testament. Vol. II. Fourth Edition."

[ADVERTISEMENT. Canterbury, April 6th, 1861.—This fourth edition of my second volume has passed under entire revision as regards (1) the critical arrangement of the text, and (2) the body of references. Both these labours have been carried on under my own superintendence by my Secretaries, the former including the re-writing of the digest of various readings, and of that part of the Prolegomena which treats of the Apparatus Criticus, by the Rev. A. W. Grafton; the latter by the Rev. R. Hake, Minor Canon of Canterbury.

I owe it to the unwearied diligence and watchful care of these my coadjutors, that I am able to express a hope that this edition will be found very far superior to those which have gone before it.

The alterations in the notes have been chiefly those which were rendered necessary by the more complete conformation of the text to the testimony of our most ancient manuscripts and versions. I may be allowed to direct the critical reader's attention to the list of ascertained readings of the "Codex Vaticanus," printed at the end of the Prolegomena.]

"Greek Testament. Vol. IV. Part I. Second Edition."

[ADVERTISEMENT. Canterbury, April 6th, 1861.—This second edition is nearly a reprint of the first, the changes being confined to the correction of ascertained errors, and a few necessary improvements in the digest.]

"Greek Testament. Vol. III. Third Edition."

[ADVERTISEMENT. Canterbury, Dec., 1861.—This volume has been now made uniform with the rest of the work as regards the revision and augmentation of the references, and the re-writing of the critical digest, and consequent occasional changes in the text.

The notes have also been in parts considerably modified and augmented.]

1862.

" New Testament for English Readers. Vol. I. Part I." First Edition.

" Greek Testament. Vol. IV., Part II., Second Edition."

[Advertisement. Canterbury, March, 1862.—This second edition has undergone considerable revision, especially in the digest of various readings, which has been in many respects made more complete. The recent discovery of the "Codex Reuchlinensis," on which Erasmus's text was based, rendered it necessary to insert in the digest notices of its readings, obtained from the tract of Professor Delitzsch.

The lists of MSS. in the Apparatus Criticus are new, and have been drawn up almost entirely by the Rev. A. W. Grafton, who has personally inspected several of the MSS. See note, Proleg. p. 271.

To him, and to my other Secretary, the Rev. R. Hake, I am mainly indebted for the revisions and the new matter in this edition.]

" Mourning and Praise: two Sermons preached in Canterbury Cathedral." Rivington. Pp. 36.

" The Good Shepherd giveth His Life for the Sheep: a Sermon preached in Canterbury Cathedral at a Consecration." Pp. 15.

" Sermons on Christian Doctrine: preached in Canterbury Cathedral." Rivington. Pp. 342.

1863.

" Importance of Scripture Knowledge: a Sermon preached at St. Paul's."

" Rejoice with them that rejoice: a Sermon preached at Canterbury Cathedral on the Prince of Wales's Marriage." Rivington. Pp. 11.

" Life's Answer," a poem in " Macmillan's Magazine."

" The Queen's English." Strahan. Pp. 257. [Sent first as articles in " Good Words."]

Articles in " Good Words" on " Meditations on Creation, Providence, and Advent." [Afterwards published in a volume.]

" Passing away," a poem in " Macmillan's Magazine."

"Church Movement in our Day: a Sermon preached in Wells Cathedral." Pp. 20.

"Greek Testament. Vol. I. Fifth Edition."

[ADVERTISEMENT, May, 1863.—In the present edition considerable improvements and additions have been made; the text has been carefully gone over, and the results of additional evidence from new MSS., and the more exact collation of others previously known, have been embodied in it.

The digest of various readings has been nearly re-written since the publication of the fourth edition. I regret that the printed edition of the "Codex Sinaiticus" did not reach me till the three first Gospels were printed. In the digest to the Gospel of St. John the whole of its readings are incorporated.

The marginal references have undergone careful and thorough revision, and will be found more practically useful, and more exhaustive of the occurrence of words and constructions than in the former editions.

The notes have, for the first time since the publication of the first edition in 1849, been subjected to entire revision. I could have wished to have taken account in them of every recent contribution to the exegesis of the sacred text, but this has been found impossible. Bleek's valuable posthumous "Introduction to the New Testament" has been consulted throughout, and many additional notices have been inserted from other works.]

1864.

"Letters from Abroad." Strahan. Pp. 269. [Sent first as articles in "Good Words," in eight articles.]

"Evening Hexameters," in "Good Words."

"Filiolæ Dulcissimæ," a poem in "Macmillan's Magazine."

Three Articles on "How to Use the Gospels," in "The Sunday Magazine." [These and the remaining articles sent in 1865 and 1866 were afterwards made into three volumes, "How to Study the New Testament."]

1865.

"Meditations on Advent, Creation, and Providence." Strahan. Pp. 124. [Reprinted from "Good Words."]

"To the Chief Singers: a Sermon preached in Canterbury Cathedral at the Festival of the Choir Fund."

"Poetical Works." Fourth Edition.

Nine additional Articles in the "Sunday Magazine" on "How to Use the Gospels," &c., &c.

Article in "Good Words," on "Three Weeks among the French Churches."

"Greek Testament. Vol. II. Fifth Edition."

[Advertisement. 1805, July. Deanery, Canterbury.—The "Codex Sinaiticus" has been collated throughout, and in certain doubtful passages of the text its testimony has now decided the reading. The references have been somewhat modified, principally with a view to render each volume independent in itself, and prevent constant cross references to the others.]

1866.

Six Articles in the "Contemporary Review:"—

1. On Church Hymn Books.
2. Mr. A. Trollope on the English Church.
3. Recent Nonconformist Sermons,
4. Cathedral Life and Cathedral Reform.
5. Felix Holt, the Radical.
6. Recent Poems. Article 1.

Five Articles in "Sunday Magazine."

Three Articles on "How to Use the Acts of the Apostles."

"Last Words in Canterbury Cathedral, 1865."

"First Words in Canterbury Cathedral, 1866."

Article in "Good Words." "A Frenchman's Impressions of England a Century ago."

"The Year of Prayer: being Family Prayers for the Christian Year." Pp. 283. Small 8vo, pp. 207.

"Week of Prayer." Pp. 83.

"True and False Guides." A Lecture given in Exeter Hall. Pp. 32.

"Easter-tide Sermons." Strahan. Pp. 124.

"How to Study the New Testament." Vol. I. Strahan. Pp. 360.

"Coming of the Son of Man; Conflict and Victory: preached at Oxford." Printed in a book with other Sermons.

1867.

"The Year of Praise: being Hymns, with Tunes, for the Sundays and Holidays of the Year." Five editions, viz.:—Large type, with Music. Without Music. Small type, with Music. Without Music. Tonic Sol-fa Edition.

"How to Study the New Testament. The Epistles: first section. Vol. II." Strahan. Pp. 278.

"The Work of Him that sent Me: a Sermon preached in Lambeth Chapel at the Archbishop's Ordination." Rivington. Pp. 16.

Four Articles in the "Contemporary Review:"—

Recent Poems. Article 2.
Recent Anglican Sermons.
Le Curé d'Ars. Article 1.
Le Curé d'Ars. Article 2.

Two Articles in "Good Words:"—

"More about the Queen's English."
"Hymns," afterwards printed in "The Year of Praise."

Fourteen Articles in "Sunday Magazine:"—

Twelve Articles on "How to Use the Epistles."
"Last Words in Canterbury Cathedral, 1866."
"First Words in Canterbury Cathedral, 1867."

1868.

"Poetical Works." Fifth Edition.

Five Articles in the "Contemporary Review:"—

1 The Union of Christendom in its Home Aspects.
2. Byways of New Testament Revision.
3. The Church of the Future.
4. Principles at Stake. No. I.
5. Principles at Stake. No. II.

Three Articles in "Good Words:"—

1. The Christian Conscience.
2. A Week on the North Coast of Cornwall. With Illustrations.
3. Cornwall Again. No. II., with Illustrations.

Two Articles in "Sunday Magazine," called "Fireside Homilies."

[These Homilies were written in a familiar, affectionate style, describing a father and mother and two little girls talking over various religious subjects on Sunday evening at the Deanery. Some family scenes and some public ones are introduced, and nearly all the Scripture pictures in the Deanery are described.]

Homily I. The Christian Enjoyment of Sunday—an approach to the State of the Blessed Dead.

Homily II. Archbishop Longley's Death. His Boy's deathbed described.

1869.

"Essays and Addresses: chiefly on Church Matters." Strahan. Pp. 195.

Four Articles in the "Contemporary Review:"—

1. The Next Step.
2. Manual of Family Prayer.
3. Cathedral Reform.
4. Cathedral Reform: a Supplement.

Seven Articles in "Sunday Magazine:"—

Homily III. Of the Infant Jesus, and six pictures describing Him.

Homily IV. Of the Child Jesus, and six pictures describing Him.

Homily V. Of Jesus a Youth. Holman Hunt's picture of Christ in the Temple described, and Herbert's picture of Christ in the Carpenter's Shop.

Homily VI. Of the Marriage in Cana of Galilee.

Homily VII. Our Saviour raising the Widow's Son.

Homily VIII. Our Saviour raising Jairus's Daughter.

Homily IX. The Raising of Lazarus.

Six Articles in "Good Words," called "Pamphlets for the People:"—

1. The Wants of Man in the Matter of Religion.
2. The Reasonableness of the Christian Life.
3. Mosaism and Christianity.
4. Right Views of Life.
5. Romanism and Protestantism.
6. Things which need to be Reformed.

"State of the Blessed Dead." Hodder and Stoughton. Pp. 100.

"The Coming of the Bridegroom." Hodder and Stoughton. Pp. 93.

"Our Lord and His Twelve Disciples. A Series of Photographs after the Crayon Drawings of Leonardo da Vinci, with a History of each Disciple." Bell and Daldy. Pp. 86.

1870.

"The Riviera. Pen and Pencil Sketches from Cannes to Genoa." Quarto. Bell and Daldy. Pp. 128.

"The Lord's Prayer. Illustrated by J. R. Pickersgill and Henry Alford." Quarto. Longmans, Green, Reader, and Dyer. Pp. 36.

Three Articles in the "Contemporary Review:"—

1. The Idylls of the King.
2. The Church and the Age.
3. Nonconformists' Essays.

Three Articles in "Sunday Magazine:"—

Homily X. Our Lord's Anathema, St. Mark ix. 39.

Homily XI. The Transfiguration.

Homily XII. The Gospel of the Children; an imaginary Scene abroad.

"How to Study the New Testament: Epistles: second section. Vol. III." Strahan. Pp. 337.

"The New Testament after the Authorized Version Revised." Strahan. Three Editions, in Long Primer, Brevier, and Nonpareil.

"Plea for the Queen's English." Third Edition. Called also "A Manual of Idiom and Usage," with many Additions.

"Biblical Revision, its Duties and Conditions: a Sermon preached at St. Paul's." Strahan. Pp. 27.

"The Compacted Body: a Sermon preached in the Chapel, Lambeth Palace, at the Consecration of the Suffragan Bishop of Dover." Strahan. Pp. 24.

1871.

[Posthumous Publications.]

"Truth and Trust: Lessons on the War." Hodder and Stoughton. Pp. 103.

Article in "Good Words:"—"The Bullers of Buchan." With Illustrations.

Processional Hymn, with Music. Novello.

1872.

[Posthumous Publications.]

"Genesis and part of Exodus, for English Readers." Strahan. Pp. 338.

"The Sons of God Known and Unknown." Hodder and Stoughton. Pp. 200. [Eight Sermons preached in Canterbury Cathedral towards the end of 1866.]

APPENDIX B.

PROCESSIONAL HYMN.

[The following Hymn is not included in Dean Alford's "Poems," or in the "Year of Praise." It was written and the music was composed to be sung at the Tenth Festival of Parochial Choirs of the Canterbury Diocesan Union, on 6th June, 1871.]

"Speak unto the children of Israel, that they go forward."

FORWARD! be our watchword,
  Steps and voices join'd;
Seek the things before us,
  Not a look behind:
Burns the fiery pillar
  At our army's head;
Who shall dream of shrinking,
  By Jehovah led?
    Forward through the desert,
      Through the toil and fight:
    Jordan flows before us,
      Zion beams with light!

Forward, when in childhood
  Buds the infant mind;
All through youth and manhood,
  Not a thought behind:
Speed through realms of nature,
  Climb the steps of grace:
Faint not, till around us
  Gleams the Father's Face.
    Forward, all the lifetime,
      Climb from height to height:
    Till the head be hoary,
      Till the eve be light.

Forward, flock of Jesus,
  Salt of all the earth;
Till each yearning purpose
  Spring to glorious birth;
Sick, they ask for healing,
  Blind, they grope for day;
Pour upon the nations
  Wisdom's loving ray,
    Forward, out of error,
      Leave behind the night;
    Forward through the darkness,
      Forward into Light!

Glories upon glories
  Hath our God prepared,
By the souls that love Him
  One day to be shared;
Eye hath not beheld them,
  Ear hath never heard;
Nor of these hath utter'd
  Thought or speech a word:
    Forward, marching eastward
      Where the heaven is bright,
    Till the veil be lifted,
      Till our faith be sight!

Far o'er yon horizon
  Rise the city towers,
Where our God abideth;
  That fair home is ours;
Flash the streets with jasper,
  Shine the gates with gold:
Flows the gladdening river
  Shedding joys untold:
    Thither, onward thither,
      In Jehovah's might;
    Pilgrims to your country,
      Forward into Light!

Into God's high Temple
  Onward as we press,
Beauty spreads around us,
  Born of holiness;
Arch, and vault, and carving,
  Lights of varied tone;
Soften'd words and holy,
  Prayer and praise alone:
    Every thought upraising
      To our City bright,
    Where the tribes assemble
      Round the throne of Light.

Nought that City needeth
  Of these aisles of stone:
Where the Godhead dwelleth,
  Temple there is none:
All the saints that ever
  In these courts have stood,
Are but babes, and feeding
  On the children's food.
    On through sign and token,
      Stars amidst the night;
    Forward through the darkness,
      Forward into Light!

To the Father's Glory
  Loudest anthems raise:
To the Son and Spirit
  Echo songs of praise:
To the LORD JEHOVAH,
  Blessed Three in One,
Be by men and angels
  Endless honour done.
    Weak are earthly praises,
      Dull the songs of night:
    Forward into triumph,
      Forward into Light! H. A.

PROCESSIONAL HYMN.

Very Rev. H. ALFORD, D.D.

APPENDIX C.

CATHEDRAL RESTORATION.

[As Treasurer of the Cathedral Fabric Fund, Dean Alford gave much time and attention to superintending various improvements in and additions to Canterbury Cathedral. Through the kindness of Canon Robertson I am enabled to give the following account of what was thus done.]

In his Report as Special Treasurer of the Cathedral Fabric Fund for 1862-3, Dean Alford mentions that the works undertaken during the year, in pursuance of the recommendation of Mr. Austin (Architect to the Chapter) and Mr. Christian (Architect to the Ecclesiastical Commissioners), were "the choir-roof and the south-western tower, with a portion of the west front."

"In repairing the tower and the carved work (of the south porch) great care has been taken not to remove any old work which could be retained. No scraping or renovating of the old work has been allowed, and only those stones have been taken out in which decay was advancing. In their case we have felt that the duty of substantial repair must prevail, however much we might prefer retaining the ancient and venerable aspect of the surface. I am happy to be able to announce that Mr. Christian, by whom the whole work has been thoroughly examined, has pronounced that, in this as in other respects, he is completely satisfied."

The Report then goes on to notice the manner in which the carving intended for the south porch had been executed by "a workman of great skill and genius," and the Dean continues:—

"A scheme of my own, to re-fill the niches of the south porch and west end with figures of Kings and Archbishops, has been very favourably received. Of the twenty-eight figures required for the south porch and south buttress-front, fifteen have been subscribed for, and are now in hand[1].

"In the Precincts, the main work undertaken has been the erection of the new School buildings from Mr. Austin's design."

The Report for 1863-4 mentions the continuation of works mentioned in that for the preceding year. The beginning of a restoration of the east side of the Cloisters, the restoration of the roof of the choir westward of the transepts, repairs of the windows, especially the great windows of the west front and of the south-west transept.

The new School-house and Head-master's house had been completed and were occupied, but "the former residence of the Head-master, which it was intended to fit up as a house for the Second Master, has been pronounced by 'the Architects' to be in a state of such unsoundness as to preclude all idea of repair."

The Report for 1864-5 sets forth the prosecution of the work of restoration, chiefly along the south side of the Cathedral.

---

[1] The number of figures already erected is at this time, June, 1872, forty-seven. The extent of the Dean's scheme will be seen from the following list of the statues:—

Our Lord as the Good Shepherd.
St. Augustine.
St. Anselm.
Abp. Lanfranc.
Abp. Cranmer.
King Ethelbert.
Queen Bertha.
St. Gregory the Great.
Abp. Theodore.
St. Dunstan.
St. Alphege.
King Alfred.
King Edmund.
King Canute.
King Edward the Confessor.
Abp. Becket.
Abp. Baldwin.
Abp. Hubert Walter.
Abp. Langton.
King William I.
King William II.
King Henry I.
Abp. Courtenay.
King Edward III.
The Black Prince.
Prior Ernulf.
King Henry VIII.
King Edward VI.
Abp. Sancroft.
Abp. Laud.
King Charles I.
Queen Victoria.
The Prince Consort.
Bishop Ridley.
Dean Stanhope.
King Henry II.
King Henry IV.
King Henry V.
King Edward IV.
King Henry VI.
King Henry VII.
King William III.
Queen Elizabeth.
Queen Mary II.
Abp. Stratford.
Abp. Sudbury.
Abp. Chicheley.
Abp. Arundel.
Abp. Warham.
Abp. Parker.
Abp. Grindal.
Abp. Whitgift.
Abp. Tillotson.
Prior Conrad.
Prior de Estria.
Prior Goldstone.
Dean Wootton.
Dean Bargrave.
Dean Percy.
Richard Hooker.

"In St. Andrew's Chapel, otherwise known as the Lay Clerks' Vestry, the sash and casement windows have been removed and the ceiling taken down, and the Norman work restored both inside and outside: also a new roof has been put to the apse.

"The South Norman Tower is now under repair, and the ashlar on the west side of it has been repaired to the height of about ten feet. In continuing the restoration of this tower, it is not proposed at present to go higher than the level of the parapet of the choir-aisles, leaving the rich old Norman work above for a future time

"An Early English embossed parapet, the pattern of which was borrowed from Lincoln Cathedral, has been placed over the south aisle of the choir."

Among works to be undertaken,—

"We purpose also taking in hand the Treasury, and hope to be able to complete its restoration and preparation to serve as the future Audit-room of the Chapter. The completion of its western front must of course await the removal of the present Audit-room, which cannot be effected until such time as the new one is ready for occupation."

In the Precincts, "the pulling down of the houses south of the Brick Walk has been completed; the road has been partially made from the Churchyard. . . . The portions of old ruin which are to be preserved have been cemented on the top, and supported and defended by railing.

"On the south side of the Cathedral the entire length of railing has been removed from the grass plots, and the (wider) road has been partially constructed.

"In the Mint Yard the new building attached to the Second Master's house (late Mr. Austin's) has been raised from the ground, and is now roofed in. The Organist's late house has been pulled down, as also the old School-house. A new Gateway and Porter's Lodge have been built at the boundary of our property in Northgate."

The Report for 1865-6 shows that restoration and improvement was vigorously carried on. The following paragraph records a change of plan since the preceding year:—

"[The South Norman] Tower, which, in its upper stages, has its surface enriched by most elaborate and beautiful ornament, has been thoroughly repaired and restored; also portions of the walls, where crippled and bulged, have been carefully taken down and rebuilt. This tower is now completely restored, with the exception of the conical leaden roof."

There are notices of the completion of improvements at the east end of the Cathedral, in the Mint Yard, &c., and of the adaptation of the ancient Brewhouse to the purposes of a Choristers' School, with "a large and commodious Singing School for the Choir rehearsals.

"These last-mentioned works bring the improvements in the Precincts to an end; and it is hoped that the whole Fabric Fund may hereafter be available for the restoration and improvement of the Cathedral itself and its appendages."

The Report for 1866-7, after recording the completion of some works mentioned in previous years, enters into a statement of the state of the Fabric Fund. Of the 20,000*l.*, with interest, which the Ecclesiastical Commissioners had agreed, in 1862, to pay to the Chapter, there remained a surplus of about 1200*l.*; and, when this shall have been expended, the Chapter would have only its ordinary Fabric Fund for restorations and improvements.

"During the summer it became questionable whether the plan proposed in my last Report of restoring the old Choristers' School, as an addition to the present Library, were feasible; and after some deliberation, it was agreed to build a new Library on part of the site of the old Dormitory. . . . The building is about half completed. It is hoped that this room may be ready for the occupancy of the Chapter as their Audit-room (the idea of fitting up the Treasury for that purpose having been for the present abandoned) by Midsummer next [2]."

The Report for 1867-8 is not in the Dean's handwriting, and the works which it records are (as might have been expected from the explanations of 1867) on a reduced scale. The chief feature is the restoration of St. Anselm's Chapel.

The Report for 1868-9, after speaking of "the absorption of

---

[2] The idea of building a new Library on the site here described was suggested by the Auditor of the Cathedral, Mr. T. G. Faussett. The building was used for the first time on occasion of the Kentish Archæological Association's Congress, July 30 and 31, 1868; and the books were removed into it in the beginning of the following year, so that it wore the appearance of a Library when used as the scene of a luncheon given by the Dean and Canons on the day of Archbishop Tait's enthronement, Feb. 4, 1869.

a great portion of the Fabric Fund in the cost of the new Library," proceeds:—

"Our attention has been chiefly directed to removing the old brick sash-windowed Audit-room, and making good the ancient walls and arcading thus exposed to view. This process has been nearly completed as regards the west face of the Treasury, the adjoining face of the Lay Clerks' Vestry or St. Andrew's Chapel, and the stump of the Norman Tower adjoining it.

"That portion of Henry de Estria's screen which formerly occupied the site of Archbishop Howley's cenotaph, has been repaired and restored, ready for erection when the masonry shutting out St. Andrew's Chapel from the Cathedral is taken down."

In the Report for 1869-70, the Dean says, "Our works have again this year been subjected to almost entire suspension on account of the determination, since the last Report, to undertake the warming of the Cathedral.

"Of the works mentioned in the last Report as apportioned to the present year, the new north staircase only has been proceeded with. That is now completed, and in use."

To this Report is appended a Balance-sheet, showing the expenditure of *all* the money which had passed through the Dean's hands as Treasurer of the Fabric Fund. The date of the Report, Dec. 8, 1870, throws a peculiar light on the fact of his having taken that opportunity to sum up his accounts with the Chapter.

INDEX.

Note.—In page 182, *for* North *read* South Devonshire.

GILBERT AND RIVINGTON, PRINTERS, ST. JOHN'S SQUARE, LONDON.

www.ingramcontent.com/pod-product-compliance
Lightning Source LLC
LaVergne TN
LVHW021240110826

845150LV00002B/370

* 9 7 8 1 4 2 5 5 6 1 7 6 5 *